D1830496

MANONIYANTRAN
[KEY TO HAPPINESS AND SUCCESS IN LIFE]

MANONIYANTRAN

[KEY TO HAPPINESS AND SUCCESS IN LIFE]

VEDANTIC VIEWS AND WAYS OF

MIND CONTROL

EDITED BY :

DR. T. N. ACHYUTA RAO

KALPAZ

Published by

Kalpaz Publications
C-30, Satyawati Nagar,
Delhi – 110052
Ph.: 011-47034999, 9811692060
www.kalpazpublications.com
E-mail: kalpaz@hotmail.com

Distribution Network
gyanbooks.com
India, USA, Canada, UK, Australia, France

ISBN: 978-93-5722-521-2 (PB)

First Published, 2024

Printed at: Gyan Press, Delhi.

Manoniyantran: Vedandic Views and Ways of Mind Control
Editor: Dr. T.N. Achyuta Rao

DEDICATED
TO
MY PARENTS
And My Brothers
Girish & Krishna

Contents

"Samudraadoormirmadhurmaam udaaradupaamshunaa samamrutatvamaanat, ghrutasyanaama guhyam yadasti jihvaa devaanaam amrutasya naabhih"

[Mahanaraayana Upanishad Anuvaaka XII, Shloka 8]

Meaning,
"The universe emanated in the form of waves from the supreme Fount that is the source of enjoyment to creatures."

Physically speaking,
"You and I, the sun, the moon, and the stars are but the little waves or wavelets, foam and bubbles in the midst of an infinite Ocean of matter".

Similarly,
"Both body and mind are but mere names or little Wavelets in the ocean of matter, the 'Samashti'; Behind that idea of the unity of the whole show, The real soul is one. There is but one soul through- out the universe, all is but one existence".
Realization lies in the fact that 'the ocean is real and its waves are unreal'. The bottom of the lake can be seen only in the absence of the waves. Similarly, Self can be realized only when the thought-waves cease.

PRAYER

"Om!   Mahat Pradhana Kala Purusha Hiranyagarbha Roopine!
Sat-Chit-Ananda Svaroopine Namo Sree Naarayane Harih!"

This in brief is the 'Truth' (Satyam) and 'Order' (Ritam), the foundation of this universe, - all about the Creator, the creation, the created, and the seeker. The supreme devotee Bhakta Dhruva uttered the above words describing the Lord when he was enlightened by the touch of the Lord Shree Vishnu's Conch. These wonderful, mystic words are the words of wisdom that explains all. Shree Hari Narayana is the Supreme Consciousness, Space, Time, Energy, Nature, all living and non-living beings as the manifest and the supreme Truth, Knowledge and, Bliss that is unmanifest in all.

II

Om! Sham no mitrah sham Varunah
Sham no bhavatvaryamaah
Sham no Indro Brihaspatih.
Sham no Vishnururukramah.
Namo Brahmane.Namaste Vayo.
Tvameva pratyaksham Brahmaasi.
Tvaameva pratyaksham Brahmaavadisham.
Ritamavadsham. Satyamavadisham.
Tanmamaaveet Tadvaktaaramaaveet.
Aveenmaam. Avidvaktaaram.
"Om, sahanaavavatu. Sahanau bhunaktu.
Saha veeryam karavaavahai.
Tejasvi naavadheetamastu. Maa vidvishaavahai."
"Om! Shantih! Shantih! Shantih!"

Meaning, May the Sun (Mitra) be good to us!
May Varuna be good to us!
May the Sun (Aryama) be good to us!
May Indra and Brihaspati be good to us!
May Vishnu of great strides be good to us!
Prostrations to thee Brahman!
Prostrations to thee, O Vayu!
Thou indeed art the visible Brahman.
I shall proclaim thee the visible Brahman.
I shall call thee just!
Om! Peace, Peace, Peace!

Agni and Vayu are the only two of the Devas that ever went very close to Brahman but could not recognise Him. Indra could know about Brahman only through the effulgent Knowledge Uma, the daughter of Himavat! When Indra asked Uma who the Yaksha was, Uma told Indra that it is Brahman Who governs this Universe; all that exists here and elsewhere derive their energy from Him. Nothing will move without His 'Will' and support. [KENOPANISHAD].

"Advaitam Achyutam anaadim Anantaroopam
aadyam puraanapurusham navayouvanam cha;
Vedeshu durlabham durlabham aatmabhaktau
Govindam Aadipurusham tam aham bhajaami.
[Brahma Samhite 5.33. Bhagavad Geeta 5.5]
Krishnah svayam samabhavatparamapumaan yo
Govindam Aadipurusham tamaham bhajaami.
[Brahma Samhite 5.39]

Meaning,
I bow to Govinda, who is the One and only Supreme Brahman, The changeless, deathless, beginningless, endless; and He who Appears in innumerable forms, the One who is praised in all The scriptures as the ever youthful, radiant, resplendent, the First-ever born and unassailable, the One who is not easily reachable through Veda, knowledge of scriptures, but can be accessible to the devotees through the knowledge of their Self. I bow down to Sri Krishna who is the Parama Purusha, the First-ever born, protector of the cows-Govinda.

Mantra

"Arvaaj trichakro madhuvaahano ratho jeeraasho
ashvinoryaatu sushvutah,
Tribandhuro Maghavaa vishvasoubhagah sham na
Aavaksha dvipaade chatushpaade!"

'Rk Veda' [1.157.3]

"O Lord Indra, Maghavan, the God of the Gods, make our family life blissful and give us success, wealth, happiness, and make our life praise-worthy, fit for others to emulate; help us to develop an integrated personality, body, mind, and soul integrated and harmonious, to bring all happiness. Let all creatures- biped as well as quadrupeds, be happy and peaceful!"

Om Shantih, Shantih, Shantih!

Preface

Mind is the thing! Mind is the zing thing! It has the amazing creative power and it is the Mind that makes man a 'human' leading him to the 'Divine'. It is the discerning and discriminating Mind that makes Man so special and separate from other animals. It is also the Mind that makes or mars our life. All our problems are due to our Mind and it is absolutely essential to know about the nature of our Mind and its behaviour. Unless we control its unruly behaviour, it is sure to land us in trouble. It is also essential to harness the enormous creative power that rests with the Mind and harness the potential in us. There are very simple techniques that help us in this endeavour.

This book: "MANONIYANTRAN" – "The Vedantic Views and Ways of Mind Control" is a treatise on Mind and gives spiritual techniques of controlling Mind and harnessing its powers for a happy, successful, and peaceful life. It ensures both materialistic prosperity and spiritual progress. It is in the Vedic tradition and implores Upanishadic doctrines to gain not only happiness in worldly life but also attain to great spiritual height that ensures liberation from bondage of Sansar, the mundane world.

By the way, one may ask: why the control of the Mind? Why 'Manoniyantran'? The aim of life is happiness and happiness is a state of Mind. It is the Mind that gives the impression of happiness or unhappiness; and, it is the Mind that normally controls our life and activity and we suffer due to our sheer ignorance and our inability to control our thoughts. Actually, it is the Intellect, 'Buddhi' that has got the discriminative power and it should guide the Mind and enable it to keep us happy and successful through the power of discrimination. This 'Buddhi' is the Intellect that gets its power of discrimination, the 'light' or Knowledge from the soul or the 'spirit within'. In the absence of this reflected light of the Soul, the 'Atman', the Mind goes on rampage, dwells on anything and everything that the senses dwell upon, and mistakes all illusory, or the 'make-believe', or the magical objects of the world as real and get us into trouble. In the absence of this intellect's guidance or discriminative power, we fail to *'see things as they are'* and get everything wrong in our understanding. This ignorance governs our lives until and unless we realise the 'Reality' of this world.

Who will guide us in this endeavour of *'seeing things as they are'* and knowing the *'Reality'* of this world? Who will lead us from 'Asat' to 'Sat', from 'Ignorance' to *'Knowledge'*? If we look back to our cultural and spiritual heritage in the Ancient Scriptures like the Veda and Upanishads, the Brahma Sutra, and the Bhagavad Gita, we realize how our forefathers lived a life of contentment, happiness, peace, and prosperity and held the 'spiritual' values in high esteem.

This book dwells briefly on the doctrines enshrined in the Veda* and

Upanishads, the Epics and the Puranas (also known as the Fifth Veda), the Bhagavad Gita, and the Srimad Bhagavata. These Ancient Scriptures are a source of Knowledge and provide invaluable guidelines in the form of sutras (aphorisms), mantra, tantras, and yantras. Only knowledgeable persons can guide us in this respect. A benevolent Siddhi Purusha, an attained person or Yogi only can help us. It is the spiritual attainments, saadhana, or spiritual power that can help us to understand the meaning of life and get us liberated from bondage. But, such a Guru or teacher of excellence who can guide us is not available so easily, with the result, we are forced to look to the Lord for his 'divine grace' and pray Him for enlightenment and emancipation.

In the light of modern science, the technique of 'mind control' is still in its early stage of development and all the progress made so far in mental sciences like psychiatry, para- psychology, psycho-analysis, neuro-science, phrenology, etc. do not help us much. They treat Mind as a separate entity through techniques of hypnotism and take recourse to medication, administred to brain, that is harmful in the long run. The treatment should be holistic treating the body, mind, and soul in its totality, unity, and homogeneity. Such a science has not yet developed.

The Ancient Indian Sages treated the Soul, 'the Atman', as the spirit or power behind the physical body and considered it as the supreme commander of the body and mind. The study of the inner world of man is better known as 'spiritual science' perfected by the Seers, the Rishis, is based on the Veda and the Upanishadic doctrines; and, this aspect does not come within the purview of modern science that concerns with the outside world. The ancient Sages considered Man as something special, made of three types of bodies- the sookshma sharira (the subtle body), the Kaarana (causal) sharira, and the sthoola (physical) sharira; rather, these are the Adhidaivika (Consciousness), Adhyatmika (Spirit), and the Adhibhoutika (Matter) sharira, respectively. Ancient Indian Sages and Seers had a clear vision of this. They could get mastery over the Mind and use the Intellect to control the entire mechanism of this human body, including the subtler aspects and they had the ability to stop breath and control the movement of Prana in the body, control pulse and heart beat. They could live hundreds of years without any physical ailments and, it is said that some Yogins live without solid food for years and years!

As already stated, modern psychiatrists and medical scientists treat mental ailments with medication that is very harmful in the long run. This sort of treating a part of the body for any ailment is detrimental to the over-all health of the body. Moreover, such treatments are temporary and the ailments recur after a lapse of time. On the contrary, the spiritual exercises are more helpful since they give a wholesome treatment to the body rooting out the cause of illness through the mind and, some sort of transformation also takes place in the long run for those who want the ultimate spiritual attainment.

Thus, there are two types of solutions to the problems of life. One is the short-term solution to the immediate problems of life that disturb our

* Veda is one and Plural.

peace of mind and cause the physical ailments. These can be treated through the practise of yoga- the Vedantic way of life, with the Knowledge of Vedic Sciences such as *'Ayur-veda'*, nisarga chikitsa (Nature Cure), pranayama, dhyana, austerities such as Sadachara-Sadvichara, japa, tapa, and vrata, niyama and upavasa (residing near God or thinking of God), and dietary restrictions to gain purity of mind and body, concentration, *'chitta ekaagrata'*. The second one, a long-term solution, is the more difficult one leading to spiritual fulfilment through Yoga- particularly Raja Yoga; this is the long-term solution to the problems of not only this life, but also that of emancipation or liberation called 'mukti', or 'moksha'. It is the ardent desire of every one, tired of this life or not, to seek a permanent solution by way of emancipation, release from the cycle of repeated birth and death- the *'metempsychosis'* - entanglement in Sansar.

Indian Philosophy believes in 'Karma'– both prarabhdha and sanchita that bother us due to our actions- commissions and omissions, good acts and bad deeds, sins or crime committed in the past lives, as well as, the present life, respectively. Just like the neem seed brings forth a neem tree and a mango seed gives the mango, our good deeds give us good life and our misdeeds make us suffer, if not in this life, in the lives hereafter. There is no escape from this Karma. It is like a Bank account. Whether you have plenty of money or loan, it does not matter; loan has to be returned with interest! You will certainly enjoy the fruits of good deeds. Time is not important here. Many people have received state honour and rewards at their ripe old age for their service in the past!

People who do not believe in 'life after death' should remember the scientific dictum that "nothing is created and nothing is destroyed and the sum total of product remains the same forever"; so also, our Soul remains here forever but take different bodies to fulfil their desires and, in the course of each life, the person suffers or enjoys the fruits of his past deeds! These fruits of the deeds are embedded in the 'germ cell' that produces repeated births, just as the entire plan of the Banyan (Peepul) tree is hidden in the small Banyan seed, or just like the sesame seed holds the oil within, or for that matter, butter and clarified butter, ghee is latent in the milk.

It is the desire- the blemish of the soul that keeps the 'germ cell' alive and active causing birth and death repeatedly, endlessly. The emancipation, or release of the 'blemished embedded soul', or redemption from bondage is achieved through intense meditation culminating in 'Samadhi' transcending time, space, and causation. Practise of Yoga- 'Hatha Yoga', Jnyaana Yoga, or 'Raja Yoga', culminating in 'nirvikalpa samadhi', and the "Realization of the Self", i.e.,'Enlightenment' is the only solution offered to the suffering souls! This book treats all these aspects in some detail.

A very interesting aspect of this study is that it leads the sincere and the devoted aspirant from 'darkness' to Light', from 'asat' to' sat' and from 'death to immortality'. It lays bare the' secrets' of life and removes the screen of avidya (ignorance) to reveal *'things as they are'*. This, indeed, is a mirror that reflects our imperfect knowledge and understanding, our bloated ego that blinds us to reality of things and prevents us from realizing the nature of our Self. Even if we are partly successful in this life attaining whatever is possible spiritually, it is a great achievement! As the Buddha puts it, it requires several lives to attain perfection and the first step is taken in that direction, now and here.

Some people believe that science and religion are two different approaches and each is divorced to other. Neither Science and Religion are two different subjects of knowledge nor the two are exclusive of each other. In fact, science, philosophy and religion are like the three main streams- the Ganga, the Jamuna, and the Saraswati – the Rivers of knowledge that unite at Sangam, the Veda.Each one is incomplete without the other two. Science is rational, philosophy is logical, and religion is spiritual and all the three go to make complete knowledge, the 'Samhita'. All knowledge is welcome and whatever that removes our ignorance and gives us 'Right Knowledge' is the right approach. But, Science as 'rational inquiry' suffers from inadequacy as it is guided by the Mind and the five Senses (that are inadequate) and the instruments (that are not efficient enough) devised for the purpose; further, all these are under the constraints of time, space, and causation. Anything that is bound by time, space, and causation is subject to change and will not reveal the 'Absolute Truth'- 'That' which is formless, deathless, changeless. Hence, science- physical, or biological, is incapable of revealing the "Truth"; it is only the spiritual science, religion and philosophy, morals and ethics that trancend time, space, and causation and gives a glimpse of the "Reality" in the form of spiritual experience. Unfortunately, unlike physical or biological sciences the knowledge and experience gained by spiritual exercise is not only inexplicable, but also' not transferable'. Thus, all discussions or arguments on this subject are useless. Any advancement in science and technology will touch only the fringe of the Subject like the tip of the iceberg. It will never take us to the center, the core. To get to the bottom of the 'Truth' is never possible and the mystery remains a mystery forever. Only the Veda and the knowledge obtained from Vedic Literature, the Upanishadic doctrines, the Brahma Sutras are useful to us in our spiritual inquiry. These will take us to the center of the Subject, the core of the Universe! It reveals all at once in a flash! But, it requires immense saadhana, daily exercise in Transcendental Meditation.

This book 'Manoniyantran', based on the Vedic pronouncements and Upanishadic doctrines, greatly help us in understanding Man and his Universe, Life and its problems, and offers easy solutions, too. The human body is the yantra like the space suit of a space traveller, and it helps to enjoy the show on earth; and, the Sages and the Seers have devised means, also called 'yantra', to keep this machine fit to achieve its purpose. They have learnt the 'Jyotish'- the Science of the 'Light of Stars' (not in the present form astrology) and knew how to analyse the influence of stars and planets. They could easily analyse the colours emanating from the stars, or the congregation of stars, at the time of birth of the person and discern their influence on the subtle parts of the body. They could reduce these colours to numbers and calculate the effect. Thus, Jyotish or Astrology is a very exact science provided one has studied it properly. It is one of the important branches of Veda that gives Man a special ability to foresee things. Also, there is the branch of Vedic Mathematics that helps us to know the intricacies of the mechanism of the Universe. Learned Vedic scholars have adopted this knowledge, Numerology to Jyotish to match the numbers with colours and devise graphic designs and formulae that would help the person to gain success in all his endeavours. It is based on the theory of waves and vibrations. Even today, there are astrologers and occult scientists who practise this system of Yantra Shastra.

Every letter in Samskrut Language is powerful and these letters produce strong or weak vibrations that cause definite effect on subtl organs of human body, mind and heart. These are wisely put in appropriate form called the 'Mantra'. These mantra produce very potent sounds and their vibrations penetrate the subtle parts of our body, whose power can help maintain the physical health. It is very useful in 'Japam' or chanting, 'dharana' or concentration, and Meditation that helps 'manoniyantran' or 'Mind Control'. *Atharva Veda* is a storehouse of these techniques and devices that help us to control Mind. The sounds of words that carry vibrations of energy and sound convey message to the brain cells, and greatly influence the physical and mental health.

An attempt is made here to bring out as much knowledge as possible from the various sources- ancient and modern, and help the troubled souls and the suffering ones to get some relief. It is a sure path to success and happiness in life. But, since it is the spiritual science that we are talking of and this knowledge is based on 'Faith'. Faith is 'Shruddha' in Samskrut Language and it means a firm conviction based on supreme knowledge and devotion (bhakti) and total surrender. Without 'faith' there is no life, there is no salvation! Here, everything depends on faith and faith rests on deeper spiritual experience and knows no rationale. It is 'Faith' that manifested from the Absolute, Abstract Silence, the Brahman. And, faith runs all through life.

TNAR
SANJOSE, CALIFORNIA
USA.
MAY 2004.

Introduction

Our Mind is our world. Each one of us think and act as per the dictates of our Mind and get into problems due to the dualities and complexities of the world. We get confused and perplexed when we face problems that we cannot understand. We often forget that Man is made up of not only matter (body, mind, and intellect), but also spirit (Soul, the 'Atman'), and, more often, it is spirituality that shows the way in times of confusion and doubt. Bhagavad-Gita is a compendium of guidelines to sensible way of living and gives the techniques of Mind control- 'Manoniyantran'. It shows the way out of this confusion of *'to be or not to be'*. The principles enunciated in the Gita are culled out of the Veda and the Upanishads.

A simple guide to life would greatly help in times of problems, confusion or distress; and, it is true that not all can take to Veda, Upanishads, Brahma Sutra and the Bhagavad-Gita. Hence, the much-awaited book is here. This is a small book, but makes a slow reading. Sometimes, it may seem difficult to understand the 'mantra', the Samskrut verses, and their meaning; it requires much patience and concentration. The English equivalents are also difficult to understand. Hence a glossary of Samskrut terms is given for a quick reference.

It is all about the 'endless quest'. Not only it is about the problems of life but it is also about 'death and after'; it is about emancipation, liberation from bondage or 'Mukti'. It is about freedom, liberation, and eternal bliss and happiness. It is about the goal of life. It is about the meaning of life. It is about the proper understanding of the problems of life as also to equip oneself to face life as it comes. It is about experience of life in its full. It is about salvation, or 'mukti', i.e., the purification of the mind. 'Moksha' is burning of all desires of impure mind and to 'dwell in Him', the Lord, and attaining to the Supreme Bliss. This does not mean abandoning the great opportunity given to man to live and enjoy on this earth, of which even the Devas are jealous. In a way, it is the Vedantic way of life, not of abandonment, but of fulfillment!

Spirituality is not divorced to worldly life nor is it opposed to materialistic prosperity as is often mistaken. It is the only sensible and sane way of living. It does not advocate rejection; on the contrary it implores acceptance. But, there is the appropriate time when Man should take to the 'sat-nyas' (the true path), the sensible way of living and leave the path of 'illusion' (Maya) and delusion. There is no doubt that this life is for enjoyment. Enjoy life and enjoy it so well that you will not hanker after it any more, taking repeated births. Enjoy your life so well that you feel happy and contented. Enjoy your life so well that it leaves no desires for further fulfillment in the next birth. Live so well, as a model for others to emulate! There is a Vedic prayer for the Grace of the Lord to enjoy good health and good life. But, the most important thing is to realize one's own 'Self' by a deeper understanding of the life and its purpose. Realisation of the Self, the Soul, and the Spirit within is the supreme goal of life. It is possible by control of Mind or 'Manoniyantran'.

A number of techniques of Manoniyantran, i.e., Mind control derived from our ancient scriptures are given in this book. Also it will help to understand the meaning of life and to lead a happy and successful life. Mind is the key to sensible living. Understanding the Mind is the most difficult thing in life.

There is need for a clear understanding of the Hindu way of life, the Vedantic way, the spiritual way, called the Hindu Religion. It has survived over a long period; it is several millennia-old, and unlike the other civilizations that are purely materialistic and devoid of soul, the Hindu Religion aims at a fuller attainment that leaves no hankering for worldly pleasures and mundane existence. All the ancient sages have experienced the trauma of life and have found out the way of getting out of the misery of this life, i.e., 'Emancipation'. This book- 'Manoniyantran', more importantly, explains the meaning of dhyana, contemplation, meditation and the mantra that help us to realize the Self in us. A number of seminal thoughts are given at the end for purpose of contemplation. This will be very useful in controlling the mind through 'awareness'. Index is given at the end so that one can pick and choose the subject of his interest for a quick look.

In times of distress, some persons think that renunciation or taking to Sanyas would solve all the problems of life. They feel that only 'Sanyas' will help to attain liberation, release from bondage of Sansar. And spiritual salvation. It is true that anybody with a determination can take to sanyas and realize his Self. But, that is not the only way! There are sixty thousand ways to salvation and each can find his own way of salvation by intuition, divine will, and Grace of the Lord. Some take to Bhakti marg and some to Karma marg; some persons take to Jnyana marg and others to Raja Yoga. It is easy for one to take to ascetic life under the initiation of a 'Guru'. But, it is very difficult to get a true 'Guru'; under these circumstances, there is a fear that one may take to spiritual practices reading books, and it is very dangerous.

There are warnings not to plunge into the unknown 'Spiritual' world without a proper preparation. May be it is marriage leading to householder's life, or 'sanyas', leading to spiritual life, both are full of dangers. None can assure instant happiness and success in life. It is the proper understanding of the meaning and purpose of life alone that can help. 'Jnyana' and 'Bhakti' are essential requirements to cross the ocean of life. What is the golden mean? One must learn the art, science and technique of living.

The question often asked is, 'whether any body is happy in this world? If the answer is in the negative, why is this world created? The answer to these two questions seems like a riddle of the Spinx. Everyone wants to be happy, and the world has been created for him to be happy. If any person is not happy with this world, it is because he does not know what is happiness and how to live happily in this world; and, may be, he is seeking his illusory happiness where it is not available. After all, happiness comes from within, from contentment, one's own satisfaction; it is a state of mind and the feeling of happiness come from within oneself. Try to remember an occasion on which you felt immensely happy and joyful. While happiness depends on external sources joy is within one's Self only.

We are all children, innocent and joyful, in the beginning and gradually grow up into 'grown-up children' instead of becoming 'individuals' and a 'personality'. A child is very happy and its needs are very few and simple. As the child grows it absorbs everything that is seen and heard and develops an insatiable hunger and thirst for all sorts of things, needed or not needed, useful or not, and finally get them only to discard them; not only that, the child cries for more! A grown-up man is like a grown-up child and he goes on struggling throughout life to acquire things, whether these things really give him happiness or not and finally he feels disappointed. He goes on blaming this world for his mistakes and for his inability to understand the meaning of life. Some are over-confident and try to bulldoze everything that comes their way; and some are afraid of facing life and take recourse to cut it short. Fear is one of the inherent weaknesses of man. Both these sorts of persons do not know their own strength and weakness.

Our life is governed by two important factors. One is Desire and the other Fear. Both these play significant role in controlling our Mind and the senses. As the datum line, at the base of these two governing factors is the 'Avidya', or Ignorance, Nescience. Desire is the '*germ cell*' that causes our cycle of birth and death. Desire is caused by Ignorance. Ignorance brings fear and knowledge gives power. When one knows the reality of nature, he becomes one with it, there is no fear of 'the other'. When one knows the realities of life there is no expectations from the' other', and hence, not any disappointment. A number of Mantra are given here for contemplation and 'dhyan'. Repetition of these Mantra will give immense strength and power. Concentration will produce extraordinary success in life. It is important here to note that each and every word of the Mantra is potent and pregnant with meaning and, contemplation on that serves as an unfailing support to life.

Mind always wants some support and it clings even to fear or some obsession of some imaginary memory. Hence, it is absolutely essential to give some support to this mind. People take to games that ultimately end up in gambling; some take to drugs for fun that turns him into an intractable addict. Some indulge in sex promiscuously, in a state of inebriation. Some fall in love with every girl he meets and some commit the folly of indulging in all sorts of undesirable means to acquire power, wealth, social status, and even resort to crime. Some revel in a state of ego and look down with contempt everybody including the Lord Almighty. They have no respect or value for anybody or anything. Ultimately, for a wise man this world appears like a lunatic asylum where all are busy searching for something that does not exist there. It is like 'searching for a black cat, that is not there, in a dark room'. Unfortunately, Indian philosophy is also described as one such utopian, unrealistic approach; but the reality is different. The Ancient Indian Seers, Sages and the Sadhus have proved that the life is more meaningful when spirituality is added to the materialistic. Austerity does not mean poverty or penury. Austerity is the most sensible way of life and it assures happiness and success without fail. It is the greed, avarice, selfishness that is mainly responsible for our discontent, unhappiness, and misery. A person of pure heart and pure mind has no problems whatsoever for him everything appears divine and he sees divinity in everybody and everything.

The meaning of life has to be carefully understood. Life needs guidance and preparation in early stages of childhood and youth. Lack of guidance leads to way-wardness and spoils the opportunities of developing our full potentialities and happiness and success. Life is a journey to be accomplished with single-minded devotion, dedication, steadfastness, and un-wavering mind; it is, as if, an offering to the Lord Almighty who created us with a purpose. Finally, it is a total merger with 'That'. It is all contemplation, mind tuned towards sublime bliss; the mind turned away from the gross, mundane, sensate world. There is no more hankering after the sensual desires once the 'Reality' is felt 'within'. The mind is under the supervision of the consciousness, 'Sakshi' the inner eye that perceives the fickle and irrational behaviour. Intellect, the'Buddhi' keeps the mind under control; the mind that puts the senses under its command to irrational errands will thus be checked.

Swami Shivananda of Rishikesh says that, "a knowledge of the ways and habits of the mind, and its operations, the laws of the mind and the method of mental control and mental discipline, is very necessary if you want to enjoy real happiness and peace of an unruffled and abiding nature. You cannot expect everlasting happiness and perennial joy in the world of sense around us. The mischievous monkey- mind plays havoc in a variety of ways and causes and cares, worries and anxieties. Money, property, women and children do not give permanent satisfaction. This is the experience of all people". The sooner one gets a glimpse of the truth behind the human mind's mischievous play offering false notions of happiness, promising escape routes to drudgery of life and thus getting us trapped, better it is. Realize the nature of mind; watch its behavior in a sense of *'choice-less awareness'*. The restless mind stops to rest for a while; continue to remain in that state as long as possible; by continuous practice one can continue to be in this state of blessedness. This is the true path from wretchedness of the mundane sensate world to blessedness of the heavenly world.

This book 'Manoniyantran' (or Mind-control) serves a much-needed reference manual for all age groups, particularly the youngsters who are eager to climb the ladder of fame and success. Interestingly, it also guides those who feel inadequate within and suffer inferiority complex and do not show much progress. Even those who achieve something very early in life fall prey to their ego and soon stagnate. These complexes and self-consciousness are the root cause for success or failure. These things are analyzed in great detail with reference to the doctrines, 'suktas' and 'mantra' obtained from the Veda and the Upanishads, Shrutis, the Puranas, Bhagavatam, the Bhagavad Gita, and other sacred works. Our ancient Sages and Seers, Saints and Sadhus, Scholars and Pundits paid rich tribute to our ancient scriptures, which constituted a store house of knowledge and wisdom. It is our misfortune that these source materials were not available to us till recently; and, suddenly now the awareness has made everyone search for these source materials.

Efforts are being made here to collect essential material that is useful to our young friends who want to know about the 'mysterious' ways of functioning of our mind. For this purpose, we go deep into the origin of the Universe and evolution of Man so that we can understand in-depth the whole intricacies of the mind. This book is of immense value to all those who want to correct themselves for, methods are given here to know how to achieve success and happiness in life.

After all, it is in the 'Mind'. If one is fully aware of his mind and moods, one can easily cross the hurdles of life. Life is what one makes out of it. It is wisely said, that it is in the 'becoming' that is more important from what is 'being'. So, go through this work carefully and take full advantage of the wisdom of our ancient Sages and make your life happy, joyful, and peaceful; enjoy the bliss. Not only the ancient wisdom but modern science too is explored here in order to understand the mysteries of modern man. In spite of all the progress made in science, the life of man still remains vain, unfulfilled, wanting, and keeps one in constant search of the real meaning and purpose of life. Thus, a number of questions are raised and answered in this book.

Modern life is full of stress. At every step man is not sure of himself and anxiety kills him. Mind control or 'Manoniyantran' is, in fact, very useful in combating illness and diseases emanating from stress. Now it is found that the much-dreaded cancer, diabetis, paralysis, and heart attack are due to stress and these can be prevented by the technique of mind control. Unknowingly tension and stress accumulate leading to illness. One has to be cautious of his pursuits in life if he wants to enjoy it in peace. It is observed that psychosomatic problems are better solved by 'placebo effect' through mind management than psychiatric treatment and medication.

Manoniyantrana Tantras (Techniques) are the 'magic' formulae. It is in the 'Bhagavad-Gita' that the word '*Maya*' is used in the sense almost of 'magical' power; and 'God, the Great Magician', is declared to cause the spirit host to resolve as by the power of His divine magic'. (*Bhagavad-Gita* Ch. XVIII: Verse 61). *'The living beings in this world are declared to be resorting to the demoniacal sort of life when God robs them of their wisdom by His power' [ibid*, Ch.VII.Verse 15]. Upanishads also refer to this world as 'illusion' or dream; and as such, the problems of such a world should have magical solutions. And, each 'Mantra' in the Veda and Upanishads is a formula. Hence, the techniques are called the 'magic formulae' here.

The mind is an amazing thing! Mind works always with the past as memories, or the future as hope. With this powerful tool we can change the memories of the past or create the future. Positive thinking, creative visualization, neuro-linguistic programming, and emotional intelligence all use some form of mental programming and restructuring to achieve amazing results. This will help us to release ourselves from the shackles of fatalistic and self-defeating concepts of fate and luck. We can control our destinies by programming our mind to achieve our goals. The power of the human mind is enormous and limitless. We can overcome defeatist tendencies and remove the stumbling blocks that are coming in the way of realizing our dreams. Although we cannot change our past, at least, we can re-program our mind and thereby change our experiences, and our memories of the past. By this way, we can erase all our painful traumatic experiences, sad memories, disappointments and negative feelings that are stored in our subconscious mind.

It is amazing that our subconscious mind is literal and trusting. It believes whatever the conscious mind tells it. It cannot differentiate the real and imagined situations. This is the secret of the mind and we can use it to change our lives and need not curse our destiny and fate anymore. Even under extreme situations that drives one to commit suicide such as failure in love, or inability to cope with a situation, the state of mind or the attitude can be changed to one's advantage and life can be made more lively. 'Failure is the stepping stone of success', they say. This is the Mind management technique.

Vedanta shows the way as to how to understand the mind. It provides the technique of gaining not only spiritual wealth but also material wealth that the 'Vasundhara' or 'Dharitri'–the Earth offers. This technique of gaining material prosperity through Vedanta is by practising particular methods of action. It explains scientifically how we could exercise our optimum capacity for efficient and productive action. Personality development experts are suggesting the use of both sides of the brain in order to harness the full potential of the human brain. But it is certain that, due to lack of mental concentration we are not able to use our capacity to optimum, let alone harness our potentialities. Our ramblings into the past and dabbling anxiously about our future kill our present. Brooding over memories of past actions and expectations of fruits of work swing back and forth not allowing the mind to dwell on the present. This is a fundamental quality of the mind.

'Vendanta' provides ways and means of controlling the mind. It helps us to live in the present and concentrate on the work on hand. It helps us to channelise all our energy, 'chitta-ekagrata' (concentration of mind) into present activity. It helps us to save the dissipating energy thereby making us more efficient, our efforts more fruitful and productive. Vedanta provides many more avenues to peace and prosperity. Vedanta provides a blue print for efficiency, productivity and prosperity. Vedanta expounds various methods of successful and practical living. It provides a very positive approach to life and presents the highest knowledge of life and practical living. If we get this knowledge, we will have power- both spiritual and material. We will gain peace and dynamism in one stretch. We will not have worry or anxiety, stress or strain, and life becomes an experience without which we are lost in wilderness.

This work, 'Manoniyantran' blends the modern with the ancient, scientific, and the spiritual, old and the new, and the oriental and the occidental methods and thus, paves way for a happy, successful, and contented life. This book is the product of a long-sustained effort to understand this world, the meaning of life, the goal and purpose of life, the secret behind the success and failure, joy and sorrow, the future of mankind and such other problems. At first, it may seem very difficult for laymen to evince keen interest in this work; also, it may be difficult to understand this work bordering science, philosophy, religion, morals and ethics; gradually he will find it very interesting touching his personal life and create a hunger for the Divine.

This book speaks a lot about Mind that governs our life and its experiences. Mantra are repeatedly quoted from the Veda, the Upanisads, the Bhagavad- Gita and Puranas. It is a gospel of truth like the Bible, or Quran, or the Bhagavad-Gita. There are mention of names purported to be names of Hindu Gods in a metaphorical way; as far as they convey certain meaning like any other words, the names mentioned like Sri Krishna, or Sri Vishnu, or Sri Hari Narayana, are all figurative. God has no name and form. The word 'Sri' or 'Shree' stands for beauty and bounty; similarly, Vishnu stands for the All-pervading, 'Vish' meaning, ' to pervade'. Hari means the 'flow', the cosmic flow of energy, 'Prana', the 'life-sustaining force'. It also means 'the sword that cuts ignorance'. Also 'Narayana' means a person who had 'nara', water as his abode. It alo means 'journey (yana) of man (nara) in space'. It also means, 'the ever expanding universe'. Similarly, 'Achyuta' and 'Krishna' mean infinite, endless, one who has no death or decay. 'Chuyti' means death and,'Krish' means, 'to wear out', decay. Hence, the names of Hindu Gods used here are the Samskrut words metaphorically conveying certain meaning. In Samskrut, Shiva means 'Bliss'; Sri Hari means 'sweetness'. It is always very sweet to utter His name; it is pleasant to hear, 'Karnamruta'. Everybody wants to hear His name. One is not tired of hearing his name repeatedly. It brings joy, happiness to repeat the Lord's (His) name. God is the 'Lord Almighty' who has no name or form. We may imagine him in our own form since. He has created us as a microcosm, replica of Himself. Man is a microcosm, a replica of the macrocosm; his power and glory made us to give Him several hands and heads and worship Him.

Mantra, especially in Samskrut language, are very potent. It is the beauty of the Samskrut language that the words are pregnant with meaning. Take for example, 'Prapancha' (the world). Here,'Pra'and 'pancha' mean that 'objective world that comes within the grip of the five senses', in other words, the 'sensate world'. So also, the syllable 'ka' which stands for 'kana' (anu), meaning the microcosm; the syllable 'Kha', on the other hand, stands for 'Akhand' meaning the macrocosm. The one-syllable word 'Om' includes the whole of the cosmic entity, the Cosmogony. Unlike other languages that are written and read from right to left, or from top to bottom, Samskrut is directly piercing the heart with out entering the mind; it is considered the language of the Gods (Devavani), the language of the soul, the spirit. The words and images are formed with the very origin of the universe with the word 'AUM' or 'Om', the sound that reverberated with the 'Big Bang'. The word reaches, rather pierces, the heart and the meaning of the word come out of the heart.

In the Veda (knowledge), each word has got inherent intrinsic power and a person with austerity and deep meditation can use them as 'mantra' and gain enormous power. For example, the letter 'Ja' in 'Japa' stands for annihilation of cycle of births and deaths and, 'Pa' stands for eradication of sins (papa). Some sounds words can cure diseases, while others console and soothen the distressed mind. Some words energise and others dampen the spirit. A slight change in the expression makes a world of difference; often the same word contains both (opposite) meanings. A slight variation in the expression of the word 'Amruta' can make a lot of difference in the meaning; 'Amruta', what is 'elixir' that produces immortality, becomes 'mruta', the dead, by just suppressing 'a' in it. While the Samskrut language has got this inner strength, other languages simply float the meaning and no words of other languages do not come nearer to, or equivalent to, some Samskrut words. For example, 'faith' is a poor translation of 'Shruddha' that includes, Jnyaana, Bhakti, and Courage of Conviction in practice. Similarly, a 'Teacher' in English and Guru in Samskrut; there is total surrender of the disciple to a Guru, whereas, the student and teacher remain apart even after several years of association. Hence, Samskrut words are used in the text here alongwith their English equivalents. Glossory with elaborate description is given at the end of the Text will be of some help.

It is the Lord Almighty, to whom we use the terms 'He' and 'Him', or the 'Divine Force', referred to as 'That'. 'He' who resides in every creature as 'Soul', the Atman is the real God and He is common to all the six-and-odd billion people as well as the billions and billions plants and animals of this Planet Earth; and, 'He' has no name and form! If you so desire, you can give a name and form to 'Him' and worship 'Him'. All these five or six thousand years we have been doing only this. Jesus Christ, Sri Krishna, Sri Rama, Gautama Buddha, and Mahavira are the 'avatars', or incarnations of the Lord. In a way, these are the persons who have purified their mind and soul, raised their level of consciousness to unite with the Supreme Consciousness and thereby developed their inner strength to become so powerful that they 'swayed the world' and have ultimately become the hope and faith of millions of people. Many spiritual leaders like Shri Ramana Maharishi, Shri Ramakrishna, have developed their inner strength, attained purity of mind, heart and soul, and they too have become the hope and aspirations of their followers. That way, everybody can attain this spiritual height by mere sadhana, practice of Sama, Dama, Dharana, Dhyan, Meditation and Samadhi.

Elaborate description of this universe and the 'world we live in' is given so that one will clearly understand the nature of his existence bound by space and time. Some of the 'Mahat Tattvas', the 'Great Principles' are explained so that persons who seek permanent happiness will abide by the Lord's Will and Trust in Him. There is no disappointment and cause for unhappiness to those who have total devotion, faith and trust in God. Some Golden Rules of Manoniyantrana taken out of the ancient scriptures are given in a separate Chapter. The exhaustive index given at the end will help locate the subject easily and quickly.

This book is of immense value to all age groups. A doctor who follows the guidelines given in this book will achieve extraordinary success in his profession for he will realize the play of the hidden hand in saving lives of patients and reducing their pains. Similarly, an engineer will realize the extraordinary meaning and depth of his profession and gains insight into the working of machines. The yogic powers are such that one can identify the faults in a machine by mere touch, sounds and vibrations, without even opening it up. All sorts of professionals can gain success and happiness from the study of this small book. One can shape his life and achieve success and happiness.

Manoniyantran Tantras, or the Mind Control Techniques, described here are based on our Ancient Scriptures. Veda, Upanishads, the Brahma Sutra, the Bhagavad-Gita, Bhagavatha, Vishnu Purana and epics like Ramayana and the Mahabharata. The ancient scriptures are the invaluable legacy of Indian spiritual history and culture. The Veda have been instructed to the trusted ones and have been handed down to us by careful renderings by memory (Smruti) with utmost care for pronunciation and accents. It is said that the Creator Brahma himself instructed the Veda to his First son Atharvan and the date of this ancient scripture is beyond all possible estimates. Each of the renown Sages and Rishis specialized in the different aspects of the Veda established individual schools of thought emphasizing different aspects of the Veda, and the Upanishads. These have come down to us as 'Vedanta' and it is an invaluable guide to us. Vedanta holds the key to not only a happy and successful life but also for emancipation, salvation, liberation, or Moksha. Besides the Knowledge pertaing to the Self and God, the study of the most wonderful thing ever-created, called 'Mind', the Techniques of Mind Control, or 'Manoniyantran', are also the major aspects dealt with in Vedanta. The Yoga Upanishads elaborately deal with these. These two aspects are taken up here for a detailed study here.

Vedic culture is the *'Sanatana Dharma'*. The ancient Indians who settled down in the Sindhu (R.Indus) Valley, known as Aryans, seem to have descended from the Arctic region where the days and nights are six months-long and came down to live over a wide area in the R. Euphrates and the R.Tigris valley of Persia (Iran) of ancient times and influenced the lives and thought of people as far as Malaysia, Indonesia, China and Japan in the East. All these countries have inculcated the Vedic culture in one form or the other. The Mind and psyche of these Asians is simply wonderful for it blends spiritual with science and technological civilization in a very harmonious way. The success of Japan and Korea is attributed to spiritual practices that can be traced to Vedic tradition and Upanishadic doctrines. Even today, Mind control through Yoga and Meditation (Zen) is practised as one of the major aspects of industrial culture in Japan. It is very religiously practised to enhance the potential of the workers and maximize their input in all avocations.

India is called the Karma Bhumi, Punya Bhoomi or the Yoga Bhoomi, whereas, the Western countries are called the 'Rajo' (Bhoga) Bhoomi. In India, people strive for spiritual progress and practise Yoga and Meditation to attain inner peace and bliss ('anand') that is not possible through indulgences in materialistic acquisitions and sensuous living. There is need for a clear understanding of the Hindu way of life, the Vedantic way, the spiritual way. The Indian or Hindu way of life that has developed over several millennia, estimated to be at least ten thousand years. This way of life is very much criticized by the western thinkers who have failed to grasp the essence of the Veda.

Some of the 'Maha Vaakyas', 'Great Principles', the Mahat tattvas, are repeated in different contexts to drive these into the minds of our ignorant selves and knock some sense to the unconscious mind indulging in mundane things. Many important mantra that are panacea for all our ills are also repeated several times. Elaborate description of the 'cosmogony' is given in order to locate the insignificant stature of 'human' life in this universe. The bloated ego of man makes him an imaginary giant who can destroy this world by his wickedness but cannot sustain it by his humility, love, piety, compassion, and fellowship.

The Hindu philosophy of life believes in 'Karma' and 'Rebirth' (Metempsychosis). Except for Charvaka, all other doctrines are united on this. It is only Charvaka, who is a materialist and secular, who does not offer any reason or theory to support his version of evolution of man and a reasoned theory of man and the universe. Nyaya, Vaisheshika, Samkhya, and Yoga believe in the authenticity of the Veda and accept dualism or Vishishta Dvaitism. Purva mimamsa, and Uttara Mimansa advocate 'Advaitism'.

Samkhya philosophy considers that Mahat (Purusha) and Pradhan (Prakruti) account for everything. Purusha is the Universal soul, the manifest form of which is the Jeeva, individual soul (of which there is an unlimited number). Primordial Prakriti is matter consisting of the twenty-four principles ranging from the three gunas-the tamas, rajas and sattvic, down to the gross earth. By the joinder of Purusha and Prakruti, spirit and matter, samsara is the result. Their divorce is the goal to be reached! Both matter and spirit are real entities that get on without any controlling force or power. However, the controlling force behind the two is the inexplicable, self-effulgent, omniscient, omnipotent, absolute and the Infinite called 'the Brahman'. Realisation of this 'Truth' is emancipation.

This brief introduction would suffice to know the cause of all the myriads of problems of the world and the problems that the individuals face in crossing the ocean of sansara. One should always remember that 'life is to live'. Life offers plenty of opportunities. Enjoy life fully; know what it is, its limitations, its futility, and then reject it as of no avail in attaining greater and permanent happiness, the 'mahat anand' ('Supreme Bliss'), eternal happiness, i.e., 'sat, chit, and anand'. At every corner of the road there is a new vista and a new road. Pause for a while, take a view at the vista point, gaze at the horizon, look to your inner voice for guidance and move on and take a fresh journey to success and happiness. Never be disheartened by failures or stumbling blocks or hurdles; these are the testing stones. There is always light at the end of the tunnel. If you do not want to travel this way again, turn to God. Make an earnest prayer to put an end to all this drama! Make your self fit to get His Divine Grace by your pure thoughts, action and total submission. He will redeem you. Realise your 'Self' yourself!

It is important that a good guide, a Guru, is required in all these matters, especially for spiritual attainments. If you get a 'Guru', well and good! You are lucky at that for he will guide you; otherwise, be your own "Guru". Prepare yourself for the great journey with very simple equipments like austerity, truthfulness, disciplene in personal life, self-less service and compassion, etc. Look within yourself; there is none better than your own Self. The Lord sits within you as '*Antaryamin*' and guides you if you sincerely seek Him and carefully hear Him. When you sincerely pray you will hear '*anahata dhvani*' in your right year at the appropriate time. He may direct a spiritual leader to guide you, or He will appear in your dream and initiate you. Such mystic experiences are common. One need not worry too much about this. But, remember, it is a very slow and a never ending process!

Again, remember, 'Brahma is your Guru, Vishnu is your Guru, Maheshwara is your Guru'. Brahma taught the Veda to Indra, Narada, Shuka, Vemana, Veda Vyasa, and many many others. Similarly, Vishnu, Sri Krishna has taught Arjuna, as seen in Bhagavad-Gita. And, Shri Rama taught the Veda to Anjaneya, as in Muktikopanishad. So also, Maheshvara taught Parvati; and, all their teachings are there before us in the sacred ancient Scriptures- the Upanishads, the Brahma Sutras, the Bhagavad-Gita, and the Epics and Puranas. Only, you have to take interest in these Scriptures and experience the doctrines.

As one proceeds with the practice of Meditation regularly, 'Revelations' come in dreams. Mystic powers appear very early in sadhana. Those who surrender to Him enjoy the Supreme Bliss. 'Shruddha', i.e., Faith with knowledge and conviction, is all that is required. '*No faith, no life*' is the rule of spiritual life! Now that a large number of young boys and girls are going away from India to various countries of the world in pursuit of economic prosperity, there is every possibility of their being left out from the mainstream of Indian life. Indian life, the Hindu 'way of life', i.e., the Vedic or Spiritual Life is very important. The Hindu Philosophy and Hindu Religion are the oldest in the world like the Chinese Philosophy and religion. It is almost ten thousand years old or may be more than that. There has been a thorough degeneration, deterioration in the quality of human life; values have changed during the last few Centuries and it is a bad sign! In fact, the quality of human life has been declining since the Krita Yuga, or Satya Yuga called the 'Golden Age'. And, all our problems are due to our neglect of 'Truth', Order, and 'Righteousness', i.e., 'Ritam' and 'Satyam'.

In the Krita Yuga, an age of illumination and harmony, it was all a transparent life of 'Ritam' (Order) and 'Satyam' (Truth). People could see through and through others and could see and understand the minds! In Treta Yuga, called the Silver Age, it was all 'Virtues', values of life; come what may, Sri Ram stood for values in life. Values started declining. Sattva guna declined giving place to prepondering Rajas. And, in the Dvapara Yuga, called the Copper Age, it was all 'Dharma' and Shri Krishna stands for 'Consciousness'. Values had declined further over the ages and we see the behaviour of Duryodhana and Shakuni in Mahabharat. Sri Krishna took birth to kill Kamsa and restore Dharma. He has been striving for establishment of 'Dharma', righteousness, values in life, as we can see it in Mahabharat. Sri Krishna says, "I will take repeated births to re-establish Dharma, (*"Dharma Samsthapanarthaya ... sambhavami yuge yuge"*). In Kali Yuga, called the Iron Age, it is total devastation of values and spirituality. It is pre-ponderance of Tamas, loss of values of life-'Ritam','Satyam' and 'Dharma'. People who want to turn this order and truth, upside down, topsy- turvy, should understand that it ultimately leads to chaos. Already one can see how the moral, social, and economic order is disturbed due to the misguided conceptions. Sri Krishna says in Bhagavad-Gita, "whastever station in life, one should work devouted and selfless and I shall take care of him". This phrase, "whatever station in life" has not been clearly understood by politicians with the result that they want social and economic justice to the under-privileged, without knowing what it means! Whether born in a high caste called 'Brahmana', or supposedly low caste, 'Shudra', all are equal in the eyes of God and all are taken care of by God. It is political glimmic that the selfish politicians offer reservation in jobs and promise to bring heaven on earth. Ultimately, it is cheating the gullible and ignorant poor in the name of secularism, social justice, reservation and the like. Vedanta only is the key and will bring knowledge and happiness to all irrespective of caste, class, and creed.

Today, life has become senseless, wayward, aimless, goalless and nobody knows what he wants; it is all confusion and complexes. Ego rules the roost. Everybody wants freedom, liberty, and independence without knowing the meaning, without understanding what it means to be free, independent. And, the result is that they are 'neither here, nor there'. They are a confused lot. The present-day children face lots of problems in their lives due to conflicting values, languages, cultures, and life styles. It is here that a sense of purpose, a sense of direction or goal is needed to make life more meaningful, make it more fruitful. Having got the human life form, it is an evolutionary process to make life more divine, spiritual, and thereby enable oneself to enjoy the 'Bliss', eternal happiness- "Sat Chit Anand".

There is, thus, no doubt that this 'make-believe' sensate world of glimmicks is the 'Leela' of the Lord! Our children, particularly those living abroad, should not get lost in this maze of material objective world! The Western world is a land of wine and women ideal for sensuous life that binds jeevas in eternal bondage. They should not lose sight of the ancient wisdom of the Sages and the warnings given in the Veda and Upanishads. It is appropriate that the knowledge and wisdom of the age-old scriptures come handy to open our eyes to 'Reality' of life. Most of the views, perceptions, and doctrines presented here are useful in contemplation and meditation. Vichara is the first step towards liberation followed by viveka and vairagya. This book strives to bring home the fact that what all we see, hear, and know is not real. Lord's Grace alone can guide us in these days of strife, darkness and ignorance. Shree Harih, Om! Tat Sat!

1
Manoprapancha
[The Sensate Objective World]

"Manonmatram Jagat, Manah Kalpitam Jagat".
"The world exists in our mind". Sage Kapila.

Sage Kapila is believed to be the first ever born and, as such, considered to be the son of Prajapati, Brahma. He learnt the Veda and gained supreme Knowledge from his father. Thus, Kapila is the most ancient and the all-knowing Sage, the first Rishi who is the perfect being. {See Svetasvatara Upanishad}. He had an extraordinary flair for numbers. He deduced the whole universe consisting millions of material objects to two primary Principles –the Purusha and the Prakriti, the two uncreated, self-existent, primary beings. The universe that appears to be a complex world of material objects is actually made of very few simple elements and compounds; literally, it is the product of the combination of Prakriti and Purusha. Sage Kapia states that the Union of these two self-existent beings is the cause of all causes, and has created all the material objects of the universe. But, here again, Kapila asserts that this universe is phenomenal consisting of three factors viz, knowledge, perception and sensations. This phenomenal universe appears to be a collection of innumerable entities due to our ignorance. He deduced that the union of Purusha and Prakriti produced twenty-four entities, including the Mind and the five senses. Purusha being the Self or Brahman, it is this Prakriti that we are dealing with here. The much-Revered Sage Kapila asserts that the perceptible material world is nothing but the creation of our mind and, as such, it exists only in our mind. It is called 'Manoprapancha'.

Sage Kapila's philosophy is known as *Samkhya Philosophy*. It explains the process of evolution very clearly. Kapila Maha Muni, as he is known, is the first to find out the phenomenal nature of the Universe and stated that three factors- the adhibhuta (matter), the adhyatma (spirit), and adhidaiva (Consciousness) go to make this phenomenal world. The perception of the objective world is made possible due to Consciousness, Prajnya, (the illumining principle). Thus, in order to perceive this matrial world, there must be a Seeker, the visible material objects, and, the illumining principle called 'Consciousness'. It is this consciousness in the mind that enables a person to visualize this universe. Hence, this visible universe exists within the Mind, not somewhere outside. In other words, the universe exists in our mind.

According to Sankhya Philosophy, some supreme power must have brought us here to serve its own purpose. This mysterious irresistible power has created this universe and man with a purpose. In this sense, we have not come here according to our will, or on our own accord. It is in obedience to this powerful being that we are here and it is impossible to oppose. We had no choice in this. If there was any choice, we would have selected much better environment and endowments for all of us are always searching for something better. We are all hungry, thirsty, needy souls and we feel weak and dependent. We have got eleven sense organs (Mind and Jnyanendriyas and Karmendriyas) under the grip of three gunas- tamas, rajas and sattva creating thirty- three hungers of the body. These thirty-three sorts of hungers and desires constantly bother us. And, each sort of desire has a million attractive objects in view. Thus, these thirty-three million objects of desire fill this sensate world and we are struggling day and night to fulfil our limitless desires in a limited time without success. This is the cause of our misery.

Jaimini has described this world as a very attractive world of desire and wish-fulfilment. This world is created for our enjoyment. It appears as though the Lord has thrown a lavish party, an eternal banquet of endless dinner over a vast limitless space for innumerable jeevas to satisfy their hunger. We are all hungry, thirsty and needy souls; in addition to the stomach hungry for food, we have thirty-three sorts of hunger- each part of the body having its own hunger like the eyes eagerly looking for beautiful sights, ears longing for melodious sound, skin greedy to have soft satisfying touch, etc. There are thirty-three million objects of desire to cater to these hunger and thirst of our body and we are struggling day and night to fulfil our endless desires within a limited time, without success. This is the cause of our misery.

Jaimini's philosophy is very clear. This world is for enjoyment and God has given everything here to make our life happy. He has created thirty-three million Deities, 'Abhimani Devatas' to look after our hunger, thirst and desires. Do not ignore them. Worship them, propitiate them, and get whatever you want and be happy. Whatever be the wish, it will be granted by these 'Abhimani Devatas', or 'Vasus', only if you propitiate the particular Deity or Lord Indra and pray for the fulfilment of your desires.

Further, it is held that the whole universe is created for the enjoyment of the jeevas. The mind and the out-going senses on the one hand, and the tantalizing and thirty-three million attractive material objects of the world on the other, make this world enjoyable. Enjoy and be happy. But, Lo! It is just not that. There are persons who reject this. They do not want to be slaves of desire. They do not want to worship these Deities to fulfil their desires. Thay say, 'Why should we be slave to these Deities? Why should we serve these Gods?' We are free and we do not want bondage. We are ever eager to get out of these senses, the mind and desires of the flesh, and be free forever. These Jeevas know that their nature is freedom, all-Bliss, and infinite and perfect for they know that happiness comes from within. Vedanta says 'nothing exists outside; God is within you, the whole universe is in you. You are the eternal, peaceful and the Blissful. Thus, a Jnyani will not fall prey to eternal bondage and knows how to get out of the clutches of this 'Prapancha'- the gripping sensate objective world.

The 'World' or *'Prapancha'*, means, *'that perceived by the five senses'*. The sensate world is the one perceived by the senses, and, man perceives this world by his mind through the senses. The senses as they are, are dispensed to outward perception and the earth being a gross body, the senses perceive the gross sensate things that come within their range. It must be always remembered that the gross body is finite and limited. All that is perceived by the human mind through the sense organs is finite and limited. As such, this sensate world is incapable of granting everlasting happiness. Inspite of this, the ignorant jeeva wants to enjoy and thereby suffers misery and cries for liberation. The day a child is born it cries for having come to this earth while the parents and all others attached to it are happy. May be, it is the memory of its former heavenly abode and the bliss the Jeeva enjoyed before arriving here that makes the child cry as is believed by the Seers and the Knowledgeable. So also, it is true that the Jeeva is happy to leave this earth at the earliest opportunity, unless it is greatly attached to its petty joys and illusory happiness. All the happiness and joy on this ever-changing material world is short-lived since this objective world is *'Maya'* or illusion. Hence, it is made very clear that this world, 'prapancha', is not the place for eternal happiness and permanent bliss. It is the 'desire' of the Jeeva that makes it to take repeated births to fulfill the desired object. Until and unless the inherent desires are fulfilled, or till the realization as to the reality of the things come to the Jeeva, it is bound to go round and round this cycle of rebirths. Hence, the cause of birth lies in the 'desire' followed by Karma.

Gautama Buddha realized that man is sensate and, as such, liberation is difficult till he gets rid of his attachments and desires. It is the desire that drives one to disillusionment and disappointments. Even when one attains his desired objects, he is not happy because there is a gap between the time when he desired and the attainment and in the mean time the desired object ceases to match his desire thereby leading to misery. So, no man is happy; whether rich or poor he is bound by his desire that can never match his attainments. Many kings and emperors, Conquerers and rulers, who desired to hold the entire world in their hands died miserably. There are the examples of Napolean, Alexander, Hitler, and the like to prove this point. But, this should not be a deterrent to 'action' man is bound by 'karma' and has to perform his action, as there is no escape from his duties as long as he lives here.

In *Bhagavad-Gita,* Sri Krishna advocates 'Nishkama Karma' i.e., *'one has to do his duty without attachment to its results'*. It is essential that all actions are performed in the name of the Lord and the fruits of action offered to Him, so that there is no scope for greed or desire in the action and thus one is released of his bondage. *This is the greatest secret of happiness and success in life.*

Some of the eternal questions are: What are the qualities of this sensate world? How to cross this ocean of samsara, carefully, wading through all the miseries of unhappines, disappointments, troubles and turmoils, sickness and ignorance, poverty and what not?

The answer is not very difficult to find. It is now and here that one can attain the Divine Bliss and be happy forever once he gets 'enlightenment'. The Buddha's *'enlightenment'* is not essential for any and everyone to be happy. It is enough if one gets a clear understanding of one's own true nature, life-his ambitions, his potentialities and abilities, his innate desires, dreams and ambitions, and methods to achieve them; or, at least, it is important to know what exactly he wants from his life. One has to be very clear about these things in order to be happy and successful. *It is mostly due to ignorance that one suffers.* The answer, in one word, is that this world is 'sensate', and all wants are 'insatiable'. Most of the time one is confused and the famous *Bhagavad- Gita's* Arjuna's 'to fight or not to fight', or as Shakespeare puts it in Hamlet as, "to be, or not to be", are the cases to remember here.

Katha Upanishad warns that, *"He who is without discrimination and whose mind is always uncontrolled, his are unmanageable like the vicious horses of a driver. The body that is at the command of the Mind sans Buddhi simply follows the dictates of the mind. The mind which is nothing but the desires, fears, accumulated prejudices has nothing to offer to the supreme Lord except what it is made of – i.e., 'thoughts'. No God would accept the fruits offered by the mind because, the fruits of the mind are misery and ignorance, and being the servant of the ego, only the self-promotion. This no God would accept".*

Life raises problems at every step. When doubts arise, we turn to the wisdom of philosophy, as to a lamp in dark, for guidance. Every individual is the possessor of a little wisdom, which helps him to negotiate life's placid waters. But, this little 'light' (wisdom) fails us when storms and stresses are set in. It is then that the human mind seeks for a steadier light. We want a steadier light (wisdom), which will stand us in all circumstances of life. Vedanta has the capacity to provide us with this light (wisdom) that will help us to keep our feet steady and our head firm.

The best teachers are those who help the disciples to solve their own problems, never imposing set solutions of their own to them. In *Bhagavad-Gita* Sri Krishna tells Arjuna, *"Thus I have taught you wisdom which is subtler than the subtlest, having examined it well, act as you think best".* The mention of a great name should not rent in the surrendering of our independence of judgment, Yama said, in *Katha Upanishad, "Go round and round and examine it well from all sides and from all points of view".* First examine the teacher and the teaching, and then accept. Sri Ramakrishna used to say to his disciples: 'Test me as the money-changers test their coins'. How few are the students who can test the teachers and the teachers who can stand the test?

The sensate world and the human mind are the two things involved here. In a sense, these are not two different things. The mind is the world. What one thinks is one's world; what one perceives is one's world. What one makes of it is one's world. *The perceiver, the perceived, and the act of perception are all one. This is 'unity'.* When there is total submission to Him, the Lord, the duality disappears; the *'unity'* or, that *'one behind the many'* is realized. This concept of unity of things is very important in the understanding of things. As Kapila puts it, the illumining principle, Self

(Consciousness) comes in between the objective world (Prakriti or Nature) and the ever-hungry Jeeva, the embodied Purusha, ignorant of the real nature of his Self. The Mind is the key to solve the mystery of this universe since the objective world is its own creation and rests within it. If the Mind ceases, the world ceases to exist. We are all under the grip of the mind and see the world through the sense organs as the mind directs them. Ultimately, it is our ignorance that makes us see and believe this world as real.

Intelligence and Creativity

Intelligence is the basic quality of Nature. There is intelligence in all creatures. This supreme intelligence and bliss pervade air, water, earth, fire, and all the great elements. The Supreme Self expresses in terms of 'Sat' (Truth), 'Chit' (Consciousness), and 'Anand' (Bliss), the vital force Prana, and the 'Intelligence'. The seat of intelligence is Consciousness and the seat of Consciousness is the 'Atma'. 'Atman is Brahman', the Absolute, who resides in Abstract Silence, called 'Atyantaa Abhava'. It knows all and it is self-referral. It is Purusha. Creative Intelligence is the quality, nature, associated with the Svaroopa of 'Purusha', the ever full and the unchanging quality of Consciousness. And, then, there is the 'Sakshin', Silent Witness to all this. That is the Self, the Tenth; "Dashamasthvamasi" meaning 'Thou art the Tenth', the Self within, the source of all Intelligence and Creativity [Rk Véda, Purusha Sukta, Mandala X]. With the attainment to this Self, the journey, the search for Truth, stops.

Maharishi Mahesh Yogi has beautifully brought out the secret of Intelligence and Creativity hidden in the Purusha in his ***"Apaurusheya Bhashya.*** He says, ' When *Atyanta Abhaava*, the *Abstract Absolute Silence*, the ***Purusha***, comes in contact with the ***Pradhana***, *Anyonya-Abhava, the Self-Referral Dynamic Silence*, where the creative force operates, the material world takes its shape in numerous names and forms. Infinite possibilities exist in this center of contact of *'Atyanta-Abhava'* with *'Anyonya-Abhaava' the seat of Absolute Silence.* Anybody who reaches this depth of Silence by Transcendental Meditation can reach the treasure of immense possibilities stored in the depth of *Atyanta-Abhava.* Deep Silence attained through contemplation and Meditation is the key to intelligence and creative activity. By virtue of the self-interacting dynamics of its unified nature, the unmanifest, the unbounded ocean of Consciousness (Purusha) spontaneously expresses the mechanics of manifesting (the waves or the intension, desire, thoughts, images and words and sound). The quality of specificity (the bubbles or material objects) comes into being without disruprting the Continuum (Existence) of the eternal, self-referral generality of Consciousness (Purusha). It is a self-referral superfluid system of expressing specificity within the unity of eternal generality. Emergence of dynamism in the Silence (Mauna) of the GAPS (Sandhi) within the nature of Consciousness- lays open the total nature of consciousness (quality of Consciousness called *Anyonya-Abhava*, the seat of immense possibilities) Bhagawan [Mahesh Yogi]. Hence, all creativity and intelligence emanates from contemplation in deep silence, Meditation'. Here is the clue to originality, excellence in performance, and all success in any avocation, may it be in research leading to inventions and discoveries or ordinary routine duties. Pĕrsons who practise silence for a few minutes daily, contemplates on the supreme Lord, shall gain all the Best in this world - name, fame, power, position, material wealth, spiritual progress, and savation, too. That is why, it is said that the Lord sits in the cave of our heart and guides us, only if we look to Him for guidance.

Now, coming to creative thinking, it is a function of the brain. Any process of thought has certain correlates in terms of the chemical and electrical behaviour of the nerve cells and their functional groups. These physical values may be measured and connected with their subjective correlates; special type of thinking that is highly creative has associated with it certain physiological characteristics in the brain. An orderly, coherent thinking and resistence to confusion at a direct neurophysiologicallevel in the functioning of the brain facilitates creative thoughts. A person of cool mental disposition is more creative than a highly excited emotional person. In fact zero degree brain temperature is idealy suited to higher creative performance. It has been found that highly creative persons show synchronous and coherent brain waves from the two cerebral hemispheres and have a capacity for integration and coordination of different brain areas. This has been experimented and measured by EEG of some persons. Anxiety is a deterrent factor in creativity. Reduced anxiety and improved psycho-technical performance and the timing of voluntary actions for creative behaviour are important factors. There is evidence of increased activation of the right hemisphere during process underlying creativity such as intuition, non-verbal idea formation, melodic composition etc.

Highly intelligent people are not necessarily very creative. Although creative people are intelligent, high Intelligence Quotient (IQ) is not necessary for creativity. In fact, high IQ may hinder development of creative ability due to self-criticism. Use of primitive forms of cognition is necessary for creativity. People are under wrong notion that use of drugs, alcohol, and such other stimulants which are highly addictive and damaging the brain take to these with the hope achieving success. But these are contrary to spiritual laws and do not go to make a harmonious development of the personality. Special physical and social environment, development of good habits, attitudes and associations may greatly help. Sattvic food, solitude and contemplative moods are highly elevative inactivity, it is said, facilitates creativity; and, more often Eureka! New ideas come on a lonely walk, in a bath -tub or in a state of relaxation. Excessive routine activity stifle mental activity and creativity; it creates drudgery and dullness. Physical exhaustion is the killer of all intuition and imagination.

Creativity comes out of inner harmony and orderliness. Alertness and discipline are the other requirements. Some artists and thinkers refuse to obey orderly disciplined way of life due to the rigidities not accepted by the mind which cries for freedom and liberty. Creativity requires hard wprk to put into practice what the creative, intuitive mind props up. This is where most of the aspirants fail to achieve their dreams. Their wishful thinking ends up in dry day dreams due to lethargy and appropriate âction at the appropriate time. Many great writers keep a notebook and pen at their bedside to quickly note down their dream sequences lest they should forget.

Thus, there is great need for Divine Grace as also the Grace of one's own mind to achieve something in life. But, the best policy is to 'let go' (free mind) and watch it with contemplative mind; Work hard to sustain the dreams and it comes by ninety-nine per cent perspiration and one per cent inspiration. There is some truth in what is called 'ashirwad' of elders, parents and teachers. The blessings uttered with pure mind and heart would go a long way in fulfilment of one's desires. When one builds up good samskara, individuality and self-reliance, strength of character, and self-confidence, the Grace of the Lord and the Grace of one's own Mind is already there. In a very successful person, the great achiever, the hero, his ego is built up to the brim so that he offers it to the Lord in total submission. That is the beauty of this creation. Total surrender to the Lord Almighty is the rule of law in spirituality. If not total Satva guna, at least, Satva-dominated rajas will entitle the person to His Grace.

Ralph Waldo Emerson, the author of 'Self-Reliance' says that, *"there is guidance within each of us, and when we look and listen we will hear the word ".*

And, then there are experts on thinking techniques and well known thought-leaders like Al ries, Tom Peters and Michael Porter, Dr Edward De Bono of the 'Six Thinking Hats'- fame who are Business intellectuals. De Bono is the architect of Lateral Thinking and has produced techniques of thinking that are simple and practical. But, remember all these experts talk of material progress in this mundane world and they are all obsessed with survival in a competitive market, not spiritual enrichment of the 'Self'. Also, remember real happiness, peace and progress does not come from topping the list in Fortune 500 Magazine, or being the CEO of the Corporate Giants that are listed in New York Stock Exchange or NASDOC. It is the man of Self-Realization who is at peace with him self and gives all his wealth to the benefit of the needy ones. It is ultimately the spiritual wealth only that counts in life.

Self-organisation

There is the principle of Self-Organisation. A living organism is a self-organising system, which means that its order in structure and function is not imposed by the environment but is established by the system itself. Self-organising systems exhibit a certain degree of autonomy. They tend to establish their size according to inner principles of organisation, independent of environmental conditions. On the contrary, they interact with environment continually, but this interaction will not determine their organisation. The two principal dynamic phenomena of self-organisation are self renewal, i.e., the ability to continuously renew and recycle their components while maintaining the integrity of their over-all structure; and self transcendence i.e, the ability to reach out creatively beyond physical and mental boundaries in the process of learning, development and evolution. This leads to the question of free will.

Free Will

The concept of 'Free Will' is an age-old concept. To the extent that a system is autonomous from its environment it is free; to the extent it is dependent on it through a continuous interaction it is influenced by environment. The relative autonomy of organisms usually increases with their complexity, and it reaches its culmination in human beings. This relative concept of 'Free Will' seems to be consistent with the views of mystical traditions that exhort their followers to transcend the notion of an isolated self and become aware that we are inseparable parts of the cosmos. Once such a state is reached, the question of 'Free Will' seems to lose it's meaning. In reality, 'Free will' is restricted to 'action within bounds'; life as dictated by Karma on the one hand, genes on the other. Environmental factors too mould the life and dictate the action within bounds of genes and karma! Thus, the answer to the major question of Fate or Luck is answered. No one can escape the bondage of karmic particles that entwain the embodied soul and keep us in eternal bondage. Hence, 'Free Will' is a myth! We are born under 'His Will' and Live under His mercy and, work at His Behest. Our joy or sorrow, happiness or misery depends on His sweet will and pleasure. "At best one can do under the circumstances is to "do one's duty and surrender to Him".

Psychologists and Neuro-surgeons believe that free will is evident from the fact that *'I can move my fingers, but not yours'*. Of course, there are Sadhus and Aghori Babas who can do that other thing also; they can make others body move as they like. That is a different matter! Here, we concerned with one very important aspect. Is it our destiny, or luck, or free will that we act and gain what we want; or, is it simply divine will and Grace of God; or, is it our strong determination and hard work; or, simply Karma, the fruits of action of previous births and the present; or, the genes are in any way responsible for the thoughts and the results of action; or, the environment- physical, social and economic, that is responsible for our life? All these questions call for an in-depth study. So far, the results of such studies are very interesting. Each one of these factors play very significant role in the life of man. Not only 'Free Will' but, the 'Genes' (heredity) and environment, as well, play a dominant role. However, Karma and desire are the driving force!

Hence, it is very clear that we all live and work within a narrow restricted field like the bullock tied to a long rope; it can operate within a certain sphere as long as the rope allows it to. However, hard it tries to work to get out of the reach, it is bound to come back to rest near the pole to which it is tied! The whole life is like that. Ultimately, we have to take shelter in Him, the Lord! Of course, we have freedom to think and act; but this freedom is tied to our past actions, Karma. There is no release from this bondage unless we surrender (our 'ego') to the Lord. Remember, the Lord Himself has said in Bhagavad Gita, 'Come to me, I will take care of you'

Freedom

'Real freedom is the freedom of the Soul'. Freedom of the Soul is the real happiness, too. All other 'freedom' is like the freedom of a person aloft the coconut tree. He can operate within the scope offered by the situation. We are bound by space and time, by gravity, by the grip of 'Maya', 'avidya' or nescience, ignorance, or perverted intelligence. We believe and feel this objective, mundane, fleeting, insentient, tantalising world as real. It is our deluded mind that is the cause of our misery. For instance, a person who moves in a fast vehicle feels the freedom from space and time in a very limited way. So also, a person who flies in an aircraft feels he has conquered time and space and has attained greater freedom. But, a person who flies in a spacecraft reaches to outer space, enjoys much higher freedom in the real sense, by going beyond gravity; but, this too, is limited. Real happiness is enjoyed by the one whose Mind is free! Real happiness comes to one who transcends space, time, and causality by transcendental meditation and reaches the state of 'Turiyaateeta Samaadhi', the state of Godconsciousness. It is pure 'joy' emanating from the Soul and just not the happiness that depends on external sources. Any happiness that depends on exernal source is bound to bring misery, but not the pure joy.

Stress

When confronted with challenges of life, or when under pressure to perform, we often tense our minds and bodies in an attempt to focus on our goal or objective. This intense condition creates mental, emotional and physical rigidity that causes us to be more receptive to the information and possibility that surround us. We become inflexible, unconscious to other people and their feelings, as well as our feelings. This tension not only dis-empowers us; it blocks our ability to perform at our higher mental and physical levels. This rigidity eliminates flexibility. Increasing tension often leads to the opposite of relaxation, which is increased stress.

Too much of stress leads to change in blood pressure, increase in adrenalin, increase in gluco corticoids- all potential destructive harmones, increase in perspiration, heart-beat, etc. One will loose his self-confidence. One in relaxed condition can maintain balance and manage stress. Stress should not lead to distress. Recent studies have shown that the damage inflicted on the body due to too much of stress is not just restricted only to ulcers and heart diseases, but also extends to the loss of immune function and memory. In the short term, stress is damaging, but over time it turns destructive-in the adrenalin glands the cortex secretes cortisol which becomes toxic to brain cells, potentially damaging cognitive ability and increasing fatigue, anger, and depression. The immune system gets weakened due to repeated supression of disease-fighting cells, decreases in blood flow leave mucous lining vulnerable to ulcers and the elevated blood pressure and heart rate damage elasticity of blood vessels. The above stress syndrome is not exclusive to high-fly executives only; it is affecting young mothers and school going children as well. To control stress and avoid all its consequences, both yoga and meditation are superb proven remedies. Sit comfortably and close your eyes. Do not think;

observe the thoughts that pass by in your mind. Finally, the thoughts cease and you feel relaxed. Thoughtless awareness is the key to happiness. Be aware of thoughts that repeatedly bother you. It is like a dog wagging its tail; the moment you stare at it, it stops.

Our culture takes pride in science, being scientific. Our time is referred to as the scientific age. It is dominated by rational thought, and scientific knowledge is often considered the only acceptable kind. That there can be intuitive knowledge or awareness, which is just as valid and reliable, is generally not recognised. This attitude, known as 'scientism', is widespread pervading our educational system and all other social and political institutions. The emphasis on rational thought in our culture is epitomised in Descartes's celebrated statement, *"cogito, ergo sum"*. "I think, therefore I exist"; which forcefully encourage western individuals to equate their identity with their rational mind rather than with their whole organism.

Retreating into our minds, we have forgotten how to think with our bodies, how to use them as agents of knowing. In doing so we have also cut off from our natural environment and have forgotten how to commune and cooperate with other rich variety of living organisms. Living systems are organised in such a way that they form multi-level structures, each level consisting of subsistence that are wholes in regard to their parts, and parts with respect to their larger wholes. The holistic approach is very important. Remember the aphorism: *'Om, poornamadah poornamidam Poornat poornamuduchyate; Poornasya poornamadaaya poornamevavishyate' (Isavasya. Upanishad)*. It is full of meaning. One has to contemplate on this mantra.

Molecules combine to form organelles, which in turn combine to form cells. However small, each cell is complete in itself. The cells form tissues and organs which themselves form larger system like the digestive system, nervous system and the like. These finally combine to form the living organisms fully equipped with memory, aminoacids, enzymes, vitamins and minerals, and proteins aided by the DNA and RNA chains keeping different parts self-supporting as also mutually supporting and in constant communion. The highest life form of the human- the man or the woman, with X and Y chromosomes, with automatic thermostatic and pressure control systems, the ability to manipulate and maintain appropriate sugar, salt, and calcium balance in the body, metabolism, constant dialysis, etc. is a real wonder! It is the mystery unveiled by medical science layer by layer, and the stratified order does not end there. People form families, tribes, societies, nations. All these entities –from molecules to human beings, and on to social system- can be regarded as wholes, in the sense of being integrated structures, and also as parts of larger wholes at higher level of complexity. In fact, we shall see that parts and wholes in an absolute sense do not exist at all.

Arthur Koestler has coined the word *'holons'* for these sub-systems that are both wholes and parts, and he has emphasized that each 'holon' has the opposite tendencies; an integrative tendency to function as part of the larger whole and a self-assertive tendency to preserve its individual autonomy.

In biological or social system, each 'holon' must assert its individuality in order to maintain the system's stratified order, but it must also submit to the demands of the whole in order to make the system viable. These two tendencies are opposite but complimentary. In a healthy system - an individual, a society, or an ecosystem, there is balance between integration and self-assertion; this balance is not static but consists of dynamic interplay between two complimentary tendencies that make the whole ecosystem flexible, open to change.

American Psychologist J.L.Holland has identified six types of personalities that are very useful here. (1)The conventional type consists of persons who are conforming, methodical, conscientious, and efficient-tending to be inhibited and not wanting to stand out from the crowd. These types of persons are ideally suited to jobs of receptionists, accountants, etc. (2)The second type is the social type, who like people and enjoy mixing with them. They make very good teachers, counsellors, therapists and management consultants. (3)The third type is the investigative type, are analytical, complex, curious, and precise. These are usually good researchers. (4) The fourth type is the artistic personalities deeply non-conformist, and original. (5)Then there is the fifth type, the realistic who are down-to-earth, natural and genuine; usually pilots and engineers belong to this type. (6) The sixth type is enterprising, very self-confident and out-going; they infuse confidence in others. All of us fall under one of these categories and more often than not a combination of these traits.

Daniel Goleman recognized the qualities of emotion such as emotional intelligence, awareness of one's own and other people's feelings such as empathy, compassion, motivation, and the ability to respond to the pain or pleasure of others and put it in a measurable quotient called Emotional Quotient (EQ). His hypothesis is that for an effective use of IQ, EQ is necessary. "It is not IQ, but emotional intelligence that matters", he said. Carl Jung referred to the growth of personality as 'individuation' and associated this with the spiritual dimension of life. Danah Zohar concluded that 'the spiritual intelligence is the basic foundation for an effective use of EQ and IQ'. Hence a new quotient called the 'Spiritual Quotient' (SQ) has come to be known as a very important aspect of the Intelligence Quotient (IQ). In fact it is the foundation of the Intelligence Quotient (IQ).

This holistic approach is important. Devoid of this sense of participation in the ecosystem, the individual and the community try to exploit the natural resources beyond their capacity to restore themselves. Thus sustainable development is not possible, particularly in an over-populated, under-developed, poverty-stricken economy.

Stress is an imbalance of the organism in response to environmental influences. Temporary stress is an essential part of life. From the system point of view, the phenomenon of stress occurs when one or several variables of an organism are pushed to their extreme values, which induces increased rigidity through out the system. In a healthy organism, the other variables conspire to bring the whole system back into balance and restore its flexibility. Preparation to fight the threat appears in the form of tight throat, tense neck, shallow respiration, accelerated heart-beats, etc. and the organism will adopt a fight or flee response. The end of threat is perceived by a 'sigh of relief' and back to a state of relaxation.

When the 'fight'- or 'flight'- response is prolonged and the organism is unable to relax and regain control over the situation, the consequences are detrimental to health. Prolonged unabated stress generates physical and psychological symptoms like muscle tension, anxiety, indigestion, insomnia will eventually lead to illness. Inability to adjust to social rules and cultural habits leads to tension and stress; prolonged stress is at the root of the problem. Although the stress and the consequent 'fight or flee' method of facing the situation is common to all the animals, it is the human beings who have to cope with another set of problems originating in their culture. A civilized human being cannot fight or runaway from the scene and his state of homeostasis is disturbed leading to prolonged stress and illness- physical or mental. People under prolonged stress develop suicidal tendency, peptic ulcer, cancer, cerebral haemorrhage, heart attack, diabetes and many other undiagnosed diseases. But the link between stress and illness is not yet well known, although it is well known that prolonged stress will suppress the body's immune system and consequently, the body's natural mechanism of self-defence against infection fails leading to illness.

Illness will arise if five elements of life, the four activities and the environment are out of balance. When the 'laws of comfort' are violated, the body becomes fragile. Stress from outside, injury, germs, viruses, fatigue or mental pressure results in inclination towards illness and diseases. It is also true that unless one wilfully submits, sub-consciously or unconsciously, to the weakness, no disease or illness will bother. It is willing submission and cooperation that leads to illness. A strong will power keeps illness at bay. A person who gets disease can also drive it away, is the principle here. The human body has an amazing capacity to cure itself; it has power of recuperation. As long as there is breath of life in the patient, there is a possibility of reversing the process of disease.

Many expert psychologists reveal to us that inner conflicts, pent-up anger, hatred, jealousy, fear, tension, anxiety and other negative emotions can give us pain in the neck, ulcers in the stomach, sugar in the blood, diseases of the heart, and other various forms of ailments known as neuroses. They tell us how, through the sublimation of the emotions (by meditation), the neurotic trend can be altered and the outer life of a patient changed.

The medical research is more pre-occupied with micro-organisms that cause disease rather than the social and cultural environment that harbor the disease. Stressful situations arise not only from personal emotional traumas, anxieties, frustrations, but also from hazardous environment created by economic and social environment. It is not necessary that the stress is induced by only negative experiences; even the joyous situations cause stress and illness. In modern life, we have hip-hopped both head-centred and heart-centred scripts. We spend most of our time of waking hours in judging others with the hidden question of "what is in it for me". This is the problem! Selfless service and love cure all illness and diseases.

It is here that the spiritual training of the individual becomes more important. Yoga and meditation can contribute to a great extent in developing a balanced personality, enhancing one's emotional intelligence, and managing stress. 'Yuj' meaning unite, Yoga refers to the uniting with the all–pervading power as well as to an attainment of inner harmony between the mind, body, emotions and the spirit, and the outer balance between the social, material, career and family related aspects in the individual. Meditation is a process of attaining 'thoughtless awareness' and not just a mental process to develop concentration of Mind, as it is often believed to be.

According to the Upanishads, *"Meditation is the route to the highest knowledge, the spiritual knowledge. When self-realization occurs, it is the integration of inner self with the cosmic Self".*

There are very simple Yogic exercises that help relax the muscles and keep the mind cool. Yoga and Ayurveda, *as a way of life*, assures a hundred years life of fulfilment and there are numerous living examples. Indian way of life is completely in tune with the Vedic utterances and Upanishadic guidelines. Patanjali, an exponent of the Yoga School has laid down different postures in Yogic exercises. These offer great relief to a strained body and mind. This is completely different from the Western way of life that is devoid of organic unity and systems approach to life.

If stress is to be managed, our intelligence is to be leveraged and additional personality traits are to be developed. It is not possible for every one to lead a stress-free life in these modern days of cut-throat competition and rat-race. Living is an art. Each individual is fully equipped with the intellect and is capable of handling the problems of life provided he avails of the facility of 'buddhi' and keeps his mind under the supervision of buddhi. One need not retire to the forests in search of self-knowledge. *Sahaja Yoga* is one such system that leads to the path of Self Realization in a simple, practical, consistent manner without altering one's style of living. By regular practice of Pranayama and dhyana for at least twenty minutes every day one can be free from tension.

Spiritual Healing

"Know that to be indestructible by which all this is pervaded. No one is ever able to destroy that immutable" [*Bhagavad Gita*]. The Vedic Scriptures make it very clear that *'the soul of man is beyond all mortal afflictions; it is free from sin, free from old age, free from death and grief, free from hunger and thirst'*. We often believe what we see as our body as real and it constitutes the whole of our being. Not that our body is unreal; our physical life is unreal. But, it is not the whole of our being. In fact, it represents only a part of our real life. We are not what we were at our child-hood stage or youth stage; we have changed in our appearance, in our ways of behaviour; often people who have seen us a few years ago, cannot even recognize us. Such is the change that comes about our life. Unfortunately, many people believe that our physical life seems to be the whole of our being and it is this misconception that blocks the steady flow of 'life-force' and we suffer in many ways. Disease always indicates

disturbance; and disorder invariably results when our physical tendencies lead us away from the direct influence of the soul, or our bodily desires gain ascendancy over our spiritual nature.

We run to medical practitioners for every ailment and swallow whatever drugs prescribed without bothering about the reactions and complications that ensue. Practically, all the modern allopathic medicines are not curative. They only try to mollify the effect; moreover, these may not suit our physical conditions. These drugs are prepared under different conditions for different types of people who are supposed to be normally brought up in good economic, social environments. The only true healing is accomplished by contact with the spiritual essence. This cannot be done in a professional way. This has to be done at individual level by spiritual healing techniques. One may not believe in prayer; but prayer heals. Prayer overcomes the resistence of the ego and opens up the channels of the unconscious to the inflow of the 'Divine Shakti', or Cosmic Prana. For this prayer must be done with intensity, sincerity and perseverance. Faith also has great healing power, because it elevates us to a plane of higher consciousness that cures all our ills. All power is of the spirit. Through whole-hearted prayer and unwavering faith one can succeed in making oneself receptive to that power. Receptivity comes from faith and will to cure oneself; and it is said, that one cannot fall sick unless one cooperates with the disease to take over the mind and the body. Hence, it is amply clear that in our sub-conscious we are willing to fall sick and we fall sick. We can resist this temptation and overcome the feeling of sickness by a strong mind and spiritual practice like dhyan and meditation.

Even today, there are thousands of Sadhus who practise spiritual healing, touch therapy and mantra techniques in the villages of the Himalayan valleys where modern medical facilities are absent. Ayurveda is still widely practiced by local Pundits and the wandering Sadhus. There are Sadhus, spiritually attained souls, who have devoted their life to spiritual teaching and healing the sick in these remote villages where modern health care facilities are rare. These Sadhus always carry Ayurvedic medicines with them.

Human Behaviour

Man in this technological civilization is feeling inwardly impoverished and empty in an environment of wealth, power, and pleasure. He is, all the time full of tension, sorrow and misery, doubt, confusion and uncertainty. We see juvenile delinquency, suicide, and physically challenged and mentally retarded children and other maladies. All these problems are just a reflection of the Mind. A person is not happy because he is not inwardly happy and contented. He is not satisfied with himself. An under-current of dissatisfaction always bothers him. He is often bored to the point of commiting suicide; he is jealous and envious to the point of madness. In fact, the Indian Seers had foreseen such a predicament and the *Svetasvatara Upanishad says*:

"Even though men may through their technical skill roll up space like a piece of leather, still there will be no end of sorrow for them

without the realization of the luminous One within". [Svetasvatara Upanishad, VI.20]. Three afflictions, *'taapa-trayas'* bother us. These are: the misery caused by oneself, misery caused by others, and the misery caused by natural phenomena. Usually all the three are combined. But, most often, we suffer most by the misery created by ourselves. It is our earnest desire to live happily, acquire knowledge, power and fame, and excel and shine. These are our true nature, the nature of 'Brahman'- truth, knowledge and bliss. These are the essence of our souls. But we fail to understand this true nature of our self due to the veil of ignorance.

How apt is the statement of Schopenhauer that, "All men who are secure from want and care, now that at last they have thrown off all other burdens, become a burden to themselves" (*The World as Will and Idea,* Vol.I, p.404). Today, man is his own major burden and problem. Usually our life is egocentric. The soul gets tired of everything, even get tired of itself amidst this thraldom, routine mundane things and looks for something more permanent, more satisfying and looks for something beyond the forms, names and functions. Thus, the real yearning for a spiritual life begins. Blessed are those who realize this inner urge and look inward for the answer to the problems of life, for sure they will find an invaluable mine of peace and tranquility within.

At first, the outside world looks very beautiful. We look at and appreciate only its form and name. But we fail to understand its true nature, the intrinsic, inherent nature 'svaroopa'. We are carried away by the ourward impressions. The reality is that everything has the capacity to force itself on our consciousness, possess a luminosity that shines in both the sentient and the insentient; in this there is a difference only in degree and not in kind. We find this abiding sense of existence and consciousness in everything. Thus, we get a glimpse of reality not only in ourselves, but in everything we perceive as outside objects.

Living as we are in a state of delusion, a world of make-believe, no wonder we all live in fools' paradise. We are living on the periphery, away from the centre of Consciousness.. Our lives are full of trivials. Days and nights pass in routine struggle, making both ends meet and it is a hand to mouth existence for most of us. Our joys and happiness are short-lived, while sorrows and misery knows no end. We are always unhappy; there is no contentment. Greed and avarice overtake our sense of austerity. Competition and jealousy make our life miserable. We do not know our limitations. Even when we get everything we want, a feeling of want, hollowness, a vacuum exists. We feel we are not living a full life. Often, we wonder where are we heading to? Still there is no satisfactory answer to the eternal question why some are born rich as it were in the USA or Europe, and some in veritable hell in Asia and Africa. There is no scientific answer to this question in the Western science; but Vedanta holds the clue. Another question is there. Is it one's Karma that fixes one's fate in this life, and if so, where can one find the balance sheet of good deeds and bad deeds of previous life so that the account can be settled once and for all? Also, it is open to question whether the good deeds will emancipate us for we do not know what lies in the future. Vedanta holds the key to happiness and success in life. Vedanta gives an elaborate explanation of all these aspects of fortune, misfortune, luck, success or failure in life, and reveals the secret of getting wealth as also how to enjoy it in good health and peace. Atharva Veda holds the key to solve all problems of life.

Due to our ignorance, avidya, we run after sensual objects since we feel that these objects fulfil our desires; to some extent, it is true that these outside objects fulfil some of our wants. We try to posses these objects since we feel the possession of these objects would enhance our position, prestige, ego, pride and this give us a sense of fulfilment and happiness. This desire for happiness is there in everybody. Sense objects draw our mind because of the idea that we derive happiness or enjoyment from them (the outside world). Our esteem depends on others' praise since we do not have self-esteem and self-confidence. We feel tempted because of the promise of happiness the objects hold but not their intrinsic value. Thus, we find that "every external object has the capacity to exist by itself to rouse our consciousness about it, and draw out our mind". But, we do not know their intrinsic value or true nature. We know them only by their name and form. The Reality they represent is unknown to us at present. Names and forms hide the truth in our-selves and in the outside objects, but all names and forms reflect dimly the glory of the reality hidden in them. This is the true self, the 'atman' of every body, everything in this world.

Vedanta has very clear answer to many of these problems. In *Bhagavd Gita* [Ch.XVII], we find the characteristics of persons in whom the three – Sattvic, Tamas, and the Rajas, are preponderant at any time and how they behave. *Sattva* dominates the man of spiritual inclination and is characterized by knowledge and harmony [*Bhagavad Gita* 14.11-13]. *Tamasic* persons are characterised by darkness and ignorance, heedlessness and delusion. *Rajasic* persons are passionate, restless, and dominating. Tamasic people eat unclean food. They are arrogant, deceitful, despondent, procrastinating and unsteady. They think they know everything. They are impatient of hearing what others have to say. They undertake task in despondence and without proper knowledge. Their actions are borne out of delusion, heedless of the consequences. They give gifts to wrong persons, at the wrong place and time, or in the wrong way. They worship without faith and they are deluded by superstitions. They harm others.

Rajasic persons are very fond of exciting food; they like bitter, sour, hot and pungent food. They are attached to their work with selfish interest. They are attached to other people and their interests. They are over-anxious about the fruits of action; their actions are for the satisfaction of their desires and vanity. They are greedy, violent, prone to fear and worry, and they are easily elated or downcast. They give gifts grudgingly, or in anticipation of something in return and always aim at the fruits of action. They worship for the sake of results or for show and their austerities are ostentatious and may be to gain power or with some motive.

Sattvic persons are characterized by good nature, benevolence and compassion. They take sattvic food, clean and wholesome, that give strength, good health and help longevity. They perform actions with detachment; they are conscientious workers and do not worry about fruits of action. Actions without desire for reward or anxiety about results are the traits and hallmark of success. Sattvic persons perform all actions with purity of mind and heart. They offer gifts with compassion without any desire for returns and they know the propriety of their actions. Their austerities are of pure mind and for spiritual end for the benefit of others. Their actions are bereft of attachment and egotism, being endowed with fortitude and enthusiasm, unaffected by success or failure [*Bhagavad Gita* 18.26]. The sattvic people are engaged in spiritual thoughts and actions; they speak truth but not harmful to anybody. They are persons with self-restraint, calm mind, and are often silent, engaged in spiritual thoughts.

These generalized characteristics described in Bhagavad Gita are to be carefully understood. One can easily understand the nature of a person by closely observing his behaviour, food tastes and habits, motivations and actions. But one should not commit the mistake of attributing any character to any person based on these observations. Persons change their habits according to their needs, circumstances, place and time.

A scientific analysis of human behaviour is necessary in order to understand the mysterious ways of human conduct, tendencies and instincts. Some scientists hold that environment plays a very crucial role in the formative years of a person and greatly mould his character. Some believe that instincts are natural impulses or urges innate in any person and are not just the creatures of environment. There is an evolutionary urge to change in every person. Some biologists and psychologists trace our instincts to childhood days and even go to the extent of attributing them to parents, close relatives and ancestors.

There are some thinkers who believe that ethereal beings are born in human bodies, complete with their own innate tendencies, desires and passions. Thomas Huxley believes that every sentient being is reaping what it has sown, if not in this life, in one or other of the infinite series of antecedent existences, this is close to what the Karma theory holds. Even Darwin, the great evolutionist, holds the same view. It is said "Karmaanusaarena Buddhih", meaning that 'every person thinks and acts according to the instincts dictated by his past actions. The actions of the present are governed by the desires and there is a divine plan behind delivering the fruits of action. It also indirectly hints at the fact that no one can expect the results of action simply based on the person's merits like the skills and efficiency. So there are certain innate tendencies that makes a person react as he does.

This whole analysis makes it more confusing and gives a false notion that there is nothing in our hands and everything is our past karma or divine plan and ultimately creates a defeateist tendency. But it is not actually so. There is another important thing that governs every life and that is 'Lord's Grace'. Those who start their work in the name of the Lord, offers all actions to Him, in all humility, shall reap bountiful returns. Lord's name will wipe out all the negative effects of past actions.

The ancestors to whom we trace our habits and tendencies are none other than ourselves. Instead of making scapegoats of our ancestors, and blaming them for all our ills, we must take full responsibility for our actions and change our habits. But this is a difficult job. Ego comes in the way. We are not prepared to change. We are not prepared to accept. That humility is not there; that total surrender to Him is not coming forth. 'I' and 'mine' dominate all our thoughts and action and we always forget that there is someone greater than us. We all forget that we exist because of Him. We trust others created by Him but do not trust Him easily. This ignorance is the cause of all our misery and unhappiness. Here the Rule of Mind Management is "Realisation of the Self is the only way to a happy and successful life'. Even 'prarabhda karma can be erased by the constant chanting of Lord's name. It is panacea for all our ills.' *Chant His name and do your work with total submission'.* This is the mind management technique for happiness and success in life.

The Karma Theory

Karma is of two types. One is the result of past actions 'poorvarjita karma' known as 'karma phala' or 'Prarabhdha' (fruits of past deeds). Second is the 'sanchita karma', the accumulated fruits of action of the past, the fruit of willful acts of omissions or commission performed now, in this present life (not of past lives). Here, we are talking of the action, kriya, at present. 'Karma' literally means action, work and activity. We act as name and form i.e., in physical body; we also act as mental continuums of the wisdom of our feeling, perception, actualization, and accomplishment within a world-view of the nature of ultimate reality. Each and every action creates strong vibrations that are resounding. These vibrations match with other vibrations and get subdued, become harmonious, or clash with other vibrations and cause dis-harmony. Further, every action has reaction that is equal and opposite. In fact, it is this knowledge of Karma (action) that made the jnyaanis implore the values of love. Hatred, jealousy and illwill create such strong vibrations that vitiate entire atmosphere and make even the food we eat poisonous! Our blood circulation is affected by our thoughts; it is no wonder, evil thoughts make it poisonous!

According to Buddhism, there are four Laws of Karma viz, (1) Karma is definite in that good karma will yield happiness and afflicted karma will produce suffering. (2) Karma always increases. A small act of virtue blooms many- fold as does a small act of meanness. (3) 'As you sow, so you reap'. Mango cannot be grown from neem seeds. (4) Like the laws of physics that govern energy in the external world, the inner world is governed by karmic causes; once created they cannot be erased. Karmic acts leave imprints or 'vasanas' in our mental continuums whose results will bear fruit, both bitter and nectarine, into inexorable ripening. Like a minor resentment to another leaves vast fields of resentment, spite and hatred. Remember, a single karmic seed gives birth to a vast tree. An act of compassion will not breed hatred; an act of abuse will not produce love. Similar seeds will give similar fruits.

Lack of understanding of the connotation of 'Karma' in the Indian context as well as the Western misinterpretations of Karma has led us to believe that 'Karma' is always passive, impotent, helpless and defeatist. It never occurs to us in our distress that Karma is dynamic, everchanging, self-actualising, and self-transcending. It is not a helpless pawn of luck at the merciless hands of an arbitrary God, but Karma allows recreate oneself in one's own image and aspirations. Karma puts responsibility of one's destiny on oneself. It is a universal experience that luck or destiny can make a sudden change. Gains turn to losses; profit turns to loss, fame to disgrace, and happiness to sorrow. Glowing radiant of health can find itself being silently eaten by cancer or heart disease. A spiritual insight shows light on impermanency of all things attached to this mundane sensate world. The causes and conditions of our physio-psychological aggregates of form, feeling, perception, volition, and consciousness are the result of our karmic actions. And in turn every act we perform every moment impacts upon the subsequent moments of our being and consciousness. All phenomena are in an intransigent state of dynamic flux, and changing from moment to moment. Nothing is permanent, including misery and suffering.

Thus, we are in an endless cycle of conditioned existence and we can end this by our own efforts without any divine intervention according to the Buddha. We ourselves create the causes and conditions of our misery and cry over it. Hence, we alone can get over it. Our acts must create those causes and conditions that can give us happiness and joy and liberate us from suffering. By creating desert of hatred and greed we cannot harvest groves of love and kindness. Our negative 'karmas' obfuscate us from seeing this profound truth. As a result, we tend to curse our fate and be morose instead of taking courage and merge ourselves in action.

A sense of dissatisfaction always lingers in the mind irrespective of our achievements. The causes of this deep-seated malady are many. It is difficult to pinpoint the source. One may forget for the time being all this and concentrate on the work on hand; but the dissatisfaction is lurking and often surfaces unexpectedly. This may lead to half-hearted attempts and, at times, cause failure in our attempts. To identify the source of discontent and get rid of the same is of utmost importance.

Modern psychology has identified the role of the subconscious in all conscious efforts and functions. The root cause of failure is the lack of coherence and synchronization of the subconscious and the conscious. While the subconscious is aiming at fulfilling its long-standing desires, the conscious efforts are at the superficial and the mundane. It is more concerned with the immediate. It has no patience or time to hear the inner voice. It is hard pressed for time for it wants everything now and here. It wants everything at jet-speed. It wants to conquer time and space. The result is very clear. The effort is devoid of intellect and 'prajnya'.

The day-to-day pursuits are driven by the whim and fancy of the mind, assisted by the senses. Thus, the fruits of labour depend more on chance factors since a number of factors conspire in shaping the result. This uncertainty is the cause of tension, frustration and disappointment. There is no assured success.

On the other hand, if the subconscious and the conscious efforts are working in unison at single-pointed goal, success is assured. It causes no tension and calm prevails. How to know the contents of the subconscious? How to derive strength from it? This is not easy. Unless one is trained in meditation and is capable of tapping intuition, it is difficult to reach to the depths of the subconscious. The easiest way to success is via the spiritual route. It is here that the role of a 'Guru' is stressed. One is fortunate if one can find a Guru to lead on the spiritual path. Under these circumstances, it is quite but natural that 'life is a struggle'.

Even if one is fortunate to get a spiritual leader as a 'Guru' and gets initiation from him, it is difficult to have him always with us to get his continued guidance. The surest way to overcome this is to find a 'Guru' in one's own Self. The 'Centre of Consciousness' is the spiritual guru and He never fails. If you can catch Him by pure mind, pure intellect and pure consciousness He will shed his full light. It is also one of the pursuits to attain Him here.

It seems as if it is a paradox of life that we get what we do not want and we do not get what we desperately need. The crux of the problem here is not that we do not get what we want, but we are not happy and contented with what we get and what we have. Here we forget that the aspects 'dharma' govern life through and through and we do not notice it in the haste of journey. There are the 'kala dharma' (time), 'desha dharma' (space), 'vayo dharma' (stage) etc. that rule the different walks of life. The frustration arises out of non-conformity of these forces. If one is to succeed, it should all be appropriate at the appropriate time, place, and with appropriate people to click. It may or may not happen. It may be sheer luck or mere coincidence. In worldly attainments, it is wisely said that 'one is not strong if he is not strong at thirty; not wealthy if not rich at forty; and not wise if not wise at fifty. The person is lost if he is not any of these at sixty'. Thus, it is very clear that the foundation of a successful life is laid well before anyone steps into life through proper education and training. This aspect is missing in our framework of thinking in our present day set up and we go on blaming others for all our disappointments, failures and misery. A proper understanding is all that is needed and this is absent. This is the root cause of all the maladies of life.

'Karma Theory' of Life

There are two important aspects of Karma Theory. One is the long-term impact of Karma that causes repeated births and deaths, called metempsychosis, and the other is the short-term impact on the fruits of our labour in the day-today life.

Jainism has a very beautiful theory that explains the concept of Karma that causes repeated births and deaths, or metempsychosis. It is the Karma particles that blemish our soul. Rebirth or embodiment of the Soul is caused by Karma, the blemishes of the soul. Pure soul is pure consciousness or energy (that is not matter). It is the impurity caused by desire that makes the energy matter. "The soul which is free from the defect of Karma gets to the highest point of the universe, knows all, and pervades all, and obtains the transcendental Bliss. [Kundakunda Panchasyakiya]. Umasvati, a disciple of the Jaina Muni Kundakundacharya has described the path to liberation in his 'Tatvartha Sutra'. Accordingly, enlightened faith, right knowledge, and right conduct are essential for liberation. Elightened faith includes the jeevas, Ajeevas, Asharva or Karma, Bandha (Bondage of Karma), 'Samvar', or shedding of Karma Particles, and moksha (liberation).

The enlightened faith is realization of or the awareness of 'Truth' or 'Reality'. This enlightened faith is obtained by the study of ancient scriptures like the Veda and the Upanishads, or by intuition. So also, Knowledge can be obtained by the study of scriptures or intuition. Enlightened conduct means a determined journey or concerted effort towards the goal of emancipation.

The theory of 'enlightened conduct' and Karma states that, our good deeds and bad deeds generate karma particles or atoms that bind themselves to and pollute the soul like fine dust particles that cling to transparent glass. The influx of temptations, desires, fantasies, images, impressions and memories cause the influx of karma particles; hence, Prevention of influx of temptation and desire will stop the influx of karma particles. This is called the 'Right Conduct'. Right Conduct is the concrted effort to ward off temptations and cast off desires. 'Samvar' or shedding of karma particles is wiping clean of the glass, i.e., wiping off the accumulated effects of good and bad deeds or the influx of Karma particles on the Soul. 'Bandha' or Bondage is the binding of the soul to accumulated Karma.

One of the aphorisms of Tatvartha Sutra of Umasvati says that, "the activity of the body, speech, and mind is 'yoga' which includes the joining of Karma with the Soul." All thoughts and actions result in the influx of karmic particles. The influx is not only of temptations or desires, but are also of jealousy, hatred, greed, hoarding, cheating, speaking untruth, incontinence, immoral conducts, ashrava, craving for comforts, prestige, power and position, imbalance in daily conduct such as staling, etc. Hence, vow of continence, ahimsa (shunning violence), and possessiveness is necessary to ward off the influx of Karmic Particles. In fact, a jeeva who observes these vows prefers to die during meditation and attain Moksha. Liberation is possible, according to Jainism, by preventing the influx of Karmic Particles and this is possible by destroying the obstacles to right conduct by constant dhyan and meditation.

This, in brief, is the long-term aspect of Karma theory that explains the cause of metempsychosis or repeated births called *bondage*. The short-term perspective of Karma is also very interesting although many rationalists do not very much appreciate this line of thinking. But Vedanta is very clear on this point. All our gains, profit and loss, misery and happiness, depends on our past Karma, called 'poorvaarjita Karma', or the fruits of present good and bad deeds, called 'sanchita karma'. Karma is responsible for our station in life and to ward off this influx of 'karmic particles', one has to adhere to his 'dharma' and discharge his duties. Bhagavad Gita is very particular about this discharge of one's duty in one's station in life, as Sri Krishna advises Arjuna. Sri Krishna ridicules Arjuna's idea of running away from the battlefield and implores that, 'one should work in total devotion to duty irrespective of the results of action'.

In the day-to-day life, we tend to ascribe the fruits of our labour to our knowledge and effort; but ascribe it to past Karma when we feel disappointed and unhappy. In poverty and misery, we ascribe it to fate or Karma and do not bother about these things if we are rich and powerful. It is either ego factor that rules our line of thinking or our passive nature to think of fate and Karma. A clear understanding of the concept of karma is very essential in orderto understand the secrets of life. 'Karma' literally means action, work, and activity. We act as 'form' in physical body; we also act as mental continuums of the wisdom of our feeling, perception, actualization, and accomplishment within a world-view of the nature of ultimate reality.

2
Manas [Mind]

"Mind, mind in itself can make a heaven of hell, and a Hell of a heaven" [Paradise Lost, Book I, Milton]

"Manah eva manushyanam karanam bandhamokshyayoh"
"It is indeed the Mind that is the cause of man's bondage and liberation"

[Amritabindu Upanishad 2]

The Vedantic view of *Manas* is more scientific and gives a more satisfactory answer to many of our questions about life on earth. The English word *'Mind'*, that is the *'Mind Stuff'*, is not the appropriate one for the Samskrut word *'Manas'* for Manas conveys a deeper meaning. However, for convenience and fluence, the word 'Mind' is used here throughout the Text. The *'Manas'*, i.e., *Mind* occupies a pivotal position in the Lord's Divine Plan or scheme of evolution, and the universe is entirely dependent on *Manas*; 'there is no Mind, there is no world'. In fact, 'Manas' is the first manifestation of Brahman. Human Mind, the 'Manas' is the crown of Lord's creation. It is the highest and the noblest of the creation gifted with the power of knowing not only itself but the Creator, as well. It has the rare gift of the ability to look to Him and get His Grace. Human beings have always wondered about this mind and, are perplexed as to its style of functioning. While physicians have dismissed the idea of including Mind in their day to day medical practices, neurologists have taken up this subject and they are trying to connect the mind to the other body organs, particularly the sense organs. They are trying to find out the intricacies of the functioning of the Mind. The psychiatrists and psychologists have taken over this subject and still grope in the dark as to know what exactly is the mystery of the Mind despite much advancement made in these sciences during the last few decades.

What is Mind?

Mind is abstract and hence it is invisible. It is the manifestation of the Brahman, the first born, Aditya or Sadyojata. It is Mahat or 'Vast' and is 'Akaash'. It is all Vibration. It is this vibration that is the cause of all causes, 'kaaranasya kaaranah'.

Mind is chittaakasha and Supreme Mind (Vyoman) is chidaakaasha, the Mind of Brahman. The universal mind is chidaakaasha and the individual mind is chittaakasha. Akaasha is vast ocean or sky in the sense that is very expansive and endless. It is 'anant'. The universal mind is pure consciousness for it is blemishless and it is pure energy. It is the cause of all causes and it is the Brahman. Thus, Mind is Brahman, Pure consciousness. The individual mind is covered by desire and fear and hence it is polluted. When it becomes absolutely pure it ceases to be mind and becomes pure consciousness. The individual consciousness of the jeevaatma and the universal consciousness, or Paramatma, become one ('yuj') in a state of samadhi, attained by yogic practices of dhyana, Turiyaateeta Samadhi through meditation.

Mind, as vibration, exists outside as well as within the adhibhoutika shareera, the physical body. Outside, it is a very subtle cover like a coloured balloon with close contact with the elements. Inside, it is like the electronic charges or neurons that are in close contact with the brain cells as well as the senses.

Mind is so subtle that it lies on the border of matter and energy and one does not know when it becomes matter or energy. Pure Mind is energy. Mind exists outside as well as within the human physical body.

Mind is matter; it is a finer subtle body like the sub-atomic particles of electrons within physical body. Behind the mind is the intellect that gains its light from Prajnya or Consciousness. In fact it is the reflection of the light of the Soul or the 'Atman', the real 'Self' of man. Man is both matter and spirit-body and mind are material; Atman is pure spirit. Mind is not prajnya or consciousness; mind is not the intellect; mind is not the Soul or the Atman. To repeat, Mind is all vibration. Mind, as chitta vrittis, is all vibration, and, at a low rate of vibration it is called matter; and, matter at a high rate of vibration is known as energy (consciousness). Thus, energy is convertible into matter and matter (Mind) is convertible into energy (consciousness).

Food is matter and food supports Mind. If a person is fasting for two weeks his body becomes weak and his mind becomes blank. Further fasting will lead to loss of memory and thinking power. He regains strength only when he eats food and his memory comes back. Therefore, it is the food that makes the mind.

Where is Mind?

We all have heard lots of stories about absent-minded Professors. They often forget their spectacles, pen and wrist watch although these are verily present on their own person. Then where is the Mind? The mind is very much present, but it is engaged elsewhere. It can do one task at a time. It cannot think of this here, as well as, of that elsewhere. It always dwells on something. Either it can chant the name of the Lord or indulge in wishful thinking. But, in fact, the mind is omnipresent in the sense that it is a part of the universal mind and each mind is connected with every other mind. Therefore each mind, wherever it may be, can be in communication with the whole world. But, then, to say, 'I was absent-minded, I did not see it, or I did not hear it' means that it is the 'Mind', the controller of the senses; and, in the absence of the Mind's active interest, the senses cannot communicate what they have seen or heard. Thus, even though the eyes have seen and the ears have heard, they have not communicated the message to the Mind, or the Mind has just not received the message. The Mind is otherwise engaged and is not responding to the particular sense at that point of time; hence it is said to be absent. Hence, it is called absent-mindedness.

But, there is another important aspect of Mind here. Yogins try to achieve a state of Mind wherein they will be able to concentrate simultaneously on all the five senses and their functions, as well as, the inner consciousness. This state of *'conscious awareness'* is very important and everyone must strive for this attainment. This way, one can explore the Mind as well as utilize the full potential of the Mind. Here, the Mind gets into a transcendental state, a state of contemplation on its own accord. This is the ideal state for meditation! One must learn to be in that state of transcendence as long as possible to realize the Self, the Atman. As to the existence of the inner instrument called 'Mind', the Brihadaranyaka Upanishad [1.5.3] clearly demonstrates how we can think, rejoice, feel, will, imagine, remember, regret without using any of the ten sense organs (Jnyanendriyas and Karmendriyas); and, that goes to prove that *there exists a distinct inner instrument called 'Manas' (Mind); it is also 'Anthahkarana', and it dwells in the 'heart'.*

The Mind can also perform the functions of the sense organs like hearing, feeling, touch and smell without actually using the sense organs; rather, mind can operate on its own and feel the touch, or hear the sound and even see things without the aid of the sense organs. Desire, resolve, doubt, faith or want of faith, steadiness or unsteadiness, shame, intelligence, fear, etc. are all but Mind only. The body consciousness is the mind in action. The slightest touch or a prick makes you aware of it through the presence of mind; and, you will not feel it in spite of the skin touching it if the mind is not connected to it. But, the scientists search in vain for a physical organ called Mind. It is essentially an organ, but a subtle one, that exists and operates round the clock. It is a terrific force that can look backward, skip and jump effortlessly in matter of no time. Thus, the question 'what is Mind' is easily answered!

Mind is said to be the *'Anthahkarana'*, the inner instrument of the knowing Self, closest to the Self, transparent, and composed of subtle matter. It is not the source of light. It is dark. There is no consciousness inherent in the mind. The mind receives the radiance of consciousness from the knowing Self, whose inner instrument it is, and illuminates all things including physical light. Though having no light of its own the mind appears to be luminous. That is why we often say, 'I got a flash of new idea!' New light is shed on a ticklish problem, and ignorance is removed (by knowledge). Shining as it does with borrowed light of consciousness, the mind is an effective instrument of knowledge.

Mind has the power of looking back into itself. With the help of mind, we can analyse the mind, and see what is going on in the mind. Just as the hardest substance diamond is cut by diamond itself, the strongest mind can be controlled by mind itself, through will power and rigorous practice. Mind is always present, omnipresent and everybody can feel it, sense it, see through it, if only efforts are made to learn the technique. One can see through the mind of the others. Mind can be transparent. The effect of a depressed mind or an elated mind is clearly visible on the face. A Jnyani or a wise man of spiritual attainment can exercise his spiritual power to know the mind of others; he can foresee things. Meditation, Dharana, Sama and

Dama, Prathyahara and such other moral, ethical and spiritual /yogic practices will bring enormous powers to read the mind.

According to Hindu Manovijnyana, constitution of the mind includes the permutations and combinations of the three Gunas- Tamas, Rajas and Sattva. This explains the variety of human nature and vascillating nature of mind. Many forces dictate the performance of the mind. Mind operates at different planes or levels like the sub conscious (lower), conscious (normal) and super conscious (higher). The last one is the pure state where it is identical with Atman. "*Pure mind is pure buddhi and that again is pure Atman*" according to Swami Sri Ramakrishna Paramahamsa.

Mind has four faculties in its operational or functional aspect.

'Manas' (Mind) is that modification (vibration) of the internal instrument (Mind) Anthahkarana that considers pros and cons of a subject.

'Buddhi' (Intellect) is that modification (vibration) of the internal instrument (Mind) that determines (discrimination).

'Chitta' (Thought) is that modification (vibration) of the inner instrument (Mind) that remembers (memory).

'Ahamkara' (Ego) is that modification (vibration) of the inner instrument (Mind) that is characterised by self-consciousness.

In every external perception these four functions of the mind are involved. These four functions are so swift that they appear almost instantaneous.

The Mind manifests itself in 'scattering' (pleasure or pain), 'darkening' (dullness which tends to injury), 'gathering' (struggling to centre itself), 'one pointed' focussed and 'concentrated' (Samadhi) conditions. Man feels dull and passive in the 'darkened' state and feels restless in 'scattered' conditions of the mind. Yoga helps to make the mind 'gathered' and 'one pointed' focussed and this is 'Mind control'. This helps to prosper in materialistic world as well as spiritual world. This helps to reach Super-consciousness. Thus, such persons who attain this ' ekaagrata' 'one pointedness' will surely shine!

Mind, or 'Chitta' is the mind-stuff or mental substance. It takes various forms that constitute 'Vrittis'. *Vrittis* are thought waves, virtually a whirlpool in the mind-lake, *'manas sarovar'*. If the mind thinks of an apple, the apple is formed in the mind-lake and if one thinks of milk, milk is formed in the mind-lake. These thoughts of objects go on rising in the form of waves and subside in the mind -lake, ocean of chitta or the sub-conscious one after the other without any break. These Vrittis cause restlessness of mind. These Vrittis, or thought waves, or modifications get transformed as parinama or effects.

According to Para-psychology, the power of thought is the greatest force. One can achieve anything with the 'thought force'. Coupled with the *'thought force'*, a strong will, determination, and a strong faith rooted in *'Ritam and Satyam'* would create wonders. Indian metaphysical science recognizes three fundamental and powerful faculties: Adhyatma Vijnyan, Para Manovijnyan, *'Yoga Vidya'*. Even one of these will greatly help solve the problems of life. Contemplation on a thought produces vibrations; as in case of telepathy, we can induce a certain thought process in another person by sheer contemplation. Pure love and pure mind alone can develop this sort of thought force. We know that radio waves can be transmitted to any corner of the world. Both radio waves and thought waves travel through ether and thus we can achieve world peace through yogic practices.

Mahatma Gandhi, Jesus Christ, Martin Luther King, Mahaveera, Gautama Buddha, and others have successfully tried these methods and have swayed the world under their *thought force*. It is not wrong to say that if a man 'wills' something and puts on it a great force of thought like one does through Yoga vijnyan then no power on this earth can stop him from achieving his goal. Mahatma Gandhi was a great yogi in this sense and he achieved freedom for the country through peaceful means. He used 'Shanti' mantra and 'Satyagraha', i.e., pleading for truth ('Satya' means truth and 'agraha' means pleading through 'thought force') to achieve this goal.

What is this 'thought force' or Chitta Vritti? And, how to harness this force? Thought force is the vibration, or waves of thoughts that generate according to our samskara, or memories in the mind. This is called '*Chitta Vritti*'.

Why do these 'Chitta Vrittis', the thought waves, arise from 'Chitta', the ocean of mind? The latent impressions (Samskaras) and the subtle *desires* or the 'Vaasanas' cause the thought waves. Thought waves are very powerful. When a Vritti subsides it leaves an ever lasting impression called 'samskara' in the subtle sub conscious mind. This 'samskara' is also the *'sanchita karma'* or accumulated karma, fruits of past deeds.

These Vrittis are of two types: (1) Higher Vrittis like kshama, love and piety; (2) Lower Vrittis like anger, lust, and jealousy. Higher Vritti can control the lower Vritti. All the lower Vrittis can be controlled. And, finally all the Vrittis can be controlled. A person who can control his Vrittis shall acquire enormous power and he becomes a 'Siddha'. Destroying Vrittis we acquire more mental strength (Manas-Shakti) and spiritual strength (Atma-bala). When the Vrittis subside we can see the real Self, just like we can see the floor of the lake when the waves subside and water becomes still. The thought waves, chitta vrittis cause the disturbances that prevent us from seeing the Atman in the heart (Hridaya Sagara) where the Hridaya Kamala (lotus) blossoms; it is also the source of sensitivity, 'Anthahkarana'.

The whole universe is created by Vrittis, the 'thought waves' of Mind only. In other words, it is our 'manobhava', or the psyche, that makes the world. Thought is a finer force supplied by food. If the food is pure, thoughts become pure. One whose thoughts are pure speaks powerfully and produces deep impression on the hearers by his speech. A pure thought is sharper than the razor's edge. Thought culture is an exact science. Thoughts should be carefully observed and controlled. Thoughts can be transmitted from person to person. One can move the world by thought force. Thoughts of great Yogis are recorded in the Aakasha. We are all surrounded by ocean of thoughts. We are all absorbing some and repelling some of these thoughts. Through yogic practices, we can change impure thoughts into pure thoughts. Due to the thought waves present in the Aakasha, Anaahata dhvani comes and these can be heard by pure dhyana and meditation with pure mind and pure heart.

Thought is as much a thing as a piece of stone. It has weight, colour, shape, size and form. We utter the words, 'I have a big idea', or 'I have got a beautiful plan'. Thought is a dynamic force caused by the vibrations of psychic prana (or sookshma prana) on the mental substance. It is a force like gravitation, magnetism, cohesion, or repulsion. Thought moves and travels faster than light. Thoughts have tremendous power; they can heal diseases and produce deep impressions. Thoughts play a very important role in one's life; that is why, it is said, *'Yad Bhaavam, tad bhavati'* meaning 'as you think, so you become'.

There are symbolic thinking and instinctive thinking like fear of death. There are habitual thinking like going to take bath or food and drink. There is impulsive thinking like lust, greed, or hunger. Instincts are more powerful than impulses and difficult to stop. Thus, human behaviour is controlled by his thoughts.

Ghora Vrittis or impure thoughts of mind include anger, indignation, resentment, rage, fury, monstrous wrath, etc. Mudha Vrittis are laziness, carelessness and half-sleep state. The three vrittis of causal body are moda, pramoda and priya, these are things that one would like to possess, enjoy and love. Ajnyana Vritti operates in deep sleep. Anger,'I' and 'mine' are egotistic. All these Vrittis are bad and these should be annihilated by the enquiry, "Who am I"? This will help totally to eradicate these vrittis. Praanayaama will help in controlling these Vrittis. If mula-ajnyana is removed, all Vrittis perish by themselves. Karmendriyas and Gnyanendriyas should be kept under control of buddhi. Meditation will greatly help in controlling Vrittis.

Man is in constant pursuit of happiness. Each and every activity of his is directed towards enjoyment and happiness. He enjoys sensual pleasures with his body; gets emotional joy with his mind, and delights in rational findings with his intellect. It is an unending pursuit of happiness. This pursuit of happiness ends in a person who has realized his Self. He is a happy, contented and fulfilled man who has discovered his supreme Self. The nature of the real Self within is infinite bliss. The mad pursuit of happiness continues till a person realizes his real Self within. He uses his body, mind and intellect towards the enjoyment of worldly pleasure since he is ignorant of the real happiness derived from the inward spiritual journey.

Where the Mind and Senses Cannot Reach

Kena Upanishad seeks to locate the source of man's being, and to expand his self-consciousness until it has become identical with God-Consciousness. It seeks to answer the basic questions like the source of all our 'being', our existence, and it leads the mind from the gross to the subtle, from effect to cause.

It is quite obvious to seek the answer to the question whether the Mind is all powerful to shape our lives; or, there is some other force guiding the Mind to our destiny. This is a very interesting question. Many times we take decisions that are determined by buddhi under the influence of 'vrittis', thought force coming from the subconscious mind. These determine the actions the consequences of which are not known to us; our descrimination fails here. Many times we fail and suffer. Hence, the questions:

"By whom commanded and directed does the mind go towards the objects? By whose command does the lifeforce, the first cause, move? At whose will do men utter speech? What power directs the eye and the ear?"

" Is the Mind all-pervading and all-powerful, or it is just impelled by some other force? Who sends forth the vital energy, without which nothing exist?"

The answer to all these questions is: *"It is the ear of the ear, the mind of the mind, the speech of the speech, the life of the life, and the eye of the eye".*

An ordinary man hears, sees, thinks, but he is satisfied to know only as much as can be known through the senses; he does not analyse and try to find that which stands behind the ear, or eye or mind. He has no Consciousness of 'That' which enables his senses and organs to perform other tasks. Immortality is attained when man transcends his apparent nature and finds *that subtle, eternal, and inexhaustible essence which is within him.*

According to Vedic Sages," the mind, in its ordinary state, is only another sense organ. This mind is limited; but, 'when it gets illumined by the light of the cosmic intelligence, 'the mind of the mind', then it is able to apprehend the First Cause or that which stands behind all external activities."

Knowledge means the union between subject and object. This union can be attained only by practise, by contemplation and not by theory. The word knowledge is used ordinarily to signify acquaintance with phenomena only. But, man must transcend this relative knowledge before he can have a clear conception of God. One who wishes to attain 'Soul-Consciousness' must rise above matter-'Spiritual Consciousness is not merely a question of mind and brain, it depends on the awakening of our latent higher Consciousness'. This explains our predicament in this sensate world.

Vedanta helps us to develop spirituality through which Self-realization is possible. Vedanta is the sum and substance of all the Vedas and Upanishads. This spiritual knowledge makes us more self-reliant, self-sufficient and independent. It puts us right on top of the world. Spirituality gives us immense happiness that no other source can offer. Spirituality keeps us ever successful, happy, and peaceful. It procures all the material happiness through spiritual practices like Dhyan, Contemplation, and Meditation. The spiritual practices elevate our status and we begin to operate at a higher level. With spirituality, the body, mind and intellect work in harmony and the vision is broadened and deepened. With spirituality, our understanding will be superb and our intuition becomes divine. Success is assured in all our worldly pursuits for success is the result of the divine grace and intuition rather than the efforts of our finite senses and our gross mind.

Aruni's son Svetaketu's spiritual education as depicted in *Chandogya Upanishad* highlights the need for, and the significance of *'shruddha'*, or creative faith, for man when confronted by the mystery of unknown behind the known. After 12 years' stay in the Gurukula from the age of 12 to 24, having studied all the Vedas, Svetaketu returned home conceited, arrogant, and proud, regarding himself as very learned. Aruni asked him, did you ask from your teacher 'for that teaching (about the one behind the many) through which what is unheard becomes heard, what is un-thought of becomes thought of, what is unknown becomes known?

"Where from all these entities are born, by which, being born, they abide; into which at the time of dissolution, they enter, seek to know that; that is Brahman" (Taittiriya Upanishad, **III. 1).**

In order to know the world, know your Mind. The Mind is the world; your Mind is your World. Prapancha is what you have created around your self, your Mind. You see the world through your Mind. There is no world for you beyond your Mind. As you think so is your world-*"Manonmatram Jagat; Manah kalpitam jagat"*. Your world is constructed bit by bit by your own Mind and you dwell in it until finally you shatter it and come out of it! The Mind is everything! It is its own creation and it is its own destruction. It is the Brahman. It is the creator, the sustainer and destroyer. It is the 'asat' always changing, dynamic and vibrant; and it is 'sat', it is Brahman, the 'Truth'. Know your Mind, know your Self that is covered by the Mind, you will know the World. That is it. Om! Tat Sat!

Mind is the repository of wealth. There is a very beautiful story about the secrets of the mind. Once the Gods were discussing where to hide the 'power that grants everything' that man wishes for. Some Gods suggested Heaven as the place; but, others said, Man can reach Heaven too, and there is no use of hiding it there. The argument went on and the Gods knew the tenacity and perseverance of Man and finally agreed to hide the power in the Mind of the Man. They all agreed that, "it is one place where he will not search". Thus, we have enormous resources, wealth that cannot be valued in terms of US Dollars or Gold, Diamond and Platignum hidden in our own Mind. But the thought waves, the 'chitta vrittis' disturb the still lake of Mind and we cannot see the bottom of the Mind-lake, *'Manas Sarovar'. When the Mind Lake is clear, undisturbed, one can see the enormous wealth in it. Meditation* will help to calm the Mind (by Sama) and see the hidden treasures!

The Nature of Mind

Human Mind, the Manas is the crown of Lord's creation. It is the highest and the noblest of the creation gifted with the power of knowing itself and the Creator. It has the rare gift of the ability to look to Him and get His Grace. Human beings have always wondered about this mind and, are perplexed as to its style of functioning. As already stated, physicians have dismissed the idea of including mind in their day-to-day medical practices, neurologists have taken up this subject and they are trying to connect the mind to the other body organs, particularly the sense organs.

They are trying to find out the intricacies of the functioning of the mind. The psychiatrists and psychologists have taken over this subject and still grope in the dark as to know what exactly is the mystery of the mind despite much advancement made in these sciences during the last few decades.

The Superme Lord, the Creator, has created Man truly in his own form. He has created the Great Elements: air, water, fire, earth, sun and moon, the stars and their planets. He has created space and time. He has created the rivers, mountains and valleys, plains and swamps. He has created the oceans. He has created from these building blocks all the plants, animals and human beings, of various forms and sizes. Having created these bodies of various sizes and forms according to functions, He gave the ways and means to experience the world of objects and beings. He has given the five sense organs that are the windows to the world of objects. He has given the support and background for experiences of sense objects in the 'consciousness'. This 'consciousness' is the part of the eternal 'Supreme Consciousness' by which man sees, hears, tastes, touches and smells. Man enjoys happiness through the means of this 'Consciousness'.

The Supreme Creator has also given 'intelligence', or 'buddhi', which pervades all creations. The ultimate outcome of all these experiences wisely enjoyed is happiness and bliss. Only for this happiness and bliss, the human beings do all righteous deeds as well as resort to crime.

Mind is the judge that decides the information that the five sense organs feed the sensations to the brain. The brain itself is one of the great wonders of creation that distinguishes man as the creator in the image of his Creator.

Mind is Brahman. Mind is one of the creations of the Creator that stays with human beings till death. Mind is matter, made of matter and deals only with matter. Mind turns everything into forms and images. Even the limitless space and the eternal time, the mind wants to give shape and form. It wants to hold eternal time and limitless space within itself. Mind has enormous space like the sky, or 'Akasha'. The Mind is made of time and place, and, the mind influences and in turn gets influenced by the environment in which it lives.

The mind exists only in relativity and duality. Since the mind is the servant of the 'ego', it promotes the body and drives the senses to achieve this superiority. Mind exists with the 'other'. Since this 'other' is the support of the mind, the mind vanishes when the 'other' is finished or merged with the person. For this to happen, mind depends on time. Since mind is a factor of time, it wants to beat time and overcome time at all costs. The chief occupation of all human beings, in addition to finding food, is to overcome time. The mind wants to be at all places at all times, exclusive for others. In other words, it wants to emulate the Self, or the Soul in us, which is one and only one, whose nature is undivided consciousness. But this universal undivided Consciousness is covered by mind, which is the cause of misery and unhappiness. This mind is like a coloured filter over the light which restricts the intensity, distorts the images and changes the

The mind distorts the sensations and the information it receives from the sense organs as good or bad, likes or dislikes, right or wrong as well as mine and others. Even though any sensation is the same to all beings, it is interpreted as pleasure if it is accompanied by mind; the same sensation turns into pain if it is rejected by the mind. If the sensation experienced is not very common, it becomes exclusive and it boosts the ego. Therefore, the humans go to climb the mountains, swim oceans, read and write volumes of books, and torture oneself standing on fire. These sensations satisfy the ego but dulls the mind and the senses.

Mind is finite and limited. It is a factor of the past and touches only upto the present. It cannot think of the unknown. It stops when it faces the limitless and the eternal. When it looks at the sky, or stares at the mountains or ocean, it stops. It looks itself and it is no more. It has become as large and formless that it has lost its 'being'. When the mind is no more what is experienced is bliss. Otherwise, whatever mind thinks is only sensation. When it is free from all thoughts, all impurities, it is no more. Mind is active when it is active or worrying. All thoughts good or bad, holy or unholy, noble or disgusting, evolving or depressing, all are impurities. To be free from all thoughts is to be free from all impurities. When all these impurities are removed the mind is one with 'pure consciousness'.

The mind is the creator of sensations. It is the super creator. It creates images; it sees images in the absence of objects. It hears sounds when there is silence. It smells when there is no odour. It tastes food when there is no food. It imagines when there is nothing. It creates during waking hours as well as in dreams.

Since it is the nature of the mind to think in terms of only images, in terms of finite and limited forms, it has no intelligence. The intellect is the tool; the mind makes use of it for achieving its goals. When the mind is associated with the intellect, it becomes thinking or planning. Devoid of intelligence, it is only worrying or imagining. The faculty of intelligence is normally made use of by the mind during the waking hours since it is not very far from reality during this waking period. Impossible things are created by the mind during the dream sequences.

Mind is time and mind is anxiety. The mind is always in becoming and reaching. Mind is never now and here. Mind is 'there' and 'afterwords'. Suppose we are in a journey and we are eager to reach the destination, the journey becomes irrelevant. We are eager and anxious to reach the destination. However, fast we are traveling, we feel it is very slow. This urge to beat the time and space and reach the destination or goal is the mind. In case we are on a holiday and we are enjoying the journey, the destination becomes irrelevant. The journey itself becomes goal and we enjoy every moment of it. The journey is here and now. When there is no desire to reach, mind is no more and there is no more 'time'. More time it takes, we are happier.

As long as our 'doing' itself becomes the goal, as long as the journey itself is the goal, we are free from time. There is no 'reaching' or 'becoming'. It is 'here' and 'now'. There is no time in the dynamic movement that is its own end. This is a very simple formula of getting rid of tension and anxiety, and, hence sickness. Here, the Rule of Mind Management Technique is: "*Enjoy whatever you are doing; Totaly involve yourself in it*".

Students who are worried about examinations should carefully note this. As long as their destination is passing the examinations and obtaining the degree certificates, they will have anxiety and tension. This very anxiety and tension will prevent them from achieving their goal. But, the moment they realize that 'learning' and not the 'examination' is their goal, tension and anxiety ceases to be, and learning becomes a pleasure. Learning should be the goal rather than the examination. When learning becomes the goal than mere passing examination, the tension and anxiety of passing examination disappears.

Mind is the filter. It blocks the reality and the truth when the mind 'is' and truth 'is not'. When the mind is present, the reality is far off. Mind is thoughts, mind is desire and mind is imagination. When the mind is working, it is not in touch with 'now' and the real. Mind is projecting, imagining, thinking and worrying. It is in the grip of illusion. Mind is the illusion and mind is 'Maya'.

Mind is darkness and is made of ignorance. Mind is the product of past. Mind is matter and all matter is gross, however pure it is. Only when the matter ceases to be, it becomes light and takes off. All matter is packet of light and energy. Mind is the mass and therefore, rooted to earth and bodies. Mind can think of bodies, forms, limited and finite; when the mind is face to face with the unlimited and eternal, it becomes silent. Mind has stopped. Only reality 'is' when the mind 'is not' there.

Mind is matter and all thoughts are impurities.

The impurities of Mind are the urges, impulses, and emotions like envy, hatred, anger, fears, jealousy, lust, greed, conceit, temptation, etc. born out of rajas and tamas- the two lower Gunas. These create disturbance in the mind by creating raga, (attachment) and dvesha, (aversion) and thus rob us of peace and tranquility. These impurities cover the pure shining 'consciousness'. The consciousness is ever present and even awake. It is one and is the purest. This mind, which is nothing but thoughts, the desire of objects and perishable things, which has no reality, covers this consciousness. Just as the pure mirror is covered by dust and smoke and obstructs vision and reflection, so also this mind covers the pure consciousness and the reality.

Mind is matter and, as such, it has weight. Mind becomes heavy or light according to situations. In depression, mind becomes heavy; and, in joy and happiness mind becomes light. When the mind is heavy due to grief and depression, due to loss of loved ones, friends or relatives, one should get out of depression by meditation. Rise above and get rid of the heavy weight or make the mind light, in the sense, make it light by japam, meditation, and prayer. It is difficult to concentrate during depression, mourning, and sorrowful occasions. The best one can do is prayer. Prayer brings peace. In times of bereavement, one should always remember that it is the physical matter that we have lost but not the spirit, the Soul. The Atma is ever present. Atma is always one only and it is always with us.

The Atma of our parents, and grandparents, as well as, the Atma of our children and grandchildren are always within us, our Atma. We are all extended soul of one supreme Soul or Atma that is ever present. There is nothing like my Atma and others Atma. It is avidya, illusion, that we see different bodies, names and forms, since Atma is capable of taking different forms. We feel the loss of physical body of our loved ones since we are attached to body; it is sheer ignorance. We should not weep and cry over the loss of physical bodies. We should cherish the memories and uplift our heavy mind by prayer.

This mind is 'Maya'. The illusion that brings about further creation of perishable and finite objects that further covers our pure consciousness. This mind cannot overcome 'Maya', the illusion, since the mind itself is 'Maya', the illusion. It cannot eliminate self. It is just like lifting our own weight by ourselves. The mind can be removed or dissolved by the 'Higher Being', the Self or the Soul. Since the mind is the creation of the Supreme Self, and the soul or the individual self has taken a body due to its inseparable attachment to mind, this Maya can be overcome only by the Supreme Self by the Grace of the Lord Almighty. If we take one step in this direction, He will take a million or a billion steps to redeem us or liberate us from this illusion or grip of the mind, called '*Maya*'.

'Avruti, the veiling power is the effect of the preponderant tamas, which makes things appear other than which they are. It is this 'aviveka' that causes the action of the projecting power. Absence of right judgment or contrary judgment, want of definite belief and doubt are the result of the veiling power due to the preponderant tamas aided by tamasic food samskara. Hence, the projecting power, the ' ignorance' gives ceaseless trouble.' [*Viveka Chudamani*, III. 13-15].

Hence, it is very clearly stated in the Upanishads that an austere life, sattvic food, and devotion to the Supreme Lord, the Almighty, and total surrender to Him will deliver us from all the troubles and ceaseless transmigration and bring everlasting peace.

Exploring the Human Mind

The study of human mind is a vast field covering all branches of science as well as religion and philosophy- encompassing the 'without' and the 'within' of Man. The holistic or the systems view of mind seems perfectly consistent with both the scientific and the mystical views of consciousness, and thus to provide the ideal framework for unifying the two. The systems view agrees with the conventional scientific view that consciousness is a manifestation of complex material patterns- a manifestation of living systems of a certain complexity. Biological structures of these systems are expressions of system's self-organisation, i.e. mind. In mystic view it is manifestation of cosmic mind- direct experience of cosmic consciousness goes beyond the scientific approach. The systems view gives a more meaningful scientific framework for approaching the age -old questions of nature of life, mind, consciousness and matter.

Human beings who evolved as social animals cannot keep well, physically or mentally, unless they remain in contact with other human beings. Human kind emerged through the very process of creating culture and needs this culture for its survival and further evolution- mutual interaction display similar patterns of self-organisation.

It is the nature of the mind to be creative. According to Vedanta, “Creative intelligence is in-born; it comes attached to the soul and the prana. It is the driving force, the sustainer, 'Vishnu', Sri Hari Narayana”. Modern science also recognizes this fact. The more the depths of the mind are plumbed, the more abundantly they produce. (Capra, pp.50-51). According to Paul MacLeen, the human brain consists of three structurally different parts, each endowed with its own intelligence and subjectivity, which stem from different periods of our evolutionary past.

The brain stem is the innermost part of the brain. It is concerned with instinctive behaviour patterns already exhibited by reptiles. It is responsible for many kinds of compulsive behavior and biological drives. Surrounding the brain stem is the limbic system, which is well-developed in mammals and in the human brain- involved with human emotions and expression.

Subcortex- the two innermost parts of the brain are strongly interconnected and express themselves non-verbally through a rich spectrum of body language. The outermost part, the neo-cortex facilitates higher abstract functions, such as thought and language. The neocortex originated in the earliest evolutionary phase of mammals and expanded in the human species at an explosive rate. It got stabilized about 50,000 years ago. This explosive rate at which it got stabilized is astonishing and unprecedented in evolutionary history.

Recently, in an interview, V.S. Ramachandran, Professor of Neuroscience, has made some interesting research in the field of Brain and Cognition. Accordingly, "Self requires embodiment, i.e., me, here, and 'Free Will', like I can move my fingers, not yours." As regards 'embodiment', Ramachandran says, "If you can actually stimulate the brain and when somebody is awake and conscious, there is no pain; some of these patients will report they are floating upto the ceiling and watching themselves. They have an out of body experience. Undoubtedly, this leads to the idea of 'Soul'- 'I will be floating there after death, as Soul'. So, the sense of embodiment depends on the Right Parietal in the Brain"

Ramachandran says, "Life is a word loosely applied to a collection of processes- DNA replication and transcription, Krebs cycle, Lactic acid cycle. Where does the sensations come from? He asks and says, 'we have all these things around us providing sensory inputs to the eye ball, - light rays hitting our retina, cells firing, chain of activity in the neurons, flux of ions- and we see the colour of the Rose'. 'Sensations must have evolved in perception for a specific biological function. They cannot be by-products of neural activity'. Lower animals may have some sort of rudimentary awareness- an instinctive feel of things around them; but, they are not aware of awareness. It sees, but it does not know it sees. But, man not only sees, but is aware he is seeing." [Mind Matters-An Interview with V.S. Ramachandran by Chetan Shah, Sunday Express Magazine, 14 September 2003].

By developing our capacity for abstract thinking at such a rapid pace, we have lost touch with the realities of life and have become the only creatures who often fail to cooperate with and even kill their own kind- not one or two, but the whole of mankind. Our evolution continues to offer us freedom of choice. We can constantly alter our values and attitudes to regain the spirituality and ecological awareness we have lost.

Living organisms are intrinsically dynamic. Their visible forms are stable manifestations of underlying processes. Process and stability are compatible only if the process form rhythmic patterns- fluctuations, oscillations,, vibrations, waves. The new biology shows fluctuations are crucial in the dynamics of self-organisation. They are the basis of order in living world; ordered structures arise from rhythmic patterns.

The components of ecosystems are inter-linked through cyclical exchanges of matter and energy; civilizations rise and fall in evolutionary cycles; and the planet as a whole has its rhythms and recurrences as it spins on its axis and moves around the sun. Rhythmic patterns allow individuals to express their distinctive personalities.

The mind is responsible for the dualities. The subject and the object; the seer and the seen, the perceiver and the perceived are all better explained as 'Maya', fleeting, sentient; but the physical science tries to go deep into these aspects in the "Unified Field Theory". The Vedantic truth of the unity of the Consciousness -Field will become revealed to sub-atomic physics when it resolves its present contradiction involved in viewing its 'observer' in terms of classical physics, while viewing its 'observed' in terms of the quantum field probabilities.

In his book, 'The Cerebral Cortex and The Mind of Man', the neurologist Wilder Penfield states:

"In a sense, therefore, the higher brain stem, together with that portion of the cortex which is being employed at the moment, is the seat of consciousness. It is the 'physical basis of mind', this hypothetical mechanism of nerve cell connections. When a man is conscious, one may conceive that, within his brain, impulses are passing along a million insulated nerve fibers that compose this complex, impulses that are some how, coordinated into the orderly sequences of deliberate thought."

"What is the relationship of this mechanism to the mind? Can we visualize a spiritual element of different essence capable of controlling this mechanism? When a patient is asked about the movement of a part of his body, which he carries out as the result of cortical stimulation, he never is in any doubt about it. He knows he did not Will the action. He knows there is a difference between the automatic action and voluntary action. He would agree that something else finds its dwelling place between the sensory complex and the motor mechanism, that there is a switchboard operator, as well as a switch board". Nature has given man alone, among all her species, the organic capacity, through his cerebral system to detach consciousness from thralldom to the organic system and refine it and raise it to higher and higher levels; and this is the role of evolution at the human stage" (ibid).

The Bhagavad Gita on Mind Control

The Bhagavad Gita is a treatise on Manas (Mind) and Manoniyantran (Mind Control). It dates back to 14th century B.C. It deals with the true nature of the individual and of the supreme reality, and knowledge and wisdom. When you come to the Gita, you have the presentation of truth in all its simplicity, which helps us to take us through life's problems. It frees us from all attachments to joys and sorrows, so that we may be attached to truth only. It gives us absolute calmness and a freedom from all conditionings- external and internal. It gives us independence and freedom; what more does one require? One who attains this remains fresh, in spite of life's aging and retains the freshness of a new- born baby till his death. This is the philosophy of Bhagavad Gita that helps us to remain fresh at the end of the journey as at the beginning.

Man wants a good deal of guidance. The Bhagavad Gita is an eternal source of strength and guidance. It gives us the whole philosophy of life in the famous oft-repeated mantra:

'Karmanyeva adhikarasthe maa phaleshu kadaaçhana'.

Meaning, *'Your rights are only in your duty, never in the fruits'. Some well-read persons have mistaken this concept of self-surrender. It is ego, sheer 'ahankaar' that makes one think that "Iam the doer'. This feeling of 'I'-ness, ego or 'aham' is at the root of human misery. The enlightened persons know that we are only instrumental and nothing moves without 'His Will'. He, the Lord Almighty is the doer and it is His Will. Of course, He is within us, as Atma.*

Our ancient sages were bold enough to ask the students to challenge the teachers. Love of truth and reason dominated their lives and works. They were undeterred by fear of blame or lure of fame. The reality, as enunciated in all Veda and Upanishads, is the product of sustained philosophical inquiry. No other religion or philosophy in the world is so open and challenging as our 'sanatana dharma', which came to be known as the 'Ancient Hindu Religion'. Its values hold good for all times to come. It is universal and more scientific and forms the basis of modern science and technology. The roots of modern physics explaining field theory, or nuclear energy and molecular biology, or psychiatry are evident in the Veda that culminated in the Upanishads, the 'Vedanta'- the sum and substance of which is found in the Bhagvad Gita.

In Bhagvad Gita, Sri Krishna stands for supreme 'Consciousness'. Krishna dominates the scene in Mahabharata. He was highly respected by one and all- the kings as well as the lowliest of the lowly men. He was totally detached. He did not want any kingdom for himself. He etched out a place for himself in every heart by his sheer love as "Gopala', the Cowheard- the Master of the Sattva Guna personified by the cow. People believed Sri Krishna to be incarnation of God, or 'avatara' of God. He gave 'divya drishti' to Arjuna and revealed the "Divya Swaroopa' of the Almighty since the normal bodily eyes of Arjuna could not sustain the power of the Lord. This is yet another clue to those who want to vision God in their normal sensate body and mind.

Mind and Action

'Akarma' is non-action. It is action without self, 'ego'. It is 'total surrender' to the Lord. This concept of 'total surrender' is peculiar to Indian religion and philosophy. It is here in India, we find that the devotee (bhakta) totally surrenders to his Deity (Deva) and the student (shishya) totally surrenders to the teacher (Guru) to get all knowledge and experience of the latter. This 'total surrender' (sharanagati) is unknown in the West. The teacher and the student will remain apart and never become united, one through learning, in the Western system of education. In Gurukula system, ultimately the Guru and his disciple become one ('yuj') by Yoga and the illumining principle. This total surrender is 'Akarma' – 'I am not the doer' and it is a beautiful concept that helps us to understand the intricacies of mind and its way of functioning. In 'Akarma', the Mind is free, free of anxiety and tension, and in total freedom, the person accomplishes everything! 'Akarma', or non-effort has its parallel in Taoism and Zen also. Both speak of perfection in terms of a life of spontaneity and naturalness; it involves no struggle or special effort and it is beyond all intellectuality. In other words, it is sheer Divine Grace by which action is performed effortlessly. All creativity and spontaneity are the fruit of the unfolding dimension of the Self or the Atman. These result in best of the life and work, morally and spiritually and the achievement is effortless.

This non-effort, 'Akarma', is different from inaction or non-action as also different from nishkama karma, 'desire-less action'. In his 'Tao of Science', R.G.H. Siu clearly brings out the distinction of rational and extra-rational knowledge. 'Rational knowledge is rational only because it is obtainable through reason. The others obtainable through means other than reason are not irrational; they are extra-rational. Broadly speaking, intellectual progress is an advancement in concepts which man had formulated and handed down.' In rational knowledge and intuitive knowledge, there is a contrast.

Discoveries play a minor role in intuitive knowledge; science has not accelerated human development in the field of inventions and discoveries to any great extent. People have recognized all that is known intuitively, generations before and the silent and formless depth of life had passed many times before the mind of man in its full sweep. These are beyond mathematical formulae or scientific theories. There is no logic in intuition since it is fuzzy and do not follow the strictures. In fact, discursive reasoning is not possible without intuition.

At one stage, the concept of the 'sage-knowledge' or the 'no-knowledge' state is introduced to overcome the inability of the rational and intuitive knowledge to solve the problems. 'Sage-knowledge' concerns an understanding of 'non-being'. It transcends events and qualities; it has no shape, no time. It is undifferentiated whole. This concept is to be clearly understood. Having -no knowledge is different from having no-knowledge; the former is mere ignorance, where as the latter is one of ultimate enlightenment and universal sensibilities. 'The mysteries of nature appear to be mysteries only to those who refuse to participate in them…'

'With rational knowledge, the scientist is a spectator of nature. With 'no-knowledge', he becomes a participant in nature. There is communion of knowledge and understanding here. One must rely on one's own ineffable awareness of the ineffable to probe or plumb the depths of no-knowledge. This is expounded as 'wu' in the east and the principle of 'akarma' in Vedanta. This is yet another great contribution of the East to the body of knowledge.

The Philosophy of non-action and the state of no-knowledge is beautifully explained in *Ashtavakra Samhita, Verses: 1.8; 4.4; 18.20, 39, 60-61, 95 and 98. [Published by Advaita Ashrama 1975 & 1998].*

"He who is beyond existence and non-existence, who is wise, satisfied, and free from desire, does nothing even if he may be acting in the eyes of the world". Here, actions are no longer actions when they are not accompanied by the feeling of egoism. The man of knowledge is absolutely free from it. He does not identify himself with his actions. He is, therefore, really inactive, even though he may seem to be acting.

"Knowledge of one's true nature as the Infinite and non-dual pure consciousness will give freedom and spontaineity in all actions. The wise one who lives on happily, doing what comes to him to be done, does not feel anxiety either in activity or in inactivity. The fool desires peace through the control of the mind, and so does not attain it. The wise one, knowing the truth, is ever of a tranquil mind". Further, "*With the fool, even inaction becomes action; but with the wise, even action results in the fruit of inaction*". Spontaineity through non-effort appears where the self is surrendered to something higher than itself, where the self has emancipated itself from stagnation of its sensate tether. Most of the discoveries and inventions have thus come from such total surrender and total involvement without any greed for fruits of action.

The Theory of Akarma (Non-Action) is better explained in the aphorism:

" Na karta Hari karta.... ", meaning, "I am not the doer; Sri Hari is the doer. I am only a medium, a tool in the hands of the Lord." This will release us from all consequences of our action, karma, and will release us from the cycle of rebirth or sansar, bondage.

What the Bhagavad Gita calls "akarma', is a very simple method of accomplishing great things by offering all our work to Him; The Lord is invoked first, "***Shree Vishnu preranya, Vishnu preetyartham, Sree Krishanarpanamstu***", meaning, "as ordained 'by the Grace of the Lord', and then the entire performance is done in 'His name' to please Him, and the fruits are finally 'offered to Him'." By this way, there is nothing that is done by this mortal man and everything is 'His Divine Grace'. Then, it is the divine force itself that comes into operation removing all the obstacles and deficiencies inherent in man and the work accomplished would be perfect. But, then, it requires enormous 'shruddha', i, e., 'faith' in the Lord.

The Chinese Philosopher Chuang-tze puts it this way:

"By doing nothing everything is done.
He who conquers the world often does so by doing nothing.
When one is compelled to do something,
The world is already beyond his conquering".

This is put in a different way in Bhagavad Gita (Ch. IV. 18):

"He who sees inaction in action and action in inaction, he is the wisest among men, he is the perfect yogi and the doer of all action."

Action is a basic instinct of human nature. It is the root of human progress and prosperity and is implicit in the law of life. No body can really remain inactive even for a moment. Inaction leads to decay and putrefaction. Some form of action is involved in the survival and maintenance of our body. But it is strange that action always leads to misery and sorrow. It is the attachment and indulgence that sows the seed of sorrow and misery in our actions. It is the sensual pleasure and material happiness that we anticipate as the fruit of our action that brings us the sorrow and misery. Anything done with the spirit of attachment, craving for fruits and under the impulses of ego, necessarily brings frustration, mental depression and moral degradation. This does not mean inaction is a better alternative. Rather, inaction would be disastrous and catastrophic. This prompted Sri Krishna to define the art of performing action in Gita.

'Perform action as a sacred call of duty and be instrumental in doing it; leave the rest to Almighty'. All our actions must be devoid of selfish motives and attachment. Sri Krishna says, "Your right is to work only but never to the fruit thereof. Be not instrumental in making your actions bear fruit, nor let your attachment be to inaction".

Vedanta presupposes performance of action incessantly and sincerely intensely. It guides the performer in all his actions laying down the golden rules. Renunciation is one such golden rule. Renunciation is a spirit of self-abnegation, 'na maman' in everything. It drives away the last tinge of selfishness in oneself. Human beings are essentially divine. Vedanta deals with this aspect of divinity and helps us in unveiling and unfolding this divinity. By recognizing the self as the part of the supreme Self, i.e., 'Self Realization', a divine experience, dawn of a true inner awakening, one realizes that one is not this body, mind or intellect. These three are inert without the Atman that energizes them to perform their functions. This Brahma Jnyana helps one to inculcate the spirit of renunciation. Renunciation does not mean giving up worldly pleasures or rejecting the fruits of one's action, or giving up desires and abstinence from consumption, but an attitude that reflects the level of renunciation one has attained. Spirituality does not forbid enjoyment. The ego and selfish motive attached to the action hampers progress and retards success and prevents serious practice of renunciation.

The principles of renunciation clearly lay down that one need not retire to the mountains and forests to practice it although, practically all early Sages and Seers retired to seek this Jnyan. Even the householders can practice renunciation, and in fact, the householder's duty should revolve round this principle. Dhyana and Jnyana govern this principle and, as such, the householder should perform all actions in utter humility and submission to the Almighty. All actions are sanctified when performed selflessly with dedication to the Lord. Such a person understands what is called '*akarma*' in Bhagavad Gita. He sees 'inaction in action and action in inaction'. All his actions are neutralised in fire of knowledge and no longer bear any fruit to torment him either in this life or in the next.

Of course, this Brahma Vidya needs initiation. In the absence of an initiator, the Guru, the pure mind of one's self is the initiator and it only needs firm determination. Ultimately, renunciation brings peace, happiness and Supreme Bliss. It is said, *"Gururbrahma, Gururvishnu, Gururevo Mhaesvarah; Guru Sakshat Para Brahma, Tasmai Shree Guruve Namah"*. The Lord himself is the Guru; He who resides in our heart shall guide us when a true Guru is not available, and one need not be perturbed about this. After all no Guru will ever be able to redeem us unless we ourselves sincerely aspire and put all our efforts towards that attainment. At best, a good, learned, sincere Guru, will help us to bring out the divine within us by imploring us to meditate on the 'mahat vakyas, the Upanishadic doctrines.

In *Ashtavakra Samhita*, freedom of spontaneity and naturalness arising from knowledge of one's true nature as the infinite and non-dual Pure consciousness is beautifully explained as follows:

'The wise one who lives on happily, doing what comes to him to be done, does not feel anxiety either in activity or in inactivity'. Further, 'the fool desires peace through the control of the mind and so does not attain it. The wise one, knowing the truth, is ever of a tranquil mind'.

'Whoever, by virtue of the realization of his true nature, does not feel distressed even in practical life as people attached to the world do, and remains un-agitated like a vast lake, with all his sorrows gone- he shines'. 'The wise one is devoid of thought, even when he is engaged in thought; he is devoid of the sense organs, even though he has them; he is devoid of intelligence, even though he is endowed with it; and he is devoid of his ego even though possessed of it'.

'The liberated one, who abides in the Self under all conditions, who is free from the idea of action and of duty, who is always even-minded everywhere, owing to his desire-less state, remembers what he has done and what he has not done'. Bertrand Russel suggested that 'there is a great need for modern man to surrender his inflated ego to something higher within himself'. When the self is surrendered to something higher than its own self (the sensate one), spontaneity through non-effort appears. This is evident in many discoveries and aesthetic as well as intellectual achievements.

The conscious self and the rational consciousness surrender themselves to something higher or deeper within in cases of *intuition*. Spontaneity manifests itself giving rise to creativity and thus, discoveries and innovative techniques are achieved. *Imagination* is the word used in such circumstances. This is also true in evolving rich and happy, inter-human relationships. Deep thinking and intuition, daring imagination are hallmarks of great thinkers and achievers. Science of human creativity and philosophy of 'non-effort' and Divine Grace are spiritually related. Super-conscious dimension of the human mind is involved in all imagination, intuition and flash of brilliance.

The super-conscious, conscious, the pre-conscious, the sub-conscious and the unconscious, are the different states of mind recognized in Vedanta. In fact, all rational knowledge is referred to consciousness.

But one should not forget that there is a great part of existence of which one is not conscious. The function goes on irrespective of our conscious application in the case of the inner functions of the body. Thus, man functions at two different planes of consciousness - one is the conscious state with the feeling of egoism; the other, is the unconscious plane devoid of feeling of egoism. There is still higher plane that goes beyond consciousness not accompanied by egoism.

The conscious working of the mind is called reasoning. This 'reasoning' works with in a small radius and it cannot go beyond that. But, everything that is dearest to heart lies outside this circle of human reasoning. Reason cannot answer questions about supreme consciousness, God, Self, etc. Similarly, there are the questions why one should be good to others, or always respect others, show mercy, pity, console, etc.; it is difficult whether science can answer these questions. One has to transcend reason to answer these questions. Super-consciousness holds the answer to all these questions. When reason fails, reason itself will show the way to higher plane.

There are different planes at which mind functions, each developing into another- instincts develop into reason, reason into the transcendental consciousness. Real inspiration does not contradict reason; it fulfills it. It is not the purpose here to go into the psychological aspects of the mind, but it suffices to state that where reasoning stops, spirituality pays; where science fails, Vedanta shows the way. It is important to note that the physical environment does play a very significant role in spiritual development as could be noted from the experience of our ancient Sages. The Banyan tree, also known as the Pipul tree, is the most sacred tree under which Bodhisatva gained enlightenment. The Riverside or lakeside or the hilltop environs suit the purpose of meditation. Some prefer caves for meditation.

The 'Principle of Least Effort' governs success. Least effort is effortless action. A Mind that is tense and anxious about the result cannot function properly. A calm, collected Mind is the Fountainhead of creativity. One should practise Transcendental-Meditation to keep the Mind calm and collected.

It is said that 'the Brainwaves from the two cerebral hemispheres become purified in frequency and correlated in phase by TranscendentalMeditation' The energy out put of the left and right hemisphres tends to become equalized, and the rhythmic activity from the two sides of the brain becomes balanced.

Anxiety inhibits creativity. Reduced anxiety improves psycho-technical performance and the timing of voluntary actions (for creative behaviour). The increased stability of brain rhythms is believed to be the basis of improved perception-motor performances. Increased activation of right hemisphere is correlated function of intuition, spatial and melodic composition, and non-verbal idea formation- all-important processes underlying creativity.

Creativity demands both intuition and a developed verbal and analytic capacity for the conception, formulation, communication, and application capacity for the conception, formulation, communication, and application of creative ideas in a simple and direct form.

Thus, it is very clear that creativity is the function of not only intuition but also its immediate practical implementation with proper co-ordination. The right hemisphere of the brain supports functional integration of the intuitive spatial skills; whereas, the left hemisphere supports analytic and verbal skill- the two function together on neurophysiological basis.

There is a second type, where the posterior cortex plays important role. Here, the Brain waves spread synchronously and coherently to the frontal region (include entire brain). Since the assocition areas are in the anterior brain, the motor controls in the central region, and the censory processors are throughout the brain, this profound ordering in terms of electrical wave synchrony has a suggested correlation with the improved coordination of thought and action and improved perceptual motor performance. This ends in expression of creativity in behaviour.

There is the Third type of Creativity. The electroencephalic ordering fundamental to creativity is seen in a more integrated relationship vertically, between cortex and the thalamus and other sub-cortical centers. This coherence between parts of the brain responsible for conscious thinking (cortical) and for the primary physiological functions (sub-cortical) has the general consequence of a closer connection between mind and body.

Transcendental Meditation (TM-Siddhi Programme) helps deep relaxation to entire system, reduced oxygen consumption, reduced metabolic state, reduced breath rate, reduced cardiactate, increased skin resistence, and a decrease in lactate (index of reduced anxiety). A relaxed person, free from distractions of anxiety and worry can more easily and more completely apply his creative potential.

The Power of the Mind

There is a beautiful account of a dialogue amongst the Gods regarding the Mind. The Gods were afraid of Man misusing this powerful instrument called 'Mind' and thought of hiding it beyond his reach. They thought of hiding it in heaven and knew that he would reach there without any difficulty. Then they thought of hiding it under the deep sea, etc. etc. Finally, Indra, the Lord of the Gods and Godesses suggested to hide this most powerful instrument 'Mind' within his heart so that he will not search for it there; He will spend all his time searching for it elsewhere. Thus, Man has got immense potential energy, the power of the Mind within himself.

So far, it has not been possible to get to the depth of the mind and measure it. Dr Alexis Carrel, the Nobel Prize Laureate and author of 'Man the Unknown' has said, "The Mind is hidden within the living matter, completely neglected by psychologists and economists, almost unnoticed by physicians. Yet it is the most colossal power of this world". Smily Blanton says, "In the deeper levels of the Mind are resources of power, strength and courage hardly imagined. To each person himself is given the task of these levels, with what assistance he can muster. There are, fortunately, untold resources in each of us if we will only find and utilize them". Mind is a storehouse of enormous energy; however, this energy is beyond the perception of our ordinary senses.

Thus, it is very clear that there is enormous power in the Mind that is yet to be harnessed by mankind. It is J.B.Rhine, among the scientific community, who recognized the extra-physical or spiritual nature of the Mind. According to the Psychologist C.G.Jung, "The unconscious gives us all the encouragement and help that a bountiful nature can bestow on man. ...It holds possibilities which are locked away from the conscious Mind, for it has at its disposal all subliminal psychic contents, all those things which have been forgotten or overlooked, as well as the wisdom and experience of uncounted centuries which are laid down in its archetypal organs. The unconscious can serve man as a guide, provided he can resist the lure of being misguided". Further, Jung says, "part of psyche is beyond time and space and is unknown to us. That which is beyond time and space is also beyond causation".

Prof. Rhine of Duke University who has done extensive studies and conducted experiments to explore the uncanny powers of the mind has come to the conclusion that "*Man has a soul*". The human Mind does indeed possess properties not belonging to Physics, as we know it. "Since space and time are the surest indications of what is physical, the mind must therefore be extra-physical or spiritual in nature". This has been elaborately dealt with in the Rk Veda and SamaVeda and all Upanishads herald the same spiritual strength of the mind and the magnetic powers of the human mind. It is a great truth that spiritual knowledge, the knowledge of the Supreme Principle hidden in man can bring about total transformation even in the most wretched and the miserable by infusing indomitable courage, conviction, strength and hope. The awareness of divinity of the soul can work wonders in all spheres and it is the only remedy to all the maladies of this world.

Maharishi Mahesh Yogi has demonstrated how all the Knowledge is available in the Abstract Silence, 'Atyanta-Abhava' (the Purusha) and immense possibilities exist in the dynamic Silence 'Anyonya-Abhaava'-Pradhan (the Prakriti). The source of all Knowledge is the self-referral Atma and it can be tapped through intense Meditation- the Transcendental Meditation-Siddhi Programme. *It is concentration, contemplation, and merging into the depth of deep Silence, the Absolute Abstract in the depth of the Atma, Soul, that unravel the 'Truth'. All the inventions and discoveries have come by this method only.*

Swami Vivekananda, tirelessly pleaded youngsters to understand the secrets of the Soul. He says, *"This glorious soul we must believe in, out of that will come power. Whatever you think, that you will be". 'Yad bhaavam tad bhavati'.*

The science of hypnosis has proved beyond doubt, the existence of memories of the past extending over previous births as also the ability of the psychiatrists to harness this source to cure many a mental illness. However, there has been very little progress in harnessing this source of power for the betterment of mankind. But, spirituality can do that job.

There are the telepathy, Extra Sensorial Perception (ESP), parakaya pravesha, mind reading, and powers of '*Samata*', '*Samyama*', etc. These are all beautifully explained in the Veda. Atharva Veda is a source of useful information on Mind. Russian scientists have devised methods and instruments to diagnose the causes of diseases that a normal X-ray machine is unable to reveal. The Kirlian apparatus can detect even a small lie uttered by us. It can assess the fluctuation in the condition of the mind and find out the origin of physical disorders. They have found an aura (of colours or light) around every human being (that are not fund around dead bodies) that will help us to analyze the personality of the persons. Besides, there are other extraordinary powers latent in the human mind. The Vedas have described these conditions. There is the sookshma sharira that has to be studied carefully; this is beyond the physical bony, fleshy substance of the physical body. These aspects are better studied under spiritual practices and higher stages of spiritual attainments rather than in biological or physical laboratories. Mind itself is a huge laboratory for the study of Man. One has to just sit and contemplate and meditate.

All the powers that exist in nature (Prakriti) also exist in Man and his Mind. There is the power of attraction or gravity; also, electricity, magnetism, heat, light, and the various kinds of motions that are found in the macrocosm are found in the microcosmic structure of Man. In fact, these forces are not in any way different from those we find in the external world, but they are the same; the only difference is in the degree of manifestation. As on the physical plane, so also it is on the mental plane. The universal mind is the source of all the powers that have been displayed by some individuals. That universal mind is called the 'cosmic mind' that has been in existence since time immemorial; rather, it is eternal.

The waves of power that are manifested in different forms of psychic forces rise from the cosmic mind that is below our ordinary conscious plane. It is the subconscious mind. The thought waves, or the psychic forces raise upto our conscious plane from the subconscious or the unconscious plane or the subliminal self. Then we become conscious of it. Then, again, these go down to the vast subconscious plane, i.e., the cosmic plane. Our consciousness lies on the crest of these waves, which are rising from the subconscious or unconscious realm. They are unknown to us at present, but, in course of time, under certain conditions and circumstances, they manifest themselves on the conscious plane. Then we come to know their existence.

The human Mind and the cosmic mind are one and the same. The cosmic mind exists in the subconscious that is very vast. Only a quarter of that vast ocean appears as the conscious mind, like the tip of the iceberg. Now and then the conscious mind is furbished with some of these forces in a very surprising manner as in the child prodigies or wizards and geniuses. The individual mind is related to the cosmic mind, and it's eddies and whirlpools are, in fact, the chitta vrittis called *individual mind*. These eddies of the individual minds are connected with other eddies through the cosmic mind.

The 'cosmic mind' is the Prakriti that is 'avyakta', the unmanifest or 'Maya'. This Maya or delusion is caused by the undifferentiated consciousness or the Brahman and is the first manifestation of the

Universe. Everything comes within the purview or hold of this envelope or cover of nescience, or 'avidya' or ignorance that makes the sensate objective world appear as real. It is the same objective world created by the cosmic mind that the human mind perceives as real due to its ignorance since the cosmic mind and the human mind are one and the same.

There is another interesting side of all this joy and happiness that we ordinarily refer to in our day to day life. Normally, our joy and happiness is short-lived. There is duality in all this; sorrow and misery follow the joy and happiness like the night and day. Why is this duality?

Mind Managament

The success and failure of a person in life depends entirely on the functioning of the wonderful thing called *Mind.* But no body knows what is this 'Mind' and how it functions. Our ancient Seers and Rishis gave much importance to the understanding of the complexities of Mind and devised ways and means of *managing,* if not controlling, the dynamic functions of the mind. Some Rishis have successfully controlled their Mind through 'Praanayaáma' and have achieved supreme powers. Mind and its thoughts are closely linked to breathing and its rhythm. Slow and uniform breathing is associated with calm and peaceful mind. Heavy breathing is associated with disturbed mind, anxiety. By controlling the breathing, the mind can be controlled and by controlling the mind, breathing can be regulated. In fact, one can attain any state of consciousness by breath control, i.e.,'Praanaayaama'. The art of breath control is taught in Raja Yoga, 'Kriya yoga', and Hatha Yoga. Yoga Upanishads give elaborate description of these things.

Breathing exercises are advocated for mind control and certain asanas are useful for this purpose. Patanjalis's 'Ashtaanga Yoga Sutra' gives all the details of this exercise. There are specialists who have perfected asanas for different purposes; so also, there are experts in different types of Yoga. Ultimately, what is important is the management of the so-called *delicate instrument*, the Mind.The Mind as a matter is volatile, hard as well as soft, assumes different states under different conditions and is closely monitored by breathing. Breathing influences the mind and moods and mind and moods affect breathing. Both are intimately connected. The Mind is at its best when it is silent, absolutely silent. The Mind performs at its best when it is cool, absolutely cool, below freezing point! Extremely low temperatures are conducive to flow of intuitive thoughts. Super conductivity state is achieved under low temperatures of brain and work wonders. Inventions and discoveries are possible in such state of cool and contemplated Mind. The brain ceases to work when it is heated up; increased molecular movement in brain is not conducive to clarity. Hotheaded persons are always confused and they tend to lose control of mind easily and quickly. Meditation is the only solution in all cases of anxiety and tension that leads to heated brain. In deep contemplation and transcendental meditation, the mind is stripped of all its impurities, i.e., thoughts, and the mind becomes pure consciousness; pure mind is pure sonsciousness. It is this pure consciousness that derives its light and knowledge from the Atma since the consciousness is the reflected light of the Atma. Atma is the divine Light and source of all knowledge that is the extended supreme consciousness. This is the secret of all success and happiness. Everyone has access to this inexhuastibe source.

'*Manonasha*' is silencing, or stilling, or calming the Mind in yogic parlance, or 'purification' of the Mind by dhyana and meditation that brings supreme happiness and success in life. As already stated, *Bhagavad Gita* is all about this 'Mind'. There are innumerable references to Mind and its functions in our Vedas, Upanishads, Puranas, Bhagavad Gita and other ancient scriptures. Our ancient Sages and Seers realized the profound truth and praised the Lord in thousand names; praised in the sense reaffirmed their faith in Him by remembering Him in a thousand names. "*Vishnu Sahasra Nama*" is the most sacred prayer to the Lord praising His glory. It has a reference to Mind in Verse 5.1 ***"Om! Salutations to the Mind".*** The Supreme Creator, 'Self' is the creator of the Mind. It is the lower nature of the Supreme Brahman. It is the Mind that differentiates human being from animal. Animals are blindly driven by instincts and urges. Man is provided with intellect and discretion, ability to think, to judge, and to choose, and to guide the Mind.

Aitareya Upanishad [1.1.4] says, *'the Mind came from the heart. We can concentrate only through Mind and we cannot concentrate if the Mind is absorbed elsewhere'. Taittiriya Upanishad* [III-IV-1] also says, that *'Concentration (Dharana) should be practiced. Concentration is Brahman. Brahman is supreme knowledge'.*

Both *Katha Upanishad and Brihadaaranyaka Upanishad* declare that 'Mind is the window to the world'. Without Mind we can live but like an idiot, like a child. There is an interesting story. Once, the Mind left the body to know how the body functions without it. The sense organs performed their functions normally without the help of the Mind. This hurt the ego and the Mind returned to the body. Idiots live without knowing this Mind. *Brihadaaranyaka Upanishad* [4-4-9] also says, that "Mind is the repository of Moon in the universe. Just as Moon in the Akasha of the space, so is the mind in the human beings. It is vast. It is thought itself and the Supreme Self pervades the Mind and the Moon as well as the body of the universe. It is All-pervading! Moon is honey to all beings; so also all beings are honey to Moon. This bright immortal being is identified with the mind in the human body. Mind is the cause of happiness and misery".

Bhagavad Gita says 'Mind is relativity and renunciation through mental austerities alone will free us from bondage. Attachment is the greatest hurdle in attaining knowledge of the Self, the Brahman. Attachment is bondage and non-attachment is freedom' [Gita 3-5]. Bhagavad Gita is the encyclopaedia of Mind.

Chhandogya Upanishad says, 'the ear is Rk', and 'Mind is Saaman'. The 'Saaman' rests on 'Rk'. The ear 'Sa' and the Mind 'Ama' make it 'Saama'. Mind is surely greater than speech. It encompasses speech and name'. 'Sama' in Yoga is calmness; it is this calmness of the Mind that one should try to establish always and this can be done by 'Ved', Knowledge or Jnyan. Rig Veda shows the Light!

Hence, it is interesting to study and clearly understand the various aspects of the human mind and learn the techniques of controlling the wayward mind and putting it to the fruitful avocations of man.

In order to understand the mind, one has to go deep into the whole process of evolution of man and the development of Mind. Vedas and Upanishads, the Brahma Sutra, the Puranas, the Bhagavad Gita etc.are the eternal source of supreme knowledge.

The Vedantic View of Mind

The Vedantic View is more comprehensive in explaining man and his mind than that of the modern science. The basic components of all creations and future creations, according to Vedanta are:

First, the Mahat, also known as 'Aakasha', or *Universal Consciousness* 'The Brahman';

Second, Ahamkara, -the 'I'-ness born of the Mahat, the Aakasha, or the Space;

Third, Buddhi, i.e., the discriminative faculty born of Ahamkara; and

Fourth, the Manas, i.e., ***the Mind***, born of 'Ahamkara', the 'I'-ness (the 'ego').

Buddhi, Ahamkara and Manas are also called '*Antahkarana*', the internal organs. Antahkarana is sustained by the vital airs: Prana, Apana, Samana, Vyana, and the Udana. When Prana exits the antahkarana ceases to function.

Paatanjali treats 'ahamkara', the ego-sense, or the 'I'-sense as the one evolved out of Buddhi (Intellect) and the process then leads to the other three - Manas, Indriyas and Tanmatras (Elements and Panchabhutas). There are –the *Jnyanendriyas and the Karmendriyas*; (i.e., Five sense objects like sight, hearing, taste, smell and touch); and, the five great elements (Tanmatras): ether, air, fire, water, and the earth. By the element earth, is meant all solid bodies including the planets and satellites known to man. Together, these Twenty-four Fundamental Principles are the products of 'Prakriti' subsisting in its three-fold divisions of forces- known as the *Sattva*, the *Rajas*, and the *Tamas*. These are the first sprouts branching off from the unmanifest Nature, '*Avyakta Prakriti*'.'*Duality*' starts here. Duality is Nescience, *Ignorance*.

Pradahana or Nature is unmanifested ether, maya, prakriti, sakshi, ajnyana (*Undifferentiated Consciousness*), etc. Its qualities are sattva, rajas and tamas. It exists in '*triputi*', i.e., Time, Space, and Causation. Nature, i.e., the universe of phenomenon, is actually existing in the Self, i.e., the supreme Consciousness, or the Knower, or the Brahman; by itself, it is unconscious or does not know its own existence. Again, it is the union of Purusha and the Prakriti that has created this phenomenal, or perceivable objective universe. It is through the infinite and inconceivable power of the Brahman that the union of Purusha and the Prakriti has taken place and the consequent phenomenal world is created. This power of creation, or the manifestation (vyakta) of the Brahman is called '*Maya*'.

Shree Krishna says, *"I make the souls forget their true nature by means of My divine maaya. Maaya limits even the limitless. None can go beyond it. Only those who surrender themselves to My mercy can cross over it" [Bhagavad Gita].*

According to Vedanta, *Vikruti* is Indriyas and Panchabhutas. The Eight-fold Nature, the *Prakrutyashtakas* include the *Panchabhutas* five elements, the *Mind* (*Manas*), the *Intellect* (*Buddhi*); and *Egosim* (*Ahamkara*). The Dhatu Ashtakas are the external skin, the internal skin, blood, flesh, bones, marrow, and semen; and, the eight psychic powers are the Aishwaryas (Ashtaishwaryas). These are Super-Human Powers that include the powers of *Brahma, Prajapati, Devas, Gandharvas, Yakshas, Rakshasas and Pitrus and Pishachas. The eight Virtues of Soul (Gunashtakas) are Daya (Compassion), Kshama (Forbearence), Anasuya (Absence of Jealousy), Purity (Shaucha) Karpanya (Poverty), Akarpanya (Absence of Poverty), Anayas (Absence of Fatigue) and Aspraha (Desirelessness).*

There are the eight mental states, the '***Bhavashtakas***' like Righteousness (Dharma), Adharma, Jnyana (Knowledge), Ajnyana (Ignorance), Vairagya (Renunciation), Raga (Attachment), Aishwarya (Super-Human Powers) and Anaishwarya (Want of super-human powers); and, there are the five Viparyas, 'Misconceptions', twenty-eight 'Disabilities' or 'ashaktis', nine 'Tushtis', Satisfactions. Besides, there are the eight 'Siddhis', or Perfections (Attainments). Generally, the individual souls get drowned in these '*ashtakas*', blemished with duality, that makes man unhappy despite his attainments. The way out of this 'Sansar' is total submission to the Supreme Power behind the creation and constant Dhyan of the Lord. All these are explained in *Sankhya Sutras III-37, 45; Sankhyakarika 47; Yoga Sutra 18; and, Brahma Purana II.2.*

We are rooted to the earth and our Mind works within its ambit. The earth has Gravity. In the Vedantic sense, the attraction of the Nature (Prakriti), "Ajnyana" (Ignorance) is so much that it holds the jeevas, individual souls in its grip offering temptations of the Ashtaishwaryas and will not loosen the grip while the jeevas hanker after reaching the higher and higher levels of consciousness, Jnyana (Knowledge) and Liberation. We are carried away by earthly attractions. This is Maya. The earth is often referred to as "Shree". Shree- Bhoo-Durga, the three different forms of Shree Laksmi, the presiding deity, stand for Prakruti. The Earth is conceptualised as a symbol of profound creative power, as the eternal source of everything; it is Dharitri; it is the repository of all the wealth, and it supports and sustains life providing food and shelter to all creatures. Bhoo Devi, as she is called, is worshiped in the form of *Maha Lakshmi*. The mantra to propitiate the Goddess is: "***Om Shreem, Rhyeem, Kleem Vasudhayai Swaaha***", ***meaning, that*** *'cosmic harmony of heaven, earth, and man brings out enormous power and strength. Om, I offer obeisance to Thee'.*

On the face of the 'dualities' that reign supreme, one has to work hard, build up a strong Mind, individuality, spirituality, a personality, and an 'integrated personality'; Then, when one is strong and spiritually mature, he or she should look up and see a greater courage and greater strength beckoning and makes one experience and say: *"Not I, but Thou; Thy will be done*". The full message of self-surrender and Divine Grace that helps one to get rid of the 'dualities' of sansar is beautifully explained in *Bhagavad Gita* Ch. XVIII. This is the philosophy of life, the grip of Prakriti over Purusha, and the method of getting the shackles broken and getting liberated from bondage as advised by Lord Shree Krishna in the Bhagavad Gita. Bhagavad Gita is addressed to Arjuna, a confused, perplexed, ignorant jeeva who represents the common man or woman. It applies to us and we can take lessons from it.

3
Prajnya [Consciousness]

"Prajnyaanan Brahma"

Prajnya (Samskr) Consciousness. This whole universe is one borne out of supreme-Consciousness, that is self-effulgent, all–pervasive, omnipotent, and omnipresent. It is this supreme-Consciousness (Parama-prajnya) that has given rise to the three other adjuncts of time, space, and causality. This is also present in the jeevas as individual consciousness. Rather, consciousness, time, and space exist in our mind. In a way, the time and space exist in our consciousness. Whatever perceived (pratyaksha) or inferred (paroksha) are in the mind. The visible universe is the projection on the mind screen; it is imprint in our mind. The Veda proclaims that 'knowledge is within our Self'. If one understands this secret, he knows everything! Consciousness that is in jeeva is not only a part of the whole, the universal Conmsciousness but it is the Whole (Poornam) by itself and such is the nature of this consciousness. It is the nature of the supreme Brahman. It is the divine light, or 'paranjyoti'. It is the '*Knowledge supreme*' called 'para vidya'. It is the goal of every spiritual aspirant to know this. The dawn of this knowledge, or 'enlightenment' is liberation. It is the 'be-all' and 'end-all' of this universe, or the multiverse!

According to Hindu mythology, it is the common belief that, the Trinity, the Trimurtis' who are concerned with the creation, sustenance and devolution of this Universe are Brahma, Vishnu and Maheswara, respectively. In fact, there is one common spirit or shakti, a divine force, behind all these three (Purusha) who is responsible for the nature of the world we are in, and it is known as the 'Brahman', as distinct from the Lord of the creation, 'Brahma'. Brahman is derived from "*Bhrht*", meaning huge, huge enough to hold the multiverse, '*Akhilaanda Koti Brahmaanda*'. In fact, Brahmaanda, or the Hiranyagarbha precedes the Trimurtis and constitutes the manifest form of the infinite, the 'Brahman'.

Thus, there is the unmanifest 'Brahm' or Brahman as the supreme Lord Almighty, 'God' and His seat is in vast deep ocean of Silence. It is beyond all causality, time, and space. It is self-existent, omniscient and omnipotent. *"Brahman is Universal Consciousness". It is the supreme force behind all creation. In modern scientific terminology, it is called the 'Self-Referral Dynamics of the Unified Field- the mechanics of consciousness Knowing Itself' (Maharishi Mahesh Yogi). It is the cause of the cause of creation; from it (the universal consciousness) emanate all the things that constitute this sensate objective world ('prapancha'), perceived by the five senses. It is the 'Natural Law' that governs all other Laws. It is all- pervasive ('vish') and as such, known as 'Vishnu', 'vish' meaning 'all pervasive'. It is the 'Avyakta, the unmanifest basis of the manifest world; it is omnipresent and omniscient. It is Achyuta and Anant; it is Narayana the cosmic flow.*

It is called 'God' for there is no other suitable word and those who do not want the word 'God' can simply call it "That". Since no other term is suitable to express these qualities the devotees ('bhaktas') call it 'Bhagavan'. Whoever has got this immense power is also called Bhagavan. God is 'Sat, Chit, and Anand' i.e., Truth, Knowledge, and Bliss, respectively. It is the 'svaroopa', nature, the inherent quality of the Lord.

The seat of supreme-Consciousness is the Absolute Abstract, the "Brahm". It is the 'Atyanta-Abhava', the deep Silence where all the unmanifest are located. In this sense of the term, everything emanates from deep Silence. Deep Silence is the WHOLENESS, 'all-knowing', hence 'self-referral', and thus the seat of KNOWLEDGE. All KNOWLEDGE emanate from deep Silence. It is the Self, the 'Brahm'. It is the supreme-Consciousness, the 'Purusha'. From this deep Silence, the single unending source of all energy emanate impulses that merge into another level of consciousness, 'Anyonya-Abhava'- 'Prakriti', and produce waves and bubbles that carry the primordial mattaer that create all the material objects of this Universe. The ocean of consciousness is real ('Sat') and the waves and bubbles are unreal ('Asat'). In this sense of the term, we, the 'Jeevatma'- embodied Soul, are all bubbles ('Asat') that carry with us an iota of consciousness, creative intelligence, of the ocean of consciousness (Supreme Brahman) to which we belong and into which we finally merge.

The Phenomena of Mind and Consciousness

Gregory Bateson proposed to define 'Mind' as 'a systems phenomenon characteristic of living organisms, societies, and ecosystems'. The 'systems view' looks at the world in terms of relationships and integration. Systems are integrated wholes whose properties cannot be reduced to those of smaller units. A set of criteria goes to make mind according to systems view of life. Thinking, willing, learning, and memory are all associated with mind. Mind is a necessary and inevitable consequence of a certain complexity, which begins long before organisms develop a brain and a higher nervous system. This definition of Bateson is closely related to the characteristics of self-organising systems.

Mind is the essence of being alive. Accordingly, mind is an essential property of the living systems. From the systems view of life, life is not a substance or a force, and mind is not an entity interacting with matter. Both life and mind are manifestations of the same set of systemic properties, a set of processes that represent the dynamics of self-organisation. The description of mind as a pattern of organisation, or a set of dynamic relationships is related to the description of matter in physics. Mind and matter no longer appear to belong to two fundamentally separate categories, but can be seen to represent merely different aspects of the same universal process. The term 'mentation' is used to refer to mental activity, to describe the dynamics of self-organisation at lower levels and the term 'Mind' is used for higher organism of high complexity. George Coghill developed the beautiful systemic view of living organisms and mind, well before the advent of *the systems view of life*.

According to Coghill, 'structure, function and mentation are the three essential and closely inter-related patterns of organisation in living organisms. Here, structure is organisation in space; function is organisation in time; and 'mentation' is a kind of organisation that is intimately interwoven with structure and function at low levels of complexity but goes beyond time and space at higher levels. From the modern systems perspective, '*mentation*', being the dynamics of self-organisation, represents the organization of all functions. At higher levels of complexity, mentation can no longer be limited to behaviour; because it takes on the distinctive non-spatial and non-temporal qualities associated with mind.

Thus, in the systems concept of mind, mentation is characteristic of not only of individual organisms but also of social and ecological systems. Bateson asserts, that 'mind is immanent not only in the body but also in the pathways and messages outside the body'. There are larger manifestations of mind of which our individual minds are only subsystems and this concept has radical implications in our day-to-day interaction with our natural environment. Man will stop exploiting nature when he fully understands this concept. All the maladies of the modern day industrial economic development exploiting natural resources instead of properly utilizing the natural wealth, has led to the predicament 'whither development?

Brain, its Function in Relation to Mind

It is very difficult to explain the nature of interaction between the spiritual and the physical aspects of the Mind and the Brain at one stretch. Mind is both matter and energy and it is very easy to convert energy into matter and vice versa. Meditation is the technique of realizing Mind as energy in its superconscious level. Similarly, it is difficult to relate the spiritual aspects of the subtle human heart, Anthahkarana generating emotions and feelings to the physical heart that pumps blood; so also, it is difficult to realize that the subtle heart and the subtle mind are one and the same. Thus, the Mind, at higher level of Consciousness and the Heart, i.e., the seat of the Lord, are extremely subtle and spiritually more powerful inner instruments called '*Anthahkarana*'. On the other hand, the human Brain is a bundle of tissues and cells that are constantly pulsating conveying signals received from the nerve centers as 'neurons'. It is a wonderful system of organisation and communication, and the network is fantastic! Images received, stored, processed and transferred; messages are convyed by vibrations of different intensities and, colours and codes to the brain from the heart (through blood) and on to the Mind, and again from the Mind back to the brain as impulses and waves, intuition and decision, etc. to be conveyed to the different parts of the body for reflex action. It does all the task of assimilation, codification, decoding, and transfer to memory, discretion, judgement, and declaration- all within split seconds! The messages and images are created and stored in cells and transferred from cell to cell by cell division or cell expansion. It is' ageing' and 'loss of memory' if the cells slow down and stop their growth; it is 'clinical death' when brain stops its work.

It is very interesting to know what happens when the brain cells are damaged; normally, the stored information, memory is lost. A part of the brain may stop working due to damage due to accident and this may cause paralysis. Loss of memory is common due to head injuries in accidents; also, memory may be destroyed by the use of certain chemicals and drugs and electric shock treatments. In all these cases, the individual will not react appropriately, that is all! This sort of stilling the mind, manonasha, will not help in attaining to state of superconsciousness, whereas the stilling of the mind by Yoga will greatly facilitate concentration, focusing, and attaining to higher level of consciousness. It is attaining to higher and higher levels of consciousness and awareness that brings about release from bondage, i.e., liberation.

Another interesting development is about the structure and functioning of the brain. It is discovered that there are two hemispheres of the brain and these two parts function opposite but complementary to each other. The left hemisphere controls the right side of the body and it is more specialized in analytic, linear thinking, which involves processing information sequentially. The right hemisphere controls the left side of the body. It seems to function predominantly in a holistic mode that is appropriate for synthesis and tends to process information more diffusely and simultaneously.

In recent years, there have been attempts to promote a more balanced view of brain functioning and to develop methods for increasing one's mental faculties by stimulating and integrating the functioning of both sides of the brain. It is said that we hardly use ten per cent of our brain. Concentration and contemplation greatly enhances the sharpness of the brain. The human mind is able to create an inner world that mirrors the outer reality but has an existence of its own. This can move the individual or society to act upon the outer world. This inner world of the individual is the psychological realm; it unfolds an entirely new level and involves a number of phenomena that are characteristic of human nature.

Self-awareness, conscious experience, conceptual thought, symbolic language, dreams, art, the creation of culture, a sense of values, interest in remote past, the concern for the distant future are some of the most interesting aspects of thinking of the human mind. Most of these characteristics exist in rudimentary form in various animal species; but what is unique in human species is the combination of characteristics fore-shadowed in lower forms of evolution but integrated and developed to a high level of sophistication only in human species. The patterns we perceive around us are based, in a very fundamental way, on the patterns within. Patterns of matter mirror or reflect patterns of Mind coloured by subjective feelings and values.

Our Mind is a synthetic whole, '*Samhita*', consisting of the faculties of cognition, visioning, feeling and willing. Our reasoning, feeling, willing and action are at war with one another and create a terrible confusion within ourselves. Unless we develop an integrated personality - in all its physical, mental and spiritual aspects, it is very difficult to live a harmonious life.

Maharishi Mahesh Yogi with the help of Nobel Laureate Dr. Tony Nader has brought out the correlative study of Veda and Vedic Literature as well as the Human Physiology in great detail. It gives a clear picture of the Natural Law that governs all laws of Nature as well as the laws that govern the Human life. All the intricate functioning of the human Mind and body can be clearly understood from this study. Maharishi advocates Transcendental Meditation to reach the supreme Consciousness and harness full potential. [Celebrating the Vision of Total Knowledge: Maharishi Mahesh Yogi, MM Vishva Vidyalaya, Jabalpore, India].

Consciousness

The vedantic conception of Pradhana-Purusha, i.e., matter and energy (Nature and Man) is all- comprehensive and includes the physical, the biological, the spiritual, in the unity of *Pure Consciousness*. In *Bhagavad Gita* (Ch.7. Verse 4-6) Shri Krishna says, '*Earth, water, fire, air, space, mind, intellect, and ego sense- this is my Prakriti, i.e., Nature, divided eight-fold'. "This is (My) Lower (Prakariti); but different from it, know thou, Oh! Mighty-armed, (My) Higher Prakriti, the principle of intelligence by which this universe is sustained; Know that these (twoPrakritis) are the womb of all beings; I am the 'Srushti' (origin),' Sthiti' (maintenance), and 'Laya' (dissolution) of the whole universe".*

Shri Shankara comments on the same as:

"Through the two-fold Nature, apara (lower) prakruti, and para (higher) prakruti, I, who am the Omniscient God (being of the nature of infinite Pure-consciousness), am the cause of this universe'.

The word '*Consciousness*' has many Samskrut (Sanskrit) equivalents viz.chit, prajnya, jnyapti, jnyana, bodha, and samvit. According to context, the meaning may be 'Infinitude', 'Pure-Consciousness', Knowledge, Truth, Wisdom, etc. The word '*Samvit*' is used to express '*Non-dual Pure Consciousness*', the Atman- Brahman. The systems view of mind seems perfectly consistent with both the scientific and the mystical views of consciousness, and thus to provide the ideal framework for unifying the two. The systems view agrees with the conventional scientific view that consciousness is a manifestation of complex material patterns- a manifestation of living systems of a certain complexity. Biological structures of these systems are expressions of the system's self-organisation, i.e., Mind. In mystic view, it is manifestation of Cosmic Mind- direct experience of cosmic consciousness goes beyond the scientific approach. The systems view gives a more meaningful scientific framework for approaching the age-old questions of nature of life, Mind, Consciousness and Matter. All these should be clearly understood.

Normally, consciousness is taken for granted and one does not bother about it. We live and work for most of the time without being aware of what we are doing, rather without consciousness. We unconsciously live and work; we are not aware of the implications, pros and cons, of what we are doing. Rather, we do not think! Some people mistake consciousness for awareness. One can be consciously aware of a certain thing or situation, where as, it is also possible to simply be aware without the application of mind or thought. One may say, he knew it but was not aware of its consequences! Similarly, it is also possible that one is simply aware, but not capable of focusing or concentration or understanding. In all these cases, the state of awareness and state of consciousness are of different nature and degree. A person of 'conscious awareness' can see *things as they are* and will have clear knowledge of reality of things. He will not be easily duped. Awareness under all circumstances is very important but higher level of consciousness only helps in attainment to spiritual attainment.

Quality of Consciousness

The entire Universe is organised and managed by Consciousness. Consciousness is the Constitution of the Universe; it is the Natural Law. Human system is also organised and managed by consciousness- both internally and externally. The Structuring Dynamics of Natural Law is present within the Self of everyone, Internally, the 'antahkarana' or the internal organs- manas, 'I'-ness, and buddhi, are managed by consciousness. Consciousness is the light derived from the Atman and reflected by Buddhi. Externally, the objective world is perceived consciously by mind and discriminative power is exercised in processing, understanding and performing actions accordingly. The role of mind and consciousness is of crucial importance in all human endeavour; human development would be impossible without mind and consciousness. By the way, one should not mistake Mind and Consciousness as two separate entities. Pure Mind is Consciousness.

There is subtle difference between Mind and Consciousness. Mind is full of impurities as is evident from the nature of thoughts entertained by the mind. It is the constant vibration that makes Mind restless and dis-oriented. Concentration would make it focussed pointed and purposeful. However, even the concentration or focusing of the Mind would be useless without the support of the buddhi (the discriminative power), intellect or Consciousness. Here, the quality of Consciousness becomes very important.

Maharishi Mahesh Yogi has enumerated 36 qualities of Consciousness other than the Veda- Rk, Saman, Yajus and the Atharva. According to Maharishi, the Atma is the source of Veda. It is 'the Brahm', fully awake in its Potentiality. It is Totality. It is Self-Referral and there is nothing else to refer to. It holds everything in its nutshell. It is omniscient, omnipotent and self-effulgent. It is smaller than the smallest and bigger than the biggest. It is Samhita. Rk Veda (KNOWLEDGE) is the Samhita, WHOLENESS. Atman is the Self of everyone that is the Knower, the means of Knowledge or the Illumining Principle, as well as, the Knowledge. 'Atman' is the Rk Veda, the Samhita of the Seer, the Rishi, the Devata (the Illumining Principle) and the Chhhandas (the Object of Perception). The Six Veda are the Rk, the Saman, the Yajus, the Atharva, the Gandharva, the Dhanur, and the Sthaapatya. These are the structuring Dynamics of Natural Law present in everybody. These are the permanent inexhaustible source of KNOWLEDGE. This is the Di Ribo Nucleic Acid (DNA) in the human physiology that carries the signals of information, structuring, and processing and is known as the 'Ayur-Veda'.

Maharishi has beautifully explained the Vedic Principle of 'Ayam Atma Brahm'- meaning, 'the Atma- Atma with the total memory of Veda and Vishwa within it- is Brahm, the Totality'. Atma, the source of Veda, fully awake in its potentiality is Totality- the 'Brahm' or the Brahman.

Atma is lively in its full potential when it is self-interacting dynamics, the thirty-seven values of the Vedic Literature, together give rise to the structure of the Veda, pure Knowledge- the Laws of Nature- the Constitution of the Universe- which in turn evolve into the physiology and the material creation 'vishwa' while ever remaining within the field of Atma.

Thus, the entire Universe is the product of Purusha and Pradhana (Nature), the former being the Unmanifest Absolute Abstract (Supreme Consciousness) and the latter Anyonya- Abhava, Absolute Silence where immense possibilities exist. The Unmanifest Supreme Consciousness pervades all creation. The thirty-seven Vedic Literature are the thirty-seven qualities of consciousnes that pervades human physiology. Every cell in the human body is pervaded by consciousness and fully represents every aspect of the Universe. It is complete with Knowledge, the Veda.

[See 'Heaven on Earth', and 'Wholeness on the Move', By Maharishi Mahesh Yogi, Maharishi University of Management, Maharishi Veda Vigyan Vishwa Vidya Peetham, Maharishi Prakashan, Jabbalpore].

Order and Harmony

Now, it is very clear that there exists perfect harmony in Naure. It is the Natural law, the Law of Nature – constitution of the Universe, -the Structuring Dynamics of Natural Law that is present in the Self of everyone that is governing this 'Ritam', order. There is perfect balance, order in Nature. This perfect order and harmony that exists in Nature also exists in the human body. The human body functions according to the Natural Law. The Natural law is the Supreme Law. The supreme commander of this Universe is 'Brahm' and it is his diktat, command that runs the Universe in perfect order and harmony. 'Brahm' is the Invincible source of this order and harmony. ***"For fear of Him, the Planets move".***

This Law of Nature is expressed as 'Ved'. The Rk Veda, the Sama, the Yajus, the Atharva, and the thirty-six Vedic Literature that are known as Vedanga, Upanga, Brahmana, Ayurveda, and Praatishaakhya, are the Natural Law that governs everything in this Universe including Human life and activity. The Veda and Vedic Literature are the values of consciousness, or intelligence. These are the Self-referral state of human consciousness, or intelligence. These are the self-sufficient source of pure knowledge and its infinite organising power. These are very well displayed in Rk Veda and the 39 Vedic Literature. These are self-evident in the human physiology, too. Every cell in the human body is a replica of the universe, that is self-containes, knows all and independent and complete in all respect. It is the miniature universe at the one end as microcosm.

Every part of the universe is represented in the human physiology in a miniature form. The same Ritam and Satyam, order and truth, consciousness works and the human body is maintained by the same Natural Law that is self-referral dynamism and this self-inter-acting dynamics runs the body day and night all through life. Since it is the Totality, WHOLENESS or Samhita, it is the source of all knowledge and immense possibilities exist here. This potential can be tapped and the immensity of the nature of the Self can be experienced in Transcendental State of Meditation.

"Yasmin deva adhi vishve nishedhuh", [Rk Veda, 1. 164. 39] meaning, 'the Home in which the Ruler of this Universe- Laws of Nature that govern (Devas), the Universe (adhi vishve) reside (nishedhuh). The heart is the seat of this source of supreme power-'Daivatmashakti'. It is reverberating as sounds of Veda. "Richo Akshare parame vyoman..."[Rk Veda, 1. 164. 39], meaning, the hymns of the Veda are unmanifest dynamism- self-interacting dynamism (Devas)- the structure of dynamic intelligence-the structure of Laws of Nature within the self-referral state of Transcendental Consciousness (Parame vyoman). The Vedic Mantra explains everything; "Agnimeele puohitam..." is the Natural Law that governs the Universe- the "Richo Ak-Share Parame vyoman... ". Veda is knowledge that is composed of Mantra and Brahmana. 'Mantra' is the expression of Law that presents specific sounds in sequence emerging from the self-interacting dynamics of unmanifest pure intelligence. The Brahmana present the inner creative intelligence, the engineering, or mechanics, of structuring sound from unmanifest pure intelligence that is heard as the Mantra of the Veda.

Thus, Veda is 'Total Knowledge', WHOLENESS, OR SAMHITA and the Human Physiology is the embodiment of all this WHOLENESS or KNOWLEDGE in its 'Atman'; Veda, that is Total KNOWLEDGE, 'Samhita'-the three in one- the Rishi, the Devata and the Chhand, is not something that is outside; it is all within the Atma. This is what Sri Krishna says in Bhagavad Gita,"I am the Knower, I am the field of Knowledge, and I am the Illumining Principle, the means of Knowing,- the Jnyeya, Jnyaana, and the Jnyaata, respectively.

'Supreme-Consciousness' ('Prajnana') is *'choice-less awareness'. 'Consciousness' is the physical basis of Mind, a hypothetical mechanism* of nerve-cell connections. The seat of Consciousness is the higher brain stem together with the portion of the cortex that is being employed at that moment. Within the brain impulses are passing along a million insulated nerve fibres that compose the complex, and these impulses are somehow coordinated into the orderly sequences of deliberate thought. What really controls this mechanism is not within the realm of sciences, but definitely it can be perceived in the spiritual experience. There is a switchboard and there is a Switch Operator. He decides things!

There are different layers of consciousness at which a person can dwell and operate. We have seen persons in coma performing their normal physical body functions without being conscious of the external world. The senses are redundant, here. The brain is functioning internally. It is almost similar to Samadhi; it is of no consequence in spiritual attainment. It is an endless sleep. So far, there is no scientific explanation forthcoming for this. Many a brilliant scholars have gone into coma under tragic circumstances and have never regained their consciousness. The exact state of such persons' mind is not known. They are unconscious.

But, an interesting observation here is that of our normal day-to-day activities in which we are scarcely aware of what we are doing. Most of the time we are functioning 'unaware', unconscious, or without discrimination, 'Prajnya'. We are not consciously aware. This is the tragedy of human life. All our misery, unhappiness, troubles are the outcome of this unconscious actions. Why can we not be consciously aware? It is a difficult question to answer. It requires Jnyan, knowledge to be consciously aware and, ignorant, as we are, we are unconscious, 'Prajnyaa-heena' at that! Our country has a population of 100+ crore population and almost all of us are in this state despite the greatness of our country in the field of spiritual attainments. "*God is in us but we are not in Him*", says Shri Ramakrishna. Realisation of the Self will lead us from darkness to light, ignorance to knowledge, death to immortality. We will be able to work consciously only when we have knowledge!

There are the layers of sub-conscious, sputa (the subtle). It is an ocean of or reservoir of samskara, impressions, memories, desires, aspirations, ambitions and what not! It is also a reservoir of noble thoughts, ideas, intuitions and stored up experiences. It is this deep and vast reservoir that is throwing obstacles in our day-to-day functions. It is this Sub-consciousness that throws up confusion, contradictions, dualities, and obstruct our intelligent and efficient functioning. This Sub-conscious should be kept under constant watch and an efficient system of retrieval of memories and experiences should be evolved in order to use the stored up knowledge. All unwanted trash should be removed from the sub-conscious and only the useful knowledge should be retrieved whenever needed. Silencing its unwanted interference in normal day-to-day functions is also important. This can be done by constant japam, meditation, and dhyan.

Super- Consciousness

Another level of consciousness is the ***'Superconsciousness'***. This is the higher level and is the most important one in human life. Scarcely we ever reach this higher level of Super-Consciousness in our life. It is difficult to rise to higher level of Consciousness without proper training and exercise. This higher level of Super-Consciousness is the source of divine intuition, 'Grace of the Lord' and Supreme Bliss. To attain this State of Super Consciousness is the "goal of life'. Super Consciousness can be attained by pure mind and pure heart. It is this that makes a Man more Human and then, Divine. According to Paatanjali's *'Ashtanga Yoga Sutra'*, the state of Superconsciousness is reached in *'Samadhi'*. ***'Samadhi'*** is attained in deep meditation when 'Dhyan' (worship), the 'Dhyata' (the worshipper), and the Subject of worship- 'Dhyeya' become 'One' (Yoga) in a state of 'Turiyaateeta' ('Nirvikalpa Samadhi'). This state is also a state of 'Supreme

Bliss' called "sat-chit-anand" for it is total 'enlightenment'; and, a person who attains this state of Superconsciousness becomes a liberated soul, relieved of all blemishes- the desires of the soul, and he attains immortality. It is also true that none can stay in this state of supreme 'Bliss' forever. It is only a for a few seconds, or at the most minutes, that one can attain this state of Superconsciousness and will soon come back to deep meditation again. But, this is enough to make a person 'Yogi' –a self-realized soul.

The Sub-conscious Mind

The Sub-conscious Mind is like the cellar or the store- room where we store all unwanted things, the trash. Often we resolve to clean this cellar and drop the idea; we do try to clean it, but soon we find it a formidable task and forget about it. Then again, we resolve and try to clean it and do not know where to begin the task. Finally, we drop the idea and the cellar continues to be filled with trash. Our sub-conscious mind is just like this cellar. It consists of samskaras, the impressions of all our past actions, memories, thoughts and what not! It need not necessarily be the evil or bad ones; it also consists of good impressions and memories. These impressions throw obstacles to our present resolutions, thoughts, and action. Hence, it is necessary to clean the sub-conscious mind of all evil and opposing ones and keep good and co-operative ones only. This way, there will be no contradictions, no internal strife in our thoughts and actions.

When a person carries out his normal day-to-day functions, he is not aware of the role played by the different layers of consciousness. Modern psychologists and psychiatrists stress the importance of the sub-conscious mind in both prevention and treatment of mental illness. They adopt methods of hypnotism to retrieve the stored memories and throw out the impressions bothering the mentally sick persons. But the ancient sages had devised very simple methods of Yoga to cleanse the subconscious of all evil and trash impressions and keep the mind healthy and fit. They suggested dhyan and chanting of the name of the Ishtadevatha to achieve this end. Meditation is the sure cure process of sick minds but the techniques are difficult to practise in later stages of illness.

In this busy world of competition, stress, anxiety and tension, it is essential to set apart atleast twenty minutes for meditation, regularly. But, there is no time, for these busy people, even for this; they are prepared to get admitted to hospital for treatment of hypertension and blood pressure problems and spend enormous time and money, but do not have a mind to listen to their own inner voice that is constantly warning them.

How to clean the Sub-conscious Mind of evil thoughts, bad impressions, and unwanted memories of ghastly incidents? It is very easy. This can be done by pouring in the good thoughts, remembering happy events and joyful moments, natural sceneries, temples and the beautiful idols, divine thoughts, chanting of Lord's name, japa, vrata (upavas) and mauna (silence), sat sang (company of spiritual persons), svadhyaya or reading of sacred scriptures like the Bhagavad Gita, singing bhajans and entertaining other holy thoughts and keeping good company. By this constant refurbishing of divine impressions, all old evil impressions are cleared and the sub-conscious will be cleansed. This cleansing of the sub-conscious Mind and the Conscious Mind will help us to attain the Superconscious state easily and quickly. Once the super-conscious state is reached the lower minds will automatically become pure. All the samskaras will be burnt out and the mind becomes pure. Pure mind is pure consciousness; pure consciousness is pure intellect, the inner light, the Self, the Atman; it is the Brahman- the Absolute and the Infinite.

Hence, controlling the mind is very important. It is a big job. It is a very difficult job. It requires perseverance, steadfastness, and total involvement. If good things do not accumulate in the sub-conscious, all trash will occupy it and create disturbances, strife, and misery. We get into inner conflicts and get lost in the process. Most of the time we act in an unconscious state of mind. The cause of the unconscious act is the subconscious where the unconscious thoughts are submerged with millions of our old thoughts and impressions. May be, there are good thoughts, actions, solutions to problems, but we will never reach them unless we clear it of the trash, the bad, and the evil ones. May be there exists some dangerous ones, too. Hence, it is very essential that the sub-conscious is clean and full of noble ideas, thoughts, impressions and support the conscious acts. In the absence of this, the conscious is full of duality, contradictions, fear, confusion and doubts.

Pure Consciousness alone will shed light on reality of life and in the absence of pure mind, we never get access to our pure intellect; our Buddhi evades us. Ignorance reigns supreme and makes our life difficult. Life becomes miserable. Often, we get into an illusion of happiness only to realize that it is leading us to more sin and unhappiness.

Thus, the importance of keeping the Mind in a state of '*Pure Consciousness*' is emphasised through out the Veda and Upanishads. The entire Treatise on Yoga, the 'Yoga Sutra', aims at attaining the state of Pure-Consciousness. Unless one takes to a very disciplined, austere, pious, simple, unassuming, ego-less, self-less, devoted life, it is difficult to attain this state of Pure-Consciousness. Pure food helps to attain pure mind; sattvic food is advised for both the body and mind in addition to the other simple means like svadhyaya, satsang, advocated as the prerequisites of this purification process. Unless the body and mind are pure, it is difficult to attain the state of pure consciousness. Spiritual aspirants take to Hatha Yoga and Dhyana Yoga to reach this state. They attain it in 'Samadhi'. Super-Consciousness is the ultimate goal of human life. It is attained by intense spiritual practice. There are several techniques like *Transcendental Meditation, Kriya Yoga,Raja Yoga or Dhyana Yoga, Kunadalini Yoga* to attain '*Samadhi*' and experience the '*Super Consciousness*'. However, it must be cautioned here, that these methods are not very very essential in the ordinary day-to-day householders' life in order to live a happy and succesful life. An inner peace and contentment is sufficient to enjoy the bliss of life. One can decide to take to this advanced Yogic exercise when he feels that the worldly life of mundane existence is enough and feels the need for higher spiritual experience. But, it must always be remembered that it is not an easy path and it is full of unpredictable problems! Moreover, a good 'Guru' is also needed to guide properly in the unknown. And, it is very difficult to get one, unless there is divine grace, will of the Lord! A Guru is one who has already attained spiritual goal of 'Self- Realization'.

The Un-conscious Mind

We are, almost, always, invariably, living in a state of Un-consciousness in the sense that we are not aware of what we are doing. Jesus Christ said, "Forgive them for they do not know what they are doing". We are not aware of the consequences of our action. In other words, we do not apply our Mind, our Prajnya, Consciousness, to the day-to-day activities. We take things for granted. It is this routine way of thinking, lack of application of Mind, lack of discrimination and discerning that brings disappointment and unhappiness. The moment Un-conscious Mind is shut off, the moment we apply our Mind, become conscious of our action, we realize what we are doing, we get the power of discretion and discernment and things will be all right. One has to be always conscious of his duties and do everything with interest. In fact, interest is memory and memory is interest; we will not forget whatever we do like intent hearing, seeing, touching, tasting, for these will go deep into our memory. Whatever we do with interest will bring instant success and happiness. Whatever we do without interest, without application of mind and consciousness, without discretion and discernment, is bound to bring failure, unhappiness and misery. It is another matter if our brain is damaged and we are unconscious; but even when we are physicall well, we are mentally ill. That is the problem! Mental fitness is the awareness, the conscious application of our Mind and skill to all our action, and that brings happiness and success.

Levels of Consciousness

While modern psychology recognizes only four states of Consciousness, viz the Conscious, subconscious, the unconscious, and the superconscious, the Vedic science recognises seven states of Consciousness, viz 1. the 'Jagrata-chetana' or waking state, 2.'Svapna-chetana' (the dream state), 3. Sushupti-chetana' (the deep sleep), 4.'Tturiya-chetana' (the superconscious), 5. the 'Turiyaateeta-chetana' or the 'Cosmic Consciousness' (Samaadhi,) or the Transcendental Consciousness state,6. the 'Godconscious' state (nirvikalpa samaadhi), and the state of 'Divya–chetana , or the state of 'Supreme Consciousness' (Total Consciousness, the 'Brahm'), i.e., the state of Universal Consciousness that is the cause, the sustaining power, and the power of dissolution of this universe. In fact GOD is the 'Almighty', 'Shakti'- the power, Supreme Consciousness behind the 'Trinity'- Brahma the Giver of Life, Vishnu, the Operator inside all Beings, and Rudra, the Destroyer, the 'Annihilator'.

In our waking state, the' jagrata' state, we are conscious of the sensate objective world. We think this material objective world is real but it disappears as soon as we get into sleep. In our dream state, 'svapna' state, when the physical body is at rest, the mind is still active and we observe movement of images. All our hopes and aspirations, anxiety, apprehensions, desires freely express themselves without inhibition as images and these images are inexplicable, incoherent, and confusing most of the time overlapping one another. All these images and impressions are projected from the subconscious mind. In deep sleep,'sushupti', the mind also goes to rest alongwith the body and the 'Prajnya', the reflector of the light of the Atma' takes over. In deep sleep, the mind and the consciousness (prajnya) are merged in the Prajnya and the Prana.Prana is prajnya and prajnya is Awareness, the awareness of 'Being', living! A spiritually awakened person can reach any of the higher levels of Consciousness, the Super-Conscious state, the Transcendental Consciousness state at will. In fact, a 'Jnyanin' or yogin never sleeps. He never distinguishes between day and night and all his time is spent in deep meditation,'samaadhi', the transcendental, or the superconscious state. He uses 'Praanayaama', breath control technique to reach this state since the mind and vital breath (prana) are inter-connected. By controlling breathing 'rhythm', Mind can be easily controlled, and vice versa. It is very difficult to reach the last two higher states of Consciousness, i.e., the Godconsciousness ('Daiva Prajnya') and the Universal Consciousness- the 'Brahm' or Divya Chetana. A person who attains to these stages is a liberated soul. He merges in the Brahm in his total abandonment of the awareness of his 'Self'.

One should be cautious in all these spiritual exercises. Unconsciousness of Mind should not be mistaken for super-Consciousness or transcendental state. A mind that is switched off is not working or aware. It is dark. That is all! In Transcendental state the consciousness is at its best- sharp and penetrating, revealing and enlightening. It is Bliss.

In contrast to the above seven levels of consciousness, the states of Conscious, the Unconscious, the Subconscious, and the Superconscious are the only four states of Consciousness taken cognizance of by psychologists and psychiatrists. There is also para-conscious state. Hence, this helps to understand the function of the mind only to a little extent. But the deeper aspects remain hidden. The Subconscious Mind is the source of all our problems and the psychiatrists try to reach it through hypnotism and other techniques. But, it is not possible to reach higher states of superconsciousness and transcendental states. As already stated, Patanjali Yoga Sutra has well-designed techniques of reaching the superconscious and the transcendental states and it brings great revelations! All the hidden secrets of the universe are revealed in the transcendental conscious state and one can transcend time and space. Reality of existence, the 'Sat' is perceived in this state. In other words, the real quality and nature of objects are revealed to the inner mind in deep transcendental meditation. It is a state of 'choiceless conscious awareness' and not the unconscious state. The unconscious mind cannot perceive anything. But, it requires long sustained practise to reach this state of superconsciousness. Raja Yoga, Kriya Yoga, and Hatha Yoga are very useful in this respect. There are a dozen Yoga Upanishads that describe the techniques of attaining superconscious states. One must be cautious in udertaking these exercises and learn properly from experts only, particularly those who do not want any monetary gains from teaching yoga. One must avoid all others who teach yoga for consideration, for yoga is a spiritual science that should not be taught to anybody and everybody for selfish gains. This is the secret.

4

Jnyaan [Knowledge]

"Nahin jnyaanena sadrisham"

Eversince Man appeared on this earth, he is bewildered and wondering 'what are all these' material objects? Are they real? The mystery deepens as one ponders over the 'goings on' and tries to make sense out of it! The five senses and the Mind (the sixth sense) fail to grasp the reality of things; they cannot see 'things as they are'. Not only the images of objects are projected on the mind screen but also images are super imposed like the snake on the rope. Further, the images are created by the Mind whether they exist in reality or not and this leads to confusion and complications. Unfortunately, even before one gets a clear view of things, his time is out and the pursuit continues in his next birth. Rather, this in-born inquisitive nature prompts him to investigate into the nature of things birth after birth, and finally he succeeds in getting a glimpse of it! This knowledge obtained from inquisitive nature may be logical, metaphysical, spiritual, or mystic experience gained through perseverance, contemplation, dhyan, meditation, and tapas culminating in 'nirvikalpa samadhi'. This spiritual knowledge pertaining to the 'Brahman' or the supreme 'Self' is the 'Higher Knowledge' or 'para vidya'. There is the lower knowledge called '*apara vidya*', the knowledge of the material objective world that leads to an understanding of the comstitution and function of this physical, chemical, and biological world. This material world and its knowledge is helpful to a certain extent to fulfil the curiosity; but in no way will it help to know the higher purpose of creation. The real purpose of knowledge is to know oneself!

Right Knowledge is a very essential requirement and, as humans, we are not fully equipped with the power of right understanding since our Mind is not pure and our senses are outgoing and wayward. We cannot see '*things as they are*', that is the problem. Our vision is blurred and mind clogged with prejudices, likes and dislikes. It is total delusion, here and a lot of purification is needed in order to 'know' the 'reality' of things.

Knowledge is of two types. One: The Higher Knowledge or the Para Vidya and, two, the Lower Knowledge or the Apara Vidya. The first one deals with the spiritual science and the second, with the material science. The material science is the knowledge of objects that are bound by time, space, and causality and hence, subject to change, degeneration and destruction. This is in contrast to the 'spirit' that is eternal, non-changing and indestructible. It deals with the Soul, the 'Atman' that is the eternal source of Knowledge, 'TOTAL KNOWLEDGE' ('SAMHITA' or the Veda).

The Upanishads declare that, "Jnyana (supreme Knowledge) is Brahman". It is spiritual illumination leading to the knowledge of the

Brahman, the Self. Ordinarily, knowledge of the mundane world such as science and technology is of no consequence here. It is the knowledge of the Self that is very important. The absence of this knowledge of Self is Avidya. It is the root cause of ego. "Egoism is the bondage of the Soul. The cessation of this egoism is Moksha, liberation. That which causes that egoism is 'Avidya', Nescience. That by which this egoism is completely turned back is Vidya, Knowledge" [*Sarvopanishad 1*]. In this sense, one may be a Nobel Laureate, but, still ignorant of the knowledge of the Self, the supreme knowledge.

Thus, "*Two are the vidyas, or sciences to be acquired by man*", so say the knowers of Brahman. The one is *para vidya*, a higher science or knowledge of the *BRAHMAN*, and the other is called the *apara vidya*, ordinary science or knowledge of the mundane or gross. The first one is subtle (spiritual) while the second one is sensate (of the senses). That is ' para vidya', or higher science by which that imperishable 'Reality' is realized. This is the source of supreme bliss or 'parama ananda', mahat ananda or 'Brahmananda'; in fact, it leads to 'moksha', liberation from metempsychosis i.e., cycle of re-birth, and gives supreme joy, eternal bliss even while we are here and now. 'Para Vidya' deals with the 'infinite' that cannot be tested by the finite- the mind and the senses. The scientists want to find this 'Infinite', the 'Brahman' with the help of the 'finite' and the limited- the mind and the senses; and, they fail here.

The Mind deals with the objects. All that comes under the purview of the mind and the senses are finite. Once this is clearly understood it becomes easy to understand the 'Sat', the real, and the 'Self'. Mind is thus conquered, for there is no scope for the play of the mind once you have attained that 'Sat', the eternal bliss. This is the purpose, or goal of life. Physical sciences, biological sciences, and all other material sciences deal only with the things that change, that are mundane, perishable, temporary, affected by time and space, often giving us a glimpse of truth, happiness always followed by misery.

Nescience, 'Avidya' is the term used in Vedanta for the ignorance that governs our lives. This has a larger meaning than the one that is associated with our general education and elementary knowledge about the mundane world. We all think we are knowledgeable persons; but actually, we are uneducated persons in the strict sense of the term. An illustration will clarify it further. A person who is really ignorant does not bother about things. Even if a piece of diamond is lying near his feet, he will have no knowledge and/or interest in it for he does not know the value of that piece of diamond. The same is also true of a 'jnyaani', a person who is aware of the nature of this world; he does not bother whether it is a piece of diamond or stone for both are same to him. There is another category of persons who turn upside down everything in order to get hold of, or possess a piece of sparkling thing, believing it to be diamond that finally turns out to be a mere piece of coloured glass. We all belong to this class of persons who are carried away by the glitter of the objects of the mundane world. It is this 'avidya' that governs our lives. This keeps us busy through out our lives and we achieve nothing out of it! This 'avidya' ultimately lands us in a cycle of birth and death, 'Sansar' and the whole life is miserable.

So, here is the clue to the essence of life and the ways and means to go about this '*samsara*' *(Cycle of birth and death)*, as also to avoid misery, disappointments, and unhappiness. 'Avidya' is the tamas and knowledge is 'light'. 'Bhagavad Gita' is an eternal source of knowledge and a compass to cross the ocean of life. Sri Krishna, who stands for '*pure consciousness*', presents himself as an '*avatara*' *(Reincarnation)* of the Lord Vishnu, the Protector. He provides the 'divya drishti', the 'Jnyana chakshus' to Arjuna and reveals His 'Viswa Roopa'. He shows the path to self- realization. Sri Krishna insists that 'one has to desist cowardliness and become a 'dhira' to face life as it comes since only a dhira can live successfully here. He first calms the perturbed mind of Arjuna and then discards all his illusions, moudhya (ignorance), raga, (attachment). He clears all confusion, doubts and complexities of the mind. He then preaches the importance of 'nishkama karma' (self-less action).

Any confused person, as almost all of us are, should imbibe the teachings of *Bhagavad Gita* to get over the complexities and attachments of our Mind.

The human mind operates at two levels: the one at the sensate level and the other, at spiritual level. At the sensate level, the mind looks to the sensory organs and gets the feed back to the experiences and memories of the sensate world, and craves for happiness, which is illusory and purely temporary, bound by space and time. The glimpse of the illusory happiness is presented as a source of eternal bliss and soon the person is disappointed when he realizes the stark reality of things. On the other hand, when the person operates at the spiritual level, his mind looks to his consciousness, which acts as a 'sakshi' (witness), and gets guidance as to the reality of things and thus avoids the pitfalls of sensate world. Thus, there is no disappointment to persons who look to 'buddhi' for guidance and functions with 'prajnya'. This simple truth is always evading common men, for the simple reason that they want to remain and enjoy at the sensate worldly level and it is sheer ignorance at that!

Katha Upanishad [**III**.3.9] illustrates the evolutionary advance of the human level employing a beautiful imagery:

"Know the 'Atman' as the master within the chariot, and the body, verily as the chariot; know the Buddhi, enlightened reason, as the charioteer, and the manas (incipient mind) verily as the reins. The sense organs are the horses, and the roads for them to travel are the 'sense objects'. The wise men recognise the 'Atman' as the 'enjoyer', or the experiencer, when the 'Self' is united with the body, the senses, and the mind. Otherwise, the foolish and the ignorant identify the body, mind, and the Prana with their own self, or 'ego'. They fail to recognize the Lord, Lord Vishnu ('Vish' meaning, the all- pervading flow of 'cosmic energy') residing in the cave of the heart, i.e., the 'Light within', the supreme-Consciousness.

The Upanishads, the Bhagavad Gita, the Shrutis, and the Puranas lay stress on the control of the Mind. Unless the Mind is under control, the boat of life sways hither and thither in a river of floods. The ship of life has to be steered clear in the ocean of sansar. He who is possessed of right understanding and with mind always disciplined, his senses are controlled like the controlled horses of a charioteer; he who is devoid of right understanding and with his Mind always wavering, his senses become uncontrolled as the uncontrolled horses of a charioteer. And, he who is devoid of right understanding, with mind not disciplined and always impure never attains the goal, but gets the repetitive experiences of worldliness. But he who is possessed of right understanding, with mind disciplined and ever pure reaches the goal whence there is no return to worldliness again.

"That person who has vijnyana, enlightened reason, for his charioteer and a disciplined Mind (manas) as the reins, he verily attains the farthest end of the journey in that supreme divine state of Vishnu, the Universal One, 'the All-Pervading One'."

This imagery tells us that man has an inner journey to perform, in the context of his outer journey in the world of space and time. The world of sight and sound, of touch, taste, and smell (the sensate world), is the environment for both the outer journey and the inner journey. The inner journey is a spiritual journey of inward penetration, by training and refining the psycho- physical energies and raising mind and consciousness to higher and higher levels. As the chariot gets its energy of movement from the horses, the body gets its energy of movement from the sense organs, consisting of the nervous system and the brain. The organs of perception and the organs of action, i.e., the Jnyanendriyas and Karmendriyas, respectively, convert the animal body into a center of the most dynamic activity in nature but at the level of the senses themselves. This activity is mostly un-coordinated and, therefore, not fit for purposes beyond mere organic satisfactions and survival. It is this coordination that is provided by Mind (manas), or incipient mentality or 'mind-indecisive'. It is even treated merely as a sixth sense organ.

As in the case of the horses, the reins meant to control them, involve a charioteer to hold the reins. In the human system, this is the function of ***'Buddhi'***, the Intellect or enlightened reason. And behind the 'buddhi' is the master, or the Charioteer, whose is the journey while the rest form only equipment of his journey. Mere external journey in the world of space and time is what is termed as 'samsara' or worldliness- that means stagnation at organic level. This is considered as spiritual death of man by the Upanishads – more serious than physical death of this highly evolved creature 'the man'.

For a successful life, the most important thing is to ensure that the initiative and control pass from the body, the senses, and the 'manas' to 'buddhi'. This cannot happen unless the buddhi and the manas are trained and disciplined and refined into their true forms.

The true form of the mind is its pure state when it is aligned with buddhi. It ceases to be a mere appendage of the sense organs (as the reins becoming a mere appendage of a horse); then only it can stand the stress and strain involved in its unique situation, namely, between the two powerful and initially opposite forces of the sense organs and the buddhi. All psychic break -down is the snapping of the mind.

The true form of 'Buddhi', Intellect is its pure state as 'enlightened reasoning', when it is independent of the mind and the sense organs and functions as their guide and master. This is the source of far-sight and foresight. It then reflects the pure Light of Consciousness of the Atman behind.

'Buddhi', the Intellect becomes pure and strong, luminous and calm, steady and sure when it is free from the inebriation of wealth, power, knowledge, and pedigree, sensory pulls, wine and drugs. Such a pure buddhi is the best guide in life's journey. It denotes the fusion of intelligence, imagination and Will in their purest forms. Its impact on life is irresistible as well as wholesome.

'Atman' is realized by the 'buddhi; but it is unattainable by the sense organs, or the 'sense-bound' mind. In Katha Upanishad (2.23), Yama tells Nachiketas that, *'Atman cannot be attained by the study of the scriptures, nor by a sharp intellect, nor by much hearing; by Him is it attained whom it chooses- to Him this Atman reveals its own (true) form'.*

These methods operate within the cause-effect relationship, again, the world of duality and relativity. But the Atman is beyond causality. It is not an object among objects. It is not an item among the 'not-self' items of the world. It is not an observed sense datum among the observed sense data of the world to be discovered by carefully worked-out means. It is, on the contrary, the very Self of the observer, of the seeker. As pure consciousness, infinite and non-dual, it is not an end product of the causal determination of means and ends; '*the unconditioned cannot be had through the conditioned*'. [*Mundaka Upanishad* 1.2.12].

Shri Shankaracharya emphasizes the primacy of 'Divine Grace' as the Self-revelation of the Atman as explained to Nachiketas by Yama in Kenopanishad:

'Whom alone, (i.e., one's own Self), this seeker seeks, longs for, by that self alone (i.e., by that seeker), one's own Self is attained, is realized'.

Here, the 'choosing' is done by the seeker by means of an earnest longing and struggle. *This seeking and struggle on the part of man is essential according to every spiritual teaching.* But it is only to draw the Light of the Atman, through a self-revelation. If meditation and other spiritual practices become the cause of the realization of the Atman, then the Atman is reduced to being an effect (i.e., relative and finite) and thus becomes non-eternal. Just like any torch or battery cannot shed light on the Sun, the self-illuminating 'Atman' cannot be realized by any amount of meditation or spiritual practices. It is the Atman that overpowers the puny light of the mind and illumines it through and through.

To repeat what Yama tells Nachiketas, '*whom alone It chooses, by him alone is It attained, to him this Atman reveals its own (true) form*'. It is true that initially the seeker seeks the Atman; but finally, it is the 'Atman' that chooses the seeker, that chooses to reveal Its' own Self to the seeker through an act of 'self-revelation'. It is as good as 'Divine Grace' conferred on the longing seeker.

We have the two planes in which the human mind works. First, it is the conscious level. In this plane of consciousness, any work is always accompanied by a feeling of egoism. Next comes the unconscious plane where all work is unaccompanied by the feeling of 'egoism'. There is a still higher plane in which mind can work. It can go beyond consciousness. Just as unconscious is beneath consciousness, so there is that reality is thus another plane at which mind works which is above consciousness and which is also not accompanied by egoism. This is the 'super-conscious' level.

The field of reason, or of the conscious working of the mind is narrow and limited. The human reasoning moves within a little circle and it is impossible to go beyond this limit. But, it is beyond this circle of reason that there lies all that is dearest to human heart.

To get any reason out of this human life 'one has to transcend reason in a slow but regular scientific methodical way'. The same mind develops into these planes and reveals the light. 'Instincts develop into reason; reason into transcendental consciousness'. 'Real inspiration fulfills reason' according to Swami Vivekananda.

Two important questions take uppermost position in this exercise of spiritual understanding. First, Who am I? Second, What is it I want? Honest and sincere answers to these two questions will solve all the riddles of life. It is not that we do not know the answers to these two questions. It is our ego that comes in the way of acceptance of the reality that brings the problem. First of all, Sri Shankara quoted from the upanishads and implored that "*Tat Tvam asi*", i.e.,"*Thou art That*". People mistook this simple statement and this led to intellectual arguments for several centuries, particularly between the 'Dvaitins' and the "Advaitins'. Some people misunderstood this statement and started behaving as God without acquiring the requisite divine qualities.

The Eternal, the Brahman, is the Mind of the mind, the Life of the life, the Ear of the ear, the Eye of the eye, and the Tongue of the tongue. He shines by His own brightness. His light illuminates all these. It is the One Light that casts no shadow. This is the Truth and one has to contemplate on this. Meditate on this 'mahat tattva'. Think and repeat "I am not body, I am not mind, I am unattached, non-doer, non-enjoyer, the'*Sakshin*' or Witness". This will, at once, elevate the mind to magnanimous heights.

Here, it is very important to understand the great Vedantic concept of *'Sakshin'*, witness or the 'ultimate observer'. This concept is absent in the Western thought; but the psychologists are using this method without being aware of this! Indian Philosophy discovered the concept of 'Sakshi', the ultimate Observer, or Witness behind the sense of individuality or, the 'ego'. The 'Sakshi' is that timeless Being which witnesses all this ceaseless flow and change in the world of thought and things. 'Sakshi-bhava' is the limited and circumscribed vision of the ego that gives the unlimited and universal vision of the Sakshi by the practice of scientific or intellectual detachment. In a way it is also the method of achieving ego-elimination. Detachment and universality are the two important characteristics of 'Sakshi'; it is the state of perfection of the Self, achieved by the process of de-personalisation. But, it is very difficult to comprehend this Sakshi-bhava since it is the ultimate Observer or the ultimate Subject. Sri Krishna syas,

"Some look upon the 'Self' as marvellous; others speak about it as wonderful; others again hear of it as a wonder. And still others, though hearing, do not understand it at all" [*Bhagavad Gita* II. 29].

When one attains the 'Sakshi-Consciousness', he gets a new perspective of his life. All the ego and false values get destroyed and the true Self is revealed. Thus, man gets rid of sorrow and miseries, struggles and joys, hatredness and competition and realizes a life of harmony; he is at peace with himself and ever calm and undisturbed. Nothing perturbs him; neither joy nor sorrow disturbs his calm disposition, and in a way, he becomes a 'Sthithaprajnya'. He is full of love, piety and compassion. He is an integrated personality, a Yogi.

William Shakespeare said, 'The whole world is a stage and we are all the actors and spectators, too'. It is this spectator-bhava, the 'sakshi-bhava' (the witnessing self) that is very important. We have to separate the spectator "I" from the actor "I". It is the realization of 'who am I' that is very important. "He who is the cogniser of the manifestation (name and form) and disappearance (merging into the unmanifested state) of the knower, knowledge, and the knowable, but is himself devoid of such manifestation and disappearance, and is self-luminous, is called 'Sakshi', the Witness. When being perceived in an undifferentiated (Pure-Consciousness) manner in the intelligence of all beings, from Brahma (the Creator) down to an ant, it resides in the intelligence of all beings, then, it is called '*Kutastha*'.

When, standing as the means of realizing the real nature of the Kutastha and others, which are differentiations by virtue of possessing limiting adjuncts, the Atman manifests itself as inter-woven in all bodies, like the thread through a string of jewels, then, it is called "*Antaryamin*", Internal Ruler. When the Atman shines forth- absolutely free from all limiting adjuncts, brilliant, as a homogeneous mass of consciousness in its nature of pure intelligence, independent- then, it is spoken of as the entity of "*Thou" (Tvam), and as the Pratyagatman, Inner Self. That which is, Satya (the Realty), Jnyana (Knowledge), Ananta (the Infinite), Ananda (Bliss), is Brahman. The Reality is the Indestructible; that which, when name, space, time, substance, and causation are destroyed dies not (remains change-less), is the indestructible; and that is called 'Sat', the Reality. And Jnyana – that essence of intelligence that has no beginning and no end, is spoken of as 'Jnyana'. [Sarvopanishad 3].*

'*Ananta*' is 'Bhuman', the Infinitude; 'It' is that which always remains in the same manner. It is the antecedent. It is all-pervading consciousness that is in all phenomena of creation beginning with the Unmanifested.

'*Ananda*' is Bliss. It is permanent in all space and time, substance and causation; it is called the Entity of That ('Tat') Paramatman, Supreme Self, Para-Brahman or the Highest Brahman.'Hari Om! Tat Sat'. 'That' is the 'Truth'.

Knowledge of the Self

Before going into the depth of the understanding of the Self, one must be very clear as to the meaning or connotation of the word 'Self'. One should always remember that the individual Self is the 'Jeevatman' and it is referred to the physical body of the person, and not the Soul, due to ignorance. When enlightenment or knowledge dawns, this Soul, or the 'Atman' becomes the 'Real Self' that is not very different from the Universal or Supreme Self, 'the Brahman', i.e.,' the Paramatman'.

Generally, all living beings are referred to as 'Jeevas'. 'Purusha' is the Self, the *Soul*'. Purusha is the spirit, and Prakriti is the uncaused cause, the ultimate source of all material things including the mind and the senses. There are as many Purushas as many living beings. Purusha corresponds to the Jiva, the individual self of the Vedanta. Sankhya philosophy, the oldest system of Hindu philosophy, holds 'Purusha' and 'Prakriti' as two fundamental categories. Vedanta has the concept of cosmic ignorance, or 'maaya', which roughly corresponds with 'Prakriti' of Sankhya philosophy. In Bhagavatam there is a prayer to the Lord:

"Receiving energy from Thee, the Purusha, of infallible power, alongwith Maya, holds within himself the 'mahat', like the embryonic state of this universe. This mahat backed by the same Maya, projected from within itself the golden sphere of the universe of various layers" [*Bhagavatam*, 13.28]. Also, *Vishnu Purana* says that, "*Purusha eva idam Sarvam*" as derived from Purusha Sukta of Rk Veda. It also means, that ***Man is the centre of the universe and around him revolves all the other things***. The products of a steller explosion, as we are, the Big Bang, or 'sphota' (explosion) that gave birth to Man and his Universe; a spark has entered the Jiva to make it a Prani (animal) and the sparks shines through as a 'sookshma sharira' (subtle body) in the sthoola sharira, the physical body. It is this spark, the 'atma jyoti', which makes man an intellectual animal capable of discrimination. The 'Light within' us is the eternal light, the Brahman.

Purushas are of two kinds, the perishable and the imperishable. All beings constitute the perishable, *Kutastha*, i.e., Maya (but, according to Shri Shankaracharya, it is imperishable). Maya is the imperishable primordial nescience. It is born with the Self. There is another, the Highest Self, the Immutable Lord, who is all-pervading and the sustainer of the three worlds. He is the 'Purushottama', or Sri Hari Narayana. It is only He who is beyond this Maya. Shree Hari Narayana plays a preponderant role in Jeeva's journey. Here, 'Narayana' means the journey of man, ('Nr' is man;'yaana' is journey of cycle of births and deaths). Lord Almighty takes care of all those who trust Him in their journey of life. One must have full faith in Him', so says Sri Krishna in Bhagavad Gita.

The inherent qualities, Gunas of man also have their origin with this 'Maya', or nescience. These qualities have their origin in the vibrations that is the causal force. These vibrations are of different wavelengths and colours and get associated with the functioning of the subtler heart, the '*Anthahkarana*' and play havoc with the life of man. Transcending these three Gunas is the only solution or path of salvation. "Nistraigunyo bhava

Arjuna" Says Shri Krishna.

Three qualities or 'gunas' are inherent in all Jeevas since it is the vibrations of these Gunas that constitute the manifest forms of the Brahman. These Gunas are: the Tamas, the Rajas, and the Sattva. It is the vibration of the Gunas that cause the creation. The three Gunas are the qualities inherent in the Creator Brahma (not to be mistaken with the "Niraakara Nirmama Nirguna Brahman"), and hence, it is inherent in all his creations, the creatures. These three Gunas are in a state of equanimity or balance at the time of Evolution. As the Lord Wills, the vibrations cause the creations and one of the Gunas predominates. The permutation and combination of the Gunas give myriads of qualities to objects; the proportion of the Gunas in Jeevas vary according to their past actions. When the Gunas are transcended by Meditation, the curtain of Maya or 'avidya' is removed and the jeeva will attain the Knowledge of the Brahman. Hence, the spiritual aspirant is advised to transcend the three Gunas and their manifestations by discipline of discrimination. Patanjali has clearly explained in the aphorism (Sutra) on 'Thought waves' that, discipline is the ability gained by practice to control the projections of the forces of these gunas thought forces are the projections of the gunas' forces. An enlightened Seer does not hate the qualities of these gunas such as the light of Sattva, or the activity of Rajas, or the delusion of Tamas. He sits unconcerned, unperturbed, undisturbed by the gunas. He knows that these gunas are the forces of creation, doers of action, and hence, he never loses his power of discrimination. He will never allow these forces to overtake his determination and dictate; he overpowers them and subdues them by mind control, 'Yoga'. He rests in the inner calm of the Atman taking both joy and sorrow as equal ("*sukha dukha samekrutva....*" Bhagavad Gita).

It is important to note that all the three gunas are required in the process of creation. All that is pure, ideal, tranquil is sattva; action, motion and violence is rajas; and, the principle of solidity, immobile, resistence and inertia are Tamas. 'Rajas' stands for repulsion, the 'Tamas' stands for attraction, and, the 'Sattva' Guna stands for balance between the two. Sattva is identified with illumination, Rajas with activity, and Tamas with darkness, inertia, ignorance, laziness and obstruction. All these three forces are involved in the process of creation. Sattva is predominant in sunlight, rajas in volcano and tamas in rocks. In the mind of man, the instability of these forces of the gunas cause different moods. Sattva causes moments of inspiration, quiet joy, disinterested affection, and meditatative calm; Rajas brings outburst of rage, fierce desire, restlessness and discontent; and, it also creates condition for better phases of constructive activity, enthusiasm and physical courage. Tamas is mental bog, laziness, lousiness, lethargy and stupidity whenever sattva and rajas cease to prevail. Bhagavad Gita gives an elaborate description of the Gunas. It is very important to remember how powerful and how vast is the mastery and control of the three gunas on the Jeevas. But, it is also true that, but for the operation of all the three gunas, no constructive, creative activity of man would be possible. Transcending all these three gunas alone, one can attain 'Kaivalya', or mukti, i.e., liberation. Beautiful example of a sculptor converting a piece of solid granite into a statue is possible by the operation of the three gunas in combination. The solid stone is the tamas, the rajas motivates the creation of the 'sattva' in the statue. At first, tamas in man also makes him indifferent, lothesome and the rajas offers a challenge and motivation and ultimately sattva prevails and the creative power becomes explicit in the statue.

Sri Krishna declares that, '*there is not a single class of Jeevas on earth, and even in heaven among the Gods, that is left unassailed by these three gunas born of Prakriti*' [*Bhagavad Gita* XVIII.40]. They represent the transition, because these exist in the primordial Prakriti in subtle forms as such before their evolution. In fact, these are derived from their own subtle forms without interposition of other intermediate forms. They are unlike other created things, which also exist in Prakriti latently.

Interaction of the gunas provides the motive power for the creation. These gunas are the creative forces and act in stages. The first stage of evolution from 'undifferentiated Prakruti is called "Mahat", the Great Cause. Mahat is the cosmic ego sense- the first drawing of differentiated Consciousness from the Absolute, i.e., from "Undifferentiated Supreme consciousness". From Mahat has evolved the 'Buddhi', or Intellect i.e., the discriminative faculty. Hence, one should reach this stage of discrimination to attain Knowledge. Only Man has got this power of discrimination. From Buddhi is evolved 'Ahamkara', the ego-sense, the 'I' – ness. From this ego-sense the lines of evolution branches off in three different directions to produce– (1) Manas, (2) Indriyas (Jnayanendriyas and the Karmendriyas), and (3) the 'Tanmatras'- the subtle (sookshma) and the gross (sthoola) - Elements and Compounds, the Panchabhutas of which the external universe is composed. This is the evolution outward from undifferentiated Consciousness into differentiated Consciousness, from Mind to matter.

The work of creation proceeds from the preponderance of Rajas, i.e., activity. The work of dissolution takes place when Tamas preponderates. And, the work of preservation and sustenance proceeds when there is the predominance of Sattva, which maintains equilibrium. In the main, the tendency of Sattva is to illumine the path and enables him (jeeva) to compass his own salvation. The tendency of Rajas is to make involved and rolling about in samsara, give him petty joys and grief, and tantalizes him midway between heaven and hell. The tendency of the 'Tamas' is to pull him and dig his grave for him in hell. All our will, knowledge, and emotions are governed by these three gunas. When the sattva prevails, it goads him towards the realization of the self, and impels him towards knowledge. A number of Gayatris are directed towards an appeal to the Deities to grant this impelling force and move from ignorance to Knowledge, The terms 'vidmahe' is to impel to propel and 'dheemahi' to enable to 'know' and 'prachodayat' to impel towards total understanding.

Here is a saying that, "The whole world knows him; alas! He himself knows not, who he is". It refers to the Ignorance as opposite to Knowledge about the Self.

Knowledge of the Self is very important. It does not occur to us to know this important thing throughout our active mundane lives. We always identify ourselves with our family and the family name, the caste and creed, the sex, the name and function or avocation. It never occurs to us that we are a part of the divine, the spirit that is the soul, or the 'self'. We always identify ourselves with the body and, we are carried away by our mind and moods, attitudes, and belief and we are all ignorant, at that!

As already stated, man is both matter and spirit; man is matter as far as his body and mind are concerned and he is the spirit, the divine spirit at that, when it concerns his Soul. Body is gross matter and it is made of the five elements earth, water, fire, air, and ether. But, all these are derived from a single source, the one single Absolute. Sciene clearly explains what is energy and what is matter, as also, when energy becomes matter and matter becomes energy. Our Mind is sheer energy in its pure form and it becomes gross matter with all its impurities of desire, memories, impressions and thoughts. All our problems lie here, in understanding this mind.

We must take some time off from our busy life and think for a while, *'Who am I'? And, 'What is it I am doing?' And, What is it I want? Where do I come from and where do I go after death? Are all these material objects I adore so much are real? The wife, the children, the kith and Kin- are they all real? Who are these and are they really mine? If I am the husband/wife, father/mother, son/daughter, brother/sister, friend/foe, this and that, through out my life, what am I, really? What is my existence?*

Who am I?

Am 'I' this physical body? Am 'I' the Mind? Am 'I' the Prana? Am I the Intellect? Am I the Creator? Am I the Controller? Am I the Doer? Am I the Enjoyer?

One must ask these questions in order to understand the 'Self'.

An Anthropologist defines man as an animal belonging to the class of hominids, species- Homo Sapiens sapiens. The word 'Man' is defined in different terms by different specialists. For a doctor, man is a living being. For a sociologist, man is a 'social animal'. For a Psychologist, man is bundle of mental complexes. Man is a thinking animal; since he has got 'mind', he thinks. Mind, or the 'manas' makes a 'Man', or the 'Manav'. A Jnyani will reject all these, the body, and the mind, as he realizes his 'Self' and this Self in all.

For all scientists, man is still a mystery. Let us see what is 'Prana' that makes man a' prani' or' living animal'. Man has got all the instincts of the animals; it is the buddhi, discriminating power that makes him different from other animals. Without spiritual knowledge, the prepondering gunas- tamas and rajas make him more vulnerable like any other animals.

Prana:

In the ordinary sense of the term, the word 'Prana' means the vital breath, the life force, i.e., the 'vital force". But, it really means something more than that! It is applied to the transcendental principle, the subtle cause, as well as to its effects, the force moving to activity the organs, physical and mental. 'Prana' is identified with the 'Atman'. According to

Chhandogya Upanishad, ***'Prana' is established in the heart.'*** *[Chhandogya Upanishad, III. 13]*

All the living beings of this world are living because of the life-sustaining force, the 'Prana'; hence we are all 'pranis' (animals) first, and then we become human beings, if at all we acquire the noble qualities of affection, kindness, love, selfless service, sacrifice, piety, compassion, equanimity, sympathy for the fellow beings, discretion, control over our senses, etc. We can attain 'divinity', if at all we develop our spiritual qualities inherent in us, in our soul. 'Prana', of course, gives energy to sustain the body whatever be the size, may be of microscopic size, or of the size of a whale or elephant. It is this one common factor 'Prana' that governs all life of living beings or animals on this planet.

The gross body of man is composed of the same components of 'matter' that constitute the terrestrial world. We all derive our food from the earth and the quality of the earth is also transferred from the food we eat, may be of plant-source, or animal-source. Since each plant or animal is bestowed with certain qualities and svabhava according to its preponderant gunas, man acquires these preponderant gunas by eating the food from these sources. Eating meat of animal, one may acquire qualities of aggression and cruelty. Similarly, plants have specific svabhava like bitterness in a neem or a bitter gourd plant, or for that matter, chillies, tamarind, mango or apple, each having its own quality. Man acquires the preponderant 'tamo guna' of the earth and the preponderant gunas of the products of the earth. All the qualities such as anger, jealousy, hatred, likes and dislikes, covetousness, selfishness, laziness, ego, pride, etc. are all acquired from the gross. We all think that we are merely the body sustained by prana. We do not question even for a moment that there is somebody who is the provider of the body and the 'prana' and 'chaitanya' in the body. This identification of the 'I' with the body is the main problem with man.

The real significance of the word 'I' has to be clearly understood. This perishable physical body, mind, prana, and senses are not the 'I'. They are the influence of 'Gunas' or qualities, nature. These have a beginning and an end. These are insentient and inert. When we speak of 'I', we merely speak of this body without understanding that it is only a cover of something more permanent, non-perishable and more attached to the 'Infinite'. In fact, this "I" stands for that cosmic force, the all-pervading cosmic flow, 'That', "Sri Hari Narayana (Vishnu)" who is a noun for which the pronoun "I" is used without being aware of this "Sat'.

The 'ego' or the 'I'-sense is the 'Ahamkara that comes with the birth. Even a child asserts and wants things exclusively for itself; it says, 'this toy is mine and I will not give you'. Where does the 'ego' come from? Ego is the Self. Ego is Rudra. Ego is 'Sat' (existence) and its assertion. As the child grows, the ego builds up into mountainous dimension until the person becomes totally self-conscious oblivious to the existence of others! Oh! It is such a adamantine wall that no one can break it. Everybody has to submit to this 'ego' and the trouble starts. Everyone wants to assert that he only is right and all others are wrong. It makes no sense to argue with such persons with bloated ego. It is sheer ignorance that reigns supreme in such egoistic persons. Vedanta upholds such a build-up of ego in early stages of growth since it gives the person a sense of self-confidence and courage to assert his existence without which it is difficult to survive. But, Vedanta also warns that excessive ego is dangerous for it destroys the person. According to Vedanta, a person should build-up his 'ego; only to surrender at the feet of the Lord with all humility. A person should be rich, powerful, famous, and serve humanity with all humanity as service to God. This is the purpose of life. Total submission or surrender to the Lord will erase the 'ego' (Ignorance) and bring enlightenment. Total abnegation of the Self is what is merging of the Self in the Lord. For such enlightened persons, the words 'me', 'my', 'mine' and the expression 'I' ceases to exist and only the term 'we' exists; such enlightened persons become 'one' with the universe and include everybody and everything in that term 'we'. For such enlightened persons, the world is one and there is no duality, 'the other'.

Persons who always use 'I' in their day-to-day life are ignorant and foolish. They do not know the meaning of the term 'I' they are repeatedly using. They identify their body ('Asat') and Mind (Avidya) with everything and they are deluded by ignorance. For instance, when a person tells you that he had had a nice sleep, ask him 'who is that' that enjoyed the sound sleep'? Ask him, while he was sleeping like a log of wood, whether he was 'aware' of the 'sleep' (nidra)? Is that the body, or the mind, that enjoyed the sound sleep (Sushupti)? If he was not aware of the world when he was sleeping, 'who is that was aware of the sleep' and says that 'he enjoyed the sleep' when he woke up. Ask him, 'who is that enjoyer'? Who had taken over the control of the functions of the body when he was in deep slumber? Where had all the senses gone while asleep? Was he consciously aware of the function of the body and mind? Contemplate on these facts.

Another very interesting thing is about dreams. We all get dreams, sometimes wake up frightened and remember the dream in every minute detail. Who is that who was constantly witnessing the sequence of events in dream? Is it the Atma roving about freely, or the mind exercising itself in uncontrolled manner? Psychologists tend to dismiss dreams as memories, hopes, aspirations, ambitions, fear, frustrations, and disappointments coming alive in sleep; some have premonitions and many find solutions to difficult problems in dreams. Even the Upanishads state that dreams are a way of protecting the jeeva. For instance, if a person has not eaten food, he will get the dream in which he is partaking food. If a person has not offered food to the departed souls, there is a dream to remind him of that. If a person has forgotten to attend to nature call, he will have a dream attending nature call (but not actually doing so in bed). It is a way of protecting the jeeva giving him premonitions. Or, may be it is upwelling of images from the subconscious mind that cause dreams. Whatever it might be, we should know who is that witnessing the 'goings on' in the so-called dreams?

Similarly, when you enjoy a melodious song, a piece of painting, tasty food, ask yourself 'who is that enjoyer' who enjoys these? Is it the ear that enjoyed the melody? Is it the eyes that enjoyed the painting? Is it the tongue that enjoyed the taste? These ears, eyes, tongue are the sense organs, merely tools to enjoy and the real enjoyer is somebody else subtler sitting inside the body.

There is another interesting fact that drives this "I" factor home. When we hear somebody saying that he is breathing, the doubt arises whether he is really *the person* breathing. If he *could* breath on his own of free will, he can go on breathing without end and, thus, he never dies! It is not that he is breathing; breathing is a happening that can come to end anytime! He is not aware of that, and his ego does not allow him to see the truth.

In *Aitareya Upanishad*, there is the account of Atman asking the other organs, who am I? [Verse 2-4-6] There are the three seats, viz, the Manas, senses, and the heart and there are the three states viz, the jagrat, swapna, and suṣhupti, and the Atman is present in all these three states and seats. When Brahman created the 'being', it was not active inspite of all the organs; so, he decided to enter into it through the seam in the top of the skull, 'vidriti'. When he thus entered the being, the jeeva started functioning. It is the same Brahman who is the 'jeevaatman' in the being. It is also stated that the Atman created the food and that became elusive; it tried to seize it by sense organs, mind, and breath and finally it could seize by Apana Vayu, the digestive vital breath. There is only Brahman and the other equivalent to it is the Atman, rather, Atman is Brahman. It is the 'I' in all beings. 'I' is the pronoun that stands for the proper noun Atman, the Brahman in all beings.

Bhagavan Shri Ramana Maharishi says, "*Our experience of the world is evoked and dissolved by the mind*". For instance, when we move in a vehicle, our body does not move. It is the vehicle that moves carrying us. Just as the movements are superimposed on our body, so also visions, dream states and even incarnations are superimposed on our real self. The latter (Self) does not move and is not affected by all these outward changes, remaining still in its own place even as the body remains still in the ship's cabin."*You are always the same and, hence, beyond time and beyond space*". In deep sleep you have no sense of time. The concept of time and space arise only when there is limitation of 'I'. Even now the 'I'-thought is both limitless and limited. So long as you think it to be the body, it is limited. At the time of waking up and before one actually becomes fully aware of the external world, that interval, timeless, spaceless, is the state of true 'I'. There is no limitation in sleep and the question arises; when you identify with the body, all questions arise. One may be surprised to know that 'sushupti' (Deep sleep) is always present in the waking state. What we have to do is to bring sleep into the waking state to get 'conscious sleep'. Realization can only take place in the waking state. One cannot realize in deep sleep since there is no awareness. Awareness comes in 'sushupti state of consciousness' means one should be consciously aware in the state of sushupti (of nature of deep sleep) consciousness. Deep sleep is relative to the waking state. This is the reason why the Yogins take to 'Yoga Nidra', i.e., always consciously aware. Yogins scarcely sleep and can sleep eyes wide open! It is only the ignorant who sleeps like a log of wood and is not aware of the 'goings on', or happenings, in the inner world.

All differences arise due to the outlook. Because you imagine that you are the seer, separate from the experience, the difference arises. Is there any difference between the external and the internal in sleep? The difference is only with reference to the body and arises with body Consciousness, the 'I'-thought. The so-called waking state is itself an illusion. Turn your vision inward then the whole waking state will be seen as Maya. *Maya is real Sattva. Consciousness alone exists*."

Now, one can realise the real significance of 'I' when we use the words 'I enjoy', 'I eat', or 'I sleep'? To repeat, 'I' is the Eternal Subject 'Brahman' whose nature is 'Sat', 'Chit', and 'Ananda'. This perishable physical body, mind, or prana, and the senses are not the 'I'. They are the effect of Gunas. They have an origin and an end. They are inert and insentient. The real 'I' is the Atman whose nature is "*Sat-Chit- Ananda*". Through ignorance, it is shifted to the physical body and other illusory appendages. This is the cause of transmigrations and miseries of samsara. With the identification of the big 'I' comes the 'Self-Realization'.

The personal 'I' is a reflection of the real Self in the mind. The body and its function are not 'I'. The senses and their functions are not 'I', either. Going deepe, the mind and its functions are not I. From where do these thoughts arise? Thoughts are spontaneous, superficial or analytical. Who is aware of them? Their existence and operations become evident to the individual. Analysis leads to the conclusion that the individuality operates as awareness of the existence of thoughts. This is ego. Who is this I and where does it come from? Sleep analysis will reveal the truth; 'I am' – *So'ham*' underlies the three states- waking, dream and sleep. After discarding all that is not-Self, we find the residue- Self Absolute. Both world and ego are objective and must be eliminated in the analysis. Eliminating the unreal, the Real survives. To accomplish this, eliminate the mind, which is the creator of dualistic idea and of ego. Mind is one form of life-manifestation.

The individual cannot exist without the Self, but the Self can exist without the individual. "I AM" ("*So 'ham*") is the ocean and the individual 'egos' are the bubbles in it. Bubbles pass away while the ocean remains. The Self is there whether you search for it or not. The cessation of false identification reveals the Self that is eternal. This is called *realisation*. The mind must be earsed out of existence (Manonasha). See who the thinker is and who the seeker is. Then abide by the dictates of buddhi, as the thinker, the seeker, and all thoughts will then disappear. That ego is pure ego purged of thoughts. It is the same as the 'Self'. It ('I') is the Star *- when 'I' is crossed out (by mark X), i.e., I is negated; in other words, when ego is dropped 'I' become a * - 'Star', the self- luminescent, the self-effulgent, and the self-existent one. Meditation is the only approach that will drive away other thoughts including the 'ego', 'I'-ness. The one thought of God will dominate others. That is concentration (Dharana). By concentrating on God, the Ishta devata, or meditating on the Self one can realize the Self.

In *Chhandogya Upanishad*, the nature of the body and soul is made clear. Indra told Prajapati, Brahma that, "*there is nothing joyous in the state of deep sleep since one does not know oneself or others; he goes into destruction.*"

To this, Prajapati said, "*O Maghavan, this body, indeed, is destructible; possessed by death, it is the dwelling place for that destructible, incorporeal self; the embodied soul is possessed by joy and sorrow; because, as long as he (the Self) is embodied, no averting of joy or sorrow is possible. Joy and sorrow do not, however, touch or afflict the incorporeal self. The wind, the clouds, the lightning, the thunder are incorporeal. These emerge from the world- space and enter into the highest light and there through emerge forth in their true form. So also this perfect serenity arises forth out of the body, enters into the highest light and rises forth in his true form. He is the highest spirit and never remembers this appendage of the body. He who has found this Self and known Him, attains all the worlds and all the wishes." [Chhandogya Upanishad VIII. 9-11]*

"That (spirit), who joyously roves in dream is the Atman. He is the indestructible one, the fearless one; it is Brahman."

"When one is in deep sound sleep and attained full serenity, so that he experiences no dreams, he is the Self," prajapati told Maghavan. "He is the indestructible one, the fearless one; He is the Brahman".

According to Sankhya philosophy, it is the 'Purusha', the 'Atman' or the Soul that is the perceiver of an object. The sense transmits the sense-vibrations to the mind, and the mind in its turn presents the vibrations to the Buddhi or intellect (the discriminative faculty) that is close to the Soul. Now, reaction comes in. With the reaction of the Buddhi manifests egotism side by side. Then the whole thing is presented to the 'Purusha' who really perceives all objects.

"Body is not Brahman. Mind is not Brahman. Prana is not Brahman. Intellect is not Brahman. The balance left is Brahman". This is the 'neti, neti' doctrine. 'Neti, neti' means 'not this, not this'.

The mind always clings to some support for it cannot exist without support. Normally, the memories, past experiences or objects of imagination form the support. If nothing is available for support, it has the capacity to create some imaginary things and dwell in it. The mind has the tools in the sense organs to fulfill its desires or achieve the objects of its desire or dreams. The mind asks the sense organs to go out and look for the sensuous things for it wants to match the experiences with its memories. Hence, the mind is not the 'I' that enjoys; it is only a sixth sense organ that coordinates the functions of the senses. The word 'I' is a pronoun that stands for a Noun; that noun, the proper noun- the name of the Supreme Purusha (person), '*Lord the Almighty*' is "*Vishnu*" or " *Sri Hari Narayana*", *the all-pervading Spirit, the Sustainer of all* bodies, the inner self, the Infinite that sits in all souls and enjoys all the bounties of this earth, 'Shree'.

There are a number of meanings to a word and atleast six of these are important. Some words gives dual meaning, both positive and negative and the meaning should be selected carefully depending on the context. The name of the Lord has almost hundred meanings. The word '*Hari*' means **'the cosmic flow'**, and '*Narayana*' means the *One who resided in 'nara'*, (nara is water here), i.e., water for sometime in the early formative stages of the earth. Nara also means Man. Call by whatever name you wish the eternal spirit, that is the real 'Self', referred to as 'I'. That is what the Upanishads meant by "*Tat Tvam asi*". Know this and contemplate on this 'Mahat Tattva', or the 'Great Principle'; you have crossed the ocean of life. It is so simple as that! We, the ignorant people, cannot understand this. We get into trouble by identifying ourselves with this gross physical body and the mind as 'I'. We identify ourselves with the perishable, the decaying, and the finite matter bound by time and space, and get into all sorts of problems or troubles. Not only we curse the God for our ignorance and mistakes but also we make Him responsible for all our ills. How often we curse God for our misdeeds and 'prarabhdha karma'!

A Jnyani will never identify himself with his perishable body or the ever-changing mind. This is the 'Truth', the'Sat' the understanding of which brings Jnyan, the 'Chit' and gives us immense 'ananda' the eternal Bliss. 'Sat' is that which exists in all the three periods of time-Bhoota, Vartaman, and Bhavishyat. 'Chit' is that which is self-luminous and illumines other things also. Ananda is that which is the cause for being extremely dear (Parama Apta). It is this 'Sat-Chit-Ananda' we call "GOD" for no other word suits it. If this is clearly understood, most of the problems of our life on this earth are understood. In a way, this is real 'mukti' or 'moksha' that everybody aspires for.

What do I Want?

The second important question one should always ask oneself is "What is it I want"? The moment you say, 'I do not want anything' you are released from bondage. It is this 'wanting' that binds us. Most of the time, we do not know what we want. It is because of the ignorance that all of us get into trouble. We want what others have and what others boast of their possessions, all finite objects, bound by time and space, perishable and thrown out sooner or later. It is their 'ego' boosted by possessions of materials that promotes our ego and an urge to possess the same. Not knowing what we want, we simply run after sensuous and finite objects and we are disappointed when we attain them. Our education has failed us. It has created more of materialistic than spiritual aspirations in us. Jiddu Krishnamurthy used to say that 'we should de-educate ourselves and restore our pure intellect'. We should recognize our own self and reside in Him.

The word '*svastha*' is used to refer to a person of stable disposition, 'sva' meaning his own self and 'stha' meaning, established' i.e., a person established in himself, a Yogi. The inherent nature of the Self is 'sat', 'chit', and 'ananda'; it is pure Consciousness. Actually, it is the fickle mind that creates problems here. The mind cannot grasp the future and the unknown. It always clings to memory and the past experiences or dwells on imagination for it is capable of creating anything and every non-existing thing. It dwells on virtual reality a non -existent phenomenon. Hence, there is a time lag between the desire and its fulfilment. Since time is the decayer of all finite objects, the desire can never be fulfilled and men fall prey to the mischief of mind. Past experiences and the dreams about future spoil our life now and here.

A 'Jnyani' always lives at the present and forgets the past, rather erases the past from memory, and never bothers about the future. But, we common people full of 'tamo guna', characterized by ignorance, always live in the memory of the past or expectations of the future and thus feel disappointed. Even when our dreams are fulfilled, we feel unhappy and discontented because it fails to thrill the mind which always expects more than what is achieved and fulfilled. Ambition, desire, ignorance, greed all these create problems. For a moment, we all forget that there is somebody sitting within ourselves. That is the '*Purusha*' *Who* knows all. We never try to hear His voice, 'the inner voice' of guidance.

Is it not strange that we repose trust in somebody created by Him, but we do not trust Him, the 'Lord Almighty'! How often we enter an aeroplane not knowing anything about who sits in the cockpit and flies the plane! Faith and unwavering faith alone can solve all our problems. *Trust in God.* Invoke His blessings in all your actions. Offer all your actions to Him. Aspire not for the fruits of your action, for it is He who is the giver. The Lord Almighty is the Supreme Master Provider. He gives whatever you want, and sometimes more than what you want. He gives you according to your past deeds and misdeeds, or what is called 'Karma'. We all have brought a vessel of certain size according to our past deeds and that vessel will always be full. It cannot hold more. So, to aspire for more is also ignorance. A 'Jnyani' will never aspire for anything for he trusts in Him and leaves everything to Him. He knows that the Lord looks after everybody who looks to Him for guidance and support. This is the simple truth. Truth is always one. And there is no 'dvaith' in it. So, the first principle of Manoniyantran or Mind Control technique is:

"Trust in God. Trust Him Absolutely. Trust in the Absolute". Often we forget the simple truth that 'the Lord Almighty' is there to take care of us; and, unnecessarily we get frightened at the turn of events that appear to shatter our lives; he a storm in a tea cup.

Real knowledge is one that makes us strong and self-reliant. A Jnyani always reminds himself, 'I am not the body, I am not the mind, and I am not the soul'. Then, who am I? 'I am That', -the immortal self; the 'Self' that has no birth and death or decay. Nothing, not even the personal God that makes us dependent and reliant on Him, is real. "Real is the Self. I am the Self, the Blissful one. I am the Existence (sat), the Knowledge (chit), and the Absolute Bliss (Parama Ananda).

Taking responsibility for one's deeds is another important tantra of happiness. It brings immense joy when we take up job on our own and complete it for sheer joy of doing it. "Nothing makes us work so well at our best and the highest as when all responsibility is thrown upon ourselves"; and, we, in turn, realize the force behind all this existence, trust Him, and perform all actions with a 'nishkama karma' attitude. Even the Duty performed without His Will and Grace will be futile. Mindless adherence to duty of the workoholics is also useless, for it is only a strain on his mind and body, unless it is tempered by spirituality. Spiritual duties are not the blind religious rituals. The day-to-day functions performed in His name as an offering to the Lord are the real duties. These are the duties that do not bind us but release us from eternal bondage. There is no stress or tension in these duties and it is all a pleasure. Any work done with this devotion will be sure success and brings happiness in life. Otherwise, any duty for duty sake is sheer bondage. Duty should liberate us; should bring freedom. Otherwise, it is not duty at all; it is slavery.

In *Mundaka Upanishad* [I.1.3-5], there are questions and answer about the '*Reality of things*'- mundane and divine. There is this question:

"What is that Reality, by knowing which we can know all that there is in this manifested Universe? Is there such a unique reality by which we can understand all the manifestations of nature, internal as well as external? Is there Unity behind this diversity, a One behind the many?

'*Jnyan*' or supreme Knowledge is Brahman. It is spiritual illumination leading to the knowledge of the Brahman, the Self. Ordinarily, knowledge of the mundane world ('apara vidya') is of no consequence here. It is the knowledge of the Self (the 'Higher Knowledge' or the 'Para Vidya') that is very important. The absence of this knowledge of Self is Avidya. It is the root cause of ego. *"Egoism is the bondage of the Soul. The cessation of this egoism is Moksha, liberation. That which causes that egoism is Avidya, Nescience. That by which this egoism is completely turned back is Vidya, Knowledge"*. [*Sarvopanishad I*]

Buddhi becomes pure and strong, luminous and calm, steady and sure when it is free from the inebriation of wealth, power, knowledge, and pedigree, sensory pulls, wine and drugs. Such a pure buddhi is the best guide in life's journey. It denotes the fusion of intelligence, imagination and Will in their purest forms. Its impact on life is irresistible as well as wholesome.

Integrated Personality

An integrated personality is that where a person functions with body, mind, and soul in unison. A person conscious of only body or mind will not function in totality of his existence for the very spirit is lacking. Mere spiritual thought and action also falls short of involvement of the body and mind that are the tools of existence, through which one has to perform the function.

Sound Mind in a sound body is the Principle. A healthy Mind needs a healthy body; rather, it is also true that only a sound healthy body can sustain a healthy Mind. A healthy body and Mind tempered by spirituality and rationality is the basis of a sound 'personality' (totality of the person). It is good to develop a strong personality; but, more important than this is to build an integrated personality- a person whose body, mind and soul functions in synchrony. Then life is a symphony, a melody.

Our modern life is more complex and competitive. To cope with such a stressful life, nature prepares the individual to develop a strong individuality capable of preserving oneself under conditions of intense competition. But, the real life situation needs a more cooperative, understanding, submissive individuals who have developed strong personality. As Bertrand Russel has pointed out, 'strong individuals are like the 'billiards' whose function is to hit, strike, and collide. Strong personalities on the other hand understand, cooperate and submit to larger interests; they do not come to loggerheads and thereby succeed.

First, one should develop a strong individuality and then should develop a strong personality, and ultimately become an integrated spiritual personality- synchronizing mind, body, and soul, and thereby become a harmonious integrated personality. All the three- the mind, the body and the soul should act in unison and then only perfection is attained.

In order to understand this 'integrated personality, we must know what is 'personality'. Personality is the conscious and the unconscious part of a person; together they go to make a person. Psychologists define a personality as 'a collection of capacities, habits and attitudes which distinguish him from other men'. What is that constant factor that persists amidst changes of body, mind, ego, and environment? In fact, every human being is a complex personality. There is a continuous struggle to understand and adjust to the outer world on the one hand, and to understand oneself and reconcile the never-ending conflicts that arise within one self. This makes life a constant struggle.

One of the most important factors affecting the development of personality is the society itself. We live in a society that does not make any concession for the weak, timid, downtrodden and the less privileged, much worse, the physically handicapped. It is all a game of 'the survival of the fittest'. In such a cruel society, to develop a sound personality of love, compassion and piety is a challenge. Obviously, mortals as we are, we succumb to overpowering forces; competition leaves us crippled. Defeatist tendency is obvious and natural. Inferiority complex, timidity and lack of courage to face the world are the real problems faced by young Minds deprived of basic necessities of life. Under these circumstances, only divine will or poorvapunya only will help.

Poverty teaches humilty, self-reliance, and infuses self-confidence if one takes it in the right spirit; otherwise, it may also bring arrogance and complexities that are difficult to erase. As it is said, 'necessity is the mother of invention'. Most of the great achievers have seen absolute poverty and distress in their early lives. It helps to see the world in its reality. Real personality is built in adversity rather than in a safe and secure environment. It helps to develop the emotional intelligence that makes one develop compassion, sympathy and understanding.

Many persons develop a split personality. They grow up in this competitive socio-economic order and end up as sadists, taking revenge on society for their childhood deprivations. It is this sort of human behaviour and social order where individuals talk something and do something else, we are afraid of. Corrective measures have to be taken at the early stages before it is too late. The children of deprived families deserve all sympathy, compassion, educational and health facilities; in this respect we must appreciate the social insurance schemes of the Western countries where rarely one goes hungry at the end of the day and compulsory health and education facilities are provided.

In the face of deprivations, poverty, and fierce competition many take to gambling and wayward life; they develop lack of respect to social order. The blue print of oneself called the' self-image' created in subconscious in these deprived young Minds remains beyond their conscious perception and work throughout their lives. These images, especially the negative ones like 'I am useless or I am good for nothing', etc. assumes proportions that go out of control. These deprived persons seem to believe their own experiences of deprivation as real and forget about the opportunities that lie ahead. They feel they are misfit in this competitive world and will never succeed in anything. Their defeatist tendency, inferiority complex, shy and timid nature will obstruct their progress. These deprived children refuse education and look at all progressive effort as a further deprivation of the poor. They become jealous of the rich. It is a real threat to civilized society. We see a lot of people take to narcotics, alcoholic drinks or get sick in order to escape from this struggle. One has to learn to fight this by understanding and develop peace within; otherwise it will lead to degeneration. Not only the deprived class, but, even the better- off or the well-off are not outside this syndrome. The rich and the powerful, the handsome, healthy and strong, too, develop their ego and look down with contempt on the poor, the weak, and the deprived. One must develop an integrated personality. It is here that the technique of meditation comes to help.

As Bertrand Russel puts it, two strong-willed persons are like the billiard balls whose function is to strike; they always collide. But strong personalities are well- integrated persons who do not get into conflicts. They always make a congenial relationship. To be able to communicate with each other, to enter emotionally into each other, to dig affections into each other and to live at peace with each other, there is need for the individual to grow into the person; and this growth is spiritual growth, and not just a physical or an intellectual growth. It is a spiritual growth because it transcends genetic or organic limitations. This development from individuality to personality is essential and everyone should acquire it by raising the level of consciousness. Our children should be taught to grow in to rich warm personalities instead of remaining at billiard ball level. If we behave as mere individuals and collide against each other like billiard balls we may easily be the agent of our own wholesale destruction. This is the process of humanization, or simply, raising the level from man to human.

Much more important than a strong individual personality is the act of surrender to the Lord. First, one has to strengthen, assert, and then sacrifice himself; it is denying oneself (Self-abnegtation) and total surrender to the Lord, through a super strength. That is the correct attitude and the right way. So, work hard; build up a strong indivividuality, a strong personality; and, then when you are strong and spiritually mature as a man, you look up and see a greater courage and greater strength beckoning you, which makes you say: '*Not I, but Thou; Thy will be done*!' This is the message of Shree Krishna, a message of self- surrender and Divine Grace. Be strong; have faith in yourself and face your problems boldly" [Bhagavad

Gita, Ch. Xi .33].

Modern psychology has introduced the concept of '*integrated personality*'. It is this discovery of unconscious that always takes an upper hand in all human thinking that has led to the study of subconscious in detail. We know very little about the wealth of impressions, memories, knowledge and information hidden in layers and layers of the subconscious. The conscious mind usually remains cut off from the unconscious mind that dominates it nevertheless. This is the cause of conflicts within the personality. It is Carl Jung who came out with the concept of integrating the conscious with the unconscious parts of the personality. 'To integrate is to form into a whole or perfect whole'. Conscious mind and the unconscious mind should work harmoniously to form an integrated personality.

Development of an integrated personality is possible by proper control of the mind. This again is a paradoxical statement. Unless one has got complete control over his mind, he cannot develop a sound personality and until one develops an integrated personality, he cannot enjoy a happy, peaceful, and successful life. But, it is true that one of the spontaneous out-come of the control of mind is 'integration of personality'. Such persons think and act in a harmonious way, with body, mind, and spirit. Such persons succeed in all their avocations even in adverse circumstances. Such persons are always calm and peaceful.

Calmness of mind brings enormous peace. Peace brings happiness and a happy person makes others happy. Such persons are always prosperous and successful and can face any problem in life boldly and courageously. They get enormous strength of mind from their spiritual bent of mind. They get strength from their inner Self, '*atmabala*' and it helps to develop strength of mind (*manobala*) and strong will power. Hence, the principle of Mind Management Technique is "to develop an integrated personality"; develop a harmonious personality- one of healthy body, sound mind, and fine spirit – a spirit of love, devotion, and sacrifice.

In physics, it is explained that molecules make matter and atoms go to make the molecules. Atoms are minute parts composed of still smaller parts like electrons, neutrons, protons and in turn, they too have still further minute parts within-firmiones and biones. Atoms are composed of protons, the positive units of electricity, and an equal number of electrons, the negative units. The protons are concentrated in the nucleus also contain neutral particles called *neutrons*. The electrons are extra –nuclear and are supposed to be constantly orbiting the nucleus. This means that each atom is like a 'solar system' with all its components uniting to form a whole. The atoms in their turn form parts of a greater whole.

Social contacts are important. Human beings who have evolved as social animals cannot keep well, physically or mentally, unless they remain in contact with other human beings. Human kind emerged through the very process of creating culture and needs this culture for its survival and further evolution- mutual interaction and display similar patterns of self - organisation.

It is the nature of the mind to be creative. The more the depths of the mind are plumbed, the more abundantly they produce. According to Paul Maclean, the human brain consists of three structurally different parts, each endowed with its own intelligence and subjectivity, which stem from different periods of evolutionary past" (Capra). The brain stem is the innermost part of the brain. It is concerned with instinctive behaviour patterns already exhibited by reptiles. It is responsible for many kinds of compulsive behaviour and biological drives. Surrounding the brain stem is the limbic system (Latin: *Limbus* means border); it is well developed in mammals and in the human brain- involved with emotional experience and expression. Sub-cortex- the two innermost parts of the brain are strongly interconnected and express them selves non-verbally through a rich spectrum of the body language.

The outer-most part, the neocortex (*cortex* means bark- *Latin*) facilitates higher order abstract functions, such as thought and language. The neocortex originated in the earliest evolutionary phase of mammals and expanded in the human species at an explosive rate. It got stabilized about 50,000 years ago. This explosive rate is unprecedented in evolutionary history! By developing our capacity for abstract thinking at such a rapid pace, we have lost touch with the realities of life and have become the only creatures who often fail to cooperate with others and even do not hesitate to kill our own kind- not one or two but the whole of mankind. Our evolution continues to offer us freedom of choice. We can constantly alter our values and attitudes to regain the spirituality and ecological awareness we have lost.

Living organisms are intrinsically dynamic. Their visible forms are still manifestations of underlying process. Process and stability are compatible only if the process forms rhythmic patterns- fluctuation, oscillation, vibration, and waves. The new biology shows fluctuations are crucial in the dynamics of self-organisation. They are the basis of order in living world; ordered structures arise from rhythmic patterns.

The components of ecosystems are inter-linked through cyclical exchanges of matter and energy; civilizations rise and fall in evolutionary cycles; and the planet as a whole has its rhythms and recurrences as it spins on its axis and moves around the sun. Rather, the center of consciousness also shifts from one part of the Globe to the other with the result some countries become more advanced or decline than the others.

Rhythmic patterns allow individuals to express their distinctive personalities. Tielhard de Chardin, a mystic whose thoughts come closer to new systems biology, is also a geologist and paleontologist. His law of complex consciousness states that 'evolution proceeds in the direction of increasing complexity accompanied by a corresponding rise in consciousness, culminating in human spirituality'. His concept of consciousness used as 'awareness' is perfectly compatible with 'systems view' of the mind. Tielhard coined the word 'noosphere' the mind layer of the planet- web of ideas and said God is the source of all beings, particularly evolutionary force.

In biology, we have the cells. The human body is made up of millions and millions of cells. Every cell is like a tiny solar system and is an organisation by itself. All these smaller units of cells go to make the tissue, and, these tissues go to make the organs of the body. In an integrated body, while all the organs have their individual movements, they all must coordi-nate with the general movement. When this is not the case, disharmony or illness is the result. So it is necessary that the organs should coordinate and function in an integrated and harmonious manner in order to facilitate the body to function. In order to function normally, all the different parts of the body must be healthy and strong and work harmoniously.

Our mind is a synthetic whole consisting of the faculties of cognition, feeling and willing. Some times our reasoning, feeling and willing, and actions are at war with one another and create a terrible confusion within our selves. The conflicts arise in priorities of duties, fixing moral standards, following spiritual ideals and we become a whirlpool of emotions. It is here, that we feel the need for a harmonious and integrated function of the mind. Here, integration stands for purity, strength and harmony.

We have the ego, the 'I'-ness. Ego is perverse and has no set stable standing and thus, goes on changing its centre of gravity. With the result, it is sometimes identified with outside things, next moment with its body, then with the senses or the mind. Ego, at times becomes too much single pointed, centred on oneself, thus become 'ego-centric'. For a while we forget who we are. We forget that we are a part of this universe, and we are a part of the world where we have to work harmoniously in a coordinated manner with other fellow beings. We forget that our survival depends on survival of others and take to elimination of others to gain exclusive control of everything for our selves. We become ego-centric, selfish and mean. In such a situation our thoughts and action become a danger to our selves, our family, and society. We do not realize this because we are too much egoistic and refuse to see the reality. What a great tragedy! We sit on the branch of the tree and cut the very roots of the tree!

There is need for perfect harmony between our physical, mental, and spiritual aspects of life. The body, mind, and spirit should work in harmony to accomplish the evolution of the personality. When there is perfect harmony, it is called '*integrated personality*'. But, unfortunately, we lack an understanding of spirituality and underscore the need for spirituality in our daily life. Even those who know the spiritual aspect do not have the slightest inclination to integrate it with their personality. With the result, something very important is lacking in our personality.

An integrated personality is one who has gained sufficient control on his physical, mental, and spiritual aspects of his life. Why spirituality? God or no God, it should be remembered that spirituality stirs up the subtle aspects of the conscious; it stirs up the soul; it stimulates Prajnya and the intellect. It shows light on the darker sides and illuminates the path. More than all these, it shuts up the idiotic and ignorant mind and gives it in the hands of Buddhi. This is the science of mind management.

There is another level of integration. That is the higher level at which the Super-Consciousness gets integrated with the Supreme-Consciousness, i.e., Brahman. This stage is realized when the body, mind and the soul gets fully integrated with the Supreme-Consciousness. Normally, yogins who activate Kundalini and raise their consciousness to the Sahasraara plexus level enjoy the *Supreme Bliss, Sat Chit Ananda*. This stage is called '*Turiya*'. Beyond this stage is '*Kaivalya*'. It is very difficult to reach this stage by ordinary mortals who are attached to this sensate world enjoying the lower levels of consciousness.

Fear

Fear is in-born with the jeeva. The '*Germ cell*' that causes our birth evolves with the desire and fear accompanies it. Thus, fear and desire are closely related aspects. In fact, desire comes first and then the fear of non-fulfilment of desires. Both these are the binding factors that make life a veritable hell and cause repeated births and hence, eternal bondage. Both these are associated with the life like the snail and its shell. And, then, the whole life is spent in finding out ways and means of getting out of the shackles of this bondage! Our Mind is always pre-occupied with a sense of fear, anxiety, due to uncertainities and unpredictability of events and results of action. Fear is the unknown. Fear is of the unknown. Fear is the other. Love kills Fear; Fear kills love. Fear is ignorance. Knowledge kills fear.

"In enjoyment there is the fear of illness; in social position there is the fear of calumny; in wealth there is the fear of losing; in fame there is the fear of humiliation; in strength there is the fear of enemies; in beauty there is the fear of old age; in scholarship there is the fear of disputants; in virtue there is the fear of traducers; in life there is the fear of death. Indeed everything in this world is accompanied by fear. Renunciation alone leads to fearlessness". Fear complex is one of the inborn qualities of the living beings. This has a tremendous effect on all activities. In fact, Shri Krishna advises Arjuna to be fearless and face life with courage. This earthly life is for the Dheeras, it is said in Bhagavad Gita. Even in Upanishad, there is ample reference to fear.

There is a prayer to ward off fear:

"Oh 'Indra', make us fearless of those (sin, enemies, hell) of which we are afraid. O Maghava, destroy that, i.e., the cause of fear that is in us, the devotees. For our protection, destroy our harassing enemies". Atharva Veda contains Mantra to keep the bad elements away, ward off fear and secure wealth. Mahanarayana Upanishad, too, has many Mantra to propitiate the Lord and secure wealth, peace and prosperity and enjoy without fear.

"The fear is in the mind and the fear is of the mind. The fear is of the unknown and the fear is the unknown. Fear is darkness and fear is ignorance. Fear is of the safety and security, of the protection of the body, protection of the progeny, and the dear ones, and the protection of the wealth, protection of the 'now' and the 'future'. Protection of the body against the diseases, protection of the property, of the wealth, house and property against natural causes." In Aparokshaanubhuti of Shri Shankaracharya, fear is attributed to 'duality' and 'imperfection'; it can be overcome only by the realization of non-duality. Even the slightest

distinction between Jeevatman and Paramatman will cause this fear and delusion. Hence, it may be construed here that as long as jeevas are imperfect fear persists. When duality appears through ignorance, one sees another; but when everything becomes identified with the Atman, one does not perceive another even in the least. In that state when one realizes all as identified with the Atman, there arises neither delusion nor sorrow, in consequence of duaity.

Our forefathers used to pray the Lord of the Lords, Indra, and the Prayer to the great elements thus:

"May 'Indra' come to our succour – Indra, who is the giver of welfare on earth, and bliss in the next world; the Lord of the people, who is the layer of vrata, who is the subduer of enemies, and giver of rain; Indra, who is the peaceable and giver of safety, the sun, the earth, air, fire and water; and the king of these, Indra, protect what is dear to all".

In reality, there is no safety and security for all things of the world are temporary and perishable in nature. What is the perishable cannot be saved and what is eternal and limitless does not need any protection. Wealth becomes a source of misery when we get attached to it.

If the body is killed, or destroyed, the vital force is not killed. And the Self, the Soul, takes a better body of its choice. Death is always for the better since the world is becoming better everyday. Wealth is not of paramount importance since the acquisition and squandering of wealth is always going on.

There is an interesting aspect of fear. It appears that we all enjoy fear. It seems we all feel a little secure in our hearts in the face of prevailing terrorism, bomb hoaxes, anthrax, and such other commotion. We cling to fear for companionship. Fear is a constant companion, and an ever-faithful one. Some deep fears are so personal that we become possessive about them and do not let them go. Fear gives us identity. It makes us feel special. We explain away, rationalize other people's fears. Our own, we nourish with the love of the self. The fear is also a strong support to the fickle mind since the latter clings to the former. Otherwise we would not spend much of our time in thinking and talking of these alarming sensational news that spreads fear. A little fear in the heart is good! *Fear of God* is the best!!

Fear talks to us. It tells us the world is bad. By negation one understands oneself as good. So it is comforting. Fear tells us not to venture beyond a point. By implication one feels persecuted by life. One feels sorry for oneself and sits back revelling in self-pity. Fear gives us excuses by telling us something is dangerous or evil. Fear gives us an alibi when inefficient. One actually thinks fear is protecting. But fear is masking the true self from the world and the world from one. The need is to conquer fear. When you are afraid find the cause of the fear and face fear boldly, courageously. It is rare to find a man who is completely devoid of fear. Discarding fear is important.

Fearlessness means being aware and having knowledge. We fear that of which we know least or do not know at all. Half-baked knowledge is the breeding ground of fear. When we have adequate knowledge, we have less fear. When we face fear boldly, nothing happens; only fear perishes. We should have faith in ourselves. Many fears will vanish with self-confidence; and, all Fears vanish with self-knowledge. The Fear is for the attached. The unattached is fearless. The attachment is for the ignorant and not for the knower. So, the prayer is for the removal of ignorance and for enlightenment. The whole world is at the command of the knowledgeable since knowledge is power.

Real strength is the 'strength' that is unaccompanied by any fear of loss, fear of attacks from enemies, fear of death. What we ordinarily consider strength is not really strength at all; it is the fear that forces us to make efforts to build up some sort of defence. Thus, in the greatest worldly security lies also the greatest fear. True strengh is attained only when we feel certain that our real Self shall not in the least be affected, whatever might happen to our worldly interests. Faith and that too, absolute faith in God is the key to get rid of fear. But, one must have a clear concept of God.

Fear is attached to soul since the silken thread of desire has caused the soul to be embodied. Both desire and fear are further contained by the karmic particles since the fruits of action guide the metempsychosis. The only way to get out of this bondage is to burn the karmic particles and desist from sensuousness and desire, and remove fear by submission to Lord.

5

'Brahm' jnyaan- The Supreme Knowledge

"Narayanah param brahma tatvam Narayanah parah;
Narayanah paro jyotiraatmaa Naraayanah parah."
[Mahanarayana Upanishad 13.4]

The *Knowledge of the 'Brahm'* or *Brahman* is said to be the supreme Knowledge. This is' higher knowledge' ('para vidya' that leads to Salvation) that concerns the Creator and the creation of this universe, and all other knowledge is considered 'lower knowledge' (apara vidya that may give temporary worldly gains) that deals with the objects of the world. What is this Brahman? And, Where is it? How to know this Brahman? These are the questions that our modern science cannot answer and where our technology is not of any help. But, the Veda and the Upanishads have answered these questions. Sadhus and Sants who have obtained supreme knowledge by deep meditation on the Brahman have experienced the power behind this creation. Persons who have gone deep into the super-Conscious state contemplating on the above questions have experienced the Brahman and have tried to give some expression or to explain what the Brahman is. But, Brahman is inexplicable. Brahman is beyond all expression and nobody can define ift.It is something what is "yatra vaacho nivartante..."(where the Mind cannot reach and return). The Brahman is beyond any expression since it is "Silence". Brahman is the supreme cause of all that exists. It is the cause of this multiverse of universes, galaxies, planets and satellites, all organic and inorganice matter. It is simply referred to as 'That'. The nature of Brahman is 'Sat' (Truth or existence), 'Chit' ('Consciousness), and Bliss (Anand). Brahman is the cause of the causes and it is with the power of the Brahman that all the Gods and Goddesses wield their power in order to control and sustain this world.

The inexplicable Brahman has specially created God *'Ishvara'* to rule this world; and, it appears, as if, He also created the *Trinity- Brahma, Vishnu, and Maheshvara* and bestowed on them the power of creation, sustenence, and annihilation, respectively. But, it is Brahman that is operating in different capacities or functions for no one knows the power of Brahman.The 'Trinity' appear as though the same God acts in different capacities at the behest of the supreme power, the Brahman. Brahman is the knower of the field (the universe) for He himself has created it (the Field) and He himself is the field (the universe). All this Brahmaanda (Multiverse consisting of innumerable Universes) is contained in Him and as such He is the container. He is unattached and stands ten fingers above and outside this Brahmaanda (Hiranyagarbha). He is invisible. He is inexplicable. He is Omniscient, He is Self-resplendent, He is Omnipotent and Omnipresent. He is everything that we ever imagine, think, or see. He is the supreme-Consciousness. He is abstract Silence the ***'Atyanta-Abhava'***.

The term '***God***' is used to what all powers that create and sustain us for we do not know anything about Him and cannot understand all these spiritual aspects since we have never made any attempt in this direction, so far. It requires 'faith' and concerted effort to understand all these spiritual aspects. Students who practise yoga can gradually attain spiritual experiences that unravel these mysteries.

Often we hear some people say, *"Oh God, if there is God! Save my Soul, if there is one!"* Sceptic as we are, we neither believe in the existence of God, nor know anything about our self or Soul. *'Avidya'* (nescience, clouded intelligence, mistaken identities, perverted knowledge, 'in ability to see things as they are', or 'Ignorance' of Reality) governs our lives. We have been bestowed with the five senses; still, we cannot see and understand things as they are! We are so foolish that we believe in others who are created by the Lord, but we do not have faith and belief in God. In fact, our God is in our Mind. Our Mind is our God. Mind is the man; Mind is the world. Our Mind can create the God it wants! The concept of God has to be clearly understood. It is for want of a clear understanding, a proper conception of God, that this beautiful world is made a veritable hell, and that too, by a very small minority of crooked, selfish people. First of all, we must be educated and trained to know 'God'. Upanishads reiterate that '*that which is worshipped here is not 'God'*. It is not God that we generally hope and 'believe it to be' in the sense we can understand or comprehend by our fickle mind or senses. The eyes cannot see, the mind cannot figure out what 'God' is since It is not an object of perception; but, God is everywhere! God is omnipresent. God is self-effulgent and is all-powerful. God is omniscient and all- pervasive. God is 'Supreme-Consciousness'. God is in you as well as in me as Prajnya', it is said '*Prajnyaanan Brahman*'. Consciousness, Truth, Bliss, and the Self, the Soul, or 'Atman' - are all manifestations of the Brahman, the supreme-Consciousness.

God is the supreme-Consciousness; God is there in the form of Intelligence and functions as divine will. When we stand before the Icon or idol of God in a temple, the image activates the subtle impulses and create the Consciousness of Truth, Knowledge and Bliss in us; and, it is quite a revelation that God exists; God exists in us.

The Vedic Gods are Agni, Aditya, Surya (Sun) Indra, Rudra, Varuna, Marut, Maitra and the like who are visible as water, air, fire, earth, thunder, lightning, rain, etc. and function under divine will in order to sustain us.

"Hiranyagharbhah samavartaagre, bhootasya jaatah patireka aaseet'
Sa daadhaar pruthveem dhyaamutemaam kasmai devaaya havishaa vidhema."

[*Mahanarayana Upanishad, I. 1.*]

Meaning, Aditya, the first-born, or Prajapati has the Hiranyagharbha as the resplendent body (golden egg), the Sun. He is

the sustainer, nourisher, the Paramatman; and, he supports earth as well as heaven. His nature of Bliss and power of creation cannot be questioned. May we worship Him, that Shining One, with our offerings The Veda recognize this supreme resplendent Purusha as the God and his eyes are the Stars! The Sun is that golden disc, the self- luminous, omniscient, omnipotent, omnipresent resplendent body.

Another beautiful aphorism, Shloka makes this point very clear:

"Eshaa hi devah pradisho anu sarvaah, poorve hi jaatah sa u gharbhe amtah;

Sa vijaayamaanah sa janishyamaanah pratyamgmukhasthishtai vishvatomukhah."

[Mahanarayana Upanishad I. 12].

Meaning, "This Resplendent body, Hiranyagharbha, praised by all the Veda, pervades in all directions- the earth, sky, heaven and the like; He is inside the universe and He alone is the manifest world of creation springing into existence and causing the birth of the world of creation yet to come. He sees everywhere and dwells as the innermost self in all, leading, guiding, and protecting them."

What all needed here to understand this is the absolute faith, a 'faith' with understanding and conviction, and it is the 'faith' that is born first in this process of creation.

The Vedanta Sutra of Badarayana (2nd aphorism) defines God as 'the One from whom the origination, etc.of the universe proceeds'. In other words, 'Brahman' is the father from whom the universe has sprung, by whom it is sustained and dissolved'. God is the cause of the causes, the universal cause. Every act, event, or occurrence has the volition as its prompter, a—will-force giving the initial impulse. It just cannot be 'law of nature' a non-intelligent principle, ultimate cause, according to Shri Madhvacharya. He is the Supreme Inteligence. What we call Karma, Maya (illusion), Mind (aberration), Kala (time), Vibrations or attributes or gunas, or Matter, the Panchabhutas cannot be the cause, for they are non-intelligent and incapable of volition. A volition proceeding from chit-intelligence is the source of every movement, of every action, of every vibration. God is the universal cause; God is the will-force that accounts for the worlds from the infinitesimal vibration of the molecules for the thrilling march of the starry galaxy in orbits immeasurable. The Samkhyas, who admit God as the 'Supreme Being', make Him an appeandage of Prakriti.

God pervades through every conceivable atom of the universe, occupies every point of space, ever engaged in creation, preservation, destruction, and, all the rest. This is known as the 'immanence of God' in the universe. Wordsworth, Carlyle and many others hold to this view. There is a similar view. "Not a blade of grass moves without 'His Will' and everything is governed by His volition, ichha, and is permeated by it. He is present nearer than the nearest, directing everything. This is the concept of 'omnipresence of God' defined in Vedanta.

In *Bhagavad Gita*, Lord Shri Krishna says, *'I am the indwelling soul residing within the heart of every creature. I pervade the earth and everything born, and sustain it by my power'.*

Shrutis, the Upanishads, declare: 'He is the hearer, thinker, ordainer, announcer, knower in detail, the inner guide of all beings'.

Vishnu, the all-pervading supreme reality, is ***'Ekamevaadviteeyam'*** the 'One without a second'. Cardinal Newman defines God 'as absolutely self-dependent 'Being' and the only 'Being' as such'.

There is a beautiful explanation in *Kenopanishad* that makes very clear the entire concept of what is God and what is not God. The disciple puts the questions,

"Who impels the mind to alight on its object? Enjoined by whom does the vital force proceed to function? At whose behest do men utter speech? What Intelligence, indeed, directs the eyes and the ears?"

The answer given to these questions needs a careful study. *"It is the Atman, the spirit, by whose power the ear hears, the tongue speaks, the mind understands and life functions. The wise man separates the Atman from these faculties, rises out of sense-life, and attains immortality".*

The general view is that the sense faculties, the Mind, and the life force- either each in itself, or as a psychophysical combination centering round the body, are in themselves the ultimate factors in personality. However, there is the suspicion that there is in us something deeper than these- an unrestricted Intelligence that ultimately guides all our mental and physical faculties. By themselves, these senses are inert. The Atman is the sole intelligent principle in man. By its presence behind our various organs, It enables them to fulfil their respective functions. But not knowing this fact, ignorant man mistakes the senses, mind, etc. to be really intelligent, and, therefore identifies the Atman with them. The wise man, on the other hand, overcomes this identification, realizes his spiritual nature and hence attains immortality. The Atman is beyond the 'ken' (Samsk.), ('why') of the senses and the mind. It being the source of the intelligence, it cannot be known as other things of the world, i.e., in an objective sense. "*One who syas 'he knows', knows not" and one who says 'he knows not', knows It*". It cannot be either imagined or expressed like other objects. And, ***"It is not this, anything, that the people worship here".***

It should be very clearly understood that the '*Atman*' is the '*Spirit within*' man. It is the source of all faculties of personality; and, it is this Spirit that governs all activities of man. The 'Atman' stands for the 'Spirit within man' and the '*Brahman*' stands for the '*Spirit behind the universe*'. To establish unity between the two is 'to know' the Reality, 'the Sat'. This 'knowing' is a continuous process and it never ends. ***"It is knowable but never known".*** Thus, the ultimate reality of the creation of this cosmic world, the Universe, is beyond the province of mind and language.

There is the 'Devatmashakti' that guides the life and activities of all human beings. Here, 'Deva' means God (of religion) and '*atma*' means the self (of philosophy), and '*shakti*' means the energy (of science). It also means the self-conscious power, which is inherent in all jeevas, and Deva meaning, the self-luminous.

'*Devatmashakti*' also means the source of knowledge, emotions, and will - the three aspects of the mind. 'Deva' stands for knowledge, 'atma' for the emotions, and 'shakti' for the will. One who puts his heart and soul into all his actions will no doubt achieve all success in his endeavour.

An ignorant man is usually concerned only with himself and the world. To him, God, the third entity, does not exist. The intelligent man soon finds out, however, that there is some unknown power behind the Universe, which is guiding his destiny. The first part of spiritual practice, therefore, is to realize the existence of this power on which both he and the world depends. At first, this realization is only intellectual.

The idea of God comes very early in the life of individuals. However, with the maturity of intellectual power comes, the real search as to the fundamental character of this power. Sadhana first begins with a separation of God from the Universe, as a being with qualities entirely different from the individual and the world. Subsequently, with the analysis of the individual and the world psychologically and scientifically, the various systems of philosophy come into being. Each system represents a stage in the progress of thought and sadhana. In the final stage of realization in the depths of samadhi, the world and the individual soul, as we know them, vanish entirely and God alone remains. The individual soul gradually acquires all the fundamental characteristics of the world, the world consisting of all dualities such as: gross and the subtle, spirit and the matter, cause and effect. The realization of oneness of Jeeva and Brahman is referred to as '*Divine Grace*'. It also means, that Lord's Grace is required for the realization of identity. One must understand that the Grace of God is bestowed on a person only after he has reached the limits of self-effort.

Matter is perishable but God is imperishable and immortal. God rules over all the perishable matters, and the individual souls, too. By meditating upon Him, by uniting with Him in thought, and by becoming one with him, there is cessation of all illusion in the end. With the knowledge of God all fetters fall off; with the waning of ignorance, birth and death cease. Going beyond consciousness of the body by meditating upon Him, one reaches the stage of Universal Lordship, become one without a second; it is in a sense, fulfillment of all desires and attaining Universal Lordship.

Even those who seek Salvation, or 'Mukti' and want to become one with Him i.e., attain 'sayujya', should realize that they are aspiring for something what they do not know. To become one with God is just impossible according to Sri Madhwacharya, who is the incarnation of Hanuman and Bheema of the previous Treta and Dwapara Yugas, respectively. What Shankara reiterated from the Upanishadic doctrines, 'Tat Tvam asi', has not been properly understood and it is widely believed that God is none else but the 'One' who dwells in oneself. In order to realize this, one has to become God, rather should acquire divine qualities and behave as God Himself dispelling all tamasic and rajasic gunas, and transcend the Sattvic guna; One should get rid of ari-shadvargas such as kama, krodha, lobha, moha, mada, matsarya, i.e., one should get rid of ego, prejudices, likes and dislikes, anger, desire, greed, jealousy, etc. and become totally affable, loving, compassionate, benevolent. One must become pure in mind, heart and soul and attain 'poorna prajnya' state, state of 'Supreme Consciousness'. This is a tall order for one who comes within the grip of the samsara, bondage and attachment to this sensate world. Hence, 'God Realization', —Sayujya— is a remote possibility according to Shri Madhwacharya. "To him, let alone merge with him, even visioning Him is a remote possibility". At best, one can be near the Lord and enjoy His —sameepya— by his total surrender, devotion and Meditation on Him.

Thus, there are four kinds of 'mukti' and there is no equality in bliss among jeevas and that there are degrees of enjoyment graduated and allotted according to the devotee's worth.

'*God is one*' and the ***'Only',"Ekamevaadviteeyam"***; He is present everywhere in the form of 'Consciousness' (*'Prajnyaana'*) – either 'universal' consciousness or 'individual' consciousness. It is this 'consciousness that has created this world and it is this consciousness that has made us what we are; 'It' is in each and every one of us. 'That' sits in us and directs all our actions. Without 'It', not even a wink of the eye is possible. God is so near us that He is nearer than our hands and limbs. He is One Supreme Omniscient, all-pervading, cosmic flow in all beings. He is the Light within us. He is the Pure Intellect. He is the Supreme Consciousness. He is the Pure Mind, Heart (Subtle) and Soul, the Self.

"Eko Devah Sarva Bhooteshu Goodah Sarva vyapee
Sarvabhootaantaratma.
Karmaadhyakshah Sarvabhootadhivaasah Saakshi cheta kevalo
Nirgunascha".

[Svetasvatara Upanishad VI. 11]

Meaning, "The One Lord (Self-effulgent) in all beings remaining hidden, all-pervading and the self of all beings, controlling and watching over all works (good or bad), living n all creatures and the Witness (i.e., neither the doer of any acts nor the enjoyer), The Supreme Intelligence, the One without a second, having no attributes". "*He is the One Intelligent (active) 'Being' among the many inactive; He who makes the many from what is one". [Brahmopanishad, Atharva Veda*]

The realization of this Reality releases one from all bondage of all codes.

Vedanta upholds that all evolution presupposes involution. If consciousness appears as a datum in evolution from the cell onwards, it must be present in the primordial, background material of the Universe itself. What is the most evolved notion that man has of this Universe? It is Intelligence; the adjustment of part to part. At the beginning that intelligence becomes involved, and in the end, that intelligence gets evolved. The sum total of the intelligence displayed in the Universe must, therefore, be the involved Universal Intelligence unfolding itself. This Universal Intelligence is what we call 'GOD'. One can call it by any name, it is absolutely certain that in the beginning there was that infinite cosmic intelligence. This cosmic intelligence got involved and later on it manifested itself, until it became the 'perfect man'. Then it goes back to its source. In Him we live and move and have our being; we come from God and go back to God. This cosmic intelligence is God. Pure Consciousness is known as Brahman or Shiva, in its transcendental quiescent aspect, and as Maya or Shakti, in its immanent dynamic aspect; one is like the bottled up state of energy and the other the released one. The philosophers call it Paramatman, the Yogis call it the Supreme Self and the Bhaktas call it Bhagavan. This unity or infinitude of the Atman as 'Pure Consciousness' is the goal of all Vedanta, according to Shri Shankara.

"Why do we use the word God? Because, there is no other word; it is the only word, the best word, in which is centered all hopes, aspirations and happiness of humanity. Great saints coined this word God; they realized its import and understood their meaning. In the hands of ignorant people the word loses its spirit and glory", says Swami Vivekananda. (Complete Works. Vol.11. p. 210).

Use the word '***God***' in the true spirit. Cleanse it of its superstition and realize fully what this great ancient word means. This word 'God', when one understands properly by the power of laws of association as associated with innumerable majestic and powerful ideas. It has been used and worshipped by millions of human souls; and, have associated with all that is highest and best, all that is rational, all that is lovable, all that is great, grand, in human nature. And they come as suggestions and cannot be given up.

Richard Armstrong in his book 'God and Soul' is of the opinion, that, "one who claims to see God and divine things with the inner vision of the soul, has a direct apprehension, as the bodily eye apprehends color, and the bodily ear apprehends sound. The method is simply contemplation; not to argue, generalize or infer; just reflect, brood and wait for light." Real Sadhus and saints deeply meditative, look mute, deaf and dull, more or less imbecile lunatics, begging for bread, but occasionally open their lips to give utterances of profound wisdom. These wandering ascetics or sadhus practice contemplation and penance to vision Reality, i.e., God.

Atman in the individual Jeeva and Brahman in the Universe are one and the same. It is the same individual consciousness a part of the Supreme-Consciousness. This Atman- Brahman, the individual and the supreme-Consciousness is the Unity of all Experience. It is the Unified Experience Field, Non-Dual 'Pure Consciousness'. Our mere intellectual knowledge leaves us far away from our true self. Self- realization penetrates deep spirituality, steadily breaks down the barriers between man and nature, and man and man. When this knowledge dawns on us, the triviality of this make-believe world will become very clear.

The nature of the self and the problem of conduct are the two important problems that absorbed the attention of Sri Krishna. The 'ego' in man is the cause of all errors and the origin of all false values. It is that 'ego' to which we refer all our judgments regarding everything in our experience; and itself being limited and circumscribed, it cannot confer infallibility upon its judgments. Hence, there occur errors. Hence, all doubts demand further inquiry. Deeper inquiry reveals the totally unreal character of this ego, thus shifting our sense of self-hood to a deeper reality. Here we come across the great Vedantic conception of the 'Sakshi' (witness or ultimate observer). There is no Western concept of this as yet. [See H.G.Wells, G.P.Wells, & Julian Huxley: *The Science of Life*, pp 878-9].

When it comes to Man and his Universe, the Planet Earth is a gross and 'sensate world' (Manoprapancha'), whereas, the human mind (Manas) is a subtle thing, and thus, there is friction between the gross and the subtle. The Universe, the Solar System, and the Planet Earth where life exists in all its variety and grandeur appear to a simple mind as a mysterious universe. There is a beautiful grandiose 'Universal Plan' conceptualized by the greatest architect, the Lord himself. The knowledge of Brahman would give a clear insight into this. Under this one universal plan the macrocosm as well as the microcosms are all created. The outer world, the Universe one perceives, is the macrocosm; and, it is this world that the physical scientists are interested in.

All the theories like the 'Big Bang' theory, the theory of Relativity of Einstein, the Strings theory or the 'p-Brane' theories of Stephen Hawkings, the Black Hole theory, or, the Field Theory in particle physics, the findings in molecular biology are all the outward fields of inquiry. All these pertain to lower knowledge, which do not hold any solutions to man's sensate life. The development in ancient Vedanta has parallel in modern physics in the revolutionary concept of the Electro-magnetic field introduced by Faraday and Maxwell. Further, the revolutionary discoveries of quantum and gravitational fields by nuclear science and relativity theory have parallel notions. The revolutionary field concept has now entered embryology too. One day, the scientists will find out the 'Reality' behind the 'unity of existence' that pervades the multiverse as "Vishnu' or 'Narayana', the cosmic flow that exists as potential energy in the atom and the 'Prana' in the living organisms, or simply 'supreme consciousness'. It is this omniscient, omnipotent, transcient, universal energy that is the creator, the protector, the sustainer, and the annihilator that is called God, the Almighty.

The Concept of 'Ishvara'

Ishvara is Brahman united with Maya. Ishvara is God personified and God with attributes. He is the personal God. Ishvara, though united with Maya, remains the master and ruler and controller of Maya. Devotion to Ishvara will make a man a saint. But one has to go beyond Ishvara to attain supreme Knowledge and Ishvara as God gives that ultimate Knowledge.

'Ishvara' is 'God'. Ishvara means, "one who grants liberation" and He, by his mere wish, can give liberation to whoever seeks it earnestly. He is the ruler of this universe. He is the one and the only supreme power. He is the embodiment of infinite source of knowledge and as such a special kind of Being, a teacher of all teachers. He can be realized by constant meditation with "Om". We can become Brahman, because Brahman is within us; but we cannot become Ishvara, because he is distinct, far above and beyond us. Vyasa Rishi in his Brahma Sutra, says that, 'no one will acquire that power of creating, ruling, or dissolving the universe, since that power belongs to Ishvara alone. If a man attains supreme knowledge, the knowledge of Ishvara, then he is liberated. In absolute reality, there is only the Brahman when the mind bcomes purified, the ego-idea thins out and the superimposition ceases; Ishvara and the world–appearance vanish in the blaze of transcendental consciousness.

There is no seer, no seen object but the Brahman, the single, all-embracing, timeless fact.

It is very interesting to know about this supreme ruler of the universe, 'Ishvara'. Brahman is the 'Reality' ('Sat'), the Absolute, and as such remains untouched by this universe and the like; He remains outside the universe and does not get involved in it. On the other hand, the power of creation of this Absolute, the Brahman is "Ishvara". Ishvara is endowed with the power of creation, sustainence, and annihilation. It is 'Ishvara' who with Maya has created this world! The union of Prakriti with Purusha has given rise to this objective world. Ishvara is the Purusha and Prakriti is maya. Purusha has derived all the power from the Brahman and, as such, He is the supreme power behind all the creation. Prakriti, by its association with purusha, has created the illusory objective world. Prakriti has no independent power as such; and its power of creation is derived from Purusha. Purusha is capable of dissociating from Prakriti at will. And, here is the clue. Anybody seeking liberation can identify the Purusha, the power within the self, and get liberated from the clutches of Maya, illusion or Prakriti! It is 'avidya' that binds man, the jeeva, with the objective world of Illusion, or Maya. Knowledge of the Self, or the Purusha will liberate the embodied jeeva from repeated births and deaths.

The Purusha resembles the Atman; it is formless, subtle, omnipresent, and it is beyond space, time and causality. It is beyond mind, senses and the intellect for comprehension. It is eternal, without a beginning and end, unborn, undying and uncreated. Its essential nature is perfection, freedom, immortality and unchangeability. Unlike the Atman, which is omnipotent, and one with the all-pervading Brahman, the Purusha is infinite in number. This is the reason why a person is liberated when the Purusha in him is realized and the rest of the persons have to strive for it.

The jeeva is the individual spirit and it is distinguished from the Purusha by its connection with Buddhi, the manas, and the senses. It is also limited by the adjuncts of the physical body. The Purusha is the pure self beyond the buddhi and the senses; on the other hand, the jeeva with its ego-sense 'ahanmkara', is its reflection in buddhi. We identify Purusha with buddhi and experience limitation, ignorance, pain and pleasure, and bondage. This is a temporary phenomenon and with the realization of the self, or dawn of knowledge of the Purusha within, we attain liberation. Thus, jeeva is, in reality, Purusha, the true self, in association with buddhi, the manas, the senses, and the body. The jeeva is bound by a gross physical body and has a subtle body of mind, senses, buddhi that are the product of prakriti. Its subtle body appears conscious due to its association with the Purusha and it is subject to Karma and rebirth. When the gross body dies, the subtle body continues to exist; all the memories are stored and transferred to a new body as flong as the Karma binds it. The jeeva takes another body according to its desire and whatever is upper- most in the mind at the time of the death of the jeeva will decide the nature of body to be taken in the next birth. But, a jeeva that dies with the name of "Narayana", or "Om" will merge in Him and becomes immortal.

The answers to man's problems lie in the ancient wisdom available in the Puranas, Veda, the Upanishads, and other ancient scriptures. There lies the greatness of Indian philosophy and religion. What the western scientific community failed to perceive even after centuries of thinking, research and experiments, the ancient saints and seekers perceived by their subtle mind, pure consciousness, and contemplation. By sheer yogic powers, the Seers could establish the 'unified theory and time-space-causation'. Time is eternal, 'Ananth'; Space is vast, endless, 'Ananth'. Both are 'Ananth', the one only and there cannot be two 'Ananths'! That itself is the 'cause'. So, there is no 'other' than 'That'. That is the One without the second, "*Ekamevaadvitheeyam*".

Isavasya Upanisad begins with the peace chant:

' Om! That the Invisible –Absolute is Whole (Infinite);
Whole is this the visible phenomenal;
From the Invisible Whole comes forth the visible one.
Though the visible Whole has come out from that Invisible Whole,
Yet the Whole remains unaltered. Om! Peace! Peace! Peace!'

Mahanarayana Upanishad [Sec.XII.16-17] declares,"In the citadel of the body there is the small sinless and pure lotus of the heart which is the residence of the Supreme. Further, in the interior of this small area there is sprrowless Ether. That is the center on which one must contemplate upon." See Brahmasutra I.3.14-21. He is the Supreme Lord who transcends the syllable Om that is pronounced at the beginning of the Vedic chantings, that is well established in the Upanishads and that is dissolved in the primal cause during contemplation. One must meditate upon this Mahesvara, risding in every heart!

One is advised to meditate upon Brahman as residing in the sun, the heart, and the eyes, because many special manifestations of divine glory are associated with these regions. One should perceive the spiritual entity behind the shining orb of the material sun. The idea of the Supreme State, realizable within the recess of the heart and having the characteristic of the Akasha, in that it holds the whole universe of evolving and the evolved is beautifully explained in *Chhandogya Upanishad.* "In the heart the Devas live, in the heart the Pranas are installed, in the heart exist the Supreme Prana and Light as also the immanent Cause with three-fold constituents and the Mahat principle". [*Brahmopanishad* III. 13].

The indefinite term "That" is used in the Upanishads to designate the Invisible-Absolute, because no other word or name can fully define It. God who is infinite and unbounded, cannot be expressed by finite, language. Therefore the Rishis and the Seers, desirous not to limit the Unlimited chose the term "That" to designate the Absolute. In the light of true wisdom the Phenomenal and the Absolute are inseparable. All existence is in the absolute; and whatever exists must exist in It. Hence, all manifestations are merely a modification of the One Supreme Whole, i.e., WHOLENESS, Samhita or Totality. It is ***'Poornam'*** and neither increases nor decreases nor diminishes. 'It' is That'!. The Whole therefore remains unaltered. "*Poornamadah poornamidam poornaat poornamudachyate'. [Ishavasya Upaanishad 1.1.*]

"Ishavasyam idam sarvam yatkincha jagatyaam jagat; Tyena tyaktena bhunjitah maa grudhahkasyasviddhanam"

Meaning, *"Om! Whatever there is changeful in this ephemeral world, all-this universe is the abode of the Supreme Lord. By this renunciation, support yourself. Do not covet the wealth of anyone."*

Ishavasya Upanishad declares that, *"All this, whatever exists in this universe, should be covered by the Lord"*. Having renounced the unreal, enjoy the Real. Do not covet the wealth of any man. Live on your own. '*Atmavan bhava*' meaning, rely on your own self. Your own self is more dependable than anything else, anybody else. Realise your own Self. Become '*Ekadandi*'; become a '*Paramahansa*'. If one should desire to live in this world a hundred years, one should live performing karma, the righteous deeds. 'Thus thou mayest live'; there is no other way. By doing this, Karma, the fruits of thy actions will not defile thee'. 'Do your Karma leave the rest to me.' [*Bhagavad Gita*].

Thus, these words of eternal truth should guide humans in all their thoughts and actions. Peace and prosperity are ensured for the righteous. Only greed and covetousness lead to temporary joy and endless misery. Sheer ignorance rules the minds of the mortals and unless effort is made to realize the truth, life is miserable in spite of all the wealth coveted from others.

Everything that we see, feel, hear is simply the manifestation of the Cosmic Intelligence'. They are all the various forms of cosmic energy such as the matter, thought-force, intelligence, and so on. The whole universe is His creation. It is all His projection, manifestation. To be more precise, it is He Himself, both the material and the efficient cause of this universe, and He it is that governs everything. He it is that gets involved in the minute cell, and evolves at the other end as God. He it is that becomes a small cell or an atom at the one end, and slowly unfolding His nature, regains Himself. This is the mystery of the universe. That is why, all the scripture teach us that," *We all come from God and go back to God"*.

Kenopanishad gives a vivid description of the method of 'God-Realisation'. It emphatically says, *"God is not this that people worship here"*. God is that force which makes the stars shine and planets obediently follow their stars. *For fear of Him, the stars and the planets perform their duties.* Ritam and Satyam govern their behaviour. God is behind every thought and action. He is behind every wink of your eye. He is the guiding spirit. He is the guiding force. He performs all functions for you. You are only a tool in His hands. It is for Him that you live here; and, but for Him, there is no place for you, there is no need of existence. Realise this '*Sat*', the eternal Truth. Say to yourself, "*Satyam Vadishyamai*". [See Prayer on opening page].

There is a beautiful description of the nature of Brahman or the "Highest Self' in *Shivajnyanamruta Upanishad [Mantra 3] "Brahman is the Absolute; He is Existence-Absolute, Knowledge- Absolute and Bliss Absolute". So He is called Svaroopa or the Essence. He is Self-luminous and does not need light from any other source; He is Light Absolute. He gives light to Sun, moon, stars, lightning, fire and intellect.*

Kathopanishad reiterates that:"The sun does not shine there, nor do the moon and stars, nor do these lightnings shine and much less this fire. When He shines, everything shines after Him, by His light, all these shine". He exists in the past, present and the future. He is beyond space, time and causation; He is immortal. He is "Adhi- Madhya- Antarahita". Fear comes from ignorance; it comes from duality. Duality is ignorance. Fear is a negative mental modification (thought). It has no existence in the presence of positive courage, mental strength. '*Meditation on Atman will infuse courage and destroy all fears*'.

"When there is only One, all-pervading, all- full Self, when there is no other seer but He, no other hearer but He, no other knower but He, no other thinker but He, how can fear exist in Brahman?

He is absolutely fearless. Fear is a thought wave, or ' ghora chitta vritti' or vibration in the mind that is caused by the attachment to body or possessions. If attachment and idea of 'mine-ness' and 'moha' are eradicated, how can fear exist in a Jnyani? [*Kathopanishad* V-15].

Do we need God?

We are born here on this earth due to the blemish of our soul, our desire, and sanskar or karma. We are ignorant and our mind is shrouded with ego, nescience (avidya), fear and desire. Our senses are out-going and powerful enough to keep us in darkness, never allowing us to look inward and 'see things as they are'. We are born weak and imperfect. Under these circumstances, it is the 'divinity' within us, the God who dwells in our heart, that shows the light. We only look to his image in the temples and confirm our faith in Him and look for his kindness, support, and guidance. So, if anybody asks, do we need God, the answer is very clear. It is an emphatic 'Yea', yes. Had we known all the answers to all our questions, had we been all powerful, if the world be so perfect that everything is fine, then there was no need for God. It is our imperfection; it is the vibration, the imbalance, disequillibrium that is the root cause of and the illusory world and it is our sheer ignorance that we believe it to be true. The moment everything becomes perfect, it (the illusory world) ceases to exist. The moment we become perfect, we become Gods and cease to exist (as humans). The need for God arises because this world is imperfect and we are all imperfect and we do not know what lies ahead, we do not know what would happen the next moment, and we want some self assuarance that there is some body who is taking care of us. We know that some one, 'All Merciful', kind and benevolent is there and we call Him, 'God'. This reassurance, this light at the end of the tunnel, this hope that one day everything would be all right keeps us moving. We hope and pray, we trust in Him and we move ahead. The moment we lose hope, there is misery, unhappiness, and delusion. We need Him, badly need Him for these uncertainties un-nerve us and kill us. It is 'He' who gives courage and strength. Not only do we need Him in times of distress, we need Him in happiness and joy, too. Man is caught up in the delusion of his being the truncated ego and its organic system and, under that illusion, behaves in petty ways and experiences suffering and sorrow, and scatters the same around in society. This is '*Maya*', and God's Grace or the Divine Grace alone will release him from this *Maya* and restores him to God. [*Bhagavad Gita* VII. 14].

Contemplate on the following Mantra:

"Om! Oh Gods, May we with our ears hear what is auspicious;
Oh ye fit to be worshipped, may we with our eyes see what is auspicious;
May we enjoy the life allotted to us by the Gods,
Offering our praise with our bodies strong of limbs. Om! Shantih, Shantih, Shantih!"

The Vedic concept of 'God' is important and more relevant today than ever. These Vedic Gods –Indra, Agni, Rudra, Varuna, Maraut, Maitra, etc. are the Deities that are very much present everywhere and one can feel their presence and effect. Veda recognize Indra as the Lord of the Gods, and, Sun, Rudra, Varuna, Mitra, Agni, Jal (water), Thunder and Lightning, and many other elements as Gods and define their duties as 'Deities' of different functions in this universe.

"Tadeva agnistadeva vaayustadsooryastadum chandramaah I
Tadeva shukramamrutam tadbrahmaa tadaapah sa Prajaapatih II
*[Mahanarayana Upanishad **I** .7]*

It is a fundamental theory in respect to the Soul that whatever appertains to it, is an un-created entity. The capacity of the Jeeva, its aptitudes and tendencies, its joys and sorrows, are the permanent attributes of the soul, undifferentiated from its essence. Hence, the bliss felt in 'moksha' is something not created and bestowed on the Mukta, but something which had all along remained latent and inherent in him and which, by the Grace and blessing of God became patent after redemption. It is the soul's essence that becomes unfolded and the manifest, the obstructions and impediments having been removed by God. Hence, redemption is self-realization, the bliss attained by a mere blossoming of the soul's essential nature, that too, by the Grace of the Lord.

"God Realisation'

"What delusion, what sorrow is there for the wise man who sees the unity of existence and perceives all beings as his own?" [Isavasya Upa.7]

The concept of '***Samashti***', which states that '*there is but one soul throughout the universe, all is but one existence*' is a great Vedantic view of existence. This concept is a leveler of all inequalities, rich and poor, strong and weak, advanced and backward; and, even the ugly and the beautiful, man and animal are included in this! This is a noble idea that heralds the real and basic solidarity of the whole universe, the ideal of ' the oneness of things'. It is this basic concept 'unity' that India offered to the whole world, the concept of 'universal brotherhood' and 'world peace and happiness', the concepts of "*vasudhaiva Kutumbakam*" and '*Sarve Jano sukhino bhavantu*", respectively. Here there is no distinction between man and beast or even the plants! This is the key to ecological balance. See the Rig Vedic Mantra given in the first page.

The first word of the first Mantra of Rk Veda is 'Ak'. The letter 'A' in this 'Ak' is the macrocosm, the Brahmanda and the letter 'k' is the 'kana', the microcosm and thus 'Ak' encompsses the whole multiverse. Anybody who understands this gets the 'wholeness, the 'samasthi' in all his thoughts and actions. His mind works in unity with his body and soul.

Adopting this basic concept 'Samashti', one can solve the present day maladies of development that have resulted in eco-degradation, environmental hazards, social inequities, and cruelty to animals. In order to understand this basic concept, one has to go to the depth of the Self, the immutable Brahman. Atman ('Being') is the Self. This Atman is hidden in all beings and it is not manifest to all easily. But it can be realized by means of the sharp and subtle reason of those who have been trained to enquire into and realize subtle truths. *Isavasya Upanisad* states that, "*He, the self-existent, is everywhere, without a body, without muscles, and without the taint of sin, radiant, whole, and pure, seeing all, knowing all, and encompassing all, He duly assigned their respective duties to the eternal Prajapatis". "The Self is one. Unmoving, it is faster than mind. Having preceded the mind, It is beyond the reach of the senses. Ever steady, it outstrips all that run. By Its mere presence, enables the cosmic energy to sustain the activities of living beings. It moves, and moves not. It is far and It is near; It is within all this and it is also outside all this". [Isavasya Upanisad.* 4-5, 8].

"Engrossment with the many without knowing the One behind it is the bane of ignorant life. 'The secret of the many is that the One can appear to be many without losing its identity. On knowing the One, the many lose their binding influence on the seer'."

Those persons who remain satisfied with the performance of the rituals only, and never strive to know the real significance of the works as explained in the scriptures, are rajasic and cannot attain to that sattvic state of life that rests upon the glorious union of the ritualistic actions with the knowledge of their full significance. But still worse are the persons who remain contented with the mere theoretical knowledge about the gods and sacrifices gathered from the scriptural study, and never stir themselves up for any action. They are tamasic, and as such, are necessarily relegated by their own inactivity to the inert state, which, of all levels of existence, is the one farthest away from the Truth. 'Mere conceptual knowledge of Brahman is not enough. It must be combined with the practice of spiritual disciplines'.

Not to speak of ordinary people, even great scholars fail to comprehend 'Atman'. Atman can be seen or realized through pure buddhi, since it is an ever-present datum of experience.

"Let the wisdom, 'prajnya' merge the speech in manas and the manas in buddhi; Let him merge the buddhi in the cosmic mind and merge cosmic mind again in the Self of Peace, the Atman, or the Purusha". Mahanarayana Upanishad [Sec.XIII. 1-5] gives a vivid description of that Supreme Reality,'Parabrahman' and implores that one should meditate on Him:

"Sahasrasheersham devamvishvaaksham vishvashambhuvam |
Vishvam Naarayanam devamaksharam paramamprabhum ||

Vishvatah paramamnityavishvam Narayanam Harim I
Vishvamevedam purushastadvishvam upajeevati II
Patim Vishvasyaatmeshvaram shaashvatam Shivam Achyutam I
Naaraayanam Mahaajnyeyam Vishvaatmaanam Paarayanam II
Naarayanam param Brahma tatvam Naaraayana parah I
Naarayanaparodhyaataa dhyaanam Naaraayana parah II
Yaccha kinchitjagatyasmin drushyate shrooyatopi vaa I
Antarbahischam tatsarvam vyaapya Naaraayanah sthitam II

'Narayana' is the Supreme-Reality designated as Brahman; Narayana is the Highest self; Narayana is the Supreme Light. Narayana is the Infinite Self. Narayana is the most excellent meditator and meditation. One should meditate upon the Supreme- the limitless, unchanging, all-knowing, cause of the happiness of the world, dwelling in the sea of one's heart, as the goal of all striving. The place of his meditation is the ether in the heart- the heart which is like an inverted lotus bud that turns towards the Sun when it is contemplated upon.

Katha Upanishad (V.12.13) presents the 'Atman', the 'Unlimited Reality' as also the 'Intimate Reality'.

" The one Supreme Controller of all the inner Self of all beings, who makes His one form manifold- those dheeras (wise men) who realize Him as existing in their own self, to them belongs eternal happiness and to none else".

"The Eternal among the non-eternals, the intelligence in those that are intelligent, who though one, fulfills the desires of the many, - those dheeras who perceive Him as existing in their own Self, to them belongs eternal peace and to none else".

" ... Glory of the Self that appears as man, the most glorious God that ever existed, or ever will exist, can never be imagined in books, scriptures, or sciences".

In day-to-day life, the Self is greedily possessed of this world. Without this Self, there is no world at all. And, yet, this conscious Self dies nightly when we sleep, and we cannot trace the stages by which in its stages it crept to an awareness of its own existence.

Normally, what we call personality may be only one of Nature's methods, a convenient provisional delusion of considerable strategic value. The more intelligent and comprehensive man's picture of the Universe has become, the more intolerable has become his concentration upon the individual life with its inevitable final rejection. One escapes from his ego by this merger, i.e., identification with and participation in a greater being, and acquires an impersonal immortality in the association, his identity dissolving into the greater identity.

According to the religious mysticism, the individual saves oneself by losing himself. In mystical teaching, the individual loses himself in the Deity; in the scientific interpretation, he identifies himself as 'Man'. The Buddhists teach that '*the individual life is a painful delusion from which men escape by conquest of individual desire*'.

"Self must be subordinated; it is a means to an end, but not an end by itself. Ego is a part of the ceaseless flow of Nature. The reality behind

this ego is the ultimate observer or 'Sakshi'. The Sakshin is that timeless being which witnesses all flow and change in the world of thoughts and things."

"Saakshin Prajnya"

'*Sakshin*' is the Supreme entity existing in a person. That is the eye of the eye, ear of the ear, taster, experiencer, thinker and all. Self is limited Man; Saakshi is the Universal (any other Man who is in similar moral and intelligent state of mind, absolute mind and unconditioned mind). The two important characteristics of the Saakshi are detachment and universality. It marks the highest point of perfection- the power of de-personalisation. In Bhagavad Gita, Sri Krishna tells Arjuna that,' *the true self of man is unborn, immortal, and eternal*'. (Gita Ch.II 16). It is also said, '*that the Sakshi being the Ultimate Subject, there is considerable difficulty in comprehending it truly*'. (*Gita*, II. 29). Further, 'when one attains the 'Sakshi'- consciousness, he finds life in an entirely new perspective. All the false values, which the ego attached to life and its functions, get destroyed. Thus life becomes beautiful and harmonious- in tune with everything else and with himself. Welfare of mankind and Universal Love becomes hallmark of such persons'. (*Bhagavad-Gita*, II 71, III 17, IV 18, XII 13-14&18-19).

There is a beautiful imagery of two falcon birds of golden plumage (Garuda, the Carrier of Vishnu), sitting on the branch of a tree, ["*Dvaa Suparna....*"] one eating the fruits, sweet and bitter, and the other witnessing this, sits immersed in its own glory [*Mundaka Upanishad* 3.1.1-2]. The bird enjoying the fruit is the man enjoying the fruits of action (Karma), the man deluded and feeling helpless. The bird witnessing it is the Self, Adorable and the Sovereign, ever free, realizing himself as but His glory. As the first bird finishes eating the fruits (of its action), it comes nearer and nearer the other bird (witnessing Self) and merges itself with the other (Realises the Self).

This is the reality that reveals itself to the discerning mind as the unchanging '*saakshi*' or witness of all the changing subjects and objects of the various states. Since it is not limited by any one particular state as the ego is, it is infinite. After realization of this truth, one does not desire to protect or defend oneself, because of the realization of non-duality and the attainment of the state of fearlessness. All ideas of hatred, offensee, self-protection, self-defense, and assertiveness proceed from fear, from a feeling of inadequacy with respect to the environment. That is why, it is said 'fear is the key'.

Realization of the Atman means realization of one's infinite dimensions and of one's spiritual unity with all; its fruit is infinite love and infinite strength. The Vedanta presents the Atman-Brahman as the 'Unified Experience Field' and, as such,"*inside all beings and outside all beings, He, therefore, is the all*".

In *Srimad Bhagavatam* VIII.3.3, it is clearly stated that:

"I take refuge in that self-existent Being, in whom is this Universe, from Whom is this Universe, by Whom is this Universe; Who Himself is this

Universe and Who is beyond this (differentiated Nature) as also beyond that (Undifferentiated Nature)".

'*Paramatman*' is Immanence and '*Parabrahman*' is Transcendence. Parabrahman when described as the cause of the universe is called "Parameswara" or "Prajapati". Parabrahman conditioned by the adjuncts of the universe is 'Prajapati', so is the 'Parabrahman'. Conditioned by the adjuncts of the body is termed a human being- 'Praja'. The same Prajapati who sustains vast oceans, planets, earth, and heaven enters as a seed or as a 'spark' and becomes the 'Jeeva' or the acting and enjoying agent on the earth. The Paramatman enters the seed and becomes the inner-most Self of all beings. Paramatman is the Supreme Self, "Virat" ensouling the universe. He that is dwelling in the body of all jeevas is the Self, the 'Atma'.

"Jeeva, the individual soul is the principle intelligence that co-exists with the Supreme Being; but it is thoroughly and absolutely dependent on Him", says Vedanta.

If the whole Universe is the product of a self-evolving cause, which Vedanta and modern physical science uphold, then that cause must be present in all its evolutionary products, which then can have no reality apart from it. This corollary follows, whether that cause is viewed as an intelligent principle- Brahman or Atman as in Vedanta, or as a non-intelligent background material, as in modern science. That one cause must account not only for all the objects of experience, but also for all the subjects of experience, and for all experience itself. The solar system being a product of the Sun, the food that we eat, as much as the human metabolic energy which digests it, the coal we burn, and the clothes we wear are all but solar energy in different manifestations. Einstein remarked that, "there is no place in this new kind of physics both for the field and matter, for the field is the only reality."

In Bhagavad Gita, Shri Krishna says," I am the *Kshetrajnya* (Knower of the field) since I am the Kshetra (the field). If one understands this concept of *Kshetra* (the illusory world) and the Kshetrajnya (the Sustainer of the world), then he knows 'God', the Supreme Power behind all this creation!

"Narayana is the Supreme-Reality designated as Brahman. Narayana is the highest Self, the supreme Light, 'param Jyoti; Narayana is the innate Self, the Infinite Self." [Mahanarayana Upanishad]

The Veda and the Upanishads recognise only one supreme Lord, Shree Hari Narayana, who pervades this universe, rather the multiverse; indeed. He is everything and there is no 'other'. He is the Parabrahman; He is the Atman; He is the Self who resides in every body. "*Whatsoever there is in this world known through perception or report, all that is pervaded by Narayana within and without" [Mahanarayana Upanishad* 13-5]

The knowledge of the 'Self' is the Supreme knowledge; it is the knowledge of the 'Brahman'. It is the attainment of this supreme knowledge that is the goal of life. It is the ambition of every Yogin to attain this goal of perceiving the "*Absolute Reality*", the "Truth"; and, it is the "Sat- Chit-

Anand". "Sat-chit-anand" is a spiritual experience that can be experienced only in nirvikalpa Samadhi. It is transcending the Gunas and establishing oneself in a state of complete annihilation of the vibrations that cause chitta vrittis, or the thought waves, i.e., '*manonasha*'. It is a state of exalted Mind of extraordinary purity that matches with pure Consciousness and merges with supreme consciousness. But, it should always be remembered that this is a rare experience that one can ever imagine! All the Veda and Upanishads hail the One who attains this extraordinary state of Mind and Consciousness, rather the one who merges in Him- the Brahman. It is the main objective of the Veda '*to know*' the Absolute, the Brahman, and merge in Him.

The Supreme Power

The Supreme power, the Creator, is referred to as the '*Mahapurusha*'. Actually there is no person or supreme person in the sense of 'Purusha' (Man) who is the Creator. It is a force that is inherent in the Absolute that contains everything in 'seed form' that appears as void, that can be experienced as 'vibrations', and is known as the 'Supreme-Consciousness', and that can be visualized as the 'Light within'. This Light is also called 'atma jyoti' and is the soul or the 'Atman'. It is called the '*Purusha*'. *Katha-Upanishad* [Verse XII- XIII] says that, "Purusha, of the size of a thumb, is like a light without smoke resides in the middle of the body (Heart), above the navel, as the Lord of the past and the future".

Brahmopanishad explains 'Purusha' as *"Brahman who shines forth as Brahma in the navel in wakeful state, Vishnu in the heart in dreaming state, Rudra in the throat in dreamless state, and Supreme Self, 'Indestructible One', in the head in the transcendental state. Again, He is the Sun, Vishnu, Ishvara; He is the Purusha; He is the Praana; He is the Jeeva, or the animate being, He is the Fire, the Ishvara, and the Resplendent; that Brahman which is transcendent shines within all these,* in Itself".

Kathopanishad [Verse VI} says that, "He who sees Him seated in five elements, born of tapas (tapas meaning heat, fire of Brahman), born before water, who, having entered the cave of the heart, abides therein, - ' this verily is'That'." Kenopamoshad goes to the extent of clarifying what is to be worshiped. It emphatically says,"It (God) is not what is worshiped here". What we worship here as the image of the Lord only reffirms our faith and trust in Him. It is a source of great strength to us in times of dire strait and turbulence in our day-to-day life. It restores our self-confidence.

Prayer

Prayer has a unique place in life. Prayer brings peace and happiness. One must pray for the peace and tranquility of one's mind; one must pray for happiness of the others. Prayer at all times is the best solution to all problems of life. Prayer can be associated with breathing exercises, though not strictly pranayama, i.e., rhythmic breathing, along with chanting of the names of the Lord, Ishtadevatha, Gayatri mantra, Vishnu Sahasra Nama or any other mantra is more productive. "Gayatri Mantra is the most potent of all the mantra". This mantra restores the disturbed mind to its natural self and brings wisdom, courage and peace. This is the way to live and be happy and successful in life. Whenever a doubt occurs in you, take to reciting a Chapter of Bhagavad Gita, or a few pages from Bible, or any sacred book you value most. Ultimately, it is your faith that is important. Each one has to find one's own salvation and it is up to oneself to realize freedom, mukthi, or moksha here and now, not in another world after death. *Meditation is 'panacea' for all the ills of this sensate world.* It is the disturbed mind that blinds or blurs our vision and blunts our capacity to think properly. This distrurbed state of mind can be restored to its natural self by Meditation. Sit comfortably, close your eyes, take deep breathing and utter "Om" concentrating on your heart. The job is done!

6

Storm in a tea cup

"Lead kindly Light amidst the encircling gloom,
Lead thou me on".

Life on this Planet seems like a long drawn drama that has neither a beginning nor an end. Each person gets an idea as to what is life accord to his ability to understand the same. But there is no one who can define the meaning and scope of life on this planet. The ancient sages contemplated over this problem for quite a long time and have come to certain conclusions that are worthy of consideration. These are clearly described in our ancient scriptures. The Veda, the Upanishads, the Bhagavata and other Puranas, the Bhagavad Gita, and other scriptures hold the key to life. Anybody in doubt can always go to these scriptures and get solutions to their problems. These are the 'mantra' that are like formulae of life.

What is life? Why life is a problem? Why is it for some life is a bed of roses and some always made to suffer for no fault of theirs? Why is it some people are born to poverty, misery, and sickness while some are born to affluence? First of all these are not at all questions that are difficult to answer. These are the questions that may be easily answered by any knowledgeable person. While it is true that taking birth in a rich family or a poor family is not in one's hands, at least it is true that one can live properly, judiciously and it is in one's own hands and there is no doubt about it. Let us analyze this aspect clearly.

It will be surprising to know that we are born here on this earth due to our own sweet will and pleasure. The cause of our birth is in our 'germ cell'. The seed of our birth is our desire and karma. We seek suitable parents whose desire and our desire wavelengths match and take birth. It is our karma and intent desires, rather the inherent unfulfilled desires, that forces us take repeated births. Somebody wants to become a prime minister and somebody wants to become a university Vice Chancellor, and yet another wants to become a supreme court chief justice and yet another wants to become a pilot or army major, and General. They all achieve their ambitions by taking birth in appropriate environment, get appropriate education and training, and achieve their goal ultimately to find it is not that what they wanted. It is thus they are driven to a real search for meaning of life and ways of self- realization. Some wise persons learn by others' mistakes. The very day one says to oneself that he is satisfied and contented it is the end of his cycle of rebirths. To reach this stage it is essential to attain a state of one hundred percent purity of the mind and purity of the soul, purity of the highest degree!

Only a blemish-less Soul has no rebirth. Desire is the blemish of the Soul. Only a hundred percent sattvic Soul is liberated from the cycle of rebirths. This state of liberation could be achieved by spiritual practices that are very hard in the present day life of all sorts of distractions. When one can reach the state of 'turiya' in 'samadhi' he can visualize the world of 'Sat-Chit- Ananda'- a state of Supreme Bliss. Thus, we are the cause of our own birth and our 'karma' as also, the cause of our suffering. A neem seed gives rise to a neem tree and a tamarind seed gives rise to a tamarind tree. Our sattvic life, our purified mind and soul render us spiritually strong and our tapas can burn all the sanchita prarabdha karma seeds, 'the germ cells' that are the source of our rebirths. A life of love and sacrifice is all that is called for here. So cursing anybody for own folly is of no use. The more one does good actions in this life and the more sattvic life one lives, one will find it easy to achieve this goal of liberation.

We are all living in what is called 'Mrutyu Lok', the land of death. Here every organism that takes birth will have to die one day; it has a cycle of birth and death and the cycle repeats till the jeeva is liberated from the shakles of desire, 'Moha Bandhan'

Some persons like Shree Shankaracharya and Shree Madhwacharya have studied deeply our ancient scriptures, have performed meditation and sadhana, and have realized the secret of life. They have spread their teachings through out the country. Hence, it is now possible for anybody to choose a path of his liking. One can live a reckless life of sensual enjoyment and suffer endlessly cursing every one, or one can choose a life of love and sacrifice and attain what he wants. The choice is in one's own hands.

The question arises why is that, this sort of a well-laid path to Salvation is never followed and people land themselves into trouble. It is due to avidya, ignorance and egotism. Both avidya and egotism are born with the person at birth; preponderance of tamasic and rajasic gunas rule the nature, or svabhava of the person that land them into trouble. Realised souls are those who develop sattvic guna and reduce the preponderance of tamasic and rajasic gunas in a slow and phased manner by spiritual exercises. This is one simple but very difficult method of getting rid of this magic or illusory world. In fact, this is the art of sane and sensible living and meditation helps in this.

Another important question is whether one can wish away this troublesome world in one birth. The answer is an emphatic 'NO'. It is not possible to get rid of the clutches of this gross sensate world in one birth. If one starts getting tuned to sattvic and spiritual life in this birth, it may take several births to get *'enlightenment'*, *Liberation, Salvation, Mukti or Moksha*, or whatever you call it, like the Buddha. Gautama Buddha or Mahaveera have taken several births before 'enlightenment'. It is important to note here that there is no doubt about 're-birth' in this concept of life on this planet.

In fact, the cycle of re-birth is the process of refinement, perfection, of the blemished, hence embodied, souls. And, it is the goal of life to wash off the blemishes of the soul and to attain fulfillment through the realization of the Self and not through fulfillment of desires. The more the desires are fulfilled, the more and more the new ones arise out of the impressions or memories or sanskar. Hence, the salvation lies in the abnegation of the self as identified by the body and mind, and its desires, cravings for the mundane, and realization of the true Self. It is a long drawn process, and evolutionary theory confirms this.

'Dukhatrayas'- Problems of life

Life is governed by '*Tapatrayas*'; 'Taapa' means heat and 'traya' is three. Three types of 'taapaas' trouble us. These are: one, created by ourselves; two, created by others; and, three, those created by nature. Those created by nature cannot be solved and only the Lord Almighty should come to help. Earthquakes, floods and famine are created by nature. The trouble created by others, too, can be solved by our tact and intelligence. But, the most formidable ones are those created by ourselves! Whom do you blame for the problems of your own creation? Most of the problems are our own creations. There are the 'Aadhi', 'Vyaadhi', and the 'Upaadhi'- pertaining to the 'kleshas' (problems) that affect the body and mind causing diseases ('dis'- ease). Kapila recognizes three sources of our misery, 'dukha'. The one created by the self, by one's action- commissions and omissions (karma); the second created by the Nature; and, the third, created by others, particularly the wild beasts. There is no easy solution to the misery created by Prakriti, such as earthquakes, cyclones, and storms, floods and fires.

Problems of life are many and varied. In fear, all these problems are really not serious problems at all. They are like the 'Storm in the Tea cup'! They vanish with time, sooner than they appear. But we have no patience we are anguished impatient. To find solutions to these problems, one need not go too far. No one needs to retire from active life and seek 'sanyas' or ascetic monkhood and retreat to mountains, unless one wants spiritual attainment through severe 'tapas'. But, to live here and now, to get rid of the pressure and heat of life, and enjoy the warmth and peace of life is the purpose of this study. Warmth of life comes from love and sacrifice; heat of life comes from hatred-ness, strife, jealousy, greed and selfishness. The formula of '*I love you, you love me*' will not work here. Love means to unite and when you love somebody you have already become a part of the 'other' in spirit, and the' other' simply does not remain as 'the other'.

A clarion call, 'Oh! God, I need you', only will help. In order to understand the tricky life, one has to ask simple questions like who am I? What is it I want from life? These two questions will solve half of, or most of, the problems. It is due to ignorance that one suffers in life.

Why Life is a Problem?

Life is a problem for those who do not know what is life. A Jnyani will not complain about life for he knows what is life and how to live it. It is all in the *Mind* and *Mind Control*. All problems arise out of 'avidya', ignorance. Only an awakening, awareness, 'Knowledge' will pave the way for happiness and success in life. For an ignorant man problems are many and they are coming as 'taapatrayas'- three forms of heat.

Although, the problems of Life are many and varied, the source of all these is the same. It is our 'desire', selfishness, greed and avarice, and our inconsiderate behaviour towards others. But, still more important is the

'Reality' that governs our lives. These are more beautifully explained in the Veda and the Upanishads than in the modern day science text- books. May it be hunger and thirst, sexual urge and marriage, children and friends, the problems are the same. The answer to the life's problems can be easily found in Vedanta, ***Vedanta is the Key to happiness and success in life.***

Hunger and Food

As already stated, Aadhi, Vyaadhi and Upaadhi are the three 'tapatrayas'. These emanate from 'ignorance', or 'Maya' (avidya) that governs our lives. Most of the problems of our physical wellbeing are created by ourselves- by our life style, our food habits and tastes, our attitudes, moods and mind.

Chhandogya Upanishad gives an elaborate description of food. It is very important that one should take care of what he is eating, because "*Mind consists of food*" [*Chhandogya Upanishad* VI 5.4]. The grossest part of food goes waste while the middle part is transformed into flesh and the subtlest part goes to form the mind. It is like the butter, the subtlest part of the curds that comes up due to churning. Pure food gives pure mind and good memory; it helps to realize the true nature of this world. Cold and stale food is tamasic and leads to indolence, inactivity, lothesomeness; and, hot and spicy food are rajasic, disturbing the calm disposition of mind leading to restlessness. Therefore do not give junk food speacially to children. Avoid junk food as far as possible.

Food is Elusive

Search for food is the most important driving force in man and it is hunger that keeps him on the move. Why is food evasive? Although food is available in plenty, it is not easily obtained by man to quench his hunger; even water is available, but not food! Why is it? The answer lies in the mystery of the origin of the universe. It is, again, illusion or 'Maya'; it is the divine 'Leela'. When the Lord created life he also created food. First - manifestation of Brahman is the Sun (Energy) and the second manifestation is the Moon (food); Moon is i.e. anything that reflects the sunlight, the food to the Sun. As regards the earth, the Sun and the moon also stand for time, the solar year, the lunar month, the Shukla Paksha and the Krishna Paksha and the days and nights, etc. The waxing and waning of moon is the consumption pattern of the Sun. In other words, the energy, space, and time are the earliest manifestations of the Brahman, the Supreme-Conciousness, i.e., the eternal 'cosmic flow'. Flow as it clearly shows is movement; the food, the Brahman in his manifest form, is evasive! When food was created in water it started moving. The Lord tried to catch it by his mind, but could not reach it; He tried by the eyes, the ears, the nose, the skin and the tongue but failed to catch it. Then He Himself entered into it through the mouth with air Vayu and reached the stomach the navel. Hence, food remained elusive and it is not within the reach of the mind or the five sense organs. If it were so, by mere thinking or thought of food, one would be satisfied! One would be happy and contented with mere sight of food, sound of food, smell of food, and touch of food. Even the generative organs cannot reach for food unless Brahman enters through the mouth as Prana in the form of air. It is only when food along with Prana Vayu reaches the naval plexus, center of consciousness, and Vaishvanara Deva, the Jataragni, consumes it, the person is satisfied; remember, the hunger continues day after day, and year after year till death consumes the body!

The whole pattern of food chain is a very tricky business, like each bigger fish swallowing the smaller fish. When the tiger falls on a deer and kills it, the Jnyani knows that there is neither the tiger, nor the deer and its death. The deer and the tiger are merely different names and forms and killing an action identified by our ignorant mind and the senses. The Veda proclaim "Annam Brahma" and the jnyani knows that neither there is an eater, nor the edible, nor the eating. It is all one 'That Inseparable Brahman'! It is the ignorance that makes us believe all that appears in this sensate world as real. Name, form, and function mislead us. Meditate on Him and the screen dissolves, illusion dissolves.

It is again the Self, the Consciousness (Prajnya), the Enjoyer of the food; for namesake, it appears like the one eaten by man; but, actually it is an yajnya. The food offered to Vaisvanara Deva, the Jataragni. Since the mantra says "Annam Brahma", the food is the visible God. Brahman manifests in different forms and rules the life on this planet earth. Hence, it is the Vedic dictum that one should never disrespect any food! Any person with spiritual attainment will not find it very difficult to get food. For him, food is available in plenty, enough and to spare! Veda proclaim, one should work hard, earn by self-effort enormous food, only to give it away to the hungry and needy.

Food sustains Prana with air (Vayu) and water (Jal). When a man is dying due to hunger, the first thing that he requires is food. Five morsels (handful) of food is just sufficient to regain the life of a man dying of hunger. With the first morsel, his dull brain will become more active (helps to regain memory); with the second morsel his closing eyes will open slowly. With the third morsel, his dying sound comes back. With the fourth his body will regain strength to sit up and the fifth morsel will make him stand on his own and he will exclaim that his life has come back! Offering a hungry man food is the most sacred duty of every human being.

Here again there is an interesting story about Uddalaka teaching his son Svetaketu by experiment how food is converted into mind. As we all know Milk contains butter; butter comes out of churning of curds (made out of milk). Butter is thus the subtlest part that rises out of the churning of curds. Similarly, Uddalaka told Svetaketu, "*That which is the subtlest part of the food that is eaten rises and becomes mind. The subtlest part of water that is drunk rises and becomes prana. Thus, my dear, the mind consists of food, prana consists of water and speech consists of fire*".

It is through sattvic food, one can develop a calm and serene mind that can perceive the Atman. A volatile mind is the cause of all the unrest, unhappiness and misery. One should avoid Rajasic food- excessively hot, sour, bitter, sweet and saline food. Similarly, Tamasic food- cold, stale, over-night stacked in cold storage should be avoided. Only fresh, balanced and agreeable food should be consumed in limited quantity, enough and to sustain the body. A Jnyani or a Wise man will take food in limited quantity like medicine. Essentially man is not the mind but the Self or Atman. The Atman is ever free, infinite and eternal. It is pure consciousness. Mind is an instrument in the hands of the Self through which man apprehends and responds to the external world. Since the mind is always vascillating, changing constantly, it makes the world appear changing; if the mind is made to be calm and serene it can reflect the Atman and reveal the true nature of the world. When one knows oneself as the Atman, there is no longer a mind needing control. Hence, sattvic food is one of the essential requirements for a happy and successful life.

Life teaches us lessons at every stage. If one is alert and attentive, he can learn the lessons to better his life. The ari-shadvargas cause misery to man and one should learn to control the senses. It is the avarice, greed, ego, jealosy, anger, and selfishness that bring misery. One should conquer fear and live a life of selfless service. One should develop equanimity towards all the fellow beings. Sympathy, compassion and helpfulness are the basic qualities of human beings that need be cultivated. This is emotional quotient that is more important than the Intelligence Quotient (IQ). Spiritual Quotient (SQ) is important in that it changes man into a 'human' and leads him towards divinity. Together, these make an integrated personality of a person.

Another important question that haunts us is that of 'luck' or destiny. It is true that God's Grace protects us by giving us strength- moral and spiritual. It is also true that one who performs his functions in the name of God achieves enormous success. But, luck alone is not in any way helpful. Absence of ego is the first pre-requisite of success and happiness in life. Pride nullifies all good actions while humility and trust in God brings success.

Absolute Faith in the 'Almighty' is a sure path to success. Devotion, total dedication, concentration, and total submission are essential requirements of a successful life.

Ultimately, it is God's Will. Since man has no knowledge of the future, it is He who will guide all persons in times of need or distress. Only those who submit totally to Lord Almighty will get His attention; in a sense He gives strength and courage to face life and provides clues to pass the test of life. Without His grace, nothing is possible in this worldly life. Even to tune oneself towards Him needs His Grace. '*Trust in God' is essential to success and happy life*.

Many people have asked the question "if God's Will be done, where is the need for human effort'? This is true. If God or Lord Almighty rules our destiny, a doubt arises as to what is our role in life. The answer is simple. '***He helps those who help themselves***'. One has to perform his duty without anticipation of anything in return. Every action is performed as if by divine inspiration and offered to the Lord. This is the secret of success and happiness. Giver is one who has plenty and he has got everything to give; but the actions of our past decide the results of our action. Each one gets according to his karma. If one has done good deeds in the past, the fruits of the good actions come sooner or later in this life. Those who do not believe in the karma theory depend on their rational mind that does not help in understanding the sublime and infinite truth. Ego speaks in such cases. It is 'I' which makes one forget the Creator. One has to do his duty and leave the rest in the hands of the Lord. Bhagavad Gita holds the key to success and happiness in life.

Now, as to the living and enjoyment of life on this earth, there is a very *simple formula.* Find out the level of consciousness at which you operate. We are living on the periphery and it is difficult to go to the centre of Consciousness. Most of us are living and operating at lower levels of Consciousness that does not require much energy. The centres of Consciousness decide about the nature of one's status in life. Those who live and operate at lower levels, i.e., the level of navel and below are engaged in fulfilling their basic instincts of life like any other animals. Probably, they are at lower scales of evolution. They are consciously aware of their 'Annamaya Kosha' and 'Pranamaya Kosha'. Some of them excel in one of these 'koshas' and achieve great success, too. A few of them rise above the level of awareness of these two layers and reach the 'Manomaya Kosha' and try to understand the mysteries of life. But those who realize higher levels of Consciousness reach 'Vijnyanamaya Kosha', and very few reach the innermost centre of 'Anandamaya Kosha' and enjoy the Supreme Bliss.

Hence, the level of Consciousness at which one operates is very important. One can excel at any of these levels by pure will power, personal efforts and Lord's Grace. It is only the enlightened persons who realize the need to rise to higher levels of Consciousness; it takes several births to reach the higher stages of evolution. Buddha says, it took five hundred years for him to reach the highest state of Pure Consciousness,

One must consciously be aware of one's spiritual status and position in life in order to move forward; but this awareness is rarely possible. Normally, everybody has not got the capacity to understand these secrets. Hence, it is advisable to take the guidance of an enlightened person or a spiritual leader. But, it is hard to find a true Guru. So one has to look inward to one's own soul for guidance and thus become one's own Guru. This is possible only by concerted sincere efforts. Develop purity of mind and heart.

Now, one very important question arises here. Is it necessary to take to *Sanyas* to attain liberation or freedom from the drudgery of life? This is a very important question that bothers most of the youngsters. To take to a more rigid ascetic life, i.e., mon hood does not come easily to one and all. Only initiated persons, may be those already initiated to spiritual life in the previous birth, can take to this course. Others who are born with an inherent desire to fulfill their unfulfilled desires have to struggle hard in this life. It is our desire, inherent desire of past lives that makes us undergo all the travails of life here. One can remain a householder, live an austere life, and gradually turn to the Lord for guidance. A very simple life, dedicated to the selfless service of the fellow beings with love and compassion is all what is required of this life. It is very true that one has to work hard to earn wealth in order to help others. But, material prosperity and the 'ego' that is growing with it should be offered to the Lord in total submission. This is the sure path to success and happiness in life.

Well, can one become wise and realize the Self within, with all the knowledge of the scriptures and the spiritual practices, is a very important question. It should be clearly understood that each one has to live and experience his life himself. One should remember the advice of Sri Krishna to Arjuna. After the divine vision of '*Viswa Roopa*', Arjuna is advised to simply forget everything the Lord has taught and shown, and revert to his simple duty. So no scripture can help in the Self- Realisation process and it is one's sadhana and personal experience that is very important. Whether learned or not, everyone can reach the goal by sheer perseverence, devotion, love and sacrifice.

Lord Jesus has stressed a good deal on this aspect of love and sacrifice, and the Bhakti cult of the Hindus stress the devotional aspect. The Buddhists try to practice a life of restraint and become monks in order to desist desire. Jainism preaches to practice compassion. So, in one way or the other, all the religions of the world preach only one thing and that is to live a simple life of love and self -sacrifice. There is happiness in giving and there is no doubt about it. Bookish knowledge is absolutely of no use, unless one practices the teachings of the enlightened souls. Not all the pages of the calendar or panchanga showing the rain-bearing stars will ever give a drop of water and no Veda or Upanishad and Puranas will show God.

A very important secret of success of life is to shift from 'Body-consciousness' to 'Soul-consciousness'. No body asks you to resist temptations of life and feel frustrated or disappointed. In fact, Sanyas (ascetic life) is not an answer to the life's problems. Only, be aware of the temptations and the way it leads you to. Live a life of full awareness and become a 'Sakshi' to yourself. Watch your thoughts and action. When you enjoy life, enjoy so well that you do not hanker after it any more. Be satisfied with what you get. Do not allow discontent and greed to take over. Once you fully enjoy what you get and do not live on its memory or hope, you are liberated. Live a happy and contented life. Do not fall prey to greed and avarice. Contentment is very important. There is no end to greed and sensuous pleasures that only lead to sickness of body and mind. Restraint from excessive sexual indulgence, or for that matter, any excessive indulgences are forbidden. That does not mean denial of the essential requirements of life. The golden rule is "*this far and no further*"

Problems of Life

There are a few things in life that are not considered problems in the beginning, but turn out to be very serious due to lack of understanding, knowledge and training. Marriage is one such. It is an inevitable course; it is intended for salvation!

Marriage

Legally speaking, marriage is an agreement for union between two persons. In modern times, it is an institution that is much abused due to lack of knowledge. Marriage is one thing that is totally misunderstood, mistaken, and misused and all our misery lies in our misunderstanding!

Marriage in Hindu religion is very sacred and it aims at union of soul with the objective of liberation, emancipation, or moksha. It is essential that one should get married and undergo all the troubles and travails in order to attain moksha. What a contradiction! On the one hand the person wants to get liberated and on the other, he has to get married, bonded to get liberated. This appears to be confusing, contradictory, and absurd. But the reality is that the man and wife are the Purusha and Prakru ti- each is incomplete without the other. The energy concept is that the male and the female must unite to attain to liberation as 'full', complete, 'being'. The body, mind, souls and the sexual energy – all together should in unison transcend to attain to liberation. This is the secret. Union of sex is the outward expression and marriage is said to be a public announcement of the private intention. There is nothing wrong in that. It is for sex, honestly, that everybody gets married. But, this hope of sexual union bringing happiness soon turns out to be disappointing and frustrating since it is body-oriented and mind-centred. It is the spiritual aspect of marriage that brings supreme happiness. The union of soul in a spirit of total abandonment of the self brings total happiness. There is no place for self-gratification and selfishness in marriage. It is all give, give and only one should not be disappointed if he does not get anything in return. Always remember the fact that marriage is between two different persons, totally opposite, physical entities- body, mind, soul, and sex. The female is down to earth in reality and the male is sky, high up, and beyond reach. It is well neigh impossible to remain united for long when each is pulling in opposite directions. The Male is always spirit, freedom-oriented, and seeks liberation, and pulls upward ('svar'), while the female is always gross, grounded to reality of material world ('bhu') and seeks to pull down. The male is attracted to the 'spirit' aspect of life, sooner or later in life, while the female is attracted to all sorts of shining material objects and she herself remains a fantasizing, tantalising and entertaining! There is no wonder the two seek to depart in opposite directions sooner or later. Only spiritual union can bind them for some longer duration of life/lives. The battle of the sexes remains.

Some people think that marriage is a solution to problems of youth and unfortunately it turns out to be the source of all problems. For some, the problems of life start with marriage whereas for others, it starts later with the children. Problems of life, more popularly called 'Samsaar Tapatraya', is actually a self-created one although it appears that our custom, social system and the elders force us into it. It is the one that we willingly embrace due to our ignorance. Marriage is treated as a solution to problem of loneliness and parents wish to see their children settled in life. It is one avidya that leads us to fulfil the carnal desires, the desire of the flesh, through the institution of marriage and family. The Upanishads warn of the dangers of this and implore celibacy for spiritual attainments. Marriage and family is the path of delusion and, sooner or later, one is sure to be disappointed. The reason is very simple. As already stated, in marriage the Purusha pulls up while the Prakruti pulls down and finally the latter releases the clutch and relieves the former from bondage of repeated births. Buddha is very clear about this and advocates absolute celibacy and monkhood if one has to attain spiritual enlightenment and liberation; otherwise, bondage is inevitable. The cause of rebirth is desire of the flesh. The cause of misery is the desire of the flesh. The cause of old age and pain is the desire of the flesh. One who conquers the desire crosses the ocean of sanasar.

It is in the fitness of things, and quite natural that when children come of age, their mind is tuned to the fulfilment of desires of the flesh. It is the natural order that opposite poles attract each other and the entire behaviour of the atom is the divine will. The most outstanding duality of this world is evident in the attracting forces of opposite qualities. Extreme opposite gunas are 'catching' and boys and girls of teens become more charming and attractive. It is the vibrations, the gunas that rule the life.

The word' marriage' means, 'agree to' and this agreement without a strong basic understanding of meaning of life create all the problems of life. With the passage of time, with affinity, and familiarity, the dark secrets of life start getting unfolded. This marriage has a nasty habit of unfolding its ugly side, as one slowly gets deeper and deeper into bondage. Unfortunately, it is the desire, Kama- one of the pusrusharthas that is considered as the very purpose of life! It is said that, No Hindu is fit for redemption unless he is married and begets a son so that he can transfer his family responsibilities and take to spiritual quest.

Marriage is an important event in life that shapes or ruins a man or woman. All of us, or most of us, enter into marriage without any preparation to embark the family way of life. There is a saying that, 'marriages are made in heaven and it is only celebrated here'. How true it is! We have seen instances where the 'divine plan' only will operate. Girls get their boys as if predetermined under strange circumstances and, families distant and unknown are united. It seems the same relations of the previous births continue in different names and forms and functions. The Upanishads declare that there is no such thing as father, mother, son and daughter; it is one supreme soul that pervades and, under delusion, creates the images of many.

It is customary to arrange for the marriages of children and then celebrate it. But, in modern days where boys meet the girls freely and come to know each other, arranged marriages have come to be treated as old-fashioned by the youngsters. In present day life, there is greater freedom and privacy than in early days and there is no inhibition in youth. However, some boys and girls still prefer to go in for arranged marriages than selecting one's own life partner.

Social status, religion, caste and sub-caste, economic status, educational achievements, professional status, are some of the important considerations in selecting the bride or the bridegroom. Personal likes and dislikes come later. It is here conflicts arise. It is difficult to match all preferences and come to amicable settlement. With the result there is always some dissatisfaction lingering in the minds of the young as well as the old. At some stage, some thing or the other has to be sacrificed, rather will have to be compromised. Still payment of dowry haunts in both traditional and modern families to a great extent. This cannot be totally wiped out.

Apart from the feelings and opinions of the parents, nearest and dearest, the feelings of the newly wed shall be considered here. Besides different social background of the couple, there is the 'stranger' feeling in arranged marriages. Language and communication problem, social background, economic background, educational staus greatly influence the first meeting. But the most out-weighing factor is the sex. Honestly, every body marries for sex. It is natural that the institution of marriage guarantees sex within bounds. It is here the problems start. Marriages that guarantee sex at body level and mind level do not succeed for the simple reason that the boy and the girl will soon find out each other's defects for, nobody is perfact. Each one has got his or her strong points and weak points. It is but natural, that strangers as they are at first in arranged marriages, both soon form an adamantine wall on some sensitive issues and marriages collapse due to ego factor and disillusionment at the earliest opportunity.

Many marriages have collapsed for the simple reason that the marriage partners cannot adjust, do not accept their deficiencies, and do not develop sense of trust, faith and mutual respect, let alone love. False prestige and sense of self- respect and ego rule their mind and no other consideration counts. If any one of the marriage partners is mature enough to adjust, cooperate and be considerate the marriage will succeed. Both the boy and the girl have formed unrealistic ideas and they are in a very impressionable state of mind. Fantasy and images rule the mind and this take them away from reality. Soon both are disappointed. Fantasies melt at the first hand knowledge of reality. No body wants their dream to be disturbed rather shattered!

Love and Marriage

Falling in love is the most common thing that we hear these days. But, rarely have we heard of anybody rising in love and enjoying the bliss of married life. The two most contradictory and conflicting basic concepts are love and marriage. Love is a state of inebriated or intoxicated mind based on fantasy or imagination of the mind. Love is a magical transformation. It is a chemical flow that is initiated by the imageries and memories and fantasies of the mind. That is why they say love is blind. When the figure or face of a person matches its image in the memory of the sub-conscious of another person, it clicks! It may be 'love at first sight' or at 'repeated sights'. There is no rational or scientific explanation for this; but love is a basic quality of all creatures. But, still, some scientists claim that the smell of a mother or father is the internal guiding factor in 'falling in love'. It may be match of gunas, likes and dislikes, mutual interests, and what not!

If love is blind, marriage is an eye-opener. Marriage is a practical solution to the man or woman's natural physical urge of sex and social security. Where the love factor takes an upper hand, the person is not in the normal state of mind to understand anything, let alone the pros and cons of their action based on it. Most of the children get disappointed very early in life as the reality of life strikes and they get a jolt; some even succumb to it! It requires two strong minds to get into permanent union in love and this is again a fantasy! No marriage is an utter success unless proved to be so to end, i.e., ripe old age. One may feel disappointed and dejected at the end of his life and this is the case with most of us. It is an illusion and blind faith that one thinks that marriage would help solve all problems and jumps into it. But, soon it would be realized that marriage creates more problems. This is because of the fact that marriage is not a solution; it is only a means to salvation. The institution of marriage is a social constraint and one is not bound by it if attainment of Supreme Bliss is the goal.

Bliss and Blisters of Love Marriage

Before we get into this subject, it is very interesting to know why we love. In marriages, whether arranged one or love marriage, marriage, i.e., union of body and mind is of main concern. In Love, it is the underlying psychological disposition that is important. One is attracted to things due to two reasons. One reason, although we cannot say it is' reasoning' in the strict sense of the term for there is no reasoning in love, it is the attraction of the object that draws our mind and makes it dwell on it. This attraction may be due to some sort of an inner urge emanating from the subconscious, or the attributes of the person like beauty, or the external qualities (behaviour) that are impressive to our mind. Sometimes, the object may not be really beautiful or attractive; but still we love it because our mind dwells on it of its own accord! It is this mind, *dwelling of mind* on a certain person, animal, place, or thing or God and becoming one (union or marriage) with that is what we call 'love'. There is no reasoning here. Just the mind dwells on it due to its previous impressions, memories or samskars. We cannot reason it out. Suddenly a flash of memory (may be of the previous birth?) drives the mind to such an act of 'falling in love'. That is why it is said, 'marriages are made in heaven'.

When we get good friends, lovers, or pets and intensely love them, it is this 'sanskar' that is responsible for such 'love'. That is one of the reasons why all our relationships are believed to be the result of the memories, impressions and sanskars, philosophically speaking. If a persons falls in love and gets married, may be it is the' divine will', fulfilment of a desire of the previous birth, and thus, an old relationship is re-established (in this life). In a sense, all the multitude of creatures on this earth, including human beings, are the results of a magic wand waved by the Lord. That is why this' Prapancha' is called 'Maya'.

When it comes to happiness in marriage, in the beginning everything appears happy and blissful. In the heat of passion, in the dream of fulfilment, married life appears to be blissful. It appears as if a heaven on earth! It is sheer ecstasy and joy, but, alas, short-lived! The bliss turns to blisters as the reality dawns! Married life is not a bed of roses. No marriage, whether arranged or love marriage, will ever guarantee instantaneous success unless sincere efforts are made to sustain the marriage by both the marriage partners. Dualities rule the game of marriages. It is especially so in the case of intercaste or cross-culture or international love marriages. When the charm fades, the reality of life stares at the face and everything that appeared beautiful, attractive earlier begins to look ugly, repulsive and intolerable. It is always the opposites and the opposites remain the same until joined by the will and grace of the Lord.

Both types of marriages, love marriage and the arranged marriage, do not assure any success. Success is not assured unless and until all efforts are made by the life partners (or, at least one of them) and, both sincerely strive to make it a success. Both love and marriage lose luster and glamour soon as reality dawns to day-to-day life problems. Threat of 'break-down' stares at every corner of life and it takes time to understand and adjust in marriage. First year, the third year, the seventh year of marriages are crucial in a person's life; they are the turning points. Birth of children may bring some relief. Joint family may or may not help in this respect. Ultimately, marriage is still treated a gamble in life.

Success in Marriage

Only spiritual union, 'union of souls', guarantee success in marriages. Both the life partners should be soul mates to succeed in married life; both must mutually strengthen the spiritual bondage and God is the only one with whom one can be reliable and happy. With every feeling of bliss of marital happiness, a blister arises and it is only a spiritual or divine blessing that can ward of this duality. This is the meaning of life; this is the reality of the world how it exists and how it works. Meditate on Him and praise the "leela of the Lord'!

One secret of success of marriage, as also, the art of living is given here. It is the recognition of the prepondering gunas and the vibrations of the person and properly responding to the same. A proper understanding and careful attention to these factors will help reduce the heat and irritations in marriage and bring some happiness to the couple. If both the marriage partners are of the same prepondering gunas, preferably sattvic guna, their marriage will succeed. If one of the couple is of sattvic guna and the other tamasic, it may be dull but gives no serious problem. But, if both the couple is of prepondering rajasic guna and the couples vie with each other for selfish ends and, ego rules their mind, such marriages create hell of a problem. The two will never compromise and sooner or later it breaks. It will be an indifferent marriage if the wife is of sattvic guna and the husband is of rajasic guna or vice versa. The prepondering gunas are what make the quality of the person and the person's behaviour varies according to the change in the prepondering guna; no person will ever remain the same.

Ultimately, it is spirituality rather than sexuality that governs a successful marriage. This is one of the reasons why the children should be given a spiritual training and should be guarded against the corrupting tendencies. Good company, family background, good moral and ethical education are the essential requirements. All these come under 'samskar' and good parentage is very important. Mimic of Western way of life of unbridled freedom and sensuality, valueless moral and social behaviour of the elders are corruptive. Many powerful evil forces are at work in our so-called modern society and children should be well guarded! Children should not get any opportunity to imbibe the character and even a flavour of the soul-less materialistic society that has already pervaded life of people in India.

Role of Sex in Life

We find that sex is a great force that pervades our life from adolescent age to ripe old age. Some are so obsessed with sex that they do not seem to come out of it. Ultimately it becomes a sickness. What exactly is the sex energy? *Kena Upanishad* has dealt elaborately with the role of Prakriti and Purusha. One view is that, it is Indra who perceived Uma, the daughter of Himavat as the symbol of sex in the place of Brahman. It should be remembered here that Uma stands for the self-effulgent knowledge and one view is that of sex symbol. It is believed that where Indra, the mind, rules, Uma or sex energy pervades as Brahman. This concept led to tantric sex and realization of Brahman through sex energy in ancient India. But, sex energy is the life force and it pervades the whole body. This is one of the reasons why ascetic life, a life of total abstinence from sex activity, is advised for the serious spiritual aspirants.

Conservation of sex energy is very important for raising the level of consciousness. It is also true that Uma stands for the self-effulgent knowledge that stands for Brahman and only three Devas, i.e., Indra, Agni and Vayu came very close to Brahman; of these, it is Indra only who had the direct perception of Brahman through Uma. Thus, it is very neigh impossible for ordinary mortals to realize the Brahman. Asuras stand for animal propensities in man and the constant fight between the Devas and Asuras mean the conflicting Pravrittis. Brahman can be realized only when man gets rid of the animal propensities. With knowledge, ignorance vanishes and with the disappearance of ignorance the problems, too, vanish. This is how one gets out of the riddles of life through realization of the Self, the Brahman. Instead of this spiritual approach that cures the man of the diseases, the Western scientists try to cure the diseases of the man. They forget that man is the centre of the problem. It is paradoxical that patients suffering from mental illness go to psychiatrists and finally fall in love with them. The Psychiatrists give a very patient hearing, show understanding and sympathy and finally fall in love with the patients. This creates another problem! Some doctors treating the mental patients become so obsessed that they too become mentally afflicted.

Western Psychologists such as Sigmund Freud and Alfred Jung go to the extent of identifying sex as the whole life and treat all problems of life as problems of sex only. The profession of psychoanalysts and psychiatrists is thriving on this concept of sex as the root of all mental illness. While it may be partly true that sex governs life and mental sickness is connected with sexual fulfillment, it is not wholly correct to say that all problems are connected to sex. Sex plays a significant role in early adolescent life and early maturity stage of life and loses its importance as and when man becomes spiritually mature and realizes the futility of indulgence in sex in the pursuit of greater satisfaction in life.

Love, affection and sacrifice should govern all transactions of life at all stages of life. This is the true meaning of marriage. It is not just the physical union of a male and female body. It is the spiritual unification of the entire family that brings meaning to life. Love should flow out spontaneously from the bottom of the heart. Mind has no business there. Where mind comes, jealousy, pride, selfishness and gratification take the place of love. There are married girls who postpone bearing children for fear of losing their physical form. They are afraid of losing the physical charm and go to the extent of denying breast-feeding to babies. The question of spirituality does not arise in such a situation. The concept of spiritual union is missing in the western philosophy of life, may be there are some exceptions, and the modern Indian families are also blindly following the West due to lack of understanding and proper guidance. One comes to know the value of things only when one loses what he has and does not get what he wants. The Western society is materialistic and technologically superior sending wrong signals. That is why there are more mentally sick people in the western countries.

The basic function of sex is procreation and the natural law of companionship governs it. The participation of male and female partners of life is stressed in all religions. It is not only a means of procreation, but it is also considered a means of liberation. Begetting a son is one of the 'purushaarthas' in life. But, it is underlined here that sex is not the sole purpose of life. Sexual energy has to be conserved at all cost to attain fuller life of spiritual attainment and self-realization. It opens up doors to many mysterious paths of this cosmic world. There is a blissful world here and now, for those who are prepared to throw away their coloured glasses and see reality; the auroras of dancing colours of cosmic rays exist.

The Secret of Happiness in Life

"To see the world in a grain of sand and the heaven in a beautiful Rose..." is the real understanding of life. Many poets like K.V.Puttappa, Keats, Shelly, Wordsworth, have realized this; they are the real Seers! Others like D.V.Gundappa and Shivaram Karanth have explored the inner beauty through their extraordinary intuition and inquiry. DVG's Mankuthimmana Kagga is a masterpiece, a Treatise on philosophy of Life, at that! What is the true path ('sat-nyas') to a happy and successful life? The true path is one of austerity, truth, compassion, love and sacrifice. It is a life of constant remembrance of the Lord and prayer, a simple life of dedication and total devotion to one's ordained duties. Whatever the station in life, one should devote oneself to duties offered to us either by divine providence, or may it be self-ordained. So the secret of happiness is very simple. '*Dedicate your life to love and sacrifice, at the service of the Lord*'. Never indulge in excess of anything, be it food, sex, or sport. Svadhyaya i.e., study of ancient scriptures like the Veda and Upanishads, Bhagavad Gita and meditation are important. Know what you want and ask yourself why you want it before craving for it. Remember that there is always a gap between the time of desire and time of fulfillment, and this

gap of time erodes the glamour, and even necessity, of the thing craved for and brings in discontent and disappointment. It may be in marriage, job, possession of materials, or likes and dislikes, there is a big gap of time between desire and fulfillment. The key to successful life lies in identification of the problem in desires and root out them as futile, for desire is the key to misery. How often we accumulate things of desire only to discard them later!

The secret of life lies in identification of the goals. There are two important goals in life; one is a short-term goal- of immediate happiness and the second is a more permanent long- term goal of liberation from the cycle of rebirth. The first and the foremost goal in life should be one of long-term permanent happiness, attainment of supreme Bliss. This mundane, sensuous, and objective world is meant for enjoyment and there is no doubt about it. But, it must be remembered that the fulfillment of this objective is of duality- always accompanied by misery, disappointments, and unhappiness. On the other hand the second objective, although very difficult to attain leads to permanent happiness.

The advice is simple and direct. Do not live like a fool and a coward; live like a hero and develop the higher levels of consciousness. Always beware the pitfalls of life that come in the form of a golden deer that put Lakshmana into trouble. To aim high is not a crime; to feel disappointed not reaching the height is. Always be grateful to the Lord for giving this life and an opportunity to know Him. Use this opportunity to know Him. He comes to you in the form of your 'Ishta Devatha' if you earnestly long for Him. Keep a certain time of the day for dhyana and meditation; always chant the name of your Ishta Devatha keeping in mind the bhava and artha., devotion and meaning of the mantra.

The Human Behaviour

Man in this technological civilization is feeling inwardly impoverished and empty in an environment of wealth, power, and pleasure. He is, all the time full of tension, sorrow and misery, doubt, confusion and uncertainty. We see juvenile delinquency, suicide, and physically challenged and mentally retarded children and other maladies. All these problems are just a reflection of the Mind. A person is not happy because he is not inwardly happy and contented. He is not satisfied with himself. An under-current of dissatisfaction always bothers him. He is often bored to the point of commiting suicide; he is jealous and envious to the point of madness. In fact, the Indian Seers had foreseen such a predicament and the *Svetasvatara Upanishad* says:

"Even though men, may through their technical skill, roll up space like a piece of leather, still there will be no end of sorrow for them without the realization of the luminous One within". [Svetasvatara Upanishad, VI.20]. As stated earlier, three afflictions, '*taapa-trayas*' bother us. These are: the misery caused by oneself, misery caused by others, and the misery caused by natural phenomena. Usually all the three are combined. But, most often, we suffer most by the misery created by ourselves. It is our earnest desire to live happily, acquire knowledge, power and fame, and

excel and shine. These are our true nature, the nature of 'Brahman'- truth, knowledge, and bliss. These are the essence of our souls. But we fail to understand this true nature of our self due to the veil of ignorance.

Schopenhauer said, "All men who are secure from want and care, now that at last they have thrown off all other burdens, become a burden to themselves" *[The World as Will and Idea*, Vol.I, p.404]. Today, man is his own major burden and problem. Usually our life is egocentric. The soul gets tired of everything, even get tired of itself amidst this thralldom, routine mundane things and looks for something more permanent, more satisfying and looks for something beyond the forms, names and functions. Thus, the real yearning for a spiritual life begins. Blessed are those who realize this inner urge and look inward for the answer to the problems of life, for sure they will find an invaluable mine of peace and tranquility within.

At first, the outside world looks very beautiful. We look at and appreciate only its form and name. But we fail to understand its true nature, the intrinsic, inherent nature 'svaroopa'. We are carried away by the ourward impressions. The reality is that everything has the capacity to force itself on our consciousness, possess a luminosity that shines in both the sentient and the insentient; in this there is a difference only in degree and not in kind. We find this abiding sense of existence and consciousness in everything. Thus, we get a glimpse of Reality not only in ourselves, but in everything we perceive as outside objects.

We run after sensual objects since we feel that these objects fulfil our desires; to some extent, it is true that these outside objects fulfil some of our immediate wants. We try to posses these objects since we feel the possession of these objects would enhance our position, prestige, ego, pride and this give us a sense of fulfillment and happiness. This desire for happiness is there in everybody. Sense objects draw our mind because of the idea that we derive happiness or enjoyment from them. We feel tempted because of the promise of happiness the objects hold but not their intrinsic value. Thus, we find that "every external object has the capacity to exist by itself to rouse our consciousness about it, and draw out our mind". But we do not know their intrinsic value or true nature. We know them only by their name and form. The Reality they represent is unknown to us at present. Names and forms hide the truth in ourselves and in the outside objects, but all names and forms reflect dimly the glory of the reality hidden in them. This is the true self, the 'atman' of everybody, everything in this world.

Many persons who have attained material prosperity have failed to get peace and contentment. Here, the ignorance that material prosperity will bring happiness is responsible for the disappointment. Material prosperity comes from outside world and, peace and contentment comes from within. Hence, it is necessary to understand the source of peace and contentment. An act of selfless service gives immense satisfaction and contentment. An act of contemplation on the source of all wealth, the Lord Almighty, gives immense happiness. So constant 'dhyan' or meditation on Him will bring immense happiness and peace. But, greed for amassing wealth and constant struggle and endless effort to earn more and more without having any time to enjoy that wealth will bring misery.

Sometimes, we feel that our material prosperity comes from our hard work. But, this is an illusion. Material prosperity and efforts to attain it have no relationship! Material prosperity is the Divine Grace and it is showered according to one's 'poorva punya'. It is the past deeds that decide the state of material prosperity. It is also evident that material prosperity will not guarantee any spiritual progress and eternal bliss. It is also true that one has to put in effort to attain material progress, purely as a necessity, as ordained by the Lord in the Karma marga. One has to perform one's duty without aspiring for the fruits of action.

There is also an important dictum, the basic rule, of 'ritam and satyam'. Everybody should strictly follow this rule in life. A table that does not have the four supporting straight legs cannot stand; or for that matter, no building where the walls are not straight can survive. How can a man or his society survive on dishonesty, lies, untruth, immoral, and unethical behaviour? Anything earned without morals and ethics, may it be in business or in any other profession, is certain to bring unhappiness.

'Ritam' is the right path and 'satyam' is the truthful path, sanmarg or sat-marg. If the wealth earned belongs to someone else and it is coveted by wrong means, it will bring untold miseries to family members, loved-ones and kith and kin and all those who enjoy that ill-gotten wealth. Beware! Never aspire for somebody's wealth. *The first mantra of Isavasya Upanishad makes this point amply clear*. There are numerous instances of persons suffering in unimaginable ways- mental and physical, due to ill-gotten wealth. The worst affected here are the ones whom you love most. Still, many people enjoy ill-gotten wealth unmindful of the consequences. Those giving away a part of the ill-gotten wealth in charity with the hope of getting punya or Lord's Grace will be disappointed for, the Lord will accept only the hard-earned money or part of the wealth earned in *sanmarg* only.

One need not offer huge amounts of money to propitiate the God; even a handful of grains will do to appease the God if the same has been earned in a right path and offered with total devotion. Hence, righteousness in all walks of life is the first principle of *Mind Management techniques (MMT)*. All those who follow the path of Dharma will come under the Lord's protection. *This is what is 'Dharmo rakshati rakshitah'. Here, one should not think that dharma is so weak that it needs someone to protect or save it. One has to follow righteousness, Dharma, in order to attain purity, purity of thought and action, purity of Consciousness that ensure success and happiness.*

Happiness and Success

According to Saamkhya Kaarika, there are eight forms of success, 'Siddhi'. These are: 1. Reasoning, 2. Oral instruction, 3. Study, 4. Three-fold suppression of pain,5. Acquisition of friends, 6. Well-wishers, 7. Charity, and, 8.Purity. Of these, the first three lead to right knowledge and that leads to emancipation. There are certain impediments to the success and these are: ignorance, disability and

contentment (complacency). These obstacles should be removed in order to attain Siddhi, Success.

"Success comes to those who dare and act", says a proverb. It is true. The daring ones and those who act instantaneously without procrastination are bound to succeed in life. Thoughts should be put into action before they evaporate. Procrastination will never bring success. But, action and success are two different aspects and there is no rule that all actions end in success; there is a time lag between the two. Luck, fate, yoga, karma, fortune, misfortune, bad luck, knowledge, efficiency, ignorance, pride, ego, jealousy, competition, stress, tension, and so many other factors intervene between the action and success. Ultimately, there is no guarantee that all actions bring success and happiness with them; even the ensuing success may be devoid of happiness and joy!

Normally, success should bring happiness; but it is also possible that success brings more problems, unhappiness, mostly due to the 'ego' or 'I'-factor. Success is like intoxication, inebriation that causes delusion of Mind. It leads to loss of power of discrimination and sense of right and wrong. True success lies in contentment (not complacency) and realization of the Self.

Of the three 'Anthahkaranas' (Internal Organs)- Manas (Mind), Ahamkara ('T'-ness), and the Budhdhi (Intelligence), Buddhi plays an important role, if not a decisive role, in achieving success. Budhdhi is a tool, instrumental to success. But, it is very important to note that Budhdhi is also responsible for the failure, disappointment, suffering, and misery. Perverted intelligence or application of budhdhi with motive- greed, avarice, inflicting suffering to others, gaining undue advantage to oneself, etc. will ultimately cause delusion. Hence, 'Dharma' or Righteousness is the only way to success. Budhdhi also suffers from infirmities due to the afflictions of the sense organs.

Budhdhi is the reflected light of consciousness. If the reflector (the mind screen) is covered with dust (desire) and other impurities (greed, avarice, selfishness and covetousness), budhdhi looses its brightness. When the mind is pure and the heart is full of love and compassion, budhdhi shines in its full brightness. On the other hand, Prajnya or Consciousness gets its light from the Self, the Soul. Hence, the Soul is the source of light that gives Budhdhi the sense of discrimination. When the person is not aware of his Self, i.e., when the person is not aware of what he is doing and its consequences, he is sure to land in trouble. Here, when the Mind dictates action of the person and in the absence of budhdhi, the action turns out to be a wasteful exercise. Here, the person's budhdhi is clouded by delusion of mind and he works unmindful of the consequences, without the awareness of his action, in total disregard to consequences, since the action is devoid of' awareness' of the Self, the 'Prajnya'. Hence, success comes to those who are always aware of the Self, i.e., the Lord who dwells in the self. It is the abnegation of the 'I'-ness, (egotism) which brings success. Ahamkara is an obstacle to success.

It is said that *"Karmaanusaarena Buddhih" meaning, 'Buddhi is directed by the results of past action'. Karma* is the fruit of virtue and vice; in order to gain the fruits of action of the past, the jeeva is directed to a particular action by Buddhi. In fact, Virtue, Wisdom, Dispassion and Power are the incidental dispositions; they are not innate endowments as the Great Sages Lord Kapila had acquired at birth. Similarly, Vice, Ignorance, Passion and Weakness are dispositions that reside in the Karana. Karana is the 'Budhdhi Tattva'. Karyam is the body. Hence, those that reside in the body is 'Karanaashrayna'. Buddhi alongwith the dispositions of Vice, Virtue, etc. takes shape at the time of conception when the seed (desire) in the semen enters the blood of the ovum that fertilizes into foctus. It is, thus, Karma that gives rise to birth to fulfill the desires of the jeeva and buddhi drives the action part. Thus, whatever a person enjoys or suffers in this life is the result of Karma and Buddhi supports the action in this direction. However, there is a rare possibility of intervention of some extraordinary luck. By God's Grace and Will one may transcend the three Gunas and cross the ocean of Sansar! So,"***Nistraigunyo bhava Arjuna***' says Krishna. It means, 'Strive hard to transcend all the three Gunas and be Liberated from all these dualities of Virtue and Vice, Wisdom and Ignorance, etc.'

However, success or failure is not the decisive factor in life. A jnyaani will not give any importance to success or failure for he is not bothered about the fruits of action. A Jnyaani performs all action as the ordained duty and trusts in the Lord. He offers all fruits of action- success or failure, at the feet of the Lord. Such actions devoid of claim for fruits of action bring success without fail. There is no anxiety, tension, fear of failure, when the person directs all his energy towards the action without the expectation of the fruits of action. When there is no expectation, there is no disappointment. This is the secret of success.

There are certain obstacles to success such as complacency, indolence, inaction, lack of interest, contentment, belief in luck, fate, etc. A person who thinks that he is helpless at the hands of Prarabhdha Karma and who believes in luck will not put all his efforts to action; either he is half-hearted in his approach or disinterested in his action. Such persons who do not put their heart and soul into action will not succeed. Some persons depend on intuition and achieve rare success! Such persons are really fortunate in their ability tapping their inner strength,'daivaatmashakthi'. Meditation on the Self for about twenty minutes twice daily will help in gaining access to this inner strength.

Ultimately, success is assured to those who perform action, their ordained duties, action disrespective of the fruits of action and this is the doctrine of BhgavadGita:"Krmanyeva adhikaarahste, ma phaleshu kadaachana". Shree Krishna says, 'you have only right to duty and no claim to fruits of action, whatsoever. To give you what I want to give is My prerogative. You will get fruits of action of virtue or vice not only of this life but also of the previous lives for there is no time restriction to the award of fruits of action. It is the Lord who awards fruits of action and it is His 'Grace and Will'.

Here is an important lesson to all those who want to make money and enjoy life recklessly as they wish. Enjoyment or suffering in life is preordained! What one gets in this life are the fruits of labour in the past (lives). Good deeds bring happiness and bad deeds bring sorrow. Suffering caused to others rebound and the sigh of the sufferer finds its wavelength and reaches back the person who caused the suffering! Ishavasya Upanishad strictly warns against coveting others wealth or property due to this very reason. Persons whose wealth is coveted heave sighs of dukha that will not allow the person who coveted the property to enjoy it in peace.

Some persons think that they get very little in return for their sincere efforts. But they need not worry for they are bound to get rich rewards, sooner or later, for their virtuous action. The fruits of virtuous actions will never be denied. We have seen State and National honours are presented at the doorsteps of persons who had rendered services sometime in the past. Many get rewards in the present life for their actions in past life. That is how we see some wicked and crooked persons enjoying life of riches, wealth and fortune. The Soul, i.e., Atma lives forever, taking birth after birth (getting embodied) bringing fruits of action, fulfilling the desires of the jeeva taking different bodies suitable for the achievement of success!

Job satisfaction

Some persons are prone to think that professional success is a source of happiness. Many persons are denied of this simple source of happiness, the happiness from success in profession. Some persons get jobs they seek and feel happy; others grumble and get on with whatever they get. Here, graciously accepting what one gets is the right attitude. Many do not mind whatever they get and they are happy. In all these cases, it ultimately the happiness one gets out of job is very important. But job stisfaction comes out of the lively mind and creativity

It is natural that people get bored of doing the same job again and again and there is no scope for innovation, expression. The job field is so narrow that there is no scope for experimentation. Repititious, rigid routine and highly specialized activity day after day is good for tuning the persons skill and attaining efficiency; but it also works as a factor that produces fatigue, loss of interest, boredom and ultimately acute mental tension. Inducing some freshness and widening perspectives will greatly help in such cases. Change of job after some time would greatly relieve boredom. Change of place, training. Refresher courses and incentives will gretly facilitate the rejuvenation and increased efficiency. But such options are rarely available in most of the Departments.

Persons occupying very high positions have cut short their life committing suicide due to hypertension, fear, and disappointments. Many young and prosperous industrialists have ended their life abruptly. Many scientists of repute have done this. Even the film stars of fame and wealth have taken to this unwise path due to tension, depression, and lack of inner strength. Mind

Control (Management) Technique lays down clearly that one must be a 'dheera', and only a 'dheera' can live successfully. One should not think of running away from the battle- field like Arjuna. Cowards have no place in this world. Read Bhagavad Gita every day and realize the truth. In times of distress Meditate and call for the Lord Almighty's help in total submission to Him. Do not loose your heart. Help will come in one form or the other. One who has faith and trusts God will never be let down. Absolute faith in the Lord is the most important Principle to be adhered to in life for a successful and happy life.

There is another secret of success in professional life. That is '*acceptance*'. *Accept whatever comes your way gladly, graciously, an d enjoy it.* This secret of happiness and success should be clearly understood. Any work that comes your way is due to the Lord's Divine Grace. Invoke the Lord's blessings before taking up the job and perform it with sincere devotion, and finally offer it to Him as your service – all in His name. Perform all duties with total devotion and without any desire of its fruits. Success is yours and happiness follows. An iota of ego will spoil what would have been a success story. Always remember that 'I', or 'me' and 'mine' are ego factors that are stumbling blocks in the path of success. All the creatures on this earth are mere toys in the hands of the Lord and only His 'Will' be done. There is nothing that one can do in the odds of life except to submit to Him. Even Sri Krishna was not exempt from his past karma during his avatar in Dvapara Yuga and the same is true with Sri Rama in 'Treta Yuga'. One has to pay for the misdeeds of the past.

The Lord Almighty, '*He*' gives everyone whatever one asks for with total devotion; but what one gets depends on one's accumulated sins or good work of the past. Poorva arjitha punya is important. God's Grace will only mitigate the effect of the ghastly sins committed in the past; not even the God can escape the 'prarabhda' aspect of life. God's Grace will give strength of mind and self-confidence to face any situation in life. It will instill courage and strength of conviction and helps to pass all tests of life.

Maharishi Mahesh Yogi quotes the Vedic doctrine and says that success comes from purity, 'Sattva'.

"Kriyassiddhi sattve bhavati mahataa nopakarani", meaning, "Success comes through Sattva, purity- pure self-referral consciousness- which being the source of everything, contains within itself all that is needed for the fulfillment of any desire".

The easiest and simplest way to achieve success is to look to inner Self for guidance. "*Yoga karmasu kaushalam*" *Yoga is skill in action*; become one (yuj) with action, concentrate totally on the job on hand, success is guaranteed. The inner Self knows all and it is the source of immense possibilities. Whoever taps this inner resource will succeed in his endeavour. "*Established in Yoga (Unity), perform action.*" *[Bhagavad Gita*, 2.48-50]. Perform action with total devotion, concentration, self-confidence, unmindful of the results; Pray Lord, derive '*Daivaatma Shakti*' in all thoughts and action by deep meditation. Success is guaranteed! Fruits of action are will of the Lord, God. Accept whatever comes your way; do not run after anything. Be happy and contented with whatever the God gives on His own accord and trust Him fully; He knows all and He knows what is best for you. He is the redeemer.

All creatures on this earth are bound by Karma -virtues and vice. If you have done good deeds in the past life, you will enjoy this life, but not without disappointments and misery. Like day followed by night, happiness comes like a passing glimpse of sunshine in cloudy weather. Be prepared for the worst for, you know not what you have done in the past and pray Lord the Almighty to protect you always from all difficulties. Always remember Him and chant His name; your 'Ishta Devatha' may even appear in your dream and assure you of His protection. Make it a habit to chant the name of your Ishta Devatha, or '*Om*' all the twenty-four hours of the day, year after year. It should be a part of your breath and this comes by practice every day. Never loose the grip and ask Him to take you by His hand and help cross the ocean of samsara. This is the secret of success and happiness. Learn this trick and make it your habit.

Contemplate on a holy thought, or a 'Mahat Tattva', or chant a 'mantra' at least a few minutes a day and experience the result of transcendental meditation yourself. What more do you wish for than realization of the presence of your Lord within yourself? What more external strength do you need to face the life than his eternal support in the form of self-confidence, fearlessness and daring ability? He dwells within your heart. He is nearer to you than your own hands and limbs if you desire to know Him. One must learn to look inward, hear the inner voice, and act according to the intuition and one's own conscience.

In times of distress, sadness due to bereavement of the loved ones, '*be brave*'. Take to Meditation and prayer. Pray for the loved ones; pray for all. It is always better to rely on Him than those who are created by Him. Take refuge in Him; He will take care of you. Remember He will not come to your rescue as long as you depend on others. Total submission alone will rescue you and your loved ones in times of distress. So, have full faith in Him. He is the creator. He is the sustainer, and He is always aware of all his creations. He exists in the past, present and the future. The lord knows what is the best for you and whatever happens happens for the best. Remember that '*every failure is a stepping stone of success*'. Every testing time is an opportunity to remember the Lord Almighty and re-assure oneself of His presence. Hard times are times of tuning oneself to the divine path and every blow is a warning to those who forget Him.

Who is 'He' whom we cannot see but trust at all times? He is the Lord the Almighty. He is omnipresent, all pervading Shakti, the Supreme power behind all the stars, the planets, the satellites, and all the breath and the prank of all living creatures. It is because of His fear that the stars shed their light and heat, the planet revolve and rotate. It is the single source of all potential energy and it is due to His Grace that the world goes on. He resides in the heart of all living creatures. Even the inorganic matter has its energy derived from Him and Him alone.

Now, it must be clear that having taken birth on this earth one has nothing but to live in accordance with the Law of Nature. It is the duty of every human being to follow the principle of Ritam (Order) and Satyam (Truth) and follow the Rule- '*live and let others live*', be it a fellow human being, or a plant, or an animal. It is easier to be egotistic and be proud, and look down with contempt on all others; but it is very difficult to practice equanimity since our ego comes in the way. Always remember that 'all are children of God and God is none other than the Cosmic Self residing as the Soul in all creatures'. '*Microcosm is the replica of the Macrocosm*' - 'Kana of the 'Akhand'; every atom, or cell is full in all respects. This 'unity aspect' of Divinity in all creatures should be realized as the datum line that governs the life and activity of all creatures on this earth.

Live a simple life. Do not get perturbed at the obstacles that pave the path of Realization of the Supreme Self in one's own self. Go slow; there is no hurry to reach Him for He resides very close to you. He resides nearer to you, nearer than your hands and limbs! Silence is the medium to hear His voice, and try to hear His voice in utter silence, meditation and dhyan. Always repeat the name of your Ishta Devatha whether you are working or sleeping. There are three ways to chant the name of the Ishta Devatha: One, chanting of 'Om', or any other mantra, loudly in a secluded place where nobody is disturbed by loud chantings; second, chanting without sound but only by lip movement; three, chanting in mind focussing an heart, without either of the first two methods. The third method is supposed to be more effective. *This will help to keep the mind under control and bring all success in any endeavour.*

The Sensible way of Living

There are two ways of living: One is living with 'choiceless awareness' living as a 'Sakshi', i.e., witness to all your thoughts and actions. This is a very sensible, a sane way of living. The other is just living unconsciously, 'without awareness' whatsoever; it is this way of life that our one hundred and odd crore of people of India have chosen to and the result is obvious. This life of utter callousness as regards consciousness and the senseless pursuit of sensuous living have led us and our country to downfall, from the status of a very great spiritual leader (upto 5th Century) to a Third World country, of virtually a dark age, today. When it comes to the general psyche of the people of India, this is evident in every walk of their life. Accumulation of garbage and mindless spitting in public places, pushing and goading through crowd are very common observations. The physical and social environment that has been created by the people in Indian villages, and towns and cities could have been easily avoided with a little conscious living. One can see how people are not conscious of their spiritual, historical and cultural past, and have forgotten the spiritual height their ancestors had reached, and the glory that was Mahabharat and behave like an unconscious, 'Prajnya-heena' lot today.

In every walk of our lives, we exhibit our foolish, unconscious, indiscreet, senseless behaviour. Every action of ours is shortsighted and selfish. There is no national fervour or social commitment in our thoughts and action. We are neither religious nor philosophical, nor rational and scientific. We have scant respect for 'Ritam' and 'Satyam', i.e., Truth and Order, the very foundation of this universe. We are unmindful of the consequences of our action. Accumulation of wealth by a few, regardless of the oppressive poverty of their brothren, is commonly seen everywhere, particularly among the rich and the famous; we have become blind to realities of life and our ego will not permit us to think of the reality. We are purely selfish to the core.

Thus, there is need for revival of our ancient culture and spiritual way of life. Unless one willfully wants to follow the western culture and enjoy that soul-less life, people should follow the path of 'dharma' laid down here. Modern life is full of stress and strain causing numerous problems of sickness of body and mind. Western life as compared with the Eastern life is now in a disadvantageous position due to this very simple reason that it lacks harmony. But, unfortunately, mimicking the west, the present-day Eastern way of life has also become a life devoid of soul, devoid of both rationale and consciousness. In contrast, the Western way of life seems to be much better; it has imbibed a system of strict discipline in social life. It has developed technological means of comfortable living. But, this has helped people only to build up physical conveniences only, and the people lack harmony within, mental peace and contentment. Hence, it is time to think about the path we have chosen. This work is relevant to all the people of the world, East or West, North or South.

Normally, everybody faces problems in life in numerous ways. It is due to mal-adjustments, mis-understandings or lack of understandings, or due to greed, avarice, selfishness and over-indulgences. Mostly, it is due to selfishness or unconscious behaviour of some members that all other family members, relatives, and friends, or colleagues are badly affected. The problems arise due to too much of attachment, and the golden rule is to realize the Supreme Reality.

Although abnegation of self is not possible at one stroke, one should learn to live with a sense of pure love and detachment; it is like a nurse looking after a baby with love, affection, and tenderness and handing it over to its mother. It is like the drops of water on a lotus leaf. The discontent within oneself is at the root of the problems. One who is at peace with oneself will be happy and contented with all his relations. High expectations in relationships cause great disappointments. Even in love, one who expects reciprocal emotional response will be disappointed and later on get into trouble. Self-less love is the answer here. In pure love there is 'yuj' or union and hence, only 'one' and no 'other'. Whoever thinks that he /she and his/her husband or children or parents are two do not know what is love. Love unites all and hatred and jealousy divides.

Love and sacrifice are the key words to remember. Here, the technique to be adopted is very simple. Find out at what level of consciousness you are operating; is it at the body level, or mind level, or spiritual (soul) level? Any 'body-level' relationship is going to collapse when bodily attractions cease. 'Mind-level' attachments also collapse when mind gets bored of repetition and looks elsewhere for more thrilling or interesting attachments. But the spiritual or 'soul-level' attachments are very permanent and no one will have regrets at that level. Hence, one has to cultivate spiritual relationships with relatives and friends and these relationships would last longer.

Living is an art. The art of living has to be cultivated. One should be consciously aware of one-self and develop the Sattvic guna. Both the tamasic and rajasic gunas are binding to the worldly way of life while the sattvic guna leads to liberation, emancipation, or mukti. The science of living is to develop a rational and experimental approach to life. Whenever doubts occur, one has to test and confirm oneself in order to accept it as truth; but actually, the majority of the people go by blind faith and irrelevant practices.

Modern life has become more mechanical and leaves no time to enjoy life despite the numerous time saving gadgets and mechanisms. In fact, modern technology has given an advantage to people to save time and use the same to meditation and spiritual practices. More leisure is not for more pleasure. Sensuous pleasure leaves void and brings frustration. This has to be realized. The fire of desire for sensual pleasures should be extinguished not by fulfilment but by repulsion, vivek and vairagya. The more one tries to fulfil the desires for sensual pleasures, the more one is disappointed. Ultimately, it is a peaceful and contented life that is more important. All possible means should be adopted to live a happy and successful life in this modern hectic world. This book: Manoniyantran Vedic views and ways of Mind control gives 'Mind Management Techniques' will greatly help in this endeavour.

Happiness in Family life

Happiness in marriage is a myth. Since a major part of the life is spent in grihastashram (family life) peace and happiness in married life is very important. In fact, marriage should bring fulfilment, a biological satisfaction fulfilment. It should bring happiness. It brings contentment only when it complements and completes the other. But, discontentment, sense of void, ego, competition, and unhappiness are what we find in most cases today. Of course, there may be some happily married couple. In general, marriage and happiness do not go well together for long. The happiness appears like a mirage. Before you feel the happiness, clouds of family responsibilities cast a gloom and disenchantment starts. In reality, there is nothing like happiness in family life. It's all a gambling. Man wants all enjoyment and no responsibilities and that is simply not possible. So also, women are highly possessive in nature and want their husband to be always with them. In these competitive days, the work takes away a major part of the time to work and women feel disappointed; doubts and suspicion arise when there is the 'other woman' on the job front. Lack of understanding and support spoils the peace at home in genuine cases. Computers have become the second wife and a target of jealousy these days. There are cases of divorce on account of the computers, too.

There is a very interesting physico-psychological secret of marriage. The moment a woman feels that her husband is happy and contented with her she starts exercising fuller control over him and makes him a slave of her. He is ready to do anything for her. This brings in an adverse effect in due course and affects his performance at job; many people fail to focus on job and all their attention is at home. Things become complicated, too, since divided attention is there. Normally, a happily married man should do well at his job; but this is not so in many cases due to psychological pressure of divided attention. Many times, husband or wife will have to work away from home for longer time and that causes psychological problems. Sometimes, the husband becomes over-dominating and create psychological problem for the wife who is meek and humble. Exploitation is the cause of misery. The moment a person thinks he or she is being exploited the under-current of discontent, feeling of strife start in sub-conscious leading to serious problems later. Further, the most damaging thing in marriage is the ignorance about sex. It should be clearly understood that marriage shall not offer unbounded free sex as most of the people believe or fantacise. Denial of sex is the worst problem in marriage. Unless the persons concerned are realistic, understanding, sympathetic and cooperative life becomes a serious problem.

The most important problem in marriage is the loss of individual freedom. Man loses his freedom for an imaginary happiness and the woman loses her individual freedom for the imaginary possession of a person, all for herself. The woman either cannot understand or forgets the ground realities of family responsibilities of her husband to his parents and brothers and sisters. Similarly, the husband cannot understand or forgets the strong ties that his wife has with her parents, brothers and sisters and their families. Each wants the other to oneself, exclusively. This creates the problem. It is the over-possessiveness and exclusiveness that create problems. Continued interest and involvement in pre-marriage relationships bring conflict. The Upanishads clearly lay down the Rule that husband's interests are of utmost importance to his wife; but, the modern girls do not pay heed to this and get into problems. Successful marriages are built on sacrifice, surrender and sub-ordination. Each one should try to adjust to the other and lack of understanding is at the root of marital discord.

'Desire of the flesh', as it is emphasized in Buddhism, is the cause of the 'germ cell' that causes 'Re-birth' and bondage that is called *Sansar*.The most mysterious aspect of life is this. Man is totally absorbed in finding ways and means of enjoyment, fulfilling this 'desire of the flesh'. He over-indulges in this pursuit and forgets the goal of life. This is delusion. Normally, a woman attains her fulfilment in marriage after the birth of one or two children and totally involves herself in the duties and responsibility of bringing up children. Man is prone to neglect this aspect.

Marriage means union of two souls for the simple goal of attainment to fulfilment in life. But, marriages have always been a game of romance and indulgences. One has to almost always make a trial and error attempt towards attainment to this goal of fulfilment. Family interest on the one hand and personal ambitions on the other make family life a battleground of conflicting priorities. Often husband or wife has to give up personal ambitions and this causes frustration. If both are working in office, one has to give up the job and usually it is the wife that has to sacrifice. She has to live a discontented, unhappy, frustrating life forever.

The attraction of a boy and girl starts in adolescence and there is no sense of judgment at that stage of life. Platonic love or physical urges count a lot and always end in distress, sometimes leading to suicides.

These children in love are not in a position to understand the meaning of life and do not care for the advice of parents and friends. Very rarely such marriages of adolescent attachments succeed. The real success in marriage comes from only one source, the spiritual source. Both the partners in life must be mature enough to know the secrets of life. One such secrets of life is the need for understanding that this *'life is not for eternal companionship'*, or for that matter, 'mutual dependence at all times'. Mutual dependence is good but it may not be in the interest of development of individual personality. Freedom of the individual is of paramount importance. Dependence on 'God, the Unknown' is far better than dependence on any person known. Circumstances in life are such that nothing can be foreseen! Only the Lord Almighty can help us in times of distress. God can be trusted at all times; hence, love God and depend on Him, rather, surrender to Him. Your happiness is guaranteed; nobody is disappointed with God.

Without going to specifics of pinpricks in marriage, it suffices to say that marriage is not a bed of roses; rather, there are more thorns than the soft petals that with or soon. Persons who do not expect much from marriage are the really lucky ones for they will have no disillusionment and, hence, disappointments!

Why Marital Discord and Divorces?

Marital discord and, sometimes, the consequent extreme step like divorce, is a common thing in open societies. The underlying causes are not hard to find; modern life is full of stress, tension, and competition. Normally, lack of respect for each other and the highly bloated ego of the married partners, in addition to lack of understanding and faith in each other contribute to the collapse of marriages. In the first place, it is two opposites that attract each other and the natural law is to repel whatever comes very close to each other. In marriage, it is two persons of opposite sex having different natural, social, physical and psychological background that come together; and it is obvious that the natural forces begin to operate sooner or later. Attraction and repulsion are the order of nature, law of nature. This duality is built-in to the mechanism since this world is 'maya', unreal. It is a 'make-believe' or magical world and there is no meaning in worrying about changing whims and fancies of persons and their behaviour. This is the truth! Forget and forgive; everything will be all right. This is the art of living! There is nothing else!

Two persons cannot agree always on everything. Further, it is natural that the opposites attract each other. A boy and a girl with extreme difference in svabhava, or nature, are attracted at first sight. A person looks for that which he does not have in himself to another person, preferably of opposite sex. But this attraction wanes when reality dawns on the persons. No two persons are of same nature and each person has a limited capacity to bear with the nature of another person when their relationships are at body level or mind level. Body chemistry or physical attractions are temporary. When the two persons are bound by spiritual attraction, their relationship lasts longer and becomes more fruitful. Thus, marital discord appears when body or sensual attractions and mental attractions wane out. Infatuation based on fascinations or fantasies and imaginary desires brings disillusionment sooner or later. When the real nature of a person is intolerable to the other person, either they quarrel and separate, or decide to end the marriage with mutual consent. Rarely a marriage succeeds when it is based on wealth, social status, power, or other worldly achievements. Marriages succeed when there is eagerness to give than to take. Marriages are always built on sacrifices and selfish persons cannot sacrifice and do not sacrifice. This is the tragedy of life. What Vedantas says about marriage is not very encouraging! It implores, marry but live alone (contemplate on the Brahman!). Discharge your marital/ householder's responsibilities, but do not get too much involved in them. Love your parents, wife and children but do not get too much involved in them for it leads to misery and unhappiness. Your ultimate goal of life is 'Realisation of the Self, the Brahman. Never forget the goal, the destination. Enjoy the journey but do not forget the destination. Remember that you have to get down from the vehicle when you reach the destination. If you want to get on to the roof, do not cling to the stairs.

Bertrand Russel gives a very interesting illustration. See the Billiards or Snooker. The function of billiard balls is to collide. A strong personality is like a billiard ball. Any two strong personalities always collide, and their ego forms an adamantine wall preventing proper understanding, mutual admiration, respect, and love. Where ego rules the roost, there is no room for submission, let alone subordination. Submission is necessary for union-of body, mind, and soul. In fact, any integrated personality is a harmonious being and he operates spiritually, rather than mentally, and easily submits. He is full of love and understanding. He knows only love and consideration for others, feelings. Here, 'love' means 'Yoga' (yuj), i.e., 'to unite'. It is Yoga, a Yajnya; and, for a successful marriage the couple should offer themselves as the fuel and burn their ego in this 'yajnya'. Only spiritual development, if not attainment, will provide an enduring relationship and happiness. There are some strange marriages that fall outside reasoning or rationale. Probably this helps us to understand the spiritual relationships better.

As already stated, eternal companionship and mutual dependence is possible only with God, the Lord of the universe; call Him Paramesvara, Paramatma, Govinda, or Narayana, or their respective consorts Parvati, Durga, Kaali Maa, Shakti, Lakshmi, or any other name for that matter. This is the reason why many ardent devotees like Ramana Maharshi, Tukaram, Gouranga, Swamy Ramakrishna Pramahamsa, Andal, Akkamahadevi, and Radha have all taken refuge in their Ishta Devatha to attain liberation and enjoy Supreme Bliss.

Here, it is important to note that, it is the marriage that is bound by spiritual attraction that is mostly successful. Both the man and his wife must be aware of the Lord Almighty's divine plan and submit to 'His Will'. He will grant all success and happiness to such persons or devotees. But who can know His Plans? Here, total submission will help. There is no place for the self here; there is no place for worldly desires here; there is no place for excesses or over-indulgences here. One has to be careful even in basic requirements like food, clothing, and shelter and should not hanker after them. One should live a life of austerity- of love and sacrifice, and possess minimum needed for the sustenance of daily life. He should eat only to keep the body and soul together. Hence, this is a very difficult proposition. But, there is no way out at all.

All persons bound by mutual attraction at body level or mind level will have to face unimaginable miseries in their lives; this is true especially of those who are attracted by bodily attractions and they will suffer more. Upanishads and Puranas give ample illustrations to prove this point. The demons mistakenly identified their body with the Atman and suffered at the hands of the Gods. Here, the reason is very simple; physical body is subject to change and deteriorates over time; and, thus the very basis of marriage (that depends on body union) disappears leading to disappointment and distress. 'Rajasic' and 'Tamasic' Gunas take an upper hand, or preponderance over 'Sattvic Guna', in such lives. Due to too much of attachment (raga), mind looses sight of realities. For example, in a state of infatuation the realities of nature are forgotten. The most beautiful face that the mind madly sought after looses its glamour for it is not spiritually enlightened. The skin looses its elasticity for it is its sharira dharma. One should always remember that all finite things, however strong or beautiful, deteriorate and disappear.

Many well-built and strong physical bodies are afflicted due to high sense of 'ego' and over-indulgences. Sickness and death, due to one reason or the other, bring the husband or wife, grief and disappointment in life. This is more to the partners who are guided by physical attractions. Divorces are common after the mutual attraction fades away. One day, the person realizes that the other person is not the same person he or she sought for so ardently, or for that matter, madly fell in love with. Hence, there is the disappointment and the misery. But here again, the marriage built on spiritual basis is stronger and there is no place for disappointment if both the husband and wife look to the Lord Almighty for guidance in life and take whatever comes as the God's Grace. 'Sattva Guna' takes preponderance in such lives. There is no place for 'tamasic' indulgences in 'sattvic' lives. Even if one of the married partners is spiritual and the other not, problems remain. Rajasic or Tamasic nature of a person makes him blind to realities of life since the mind under these prepondering gunas will cloud the sense of judgment with false notions of life.

The second category persons who operate at the mind level also face the same problem. Mind is always fleeting. Mind is always changing and looking for interesting or thrilling objects. Mind operates on the basis of imagination or memories. In both these cases, the persons lose sight of the realities of the present and feel disappointed when they do not get what they imagined or what they wished for. Further, if the marriage is not based on mutual understanding, mutual respect, trust, faith, love and sacrifice, such marriages are rocked at the earliest realization of the reality. If one of the partners is spiritually oriented and knows the reality of life, the marriage is sustained for a longer period. In all these cases, spiritual bent of mind will greatly help. Ego has no place in marriage. But in almost all cases of unstable marriages ego is the destabilizing factor. Wealth and fame are not the guarantors of a successful marriage.

Sex, as many believe, does not play any predominant role in marriage. Although it is true that the purpose of marriage is sex, sex is not everything in marriage. This is how duality exists in everyday life. Mind dwelling on fascination and imagination is very dangerous. Mind has the ability to create things that are not real and thus dupes the persons offering him or her unlimited sexual happiness that is only imaginary; such an unlimited happiness is never possible in real life for the simple reason that the human body is limited and finite. Infinite happiness can be achieved only by spiritual practices. The role of sex is well defined in the Veda and Upanisads. Although sex is important in life, it should be understood within the definition and scope of life as defined in the ancient scriptures.

Vatsayana's Kama Sutra has been completely distorted by modern interpreters with the sole aim of 'en-cashing' on it. It is impossible to strictly follow all the conditions that are laid down in Kama Sutra in modern day busy life. Purity of thoughts and purity of heart underlie the relationship of sex-partners that is hardly found in present day life. It requires a very different way of life than that exists to day to live by 'Kama Sutra' way.

If householder's way of life does not conform to the rules of 'Grihastashrama' dharma, it does not lead to fulfilment. In Grihastashrama, the role of wife is well defined and, sex is a part of duty within the bounds of Grihastashrama dharma. Ultimately, excessive sexual indulgences are forbidden for it turns out to be a mere wearisome physical exercise without fulfilment. Mere body union is meaningless without spiritual union. Marriage of convenience also fails in the long run. Since, mind is the guiding factor in sex, its dominance shall have to be restricted by invoking buddhi, or intellect, vichara and vairagya. Spiritual practices greatly help in controlling the mind.

The spiritual path to life is a sure path that makes life more complete and satisfying. Although sex is important as far as biological urge, and the mind's obsession of it is concerned, its role should be understood clearly. No doubt it is a significant factor in life and its role is great in the early stages of life. But, sex is not the whole thing, the main goal, in life. As already stated, reducing the rajasic tendencies and attaining Sattvic guna will reduce the heat of passion and sex. Here a gain, sad-vichaara, viveka and vairagya will help to gain control over the sex-obsessed mind.

Of all the obsessions, sex-obsession is the strongest. Unless the person has a spiritual samskara and practices yama, niyama, and prathyahara, it is difficult to overcome the power of mind full of sexual thoughts and infatuation. This is one of the major aspects of youthful stage of life in every person that needs physical and psychological discipline and spiritual guidance. Prathyahara, or obstruction, or restraining obsessive thoughts of sex will help to control the body and mind. All the Jnyanendriyas and Karmendriyas should be constantly kept under vigil (Saakshi) and perfect control. Brahmacharya or continence should be practiced before entertaining the idea of marriage for happiness and success in life. This aspect is mostly ignored as at present.

In Hindu philosophy of life, the role of sex is limited to begetting one, or at the most two, off springs to fulfil familial (biological) obligations. It forbids excessive indulgences in sex unmindful of the purpose and goal of life. Joint family system provided a social environment to fulfil this obligation; but as the individuals set up their own families away from the parents and close relatives, opportunities like freedom, privacy, and time and resources became available for a reckless private life. This has led to many unwanted problems.

It is repeatedly warned here that, over-indulgence in anything is bad; this is true particularly in sex. Normally, persons who are in the grip of sensuous life think life is for enjoyment at any cost! It is true that, life is for enjoyment; but, it is definitely not *at any cost*. Life is sheer pleasure when it is sensible, when it is full of love, a Conscious enjoyment. Enjoy so well that you will not hanker for it afterwards. Do not make it an obsession.

One who enjoys life fully will have no regret to these small things, including sex. So one should enjoy sex to the satisfaction of both the partners and the success of marriage lies in its consummation. Acharya Rajneesh says that 'a sexual union with the beloved in a 'total abandonment of the self' will give immense satisfaction. It is Yoga (yuj) and brings total liberation not bondage! The sexual union with the beloved that lasts for three hours at a stretch in a night will be totally and permanently satisfying and such persons will not hanker after sex anymore'. But it is rarely possible. Some people who have had this experience (may be in their previous birth!) do not hanker after sex any more. Thus, it is believed that sexual satisfaction that is quite lasting is important and it can be attained. It is sheer extasy and contemplation in the act that releases the bondage. Sex should not be an obsession. It hinders all other creative thoughts originating from an intuitive frame of mind.

The heat of sex, or passion is reduced with avoidance of lust. Ultimately, a sense of complete satisfaction or fulfilment, although not possible ordinarily, leads to vairagya and aversion to sex. This is called 'Pratyahara'. Hardly three per cent of our life- time is given to sex. But fools want to revel in thoughts of sex throughout life. Continence is important if one has to gain spiritual strength. It is said that 'ojas brings tejas'. Continence or avoidance of sex in married life is also very important in order to conserve the 'dhatu' (semen) and use this conserved energy for spiritual attainments. A strong heart, lungs, and nerves derive their strength from the conservation of energy from this source. A man with a strict disciplined sexual life is more attractive, strong, and self-controlled. He gets a special shine, radiance on his face.

Inadequacy of partners in marriage is an important destabilizing factor. Due to lack of proper guidance at the right time many youngsters go astray and later on suffer inadequacy in married life. An unhappy wife will become quarrelsome and revolt causing marital discord. Many marriages have ended in divorces due to this factor of inadequacy. Lack of preparation and training before marriage, such as Brahmacharya is primarily responsible for failure or inadequacies in marriage. Carefree life in youthful stage brings in unimaginable problems in later life. The true meaning and purpose of life has to be clearly understood in order to live a happy and successful life. Hence, the golden rule is '*practise restraint*'. Marriage counselling is very important, here.

Normally everybody operates at the lower levels of consiousness such as the navel plexus (chakra). An important technique of attaining sexual satisfaction is through raising the level of consciousness. Much less energy is required for sexual arousal and indulgences, whereas, more energy is required to attain spiritual experiences. With the advance in spiritual practice, the aspirant will come to experience happiness that is superior to the happiness derived from sexual indulgences. As the level of consciousness is raised from the navel plexus (chakra) to the heart level, the aspirant experiences true love. As and when this level of Consciousness is further raised higher to the throat level and the 'ajnya' (between the eyebrows) level, and 'shiras' (head), the experience will be one of supreme bliss, much superior to anything experienced so far. Hence, one should rise to higher and higher levels of consciousness through spiritual practices. Thus, life becomes more interesting and more satisfying.

Apart from sex, there are other numerous problems that create instability in married life. Lack of mutual respect, insecurity in job, social insecurity, new surroundings and strange environments, loneliness and brooding, lack of social life and lack of trusted good friends and neighbours, etc.– all create emotional stress that gradually build-up to become major problems. One solution to all these is, no doubt, pure love, a selfless one at that; lack of self-confidence is also a factor. Meditation is a panacea to all problems. A simple technique of deep breathing (Pranayama) along with japam, chanting the name of *Ishtadevatha*, will help calm down the nerves and keep the mind cool. Pranayama and chanting the Lord's name at least ten minutes in the early morning and ten minutes in the night before going to bed will greatly help. Remember, there is none greater than 'Him' and none better than 'Him' and 'He' comes to your help if you sincerely, earnestly call 'Him' in times of distress.'He' is the protector, 'Lord Sri Hari Narayana'! 'He' is Visveshvara, the most dependable and 'He' resides in the heart! "Realise That"!

Parents and Children

One of the ardent desires of couples, and also the purpose of life is to beget children. It is true that without children, life of couple seems void. Parents particularly the mother, aspires for children with the hope that many of the unfulfilled desires are fulfilled by children. Elderly parents look to children for their safety and security. For every mother, her son is a reservoir of hopes. These parents feel disappointed when their children do not come up to their expectations. Parents should realize that they are the past, dwell in the past, cherish their memories and expect the same to continue forever. But, children, on the other hand, live on hopes, live on dreams and aspirations. The children have got a future of great uncertainties, change, and constantly strive for turning their dreams to realities; many of them succeed too. Both would never meet in matters of likes and dislikes, style of life and values attached to life; and it is called the 'Generation gap'.

In the first place, it should be understood by all parents that the secret of happiness derived from children is due to love and selflessness, and not imposition of one's own likes and dislikes. Respecting children and their wishes would bring in more love and happiness in the family. Always remember, that some children want to learn their lessons by hard way. Moreover, it is the impressions of their past life that drives them that way. It is said, 'Karmaanusaarena buddhi'; it appears that every jeeva is designed and planned in a particular way to suit its needs, to fulfil its goal.

Love is a one-way traffic and knows only giving. This simple Rule of Love is not properly understood by many people and they expect love to be reciprocal. This leads to terrible disappointment. Another Rule of Love is that it (love) ceases when *judgment* takes its place. Love and judgment are inversely proportional. As love increases sense of judgment decreases. This is evident from Mahabharata. Excessive love blinds parents as to children's follies. Similarly, when wife starts to judge the husband her sense of pure unconditional love gives place to nagging criticism and quarrelsome behaviour and life becomes miserable. A devoted wife never finds fault with her husband and has all admiration since her love is unconditional, absolute and pure. An egoistic wife who puts her self-interest before others' interets becomes the cause of all problems.

Thus, love decreases as sense of judgment pervades relationships. Children, as they grow into mature life, start judging parents when their love for parents decreases; this does not mean their concern for parents also decreases. Love and mutual concern are two different things. One can have concern without love or attachment. In fact, the true meaning of love is also 'Yoga', ('yuj' meaning, to unite or become one). When you become one in love, *the other* does not exist.

Mind and moods rule over the heart. Mother and daughters, father and sons get into problems for want of total submission to love factor; when children start judging parents, they start evaluation that leads to misunderstandings, frequent quarrels, and often difference of opinion leading to separation. Where spirituality and love rule the relationships, the relationships grow stronger and stronger. Love and love alone thrives.

Problems of our Modern-Day Life

Our life style has changed over the Centuries and much more has changed during the last few decades than ever. We tend to give more importance to things mundane and do not care for spirituality. There is a mad rush for things that really do not give us happiness and peace. We are the 'gold diggers' and the 'lotus eaters' at that! We want instant riches; and, do not care about our own health. We work so hard to achieve material prosperity that we do not have any time to enjoy what we earn; we work so hard that we do not have time to eat our food and sleep enough to recoup energy, with the result we end up with all sorts of problems. The first symptoms of this are seen in small irritations, lack of patience, anger, and emotional outbursts. As and when things aggravate, pain appears in the neck, back, spinal chord and disc, legs, and finally end up with nervous breakdown. Headache is the common ailment in persons who do not have enough rest and proper nutrition. Overstraining the body is one thing and constant thinking and worrying about things is the other; both are harmful. Overheated brain and lack of time to recuperate the dead cells, and overstraining the tissues and muscles of the body cause irreparable damage to the system.

Emotion

Emotion is bondage; it binds us. We are normally governed by emotions that rise from the heart rather than the discretionary power of the Mind. At times, the heart rules over the mind and in the end gives rise to certain problems. Emotion has its root in ignorance and discretionary power comes from budhdhi. If we are emotional and do not use our discretion we trust and place our faith in unscrupulous persons that ultimately leads us to problems or disappointments. We take decisions under some compulsion, impulses, emotional state that are not decided by the discretionary power of the mind or budhdhi. Emotion motivates where knowledge is absent with the result we may have to worry, resent or feel the guilt later. All these three, i.e., the worries, resentment or regret, and guilt are harmful to our state of health for they create tension, build-up stress, and lead to diseases. Regreting the past deeds, or worrying about the results of past action, or guilt of commissions and omissions create disturbance in the subconscious mind and continue to haunt and trouble us. Unless we get rid of the emotionally disturbing guilt complex, or the worrying nature, we cannot function normally. The solution to the problem lies in taking precaution not to fall into the pits of emotional traps. It is our weakness that others emotionally blackmail us; others trap us in emotional chain for they know the weakness of our mind. They put seeds of fear, worry, and guilt that emotionally traps us and force us to submit ourselves to will of others. There are no easy solutions to these problems.

Acceptance is a good solution to the problem of resentment. Gracefully accept whatever comes to you as a gift of God. "Whatever happens happens for the good." The Lord Almighty knows everything and knows what to give and what not to give; similarly, when we ask we ask for things we don't have full knowledge of; we may ask for things that may bring us more problems, misery, and disappointments. He knows best, so trust Him; accept graceful whatever He gives. That should be the right spirit and that will solve all problems.

Vichara (thinking about pros and cons), Viveka (budhdhi), and vivechane (discretion) are the three 'V's that we should constantly be aware of in our day-to-day life besides trust in the Lord. We get into emotional traps or pits due to our ignorance, weaknesses, rather our goodness and kindness which other unscrupulous persons misuse. If we trust in the Lord, things will tide over. The best one can do under the circumstances is to take to Meditation. Meditation removes guilt, worry, and resentment. Meditation also removes anger, jealousy, and hatred that are consequential; for we become angry, tend to hate, and become jealous of persons who emotionally blackmail us. All these problems can be solved by Meditation.

Depression and Suicide

Depression is caused due to many unknown factors. There are short-term depressions and long-term depressions. Short-term depressions occur due to our low energy level and moods. It is normal like the waves and tides, ebb and low of tides for Mind is a kin to waves. It is the tendency of the Mind to flow in waves and tides of ebb and low are common. A change in the social environment or physical environment will help to correct the problem. Depression is not a problem unless it prolongs beyond a certain time. There are different types of depression that are associated with sickness, loss of kith and kin, failures and disappointments and all these disappear sooner or later. But there are some serious types that persist and this needs medical or psychological attention and medication. The worst type of depression occurs in highly emotional persons, particularly dejected or jilted lovers, and persons who fail to get job, in loss in business, etc. such persons need sympathy and love. Good company and proper advice will greatly help in such situations.

There is another worst type of depression and that is the depression in aged persons. Some aged persons feel neglected by family and friends and get into depressed states of mind that is difficult to recover. Old age depression need not have any cause. Some experts are of the opinion that depression is hereditary and comes in genes. Circumstances in day-to-day life also have a play since mind has a certain capacity to bear the stress and strain and weak-minded people are easily susceptible to depression. Failure, low esteem, competition, etc. cause depression.

Depression may be of short duration or long duration. The suicidal tendency of a depressed person depends on the version of depression inherited (Gene identified as 5.HTT). The shorter version (Genes 5.HTT) is dangerous. The longer version inherited (gene 5HTT) is considered to be not that serious. Universities of Wisconsin and Pittsburg are looking into the DNA factor also. Interplay of some mysterious genes that reside within the 19 different DNA sites is being studied. Serotonin is believed to be the cause of depression and the symptoms of depression are controlled by regulating serotonin. Drugs like Prozac, Wellbrutin and Anaframil are used as anti-depressants. Many Ayurvedic preparation made of certain flowers are also available. The allopathic medicines have serious side effects since medication is administered to brain and it is not the answer to the problems of mind, here. Under the spell of depression many out-standing achievers have committed suicide. There are instances of rich and famous film personalities, successful industrialists, and scientists have committed suicide under depression. Some of the common causes for depression is brooding; brooding over loss, bereavement, disappointment, fear and anxiety, or failure. Many take to intoxicating drinks or drugs to overcome depression and turn out to be addicts. There are much safer anti-depressants in Ayurveda and depression can be controlled by Yoga. Some take to sleeping pills and, often, higher doses are dangerous. But, the much safer and saner method is meditation.

Suicide is forbidden in all religions. It is sin to commit suicide. Indian holy scriptures condemn suicide and warn that any person who commits suicide will repeatedly take birth and repeatedly end life abruptly without fulfilling the desires. The dissatisfied soul wanders in search of a host and it is not easy to get one. Suicidal tendencies are present in some persons and it is said that it is the strong memory of the previous life; once a person commits suicide, the tendency continues life after life. Hence, one should not cut short his/her life under any circumstances.

It is the desire of all parents to beget children who are happy and successful in life. It is a great tragedy if children commit suicide for silly reasons like failing in examination, loss in business, or rejection in selection for appointments or, in matter of love and for such other reasons. There is also the belief that the soul of a person committing suicide will never rest in peace. These are always in transit. Persons who are afraid of facing life will take to suicide. They often forget that success or failure is not important in life; it is living that is important. The very meaning of life is struggling for survival. One has to live and struggle in life, realize the meaning of life and attain the goal. Evolutionary process must go on. It is always important to remember that it is the soul with blemishes (desires) that seek rebirth. The seeds of rebirth lie in the desire and, to break the cycle of rebirth, the seed of desires should be burnt with Realisation of the Self through constant dhyan and meditation. One has to live a full life in order to attain this Self Realisation. Hence, suicide is not the answer for the life's problems. Self- Realisation is the answer.

The golden Rule of Mind Management Technique or mind control is that with maturity and experience in life, one must develop 'vairagya', the sense of detachment. The coconut is a good example. In the beginning the water, the pulp and the shell one all one. As the tender coconut becomes ripe, the inner copra separates from the outer shell. Always remember, *Vichara, viveka, and vairagya* are the three 'V's of Victory in this war against ignorance of life. All relationships are governed by the principle of 'maya' and 'Lord's Grace'. Deriving happiness from wife or husband, brothers and sisters, children, and other relations and friends depends on 'His Grace'. Love knows only sacrifice. Another important thing is that many parents do not realize that their children are not their children. They are only passing through their life, through a medium, and nothing more than that! Parents have their past and children have their future and the two will not stay together forever. This aspect needs a proper understanding and that should lead to the sense of un-attachment (not total detachment like disownment); it is like the water drops on the leaves of the Lotus. Infact, there is a religious function of 'Upanayanam' wherein the mother feeds her son for the last time, symbolically, so that the Brahmachari son will adhere to the rigid rules of that station in life. Too much of attachment is thus discouraged. This is the secret of happiness in life. The Vedantic way of life has many built-in safeguards to make this life worth living and one should enjoy life fully.

Cheerful Disposition

It is very important to keep a cheerful disposition even in the face of all the 'taapatrayas' that bother us day in and day out. Cheerfulness is a healthy state of mind and everyone, particularly doctors, advocate this disposition of mood. In fact, there is a doctrine of dharma that insists on cheerful disposition.and the spiritual leaders and teachers advice their disciples to be always cheerful. But it is the most difficult thing to be cheerful, or joyful, under the pressing problems of life; stress and tension rule our daily lives and there is no scope for joy or happiness. Hence, it is more important to have a cheerful disposition and keep everyone happy. It is also true that some may think that there is nothing to be joyful or happy about in this world full of misery. The best remedy in such a situation is dhyan and meditation. But, here lies the wonder of the wonders! When one reaches the state of supreme-consciousness and comes out of the Samadhi, the whole world appears more beautiful. Such yogins will be always cheerful.

Death and Immortality

Fear of death lurks at every corner and it is a source of much tension in day- to-day life particularly with mounting accident rates. Normally, this fear of death is innate or inborn and all jeevas have the impression of previous death very clear in its sub-conscious. It is this impression of the previous life that makes one fearful of death. But, the Scriptures like the Upanishads and the Bhagavad Gita repeatedly reassure that one need not worry too much about this. One should have a very clear idea about all this drama of life and death in this world.

"There is neither death nor birth, neither a bound nor a struggling soul, neither a seeker after Liberation, nor a liberated one. This is the ultimate Truth" [Amritabindu Upanishad, Sloka 10; Viveka Chuddamani, 574].

It is in *Katha and Kena Upanishads* that we come across Death and Immortality, respectively. Nachiketas was watching the Visvajit sacrifice performed by his father Vajasrava for heavenly rewards. At the end of the sacrifice, Vajasrava offered cows and other gifts to Brahmins. As a boy of tender age, Nachiketas was sceptic about these offerings, of these Cows that ceased to yield milk. He thought that the Visvajit Sacrifice (Yajnya) would not be complete without offering everything in his father's possession including the son, me Nachiketas. He asked his father, 'to who wilt thou give me?' Vajasrava did not pay heed to his son. When Nachiketas went on asking him, he angrily said that he would give him to (Yama) Death. Nachiketas went to Yama, the God of Death, to know what is Death. Yama refused to divulge the secret in the beginning; finally Yama conceded to reveal the truth due to Nachiketas's shruddha, bhakti and other noble qualities.

Yama said, "The wise, who by means of the highest meditation on the Self knows the Ancient One, difficult to perceive, seated in the innermost recess, hidden in the cave of the heart, dwelling in the depth of inner being, (he who knows that One) as God, is liberated from the fetters of joy and sorrow"[Kathopanishad: Verse XII].

Yama went on to say that," whoever knows the word 'Om' 'Aum' as Akshara Brahman and meditates on 'Aum' would obtain whatever he desires because God is the fulfilment of all desires. This sacred word is the highest symbol of the Absolute. Further, 'Aum' is indeed the Supreme, the Self. This self is never born, nor does It die. It did not spring from anything, nor did anything spring from it. This Ancient One is unknown, unborn, eternal and everlasting. It is not slain even though the body is slain. Although this Atman dwells in the heart of every living being, ordinary mortals cannot perceive it because of its subtlety".

"He who is free from desire and free from grief, with mind and senses tranquil, beholds the glory of the Atman. Though sitting, It travels far; though lying, It goes everywhere. The wise who know the Self, bodiless, seated within perishable bodies, great and all-pervading, grieve not" [Kathopanishad II-20-2].

"A wise man should control speech by mind, mind by intellect, intellect by the great Atman, and that by the Peaceful One, the Paramatman, the Supreme Self". " Knowing that which is soundless, touchless, formless, undecaying; also, odourless, tasteless, and eternal; beginningless, endless and immutable; beyond the unmanifested; knowing' That' man escapes from the mouth of death" [Katha Upanishad, III. 13 & 15].

"He is the sun dwelling in the bright heaven; He is the air dwelling in space; He is the fire burning on the altar; He is the guest dwelling in the house; He dwells in man. He dwells in those greater than man. He dwells in sacrifice. He dwells in the ether. He is all that is born in water, mountains, earth and sacrifice. He is True and the Great. He it is who sends the incoming life-breat, Prana upward and throws the out-going breath downward. Him all the senses worship, the adorable Atman, seated in the center, the heart. When this Atman, which is seated in the heart goes out from the body what remains then? This verily is 'That'. No mortal lives by the in-coming breath, Prana or by the out-going breath Apana, but he lives by another on which these two depend. As the intelligent man realizes the splendour of this Supreme-Spirit, he becomes free from that part of his nature that grieves and suffers, and thus he attains liberation"[Katha Upanishad, V 1-5].

What after Death?

Many people ask this question. Some of the research findings have brought out queer happenings and strange experiences as narrated by persons who had a brush with death. Some have departed from the body and observed their own body under treatment in the ICCU of the hospital. According to many neuro-surgeons such experiences are not rare. There is a particular part in the brain, when activated would give this feeling of 'observing oneself', 'as if the soul is watching its body'. The author of this book had a rare opportunity of witnessing this event. Many persons have departed only to come back and join their body. Is it the Consciousness that stands apart and looks at its mortal self? It is quite possible!

Yama relates this important secret about ' what happens to Self after death', to Nachiketas. He says:

"Some Jeevas enter wombs to be embodied; others go into immovable forms, according to their deeds and knowledge. The Being who remains awake while all sleep, who grants all desires, That is pure, That is Brahman. That alone is said to be immortal. On 'That', the whole world rests. None goes beyond 'That'. This verily is' That' [Katha Upanishad V 7-8]". "Immortality is attained when man transcends his apparent nature and finds that subtle, eternal and inexhaustible essence which is within him" [Kena Upanishad I- 2].

Thus, at great length, *Katha and Kena Upanishads* describe the essentials of existence and show the path to immortality. In the real sense, there is nothing that is perishable or imperishable for everything is illusion. That unicellular amoeba, which made its first appearance, has multiplied itslef into innumerable self and the result is the vast multitude of living creatures of different names, forms and functions. If that is not immortality, what else is immortality? Our parents live in us and we live in our children, then where is the question of death? It is the illusory body that perished under His will. Ultimately everything is gobbled up by Him. Everything is wasting and waning over time and we do not realise this Truth due to our ignorance.

Death is an illusion; so also is birth. Since the whole life is a drama, leela of the Lord, where is birth and death? It is He who enters in and out of bodies at His will. This transmigration of souls is the eternal game played by Him, the Supreme Spirit, Brahman. It has already been pointed out that it is He, the Brahman, who 'willed' it . He created the cow and He himself became the bull; for all practical purposes, there is neither the cow nor the bull. It is a make-believe, magic of the Lord. He pervades the whole macrocosm and every atom of the microcosm; He is the One and only; He is the both. So death is a matter of transition from one state to the other. It is transmigration, transformation. The physical law is 'nothing is lost when a candle is burnt'. So, also nothing is lost or gained when a soul discards the unwanted body and enters another. It is His will!

Often we hear that such and such a person is no more. Sometimes we say, in fact, that person was with me till late in the night yesterday, and he is no more in the morning. Such news come as rude shock, a surprise. It never occurs to us that it is all His leela. Still we laugh over birth and cry over death! Even after people die their memories live. Even after people physically die, their genes are already transmitted and thus they live in some other name and form! So, virtually none dies and nothing lies after death since death is an illusion for a Jnyani and, an apparent reality for an ignorant person. Hence, the art of Manoniyantran is "*Fear not Death! Face it Boldly. You have conquered the world*".

Death is for celebration. It is an auspicious thing to celebrate death. That is the reason why 'Vaikunt' is celebrated as a grand feast in the memory of the departed soul on the thirteenth day of death. What happens after death is another interesting story. The physical body, made of the elements disintegrate and merge into their original state. The hair becomes the root of plants; the flesh and bones merge into water and earth. Thus, unto dust goes the body that was shaped out of the elements! Remember, anthankarana merges into the soul.

The departed soul finds its own level of existence in the macrocosm according to its purity (atomic weight?). Purer the soul, devoid of desires, and the gunas tamasic, rajasic gunas and, sattvic guna, the soul rises higher and higher into the sky. It may cross the lower levels of Pitru Lok, Deva Lok, Swarga Lok and reach Nakshatra Lok or Brahma Lok. Whatever might be! But, it is a fact that all departed souls from this Mrutyu Lok will find their own levels in the sky, the cosmic world. Some dissatisfied souls or unfulfilled souls remain nearer their homes or even within their homes till their desires are fulfilled. Some souls might be revengeful and some benevolent; and that depends on the 'fear complex' or 'guilt complex' of the living, more than the dead. Some souls wander in search of a suitable body to fulfil their unfulfilled desires. Ultimately, it is the unfulfilled desires that make the soul go round and round. A fully satisfied soul takes refuge in the Lord, the Supreme-Consciousness (Brahman) and remains there forever. Individual consciousness merges with the universed consciousness.

Desire is Brahman and desire is the cause of birth. It is the sweet will and wish of the Soul to take birth after birth, unless it is tired of it and finally decides to call it off. This is liberation of the soul; this is mukti to the departed soul. Some departed souls may be hankering for love and respect from their children; others may be waiting for the fulfilment of some of the unfulfilled desires. Hence, it is the duty of every human being to satisfy the departed souls by just remembrance with Shruddha and Bhakti, whoever it might be. The modern day busy life may not permit elaborate functions to celebrate anniversaries; atleast, a well-disposed mind and an act of self-less service will do to propitiate the departed souls. A glass of milk and a fruit will be enough to satisfy the departed souls. They always shower their blessings on their wellwishers. This knowledge is beyond all reason and science; it belongs to the spirit. Rituals or no rituals, the souls sustain on their own, i.e., desire.

Professional Excellence

It is the desire of every person to excel in his avocations, rather, in everything he undertakes. It is the inherent nature or 'swabhava' derived from the Atman. But, the prepondering guna, particularly the tamas, comes in the way. The spirit desires, but the mind and the body do not act. There is the desire, but the will is not strong enough to drive the other forces such as the body and mind to work. So, many of our dreams remain unfulfilled for want of timely action. It is good to dream, but it is essential to act. Timely action is very important to achieve ones desire turn dream into reality. But, fulfilment also depends on the past deeds, impressions, karma or sanskar propelled by the sub conscious. These are, again, vibrations that create strong will power and drive one to action. Thus, a number of factors are involved in the success or failure of a person. But, all these can be overcome by one simple magic formula; and, that formula is '*trust in God*' and 'Sharanagation', total surrender to Him. Do your duty and leave the rest to the Lord's will. The lord will take care of you; of course, Karma still binds you and the Lord will not interfere in the course of your Karma. What one had sown in the past he has to reap the harvest of those seeds, sweet or sour.

There is another important formula of success. Professional excellence is an obsession. As soon as one forgets "I am the doer- sense', he achieves it! One thinks that ' I should do this', 'I should do that', and such thinking will not help in doing it for the simple reason that thought and action are two different things. If you think too much, you will not act. If you act, you are not thinking about that. This is the nature of mind; one thing at a time, either it thinks or it acts. In examination, if you are thinking about the answer, you are not writing it. Action, as if in a trance, is what we observe in some hardworking, sincere and devoted people. These are successful people; people at the top. This is, again, the '*Akarma theory*' (*See details on* check up!). As long you are obsessed with it, you have no free will and will not be able to tap the hidden talent in you. You have to allow the mind to be calm and serene, so that ' intuition' takes over to provide you the much needed originality, perfection and excellence. Hence, the best one can do in the circumstances is to have an overall comprehensive view of things and put your whole energy and soul into it with devotion and surrender to the Lord Almighty. Slightest ego will spoil the whole exercise.

Some people have the knack of buldozing every thing that comes in their way. They assert with pride and ego and seem to succeed. But, ultimately, it is the humble and the submissive ones that succeed. The weak, the timid and the shy submit to Lord's will. The Lord will take care of everything; there is nothing that the Lord does not know. Persons who submit to Divine Will will have full faith in Him. They are not perturbed by small disappointments. Even small failures lead to successes in the long run. But, the strong egoists do not bend; their ego forms an adamantine wall and does not permit the vision of the Lord's hidden hand. Total involvement is what is needed here.

Professional excellence can be achieved by a simple technique of 'mind control' mind management. *Just study your mind and its movement dispassionately while doing work.* Watch and see how it is engaged in all sorts of trash and even harmful thoughts. Watching your mind can help gaining control over the mind to a great extent. The brain fibers become lighter and lose much of inertia when the mind is under watch by oneself. This is the 'sakshi bhava', 'self-witnessing' technique. '*Choiceless awareness*' is very important. One should be consciously aware of what he is thinking or doing. This helps us to use our discretionary power in a proper way. Most of the time we are indulging in mindless activities and lose sense of discretion. We have to watch ourselves, watch our thoughts, and watch our mind and watch our action.

Normally, one does not bother to know how the mind works. Actually, it is important to know how the subconscious, super-conscious, and the conscious work. The unconscious activity is going on with out any aim; the conscious activity is with an aim or purpose; the higher conscious works with normal consciousness. Always higher conscious should be involved in all conscious activity in order to get the best result. A sense of inner awareness develops with the involvement of the higher conscious in normal conscious activities. This comes by practice. There is a great difference between the work done by a spiritual person and an ordinary person. This is the '*Poorna Prajnya*' *technique of mind management*. This is very important for success in all activities; and, ultimately it is this approach that brings success, immense satisfaction and happiness in life.

Remember the Mantra: "*I am not the doer. I am not the enjoyer. I am not the cause of the success or failure. There is a 'Guiding Force', a cosmic force that pervades everybody and guides towards destiny*". One is mistaken if he thinks that he is the cause of success or failure in life.

There is an Upanishadic doctrine that states, "One who thinks he knows, knows not; and one who thinks he knows not, knows it". "He understands It who conceives It not; and he understands It not, who conceives It. It is the unknown to the man of knowledge, but to the ignorant It is the known" [*Kenopanishad* 3]. If a person thinks he knows everything, he is stupid; he is living in the past. Even if he says that he knows God, he is living in the past. Even those who say that they had God-vision are living in the past with their memory. They are not living in the present. Having known God one has already transcended God and, remember, it is not possible to transcend Him. So what is it he is speaking?

The more one knows of religious knowledge more it becomes unknown. The more one feels it is very difficult to know, more one feels he is too ignorant and helpless, the more God moves nearer to him. When someone really enters the divine, he comes to know that He is unknowable. He comes to know that there is no possibility of knowing Him. He always remains unknown, unknowable. He, the Lord Almighty, comes very near and still stays far, far beyond reach. He is within a wink of your eye and you can perceive Him in every lightning and thunder! He is like the fire in the molten lava, the magma. He is in the sun and beyond the sun. He is knowable and the unknown, as well as the unknowable and the known! One has to constantly strive for understanding Him, knowing Him, reaching Him, experiencing Him, realizing Him! The moment I realize or know Him I am not there; I become 'That'. Similarly, the world is the other and the moment we know it it becomes our Self and the 'other' ceases to exist. The World of illusion ceases to exist! This is the secret! He sits in us and directs all our actions according to our destiny.

7
The Art of Creative Living

Living is an art. Living as we are in a state of delusion, a world of make-believe, no wonder we all live on the periphery of consciousness. Our lives are full of trivials. Days and nights pass in routine struggle, making both ends meet and it is a hand to mouth existence for most of us. Our joys and happiness are short-lived, while sorrows and misery knows no end. Often we wonder where are we heading to? Still there is no satisfactory answer to the eternal question why some are born rich as it were in the USA or Europe, and some in veritable hell in Asia and Africa. There is no scientific answer to this question in the Western science; but Vedanta holds the clue. It is repeatedly made clear that it is due to our desire and Karma that we take birth and to terminate the eternal cycle of birth and death is in our own hands.

One may ask, 'Is it one's Karma that fixes one's fate in this life, and if so, where can one find the balance sheet of good deeds and bad deeds of previous life so that the account can be settled once for all? It is said that the Chitra Guptas maintain the account of every winking of our eyes! What more is required? Also, it is open to question whether the good deeds will emancipate us for we do not know what lies in the future. The answer to this doubt is also obvious. Any sensible person who has discrimination knows the consequences of his acts of commissions and omissions. The question of what lies ahead does not arise as long as one surrenders to the Lord. Surrender the ego and be free from all anxiety and tension. Vedanta has very clear answer for all these questions. Not only this, there are solutions to many other problems. The answer lies in cleansing the backyard, the subconscious; cleansing the memories, getting rid of the accumulated vasanas and resisting temptations of desires of flesh and sensuous life by adherence to austere way of life. Constant remembrance of the Lord, 'Harinama Smarane' is one simple technique

Life is what we make of it. We are our own masters. We have got 'Free Will'. We grow as we like and very little of external influences can affect very significantly the way of life we choose and live. Ultimately, it (life) is of our own making! Raja Yoga tells us that we are the creators and we create what we want and discard what we do not need. What significantly affects our life, at the most, is our Karma. What deeds we have done in the past is the root cause of our existence here on this earth now; and, it is also within our hands to gradually put an end to all this, life. Without a proper knowledge of all this, we are simply rushing! With the result, we accrue all sorts of unwanted things and suffer. All our problems can be summed up in the following.

The Concept of 'Maya', Illusion

We are all bubbles in the foam and waves of the cosmic ocean of the universe and, as such, our whole existence is a 'make-believe' world or magic. What all we perceive is just an image on the screen, on the retina. Remove the screen the objects disappear. Close the eyes, the world disappears for you. The sensate world is finite and perishable subject to degradation over time. It is our 'avidya' or ignorance or perverted intelligence that gives us an impression of an eternal existence; rather, it is the true nature of the Brahman that makes us believe so. We all believe that this sensate world is true and eternal. But, in a few billion years, the Sun would be completely devoid of all energy; and, it would expand and cool so much that all life forms on this earth would cease.

'Avidya' (Nescience) or 'Maya' is the power of the Lord. It is also called the 'Undifferentiated Consciousness'. A perfectly balanced state of Mind is the one when the three Gunas, Tamas, Rajas and Sattva are in a state of equilibrium. Here, one should remember that, in fact, evolution is caused by the disturbance of this equilibrium. This 'Maya' is an illusory or the 'make-believe' state since the power behind this is beyond all cause and effect, not affected by the change; neither it is non-existent nor does it exist; neither it is same or different, nor both. And, it is beautiful and indescribable! It is neither an indivisible whole, nor is it composed of parts. It is called Prakruti according to Samkhya Philosophy. It is insentient and at the same time independent. Such a 'make-believe' world of Nature we live in is nothing but the act of the Lord; it is His leela! What else should we call it, but Maya? It is like the large screen on which we witness the progress of a film story in a cinema Hall. The moment, the screen disappears the film also disappears. Our Mind is the screen on which we witness the drama of life, the so-called world we witness and the moment our Mind becomes still, the drama of life ends!

With '*manonasha*', the Maya is conquered. Maya can be destroyed by the realization of the Pure Brahman, the One without a second. Even the wise and the learned men and men who are clever and adept in the vision of the exceedingly subtle Atman, are overpowered by tamas and do not understand the Atman even though clearly explained in various ways. This is the 'Avriti-shakthi' of Tamas, the over-powering Guna! Let alone the mortals, the human beings, even the gods failed to perceive the Brahman who stood before them in the form of a Yaksha!

Kena Upanishad has a beautiful story. Once, the Brahman comes in the form of Yaksha to teach the proud Devas a lesson. The Devas were taking all credit of winning the fight with the Asuras, the Danavas (demons). They were elated and forgot all about Brahman. When Brahman appeared before them a Yaksha they could not recognize Him. Indra sent Agni to find out Who He is. Brahman placed before Agni a piece of straw and asked him to burn it, Agni used all his force and failed. He returned pale face. Indra sent Vayu to find out who the veritable Adorable Spirit is. Again, Brahman placed a piece of straw and asked him to blow it. Vayu used all his force and failed to move it. He returned disappointed. Finally,

Indra himself came, but found a beautiful woman, the wondrously effulgent Uma, the daughter of Himavat in the place of Yaksha!

Here, Indra is the Mind and where Mind enters, the Supreme Spirit disappears for the simple reason that mind, the finite, cannot perceive the Supreme Spirit, the Brahman (Infinite). The eyes and ears, whose deities are Agni and Vayu, respectively, failed to perceive the Brahman for the same reason that the Infinite cannot be perceived by the finite. One can feel the presence of Brahman with the help of the indriyas but cannot perceive it with mind. If you want to test this simple fact, take the hand of a child when it willingly offers you a shake of hand and feel the cosmic energy flowing! Also, take the child's hand by force when it is unwilling and feel the difference!

This story goes to show how we fail to recognize the indomitable Spirit, the cosmic flow, the Supreme Spirit that is behind all of us and we simply take credit to ourselves. It is strange that we take all credit if we succeed and blame the world for our failures! Why not give credit to Him for all our success? Why do we not remember that failure is our weakness, our mistake due to ignorance? Our ego prevents us from accepting our ignorance, our weaknesses. Ego is the adamantine wall; it is governed by the mind. So, remove the mind, ego disappears! Ego is ignorance; mind is ignorance, darkness. Mind and ego go together, each strengthening the other. A little bit of knowledge or awareness (Consciousness) of 'who we are' will drive away the ignorance. So, be consciously aware of who you are. You are 'That', that Indomitable Spirit, the Self!

Undifferentiated or unmanifested prakruti is called '*Maya*'. It is 'Avyakta' and hence, it is to be inferred from the effect it produces. Prakriti, with the Purusha, has brought this universe into existence by its sheer Sattva. Prakriti or 'Maya', unlike Purusha, is not '*Adi-madhya-anta rahita*' i.e., beginning-less and endless; it has no beginning but has an end to a Jnyani who has knowledge of the Self. Matter, energy and sound exist in 'Maya' in an undifferentiated state. The whole world exists in 'Maya' in a seed- state during cosmic pralaya, or dissolution of the universe. 'Maya' is the causal body of 'Ishvara'. It is under the control of the Lord Brahman.

This Mind is 'Maya', the illusion that brings about further creation of perishable and futile objects that further covers our pure consciousness. This Mind cannot overcome 'Maya', the illusion since the mind itself is maya, the illusion. It cannot eliminate itself. Hence, one should have a clear sense of the world he lives in and strive for understanding the 'Sat' or the truth. This is the path of redemption from cycle of births and deaths. All the worldly achievements are of no significance for a Jnyani. Hence, every person should know what he wants and why he wants that. Otherwise it will be a mad pursuit in this illusory world. It is so sad that many people die with all honours and worldly recognition but not knowing their Self!

There is a beautiful story of evolution in our Puranas. This should be taken in its proper perspective. Brahma created Saraswati and fell in love with her, his own creation and married her! Purana says so. Who is not enamoured with one's own creative force? A painter loves his own painting. An artist loves the object of his own creative skill. So also Brahma; but what is this marriage with Saraswati? It is the marriage, the union, of the consciousness of the individual self with the Supreme-Consciousness, the Cosmic Self. Further, Brahma created the cow and he himself became the Bull; the bull ran after the cow and the cow ran to hide and invited the bull. Finally, the cow and the bull became the cause of further creation. The story goes on and on like this to create this world of 'make-believe', 'Maya'! One should not get into the details of this story of creation. It is figuratively clear that we are bound by mamata, moha, and forget the real Self in us. The whole life on this earth is a drama like the bull running after the cow and the cow hiding to invite the bull!

Knowledge is elusive. Ignorance binds, rather it blinds. We get infatuated looking at a beautiful girl. We fantasise her. We long for possessing her. We forget for a moment that the girl is also a human, of flesh and blood, of mind and moods, and likes and dislikes. We love ourselves in her and we are ever eager to enter her. When we get possessed of her, the reality dawns on us. We realize that she is not what we longed for; she is not the person we so earnestly desired for. She is just like any one of us and disillusionment starts; her shortcomings appear glaring. Her ego may become intolerable to such an extent the ego-clash becomes inevitable. Ultimately, her presence becomes so intolerable that we start finding out ways and means of getting rid of her. She is Illusion. She is maya. She is delusion that sweeps away our existence.

Avidya or Nescience

Avidya or Nescience is false knowledge. ***Kapila's Samkhya Philosophy*** recognizes eight types of false knowledge or ignorance. Imposing spirit on non-spirit, Unmanifest, Mahat, ego or "I'-Principle and the five Primary elements. This is known as Tamas or darkness. Tamas is eight-fold; it connects to eight forms of moha or attachment (due to ignorance). Delusion, also the result of Ignorance, is caused due to egotism and it is also eight-fold. Extreme delusion is ten-fold. Attachment to sense objects such as taste, sound, sight, etc. are ten-fold and these are mundane (earthly) as well as celestial. Sound, taste, sight are delightful. There are eight super-natural powers that are means to acquire the delightful objects. It is also important to note that the objects of senses are mutually suppressive. The eight-fold occult powers that are means of obtaining sense objects become incensed due to the intense desire and craving of the jeevas. Thus, the eight occult powers and ten sense-objects together become eighteen objects and these are objects of aversion like sound, taste, sight, etc. Clinging to objects of desire is of the nature of blinding darkness. Hence, attachment or Moha leads to total loss of discriminative power. That is how delusion is caused due to ignorance.

The Source of Ignorance

Ever since the child has tasted its mother's milk, the sensate world has taken a firm hold over the life of the child. As the child grows older, the hold becomes tighter and tighter fed by the food derived as it is from the minerals, water, vegetation and other earthly sources. All the 'ari-shadvargas' - raga, dvesha, krodha (anger), moha, mada, matsarya that obstruct, or hinder, the realization of the Self takes firm root in the body. The different juices of fruits and vegetables, or anything derived from the vegetative sources take control of the senses and dictate the moods. The 'tamasic' and the 'rajasic' juices (food) make the grip much firmer and it is very difficult to get rid of this sensate world. It leads to a state where the sense of discrimination is lost and we reach a state as one can put it, 'the pigs are happy in mire'; happy and contented as they are, persons do not have the thirst or hunger for the Lord. Is it the result of 'His Grace' that you forget Him? May be! But the sweet memories of Him is lingering somewhere in the subconscious. Immersed in the worldly affairs, forgetting Him for a while, a rude shock or a jolt shakes persons out of complacency now and then to remind this. Once in a while, this changes the direction of life of some people, but may not alter the lives of many others! This is the way the Lord cleanses our mind and makes our hearts pure; this is the way our ego is curbed and realize our Self and thus He makes us see Him in all, not merely in a few kith and kins or loved ones.

The grip of 'Vasudha', Raga or attachment of the mother earth is so great on the mortals that it is difficult to get out of it. Even Sriman Narayana was not spared; He got into the grip of ' Shree Vasudha' when He came to rescue her in 'Varaha Avatar'. It is believed that Goddess Lakshmi, the earth, was hidden in ocean and the Lord came to rescue her in 'Varaha avatar'. Since he resided in water for some time with Laksmi, he is known as Narayana, ['nara' meaning water, and 'ayana' meaning abode]. On insistence from all other Divine Souls in the Heaven, Sri Narada had to come down to earth and remind Sriman Narayana of His purpose of the visit to earth and prod Him to return to Vaikunta. The Lord had forgotten his abode 'Vaikunta' for a while! If this is the state of the Lord under the grip of the sensate world, how strange it is to expect the mortals to get out of the grip of this sensuous world?

We all live on the periphery. We are governed by the sensuous life directed by the mind. The mind controls the senses and sets them on their errands of search for happiness in small things. The supreme goal of life is happiness. This happiness has to be gained by the senses and the senses get satisfied as per the dictates of the mind. It is an outward errand and the senses go out to reach for the source of happiness. Now and then, the stint of happiness enjoyed, a 'make-believe state', is attained and the ignorant mind takes it for real happiness until it gets bored of it and strives for a different source of happiness.

Thus, the mad pursuit for the 'make-believe happy state' continues and this state of illusion is '*maya*'. All of us are carried away in this flood of illusion; once we are knocked down by the 'prajnya' or realisation, we come to our real senses. The mind takes the guidance from the 'buddhi' or intellect' and looks inward for its guidance The senses are asked to keep quite and allow the mind to take to the inward journey. The same sensuous mind turns to the intellect and the consciousness guides it to better understanding of the real happiness through 'self- realization'.

Here, it is very interesting to note an episode that took place during the churning of the ocean for the sacred 'amrut'. When the demons realised that they were cheated in the distribution of the divine elixir, the amrut, they tried to control the five senses of the mortals and prevent them from turning to God. Whenever man turned towards the spiritual sources for his happiness, the sensuate mind was diverted to the opposite of all that is good. Thus came the habbit of seeing and hearing sensuous sights and sounds, taste rajasic (hot) and tamasic (cold) foods and drinks, and dwelling in sex, in mad pursuit of sensuous life. This plan of the "Asuras' is to keep off the mortals from the attractions of the 'divine' and denying them a chance of enjoying the 'Supreme Bliss'. Thus, it appears as though 'evil prevails over good'. This is again 'maya'. This is just an illusion for, it is 'Sat' only, that prevails.

The concept of '*Maya*' is beautifully described in *Brahma Rahasya Upanishad* [*Mantra*, 13]. Maya is called '*Avyaktam*' (undifferentiated or unmanifested), or Prakriti. This can be inferred from the effects it produces. It is this Maya that brings forth this whole universe. *Maya* playing upon Brahman causes the first manifestation of *Hiranyagarbha* (Cosmic Space) in the beginning of the cycle. He, in turn, creates the whole universe. [*Isavasya Upa*. 12]. Maya is Shuddha Sattva (pure, devoid of passion and inertia). Brahman is beginning-less and end-less (Anadi-Anantam). But, Maya is Anadi-Santam (beginning-less but has the end) only for the Jnani who has the knowledge of the Self. Maya can be realized only after the heart-knot is released. Unless one is fre from mamata and attachment maya cannot be realised. It is very difficult to realize the Maya and once Maya is realized there exists no world or sansar for the released one, the 'Jnyani'.

Matter and energy, and sound exist in Nature (Prakriti) in an undifferentiated state. As already stated, the whole Universe exists in *Maya* in a seed-state during the cosmic Pralaya (dissolution). Maya is the Upadhi or causal body of the Ishvara. It is under the control of the Lord. Swami Ramakrishna Paramahansa puts it in a very interesting way. Accordingly, *"the truth is that, 'God alone is real and all else unreal'. Men, universe, house, wife, children- are all unreal; all these are like the magic of the magician. The magician strikes his wand and says, 'come delusion, come confusion'! Then he says to the audience, 'open the lid of the pot; see the birds fly into the sky'. But the magician alone is real and his magic unreal. The unreal exists for a second and then vanishes*". Swami Shivananda puts it in a different way. He says, "*All visible things are Maya. Maya will vanish through the effect of knowledge (Jnyana). One must strive to get rid of Maya that devastates the mind; the destruction of the mind*". Some believe that destruction of mind, manonasha is not possible. '*Manonasha*' means the annihilation of *Maya*, ignorance that covers Reality. "*Meditation is the only way in which to dominate maya*". It is possible to get out of this 'make-believe' world by meditation, contemplation, dhyan and samadhi. In other words, transcending causalty, time and space and contemplating on Brahman will bring this delusion of Mind to an end.

Desire

Now coming to desire, it is the desire that is the root cause of our existence. Desire is the 'germ cell', the cause of life. But for the desires we would not exist here even for a moment. It is the desire that keeps us breathing. It is our desire that makes us restless and run hither and thither entertaining all sorts of thoughts forcing us to action, consciously or unconsciously and sub-consciously.

Desire is Brahman. Desire is the Self. Desire is for the Self. This is the desire of the soul. All factors work united towards the achievement of the desire of the jeevas. If one desires for the 'Supreme Bliss', the 'Divine Grace' will operate in that direction. One has to be very clear in his goal. No half-hearted efforts will ever yield any desired fruit. Although it is not in one's hands to take birth in a place of one's choice, or in an opulent family according to one's wishes, definitely it is possible to turn an adverse situation and environment into an advantage. It is easy to realize one's goal, provided he works in that direction, strives for it single- minded, and leaves it not till his goal is reached. It is possible to realize the dreams by mere faith and concerted action. Lack of resources may not be a major constraint; it may be an irritant. Poverty is a blessing in disguise for most of the great achievers.

As already stated in the Karma theory, it is the desire that is the cause of our birth. Our unfulfilled desires are the karmic particles adhered to the Soul and these drag us to the whirlpool of samsara. Know the cause and fry the seed of cycle of birth called 'desire' and win over death by Realization of the Self through tapas Meditation.

Desire comes in the form of deep impressions of past life. One has to constantly remember that Mind works on memories and most of the desires are the memories of the past and the fulfilment of these desires is not possible since there is lapse of time between the conception of desire and fulfilment of the same. Hence, the first technique of Mind Management is to define this '*desire*'. '*Desire*' is the driving force of life. It seems paradoxical that desire fulfilment is the goal of life of ordinary people; but desires kill them. Most of the desires are innate, sub-conscious, and become the cause of the repeated cycles of births and deaths. But, no one is prepared to accept this truth.

Desire and activity cease only when all wants are fulfilled. Ignorance begets desire and desire generates activity directed towards ephemeral ends, which in course of fulfillment produce good and bad tendencies, pulling up the individual self to higher births or dragging it down to lower life.

The person is the desire, rather embodiment of desire. It is the desire that makes the soul take birth repeatedly. It is the desire that is the driving force behind the formation of the body that is the means for the soul. The great elements guided by the supreme intelligence forms the body to perform this function. This is the supreme order the power of creation is the power of the Self.

The soul has the outer coverings and shines through these coverings. These coverings are the five sheaths of desire- annamaya kosha, pranamaya kosha, manomaya kosha, vignyanamaya kosha, and the anandamaya kosha. What the soul wants, it gets it. For it is the giver, that is the taker, that is the creator, and that is the 'enjoyer'. That is also the enjoyed and the 'enjoyment'. The body and mind are medium for its activities.

Till the soul is free from all types of desires, including desire for 'liberation', it goes on taking any number of bodies, transmigrating through bodies till it experiences all desires. The soul goes through different bodies *evolving* at every stage depending upon the nature of its desires till it attains supreme knowledge.

'Whatever may be the nature of desire it shall be fulfilled, since the desire itself is the Brahman in its true nature, i.e., 'Bliss', or 'Anand'. This is the Supreme Order.

"Kaamagney Namah". *'The Supreme Self purifies the person from all desires'. [Vishnu Sahasra Naamam]*

The 'ari-shadvargas', Desire (Kama), Anger (Krodha), Attachment (Moha), Greed (Lobha), Egotism (Ahamkara or Mada), and Jealousy (Matsarya) can be destroyed by Japam, Dhyaan, Prayer, Worship, and Meditation and firm resolve (Sankalpa). Mind is so attached to these qualities- raga, dwesha, moha, lobha, mada, etc. that it is very difficult to get out of their clutches. The desire is the fire that destroys reason. It burns out the body and the brain cells. It promotes animal propensities and makes man an animal. Yoga helps to get out of the grip of desire but there should be a firm mind, a strong will power.

The Supreme Self is the creator of the desires. All desires are the reflection of creativity of the Supreme Self. These desires for the objects are the conscious desires of the ignorant soul to reach its destination. It aspires for the perishable objects due to ignorance; and when it attains knowledge it attains desire and its own true nature, the 'Bliss'. The attainment of desire, ultimately, is the union of the desirer with the desired and this is possible with the help of the Lord, His Grace. For Jnyaani who has attained his Self, there is neither the desire nor the desirer for both are merged into One.

The Supreme Creator is the creator of desire. The desire is the illusion or 'maya', ignorance. Only by the 'Lord's Grace', a person is freed from this desire, this illusion, this ignorance.

The seat of desire is the mind. Mind is the desire. Senses are a medium for the experience of this desire. The senses coming in contact with the objects experience the quality of the sense objects that are termed as pleasure or pain. The intellect is the sharp edge of the mind. It is the guiding arm of the mind as per the dictates of the mind.

'The senses, the mind, and the intellect are said to be its seat through which these delude the embodied by veiling his wisdom'. [Bhagavad-Gita III-40]

"Manonasha"

Although literally 'Manonasha' or destruction of mind is not possible, quietening the mind (also called manonasha) is possible by

'Meditation' and Tapas. 'Manolaya' which is only temporary absorption for a short time in the object of meditation cannot give freedom. 'Vasanas' are destroyed in 'manonasha'. Pranayama can check the velocity of mind. It can calm and steady the mind. It cannot annihilate the mind. The enquiry of 'Who am I' or Brahma Vichara will bring Manonasha. Atman and Mind are two different entities. Mind can be annihilated but not the Atman.

So, kill the mind, the destroyer of knowledge. It is not possible to kill the mind; killing the mind is stilling the mind. It is quietening the mind and stopping its vibration. When the vibrations that cause chitta vrittis cease, automatically, the mind comes to rest. This is the right state of mind to transcend time and space by contemplation. But this is not an easy task. The mind is ever active and, the mind and the senses always search for new thrill and excitement and the intensity and velocity of vibrations increase. Moreover, the supreme Self goes on creating the universe in newer and bewitching forms so that the persons are always enamoured about to live in this world. The Lord Almighty has made breathing a pleasure, all sense objects pleasurable, so that nobody wants to leave this world. Persons are so much attached to this world of bodies, the perishable bodies at that, they forget about their own true Self. They are attached to the body that is the means of bondage that eventually leads to disenchantment and disillusion. Attaining Self is the means of breaking this cycle of life and be liberated into freedom. *Only the Self is capable of controlling the mind since the Self is the master of the Mind. Contemplating on Mind in dhyan and meditation is the right way to control the mind. Just sit in a comfortable position, breath in and out slowly concentrating your mind on the heart and chant the Pranava "Om". Slowly, the agitated mind coms to rest.*

It is important to note that *'Anthahkarana'*, the internal organ (sensitivity?) that includes mind (manas), intellect (Buddhi), and Heart will not assume the form of objects. It will be free from vrittis. 'Vrittis' are virtual 'whirlpool' in the mind-lake, thought waves in manas, or mental modifications. It will be in a state of resistence (Nirodha), or control. In saroopanasha, the Rajas and Tamas gunas are eradicated and the Sattva Guna remains. On account of this sattva Guna, a 'Jeevanmukta' possesses Sattvic virtues such as Maitri (Friendship), Karuna (Mercy), and other good qualities. In a Videhamukta, like the king of Videha, Janaka, even Sattva Guna is annihilated. Therefore, *'aroopanasha'* of mind comes in.

The attributes of the three Gunas are to be clearly understood in order to achieve '*Manonasha*'. Mind is formed out of the sum total of Sattva portion of Tanmatras, the subtle elements. It is not self-luminous. Because, it is very near Brahman on account of its subtlety, the light of Brahman is reflected on it. So it thinks, it doubts, plans and speculates. Just as there is death for this physical body, there is death for this mind also, 'manonasha'. When one gets knowledge of the Self, mind gets absorbed in Brahman, just as the drops of water get absorbed in a hot pan. Mind gropes in dark; it is unable to explain the Whys and Hows of the riddle of the universe.

Mind is a finite and a frail instrument that is conditioned in time, space, and causation.

Here, it is necessary to remember one thing. Manonasha literally means killing the mind that is dangerous. A mind that is dead makes a person almost a vegetable. In yoga, mind control is practised to attain higher spiritual experience that transcends the ordinary conscious state of the mind. Mind is set aside only to attain super-consciousness state from the ordinary consciousness. In other words, all stray thoughts that repeatedly occur in mind are laid to rest by observation or witnessing self. Once the thoughts or chitta vrittis cease, the vibration also ceases leading to manonasha. *'Manolaya' and 'Manonasha' are yogic terms that should not be mistaken for ordinary meaning of the terms.*

The Gunas

In *Bhagavd Gita* [Ch.XVII], we find the description of the qualities inherent in man and the consequent characteristics of persons. There are the three main types of Gunas – the Sattvic, the Tamas, and the Rajas, of which one or the other is preponderant at any time and a person's behaviour is very much depending on this preponderant Guna. However, these Gunas are subject to change with time depending on many factors. The actions of previous life, i.e., the Karma, decide the prepondering guna to a great extent followed by the intent desire of the jeeva and the inherent genes. Further, buddhi acts according to the dictates of the Karma and as they put it, ***"Karmaanusaarena buddhih"***. Thus, how a person behaves is subject to a number of factors that is beyond the ability of man to understand since it is governed by the preponderant guna, the past karma and the intent desire of the jeeva as well as the environment and the genes.

However, certain generalizations have been made and this helps us to know the type of persons. "*Sattva dominates the man of spiritual inclination and is characterized by knowledge and harmony*" [*Bhagavad Gita* 14.11-13]. Tamasic persons are characterised by darkness and ignorance, heedlessness and delusion. Rajasic persons are passionate, restless, and dominating. Tamasic people eat unclean food. They are arrogant, deceitful, despondent, procrastinating and unsteady. They think they know everything. They are impatient of hearing what others have to say. They undertake task in despondence and without proper knowledge. Their actions are borne out of delusion, heedless of the consequences. They give gifts to wrong persons, at the wrong place and time, or in the wrong way. They worship without faith and they are deluded by superstitions. They harm others.

Rajasic persons are very fond of exciting food; they like bitter, sour, hot and pungent food. They are attached to their work with selfish interest. They are attached to other people and their interests. They are over-anxious about the fruits of action; their actions are for the satisfaction of their desires and vanity. They are greedy, violent, prone to fear and worry, and they are easily elated or downcast. They give gifts grudgingly, or in anticipation of some thing in return and always aim at the fruits of action. They worship for the sake of results or for show and their austerities are ostentatious and may be to gain power or with some motive.

Sattvic persons are characterized by good nature, benevolence and compassion. They take sattvic food, clean and wholesome, that give strength, good health and help longevity. They perform actions with detachment; they are conscientious workers and do not worry about fruits of action. Actions without desire for reward or anxiety about results are the traits and hallmark of success. Sattvic persons perform all actions with purity of mind and heart. They offer gifts with compassion without any desire for returns and they know the propriety of their actions. Their austerities are of pure mind and for spiritual end for the benefit of others. Their actions are bereft of attachment and egotism, being endowed with fortitude and enthusiasm, unaffected by success or failure [*Bhagavad Gita* 18.26]. The sattvic people are engaged in spiritual thoughts and actions; they speak truth but not harmful to anybody. They are persons with self-restraint, calm mind, and are often silent, engaged in spiritual thoughts.

These generalized characteristics described in *Bhagavad Gita* are to be carefully understood. One can easily understand the nature of a person by closely observing his behaviour, food tastes and habits, motivations and actions. But one should not commit the mistake of attributing any character to any person based on these observations. Persons change their habits according to their sex, age, needs, circumstances, place and time.

Guna is vibration. The intensity and velocity of the chitta vrittis decide the character and conduct of the individuals. One must understand the prepondering Gunas in a person, because these Gunas go to make him what he or she is. Ultimately, one must try to transcend all these Gunas by an austere way of life. There is no other alternative for salvation!

The characteristics of pure '*Sattva*', unmixed with Rajas and Tamas, are harmony, knowledge, bliss, supreme peace, cheerfulness, balance of mind, purity of nature (Shùddha Bhava), contentment, constant devotion unto the 'Atman', absence of pride, hatred, hypocrisy, lust and anger, desire for liberation, divine tendencies, faith, turning away from the unreal, discrimination, enquiry, meditative mood, etc. Pure Sattva is like transparent crystal. Reflection of Atman can take place in Sattva only, like reflection of objects that can take place only in a clear mirror. When Sattva is mixed with Rajas and Tamas, it becomes impure Sattva. It is 'Avidya' or ignorance. This becomes 'Upadhi' or the limiting factor, the limiting adjunct of Jeevas. Transmigration takes place in this condition. Self-Realization comes when the Sattva Guna is raised to one hundred percent, reducing the proportion of Tamas and Rajas, and the transmigration also ends with it when one transcant it. Eradicating the Sattva Guna takes one to Kaivalya- a state of mind in turiya, and makes Jeeva, a Jeevanmukta. Transcending all the Gunas is the culmination of Samadhi. All waves, all vibrations cease to exist at this stage.

'*Rajo Guna*' has got the projecting capacity or '*Vikshepa Shakti*'. The phenomenal world manifests through this Vikshepa Shakti. Rajas cause attachment to objects and various sorts of activities. This brings grief or sorrow and misery. Preponderance of Rajo Guna is the cause of bondage and induces worldly tendencies. Lust, anger, greed, arrogance, hatred, pride, hypocrisy, jealosy are the attributes of Rajas.

'*Tamo Guna*' is at the root of all the problems of the Jeevas of this world. It is a veiling power. Ignorance or moudhya, carelessness, sleep, laziness, lassitude, and dullness are the attributes of Tamas. Tamas causes perverted intellect. Intellect is rendered blind. Preponderance of Tamas causes repeated transmigration. It makes things appear differently from what they are. It projects things that are non-existing. Even the learned persons are under the clutches of Tamas and lose their sense of right judgment. They lose their understanding and become seekers of pleasure. They suffer under sense of deeper attachment to worldly things and perishable objects. They mistake unreal things as real. They get swayed under the power of money, power, and authority and regard them as eternal. They regard body, wife, children, brothers and sisters as self and mistake them for Atman. These learned persons suffer grief and misery when these pleasure centers are withdrawn. Tamas is very powerful as a veiling shakti, that makes even the learned persons lose their sense of discretion and treat this 'make-believe' world as more real.

There is another interpretation of these Gunas and Samkhya Philosophy attributes all qualities to one, the prepondering and the other, suppressed gunas. At any time, any one of the two gunas is predominant- either the Tamas or the Sattva. The Sattva and the Tamas by themselves are inactive and useless unless the Rajas activates them. Rajas is the activating force, the Rajas that is at the root of all qualities.

Although the prepondering Guna of a person can be easily identified, it is not the decisive, final and determining factor. A scientific analysis of human behaviour is necessary in order to understand the mysterious ways of human conduct, tendencies and instincts. Some scientists hold that environment plays a very crucial role in the formative years of a person and greatly mould his character. Some believe that instincts are natural impulses or urges innate in any person and are not just the creatures of environment. There is an evolutionary urge to change in every person. Some biologists and psychologists trace our instincts to childhood days and even go to the extent of attributing them to parents, close relatives and ancestors.

There are some thinkers who believe that ethereal beings are born in human bodies, complete with their own innate tendencies, desires and passions. Thomas Huxley believes that every sentient being is reaping what it has sown, if not in this life, in one or other of the infinite series of antecedent existences; this is close to what the Karma theory holds. Even Darwin, the great evolutionist, holds the same view. It is said "Karmaanusaarena Buddhih", meaning that 'every person thinks and acts according to the instincts dictated by his past actions. The actions of the present are governed by the desires and there is a divine plan behind delivering the fruits of action. It also indirectly hints at the fact that no one can expect the results of action simply based on the person's merits like the skills and efficiency. So there are certain innate tendencies that makes a person react as he does.

This whole analysis makes it more confusing and gives a false notion that there is nothing in our hands and everything is our past karma or divine plan and ultimately creates a defeatist tendency. But it is not actually so. There is another important thing that governs every life and that is 'Lord's Grace'. Those who start their work in the name of the Lord, offers it to Him, in all humility, shall reap bountiful returns. Lord's name will wipe out all the negative effects of past actions.

The ancestors to whom we trace our habits and tendencies are none other than ourselves. Instead of making scapegoats of our ancestors, and blaming them for all our ills, we must take full responsibility for our actions and change our habits. But this is a difficult job. Ego comes in the way. We are not prepared to change. We are not prepared to accept. That humility is not there; that total surrender to Him is not coming forth. 'I' and 'mine' dominate all our thoughts and action and we always forget that there is someone greater than us. We all forget that we exist because of Him. We trust others created by Him but do not trust Him easily. This ignorance is the cause of all our misery and unhappiness. Here the Rule of Mind Management is "Realisation of the Self is the only way to a happy and successful life'. Even 'prarabhda karma can be erased by the constant chanting of Lord's name. It is panacea for all our ills.' *Chant His name and do your work with total submission*'. This is the mind management technique for happiness and success in life.

The *Brahmarahasya Upanishad* describes the method of attaining Self-Realization. '***By constantly thinking of Him one can attain Him***'. One can attain 'Brahm Jnyana' by eradicating or annihilating the Tamasic and Rajasic Gunas and transcending the Sattva. All vrittis, such as the Ghora vrittis (impure thoughts of mind), Mudha vrittis (stupefied) and the pleasure creating vrittis, Ajnyana Vrittis (ignorance), egoism – all should be annihilated. The source of all these vrittis is the samskaras or impressions of various vasanas in a seed state. If the seed-body or mula ajnyana is removed all vrittis perish by themselves.

Practising Pranayama will help in the annihilation of all vrittis (thoughts). Constant inquiry as to '*Who am I*?' will help understanding oneself and annihilation of vrittis. Whenever a vritti rises up, put this question; the vritti disappears. Do not try to fulfil the desires; the vrittis disappear. Because, fulfilment of the desire leaves a deeper impression that the mind lingers upon again and again leading to frustration and delusion. Fulfilment of desires is not the answer; repeat the question whether this will give an everlasting happiness. If it is not giving permanent happiness, discard it by 'prathyahara' technique, i.e., withdrawing the mind from the object. ***'Meditation' is the technique of rooting out 'Ajnyana'.*** *Meditate on the Srutis; here, the Mahat vakya is:*

"AHAM BRAHMAASMI", ["I AM THE SELF, THE BRAHMAN"] "SARVAM KHALVIDAM BRAHMA NEHA NANASTI KINCHANA", *meaning,* ***ALL INDEED IS BRAHMAN, THERE IS NO SUCH THING AS DIVERSITY***". *It is worth contemplating on the meaning of the mahat vakya, 'I am Brahman'. What is wrong in the supreme Lord sitting within the cave of the heart of man as 'Antaryamin' saying 'I am Brahman', the*

Absolute? Of course, He will not say it! Where is the need to proclaim Himself as the Supremo? Here, 'I' stands for the Self, not the body or mind. It is the Upanishadic doctrine taught to the pupils by their revered Sages and teachers, saying: "Go out and realize your Self, the Brahman 'within', and say, "Aham Brahmasmi", as also, realize "all that is and that will be are Brahman, indeed"! Remember the doctrine: "Ishavasyamidam sarvam……… ".

Realising the Brahman in the Self, i.e.,"*atma sakshatkara*" is not an easy proposition. It is indeed, the hardest task and it invariably requires a spiritually attained Yogin to teach! No ordinary teacher will do. Atmasakshaatkaar is attained by "Shaktipaata' the Grace of the Lord flowing through the Yogin. Even to think of all these is yoga; it does not come quite easily to mortals. It involves sadhana, practicing yogic exercises and imbibing the techniques of different types of yoga. In the long-run only a determined sadhaka will attain it. There are many obstacles to practicing these simple spiritual techniques."*When meditation is practised, obstacles such as absence of right enquiry, impatience, laziness, inclination to enjoyment, absorption in sensual and impure thoughts arises. Remove them through right enquiry and discrimination*" [*Mantra* 18]. Use sense of discrimination, viveka, vichara, and vairagya by asking the question 'who am I'? Meditate on vichara. Sama (serenity or calmness), dama (control of senses), and uparati (abstraction) should be practiced constantly; thoughts of Atman will remove impure thoughts. Asana, Pranayam, and right sattvic diet will help reducing tamas and rajas. 'Brahm Jnyan' is the release from the trammels from one's own mind. Such a release alone leads to the attainment of moksha or liberation. One who practises contemplation or meditation on the above mantras will surely conquer his mind and attain '*Brahm Jnyan*'.

"*If one regards the world as unreal, all vasanas will vanish by themselves. Ignorance, Ajnyana will perish slowly. One has to realise the 'Brahman' as one's own very Self. This is theBrahma Rahasya*". [*Mantras* 15-20].

It is very interesting to know that the individual mind is in touch with the cosmic mind and our mental energy comes from a cosmic source. We should know how to control and direct this psychic energy. Control is necessary to prevent the energy from flowing into lower centers, from flowing out through our sense organs and getting wasted through futile thinking and worrying and useless talk. This cosmic energy should be made to find expression at higher centers, the heart, the throat, and the ajnya (between the eye brows).

Unconscious control is called repression, and some forms of repression are harmful to certain people. But, conscious, intelligent control is beneficial and essential for all people, not necessarily for the spiritual aspirants.

Spiritual Healing and Touch Therapy

Almost all the Sadhus who live in the Himalayas who regularly practise intense Meditation have acquired the power of 'spiritual

healing' and the villagers who live nearby have been greatly benefited by this. They can go to the extent of reviving the dead by a mere touch depending on the condition of the dead body. It is the siddhi gained from intense sadhana of particular yoga like Hatha Yoga that certain mystic powers are gained for self-less servie.

While the body degenerates and decays, the embedded soul is eternal, permanent and, transmigrating."*Know that to be indestructible by which all this is pervaded. No one is ever able to destroy that immutable*" [*Bhagavad Gita*]. The Vedic Scriptures make it very clear that '*the soul of man is beyond all mortal afflictions; it is free from sin, free from old age, free from death and grief, free from hunger and thirst*'. We often believe what we see our body as real and it constitutes the whole of our being. Not that our body is unreal; our physical life is unreal; but it is not the whole of our being. In fact, it represents only a part of our real life, When we are old we are not what we were at our childhood stage, or youth stage; we have changed in our physical appearance, in our ways of behaviour; often people who have seen us a few years ago cannot even recognize us. Such is the change that comes about our life. Unfortunately, many people believe that our physical life seems to be the whole of our being and it is this misconception that blocks the steady flow of 'life-force' and we suffer in many ways. Disease always indicates disturbance; and disorder invariably results when our physical tendencies lead us away from the direct influence of the soul, or our bodily desires gain ascendancy over our spiritual nature.

The only true healing is accomplished by contact with the spiritual essence. This cannot be done in a professional way. This has to be done at individual level by spiritual healing techniques. One may not believe in prayer; but prayer heals. Prayer overcomes the resistence of the ego and opens up the channels of the unconscious to the inflow of the 'Divine Shakti', or Cosmic Prana. For this prayer must be done with intensity, sincerity and perseverance. Faith also has great healing power, because it elevates us to a plane of higher consciousness that cures all our ills. All power is of the spirit. Through whole-hearted prayer and unwavering faith one can succeed in making oneself receptive to that power. Receptivity comes from faith and will to cure oneself; and it is said, that one cannot fall sick unless one cooperates with the disease to take over the mind and the body Hence, it is amply clear that in our subconscious we are willing to fall sick and we fall sick. We can resist this temptation and overcome the feeling of sickness by a strong mind and spiritual practice like dhyan and meditation.

The Power of Love

Love is 'Brahm' and as such it has its source in the cavity of the heart. It is something that cannot be reached by the mind or the senses. It is beyond all rationale and logic. Its power is immense.

Love is the most misused, abused and confused word these' days. There is the danger that soon the corrupt form of the usage becomes more popular under the influence of the entertainment media and the true spirit of love is forgotten. There is a desire in all of us that others should always love us. We do not want that others should show scant respect or hate us.

But, the opposite is not always true. We do not want to love others unless there is a special relation with us. We do not hesitate to show disrespect to others, especially when they are less fortunate and deprived persons. Our ego does not permit us to show respect to such persons. We love only our superiors for fear of repression, or for favours. This is normal human behaviour that we observe in our day-to-day life. Hence, the question of unqualified universal love does not arise. Honestly speaking, love in its true sense, does not exist. Otherwise we would not see so much of strife, jealousy, hatred, intolerance, wars and unrest everywhere. No two countries can co-exist peacefully with all their no-war pacts, for 'fear of the unknown'! This is the situation in the world today. As psyche of the people, this applies to relationships between States, between cities and towns, between communities, and even families within towns and villages. Some attribute this to the influence of Kali Bhagavan since this is Kali Yug. But the reality is that our heart is not pure; our mind is not pure. We are possessive in nature. We are selfish and we want everything exclusively for ourselves whether we need them or not. We are jealous of others. The arishadvargas have their play for there is no control over them. Man is not bothered to control his mind; that is the problem.

Love is a very precious thing that we do not want to shower on everyone recklessly. We reserve it to a chosen few and that also for a limited time; may be till our desires are fulfilled with that person. It requires a Jesus Christ to shower love and compassion recklessly. We look at Shree Krishna's love for the Gopikas also with suspicion, lust in our mind! This is the situation today. When they say, Lord Krishna had 16,008 damsels as His lovers we literally believe it and envy Him! It is a great tragedy that our mind will not rise above a certain level (below navel) of consciousness. If God cannot redeem the troubled souls who else can? We do not realize that Lord Krishna redeemed all those damsels in distress after the Mahabharata war who earnestly worshiped Him with Love; you also worship Him with Love. He will shower His Grace on you!

Love is defined as 'Yuj' meaning union. It is the union of souls. Any person, who loves the '*other*', sees himself in that 'other' (person, place, animal, or thing). When we love our pet birds or animals, we identify ourselves with them. We do not see any difference between our selves and our pets. We become one. That is the reason why we see some fortunate pets get luxurious treatment from their adopters and inherit huge property bequeathed to them by their rich owners. The opposite of love is hatred. This should not mean that if we cannot love we should hate. Many parents hate their children and children hate their parents for various reasons. Here, absence of love is the basic thing. Selfishness is the other important reason for this. Many a parents dis-own their children and deprive them of ancestral property; they give it away in charities and public trusts.

Mother's love for children is true love. It is true love without blemish, without selfishness, without any desire for returns and it is not even reciprocal. However, some human minds are so wretched that we find some exceptions to this, too. Paternal love is filial and, very rarely we find some fine sentiments and deep love between parents and grown up children. Some parents love their children so much that they close their eyes to all their follies and weaknessess. More often, children are in the grip of their own desires, likes and dislikes, and love has no place in such afflicted minds. *Pure love exists where spirituality reigns supreme!*

We often see some doctors and nurses showering love and affection on patients in hospitals and it works wonders! Love has great power of curing sickness of body and mind. Love is God for God comes in the form of love to the sick. It is extremely difficult to say that love is a constant factor in our day-to-day life. Our love is at best conditional reflex and we hesitate to love even those who love us; hence, it is not even reciprocal. It is this kind of development of man that makes the future of this world bleak. The concept of universal love is too much to ask for in this materialistic world. With so much of jealousy, intolerance, greed and avarice, cruel and merciless attitude of people, it is frightening! It is this fear that prompted Jesus Christ to preach universal love and sacrifice. Unfortunately, even today, his preachings are not taken seriously; we are eager to accept his 'love thy neighbour' concept, that too in a very narrow and limited or restricted sense of the terms. Hence, the question, 'where is pure Love'?

You can love only the Lord Almighty with pure heart and none else! Love Him whole-heartedly. This is an important 'Manoniyantrana Tantra, the Mind Management Technique. ***Do It. Experience the joy of Love of God. Enjoy the Supreme Bliss.***

Nature teaches the lessons of love and compassion and man learns discrimination. The dualities inherent in this illusory world are responsible for the nature of man and his behavioural tendencies. Memory on the one hand and arishadvargas on the other create such a complexity in man that his actions are highly influenced by his likes and dislikes. If he likes some persons or things, his love, sympathy, benevolence, compassion, anthahkarana, overflow; if he dislikes someone, he starts hating not only him, but, everyone and everything associated with his enemy. Such is the nature of afflicted mind. This is due to ignorance that shrouds the Reality.

Love dissipates when Man loses his sense of God. Extreme ego, identification with oneself in his body and mind and the earthly possessions makes him blind. It is this blindness that is the cause of all problems of life. Pure, unconditional love is associated with spirituality. Science and rationality know no love; and, love is a divine quality, the attribute of the Brahman. Love brings bliss, total bliss at that! Home is the place of love and temple is the place of peace; we should make our homes a temple of love and peace so that our children develop integrated personality and never suffer from want; our daughters should shower love, peace and grace of the Lord wherever they go and our sons should be personification of the Lord Himself. This is the aspiration of all spiritual parents.

Love and Peace go together; where there is love, there is peace. If the nations are to prosper, there should be peace; peace is the prerequisite of progress. If the society is to prosper, it should develop mutual trust and love; only mutual trust can give the strong foundation of love. And, all these progress and development depend on the prevalence of peace that comes out of love and love comes out of spirituality. Prosperity cannot be achieved with what is called secularism; secularism is devoid of spirituality. Spirituality establishes the concept of 'unity', the 'One'; spirituality stands for the Lord who is 'One without a second'. National leaders without spirituality cannot establish peace and progress in any country. They cannot make the country great, unless they become great by spiritual attainments, love and sacrifice. The present day maladies are due to the absence of spirituality in our leaders. The first priority in India is to establish Dharma, the foundation of our MahaBharat. Truly, it will make our country great and our people great. A strong spiritual base is the only solution to our problems; it delivers peace and progress.

Hence, our constant prayer should be "*Sarve Jano Sukhino bhavantu*". Om! Shantih, Shantih, Shantih".

Thus;"***We all live on the periphery and should try to reach the Centre of Consciousness***". There are many obstacles that prevent us from attaining the Brahman in one life. Even Gautama Buddha remembers his five hundred past lives and says that he had to take twenty-one lives in different forms like the crocodile, elephant, etc. before attaining 'enlightenment'. So, to make an earnest beginning is the first step in this direction.

Love and Friendship

The relationship between Sri Hari, in his incarnation as Lord Krishna and his childhood friend Sudhama in Dvapara Yuga is well known. It is worth remembering here the episode of Sri Krishna visiting His childhood friend Sudhama, a poor Brahmin. Sudhama, with no source of worldy income and wealth, had nothing to offer the Lord except a handful of parched rice; this, the Lord accepted with love and affection and offered a little to his consorv Lakshmi,! Lo! What change it brought to life of poor Sudhama! This is the beauty of the essence of Love, love that knows no bounds.

The episode reminds us of our childhood friends and our feelings that are beyond any reasoning. We love our friends so deeply that there is no scent of selfishness or desire. It is all so spontaneous that our heart is thrilled at the sight of our old friends. There is no 'give and take' here. It is this love, spontaneity of its expression, that cannot be explained but only to be realised. The basis of friendship is pure love. This is expressed at its best in situations like distress in times of war, or on board a ship in mid sea that has turned turbulent. Comrades as they are each is ready to sacrifice himself for the other! Friendship knows no barriers. True friendship is true love and true love that blossoms in the lotus of our heart is the true God within us.

Love and Sex

Sigment Freud and the Psychologists of this school of thought always interpreted love as sex and they treat love as a technique of indulging in sex. For them, love is either foreplay or after-play of sexual indulgence

that is not true in the real spiritual sense. Love and sex are two different sources of power. Love is centred in the heart and it is a higher level of consciousness. Sex is a lower level of consciousness and it is located below the navel, i.e., the lower part of the body. The effect of love and sex, as energy sources, is exactly opposite. Love is energy that hits gently at the heart, as if tapping the heart to open up and spill the joy in it; It is sheer Bliss. Sex energy, on the other hand is a very powerful energy that directly hits at the sex center and opens up the heat of passion, creating a higher temperature in the body, builds up blood pressure and creates a hell of madness in the mind and the afflicted person rests not until all his pent up energy gushes out alongwith the semen, the source of creation. This is a destructive force that spends up energy leading to hunger and calls for repeated sexual indulgence that is tiring and exhausting never satisfying, never fulfilling, causing downfall; that is the reason why it is calld 'falling in love'.

True love is that which brings joy, fulfilment, and needs no external support, whereas sex brings happiness with the support of a lover; the happiness derived from the lover is short-lived unreliable and addictive. It is heat and passion that is exhausting, tiring and dissipating, never fulfilling! Love is satisfying, permanent, and energizing. Love brings joy that knows no bounds and never depeletes physical or mental energy. Love operates at higher level of consciousness and brings emancipation whereas sex brings bondage and entanglement in Sansaar. But, there is a secret in sex energy. The sex energy is capable of taking us to highest level of consciousness from the lowest level of consciousness through Dhyan and Meditation or Praanayaama or Breath control. Enlightenment can be attained by directing the sex energy to reach 'sahasraar' through the navel, heart, throat, ajnya between eyebrows, and the center of the head. Hence, Sexual indulgence is prohibited in Buddhist monks and continence or Brahmacharya is advocated in Upanishads to attain to spiritual goal. Sex energy can be transformed into true Love that transcends space, time, and causality; it is pure; it is Brahm. Hence, sex is the means of attainment of liberation.

The Ari-shadvargas

The enemies of man are not outside but they are within him; they are born with him alongwith the 'Gunas', the vibrations at birth as well as his desire and karma alongwith anthankarana. This is very important since the nature of the person is decided by this 'enemy within'. These enemies are hidden in the heart and some like jealousy in stomach, and moha in throat, and it is very difficult to kill them. Unless you kill these hidden enemies, it is very difficult to live in peace. Happiness and success in life depends on how you conquer these enemies, if not kill them.

Hatred: Hatred, extreme dislike or active 'ill-will' or 'Dvesha' is one of the worst enemies of man. It creates ill- will and rage at the very mention of the person, place, animal or things we do not like. The reason for hatred is self-interest. *Ishavasya Upanishad* clearly explains the cause and remedy of hatred [Verse 6]. "*The wise man who perceives all beings as not distinct* *from his own Self at all, and his own Self as the Self of all – he does not, by virtue of that perception, hate anyone*".

Hatred is the vibration of the mind at a certain degree. In order to overcome that vibration, we have to generate vibration of a different kind at a higher or lower degree. When a new vibration is created, the old vibration is cut off and new vibration starts. For example a person who is fiercely angry may suddenly cool down when he sees an old friend; so also, a sweet chatterings of a child will create a new vibration when the mind is agitated and the vibrations are forceful. Thus, one type of wave (of higher intensity) that generates anger, hatred, and jealousy may be conquered by creating another type of wave (of lower intensity) which produce love, prayer, sympathy, compassion etc. These mental waves or vibrations are the product of mind substance or mindstuff and hence, are not our true self. These waves or chitta vritis are finer particles of matter in vibration. These particles are finer than atoms and electrons and they are always vibrating where as, our 'true self', the Purusha, or the 'Atman' is different and distinct from these mental conditions. The latter is pure and perfect and stand out as exclusive to the operations of chitta vrittis. That is why one who is established in oneself is not perturbed by these chitta vrittis. He will just watch the behaviour of the waves and the waves cease to exist.

When the unconditioned state of consciousness is realized the wise man recognizes that the one Conscious Principle, the 'Self' or the 'Atman', which witnesses the modifications of the body- mind combination, that is specially called his own, is the same as the Conscious Principle witnessing all other entities from the higher to the lowest. The feeling of separateness and the self-interest cause hatred when the 'other' is not agreeable to the self and goes against the self-interest, greed, possessive, craving for self-gratification. When there is a fear that things are going against one's interest, it gives rise to anger, jealousy and the mind loses its balance and sense of discrimination. Hence, it is very dangerous to entertain the very idea of hatred, even with the enemies, for ultimately it destroys balance of mind and peace of the very person who hates. "*A person who sees unity of existence and perceives all beings as his own Self will not have any sorrow". [Isavasya Upanishad*, Verse 7]

Greed and Avarice: Greed and avarice are the worst enemies of man. It is the mean-mindedness of the person that drives him to not only covet some others property but, hides them without sharing them with others. This attitude develops very early in the childhood and continues till death unless spirituality is developed. When greed takes over, people behave like animals; and, cruelty, cunningness, falsity, cheating and other bad qualities take preponderance over sacrifice, compassion, love, piety and kindness. Lobha (greed) is one of the arishadvargas that should be guarded in spiritual practices.

Anger and Jealousy: *Like hatred, anger and jealousy are very forceful negative tendencies that create serious health problems. It has been scientifically proved that eighty percent of our illness such as ulcer, rashes, neck pain, the backache, and diabetes are caused due to the*

defilements caused in the mind. The cause lies in the mind and medication is only superficial treatment.

Anger (Krodha) is the worst enemy of man. It is fire and it burns. When a man is angry he has lost his balance of mind. He is not in his senses; he is prepared to go to any extent. He may even kill others in fitness of anger. The cause of anger is selfishness. When a person does not get what he wants, his reasoning fails and anger takes over. To control anger is very difficult and even the great sage like Doorvasa could not control his anger in front of the Lord of the Lords! Anger is associated with Rajas and unless Sattvic guna is cultivated, it becomes very difficult to control anger. Meditation is the only answer.

Turning anger on oneself is the best solution for it helps to study onself and correct this disorder. Normally, anger comes from the heart for, the blood rushes to face in fits of anger. It is also possible that anger is inherent in the jeeva due to its samskaar or memories or past impressions! Rajasic food and sensuousness cause this anger to overpower the reason. Toxic chemicals are released in the body at times of anger and jealousy that ultimately cause intestinal disorders. Hence, one has to guard against this enemy that resides within and harm us.

Jealousy is the cause of discontentment. It arises from the sub-conscious and unconsciously compares oneself with the others. If others are happy, the vibrations erupt causing either happiness or unhappiness depending on the state of prevailing mood; if one is in an elated mood, happiness of others beget happiness and if negative tendencies prevail, others happiness brings unhappiness to oneself. It brings out the discontent within. A sense of feeling of void within is the cause of jealousy and this void can be replaced by love. So, meditate and control all the ari-shadvargas; develop a sense of love and sacrifice, everything will look beautiful!

Sin: Sin is not that what we generally think as telling lie, hurting others, coveting other's property, or killing, etc. It is the feeling of guilt. It is the feeling of weakness- physical or mental. It is the feeling of helplessness. It is the feeling that others would do harm to our interest and we would be helpless. Rather it is lack of faith in the Lord. It is a great sin if we cannot help others in distress. It is a sin to be selfish and disregard the needs of others. It is a sin to engage in sensuousness and yield to the passion and the desire of the flesh. It is a sin to forget the Lord!

The Manoniyantrana Tantra here is:

Do not live on the periphery; enter the center of consciousness. Conquer your ari-shadvargas- Kama (Desire), Krodha (Anger), Lobha (Greed), Moha (Attachment), Mada (Ahamkara, egoism), Matsarya (Jealousy), by techniques of Dhyana, Japa and Vrata (Mauna, vow of silence). Develop Sattvic Guna by cleansing both body (by sattvic food) and Mind (by constant Meditation). Ethical and moral practices like the sama, dama, dharana are all the basic requirements and should invariably be practised without fail. Live a simple life, an austere life. Engage yourself in the study of the Holy Scriptures like the Upanishads and the Bhagavad Gita. Always think of divine things. Do not allow the senses to take control of your weak mind. Strengthen your mind by strong will and give it in the hands of Buddhi, the intellect. Let your consciousness guide your mind. Contemplate on the Mahat Vakyas and chant holy mantra. Always remember Lord, the Almighty.

The arishadvargas are the negative forces that cause discontent, unhappiness, and void in us. They promote vanity, pride, prejudices, and create unhealthy competition. It is also the root cause of our downfall despite much materialistic progress. Once we understand the meaning and purpose of 'life', it is not very difficult to enjoy life peacefully, joyfully, and happily. But, we do not know the meaning and purpose of life. We want success in our endeavour; but we do not know what this success is; we do not know whether this success brings happiness or more problems. We have seen many successful men have committed suicide and a closer study of such cases reveal what lies under the guise of this 'success'. A sense of void is created despite this success for want of love and sense of sacrifice and surrender to Lord. Worldly success is again 'Maya', or Illusion and it is 'make-believe! It is not real, not the truth. A few people garlanding and praising you may boost your ego and you feel happy for the moment. When the same people boo-boo and pelt stones at you for no fault of yours, you feel miserable. This worldly success is the devil that haunts us throughout our life. It arises from false values.

We want honour, fame, wealth and all these are the qualities of the Brahman who shines in us. There is nothing wrong in aspiring for these qualities. Even the Veda and Upanishads advise us to gain worldly success, achieve material prosperity, and promote your ego; but, promote 'ego' only to surrender it at the feet of the Lord! Worldly success is important. But, every success in life, every accomplishment in life, is to be treated as the means to an end; and, the end or goal of life is Self Realization, 'Atma Saakshaatkara'. This does not come easily to mortals in one or two lives; it takes hundreds of lives to purify the blemished souls, get rid of all desires, surrender the bloated ego to the Lord and live a life of pure heart and realize the Self.

The golden rule is: 'keep yourself happy; keep your family happy; keep your relatives happy; keep your friends and social circle happy; keep your world happy by understanding the intricacies of the functioning of the mind'. Achieve the full potential of the human brain by integration of body, mind and soul through the application of principles of Yoga. Gain self- control and get mastery over the skills that will help to excel in all fields. This will give the joy, the happiness, peace that cannot be achieved by any other means. 'Manoniyantran' tantras or the Mind Management Techniques advocated here are very simple and useful.

The Concept of 'Yad bhavam tad bhavati'

There are innumerable ways of attaining what one desires. Rather, one gets whatever he aspires for. Whoever wants wealth, power, name and fame, and innately desires to achieve these will definitely get them. Here, the secret is that, the desire is 'Brahman' and, His nature is Bliss. For us, the ordinary mortals, it appears that it is impossible to fulfil our dreams in this life. May be it is true that all our wishes cannot be fulfilled in one life. However, it is true that by divine grace and Will of the Lord, environment and circumstances will be created towards this end, fulfilment of dreams; and, entire effort will be directed towards the attainment of these; and, the person is driven in that direction and forced to act. There is a saying:

"*Yad Bhavam Tad Bhavati*", or "*Yachchintayasi tadbhavasi*"
"As you will, so it happens" or, "Just as you think, so you become".

This is a great truth or 'truism'. If you think you are strong, you will become strong. If you think you are weak, you will become weak. This is the secret of 'auto-suggestion', too. Tell yourself you are strong, you become strong, no doubt. Tell yourself you are feeling weak, you feel weak. Man always lives in a world of thoughts. Every man has his own thought-world. Imagination works wonders. Thought has tremendous force. Thought is a solid thing. Thought alone moulds and shapes a man. Your present is the result of your past thoughts and your future will be according to your present thoughts. If you think rightly, you will speak rightly and act rightly. Speech and action simply follow the thoughts. One should cultivate right thinking and should drive out all sorts of vain and worthless worldly thoughts. Let alone moralists or Vedantins, even the modern psychologists lay stress on purity of thoughts. Thought-culture is an exact science.

Do not entertain evil thoughts. Evil thoughts pollute the thought-world. He who entertains evil thoughts will not only harm himself, but harms the world-at-large as well. Evil thoughts are the direct cause for all sorts of diseaes. All diseases take their origin at first from an impure thought. He who entertains good thoughts, sublime and divine thoughts, will greatly promote the health of himself and the environment surrounding him. He can radiate joy, hope, solace, and peace, contentment and happiness of his kith and kin around him as well as those loved ones who are far away from him. But evil thoughts take an upper hand and do great harm. It is very difficult to suppress the evil thoughts and entertain only good thoughts. Only a person with enormous Will power and spiritual strength can always think of good thoughts. If one wants to enjoy supreme happiness, he has to rise above this, rather transcend all thoughts- good or bad, and reach a state of thought-lessness (Nirvikalpa state). Then, one can achieve much greater strength and power. Thought-lessness is the process of inward journey to reach the Atman, i.e., Brahman, the supreme Lord of the Universe.

8
Manoniyantran [Mind Control]

"The mind of man alone is the cause of his bondage and is also the means of his liberation"

[Amrutabindu Upanishad 2]

The Mind is the zing thing! The amazing thing that gives us all the impressions about the objective world, the sensate world, is the Mind; in fact, it is the Mind that makes this world; and the Mind itself is the world. But for the Mind, there is no world. Mind is the cause and Mind is the effect. It is the Mind that drives us in search of happiness that eludes us life after life and finally makes us feel 'enough is enough'. Sree Ramana Maharishi says,"*Conquer the Mind; you have conquered the world*"

How can the rebellious Mind be brought under control?

Mind control, or 'mind management' as we call it here, is very essential in the modern day busy world full of uncertainties and stress. The Japanese and Chinese have realized the importance of proper control of the Mind and the ancient Indian scriptures deal at great length the nature of mind and methods of controlling it. Some Sages go to the extent of killing the mind, total annihilation of mind (manonasha) by Hatha Yoga to attain the spiritual Bliss; '*Manonasha*' is not what we want here. We want a very cool, well-composed, creative, energetic mind that can help us to carry out our day-to-day life in an orderly, peaceful way. This is evading us due to our ego, due to our ignorance, fear, uncertainties, greed, vengeance, jealousy, competition and lack of Consciousness or 'Prajnya'.

The human mind is the product of a long, well-designed, strenuous effort of Nature to equip man with a very strong but useful tool to Realise Him. But this tool is misused for selfish ends. It is the unconscious mind that has complicated this beautiful life and brought us untold misery. To overcome this predicament, we have to go back to our ancient Sages and find out the methods by which they attained Supreme Bliss.

Mind is always active unless it is merged with the consciousness as in deep sleep or in Prana in unconscious state. Thus, Mind can be made to rest and kept under the control. The easiest method of manoniyantran is through 'Dhyaan', Meditation. Since the Mind can perform one task at a time either it can go on chanting the Lord's name, or engage itself in any wishful thinking, or dwell on the memories of the past. Unfortunately, it never concentrates on the present; that is the real problem. Hence, the best way is to give the unstable mind some sort of support like Meditation, chanting of the Lord's name, or "Om". Automatically, it becomes a habit with the mind to revert to this state of Meditation whenever it is bored of other things. The best way to control mind is through 'Mauna', or Silence. When a person gets the ability to 'keep quiet', he has already conquered the Mind!

Methods of Mind Control

There are several methods of Mind Control. But, Mauna and Praanaayaama are important. Shree Ramana Maharshi advocates a very simple method that of Pranayama.

1. *Restraint of Breath or 'Pranayama' will control the fickle Mind. The Mind is the rider and breath is the horse. Pranayama is the check on the horse, by that the rider is checked.*
2. *Thoughts are controlled by breath control, i.e., Pranayama.*
3. *Both the Mind and the breath spring from Heart, Consciousness. They have a common root and they are the branches and thus interlinked. Control of the one leads to simultaneous and automatic control of the other. Once the Mind is made silent by breath control, Pranayama, the harnessed Mind should be pushed within by self- enquiry, by enquiring about the source of Mind. Thereafter, one abides in the Heart from which both the thoughts and breath emanate.*
4. *Watching the flow of breath with the Mind is restraint of it. Constant watching of breath steadies the Mind.*
5. *If the Mind lacks the necessary strength for consistent watching of breath, then restriction of breath by hata-yoga practices is essential. Hata yoga lays down forcible inhaling, retention and exhaling of breath in a certain ratio. Exhale (Rechaka) one unit, may be in seconds, and gap (Shoonyaka) one unit; inhale (Pooraka) one unit and retain breath (Kumbaka) four units. This forcible breathing exercise will purify the channels or Nadis through which the breath flows. Watching the breath is preferable, if one is able to do so, because then the subsidence of the breath comes about naturally, whereas, Hatayogic practices bring it about by force.*
6. *However, depending upon the temperament of the persons, the different practices may be adopted.*
7. *But, it is important that one must get back to the source, the Heart. This technique is: Rechaka or Exhaling- contemplate on "I am the body"; Pooraka or Inhaling- "Who am I?" and, Kumbaka or Natural Subsidence- "Abidance in the Heart".*

The root cause of mental distractions is "Ego" identified as the 'name (nama) and (roopa) form. Once we get rid of this ego, we get in to and rest in the Heart. i.e, the Mind is absorbed in the Heart.

Mind control is also possible by chanting of sacred syllables. The syllable, "Om" brings our Mind and Breath become oneness in deep meditation. The merging of the Mind and breath is "Dhyan" or

Meditation. When 'Dhyan' is deep and firm, the natural state, the 'Self', is established. The Heart is the seat of the 'Self'.

Chanting of the sacred syllable, or the name of 'Ishtadevatha' (personal God) like "Om Namah Shivaaya" or "Om Namah Naarayanaaya" is called 'Japa'. Japa will help Mind control.

Bhagavan Shree Ramana specifically recommends to find the source of the sound of the 'Mantra' and to merge there. "Either seek its source so that it may disappear, or surrender so that it may be struck down. One must get to the very bottom of that from which it rises, and root it out along with mind and desires".

Of Mind Control, Gautama Buddha says:

> *"If one man conquers in battle a thousand men a thousand times and, if another conquers himself, he (the latter) is the greatest conqueror". [Dhammapada 103]*

Controlling the mind is the most difficult task in the world. It is a 'dheera's task. What is at stake in non-control of mind is simply unimaginable; at worst, it is insanity. An entire civilization would be lost in the collective insanity of a nation or people. Wars are nothing but the insanity of the rulers who thrust this on the innocent people in the name of nationality that is against the Vedic Principle of "*Vasudhaiva Kutumbakam*", 'Universal Brotherhood'. At the individual level it obstructs the development of an integrated personality. Mind control is of invaluable help in attaining the Self, the illuminated state of being, the highest blessing. It makes us shine. Practice of meditation helps mind control and mind control helps meditation.

Some thinkers do not believe in mind control; they are of the opinion that mind cannot be controlled, because, it is the Mind that should control itself. But, it is true that nothing is difficult for a person of strong mind or 'Will'. Mind or 'chitta vrittis' can be controlled or modified. Mere observance of the rising thought waves is enough to stop the chitta vrittis. There are numerous techniques to keep the mind under the supervision of Buddhi and thereby avoid the pitfalls. One of them is 'Yoga'. "The state in which the mind succeeds in stilling the clamour of the sense organs and itself becomes pure, steady, and still, is called Yoga". Normally, the mind tries to take full control of the senses and use them to match the memories of the past.

How to control this mind that always dwells on the unreal? Controlling the sub-conscious one can control the Mind. Sub-conscious is storehouse of all memories, desires, and urges, impulses and such other impurities. Selfless acts and moral practices are the only means or stepping- stones to the purification of the mind. These are not the end by themselves and will not take us anywhere. Our ultimate goal should be 'Self Realization', to attain Supreme Consciousness and Bliss that are within us but covered by the impurities of the mind. The Self shines forth when the impurities of the mind are removed like a lantern that gives bright light when its glass is cleaned of dust and smoke. Wrong passions and bad thoughts are the impurities of the mind. In a way, all thoughts, good or bad, are obstacles in the path of concentration and attainment of the Self. Not only the destruction or sublimation of bad thoughts and impressions but, the good thoughts and impulses as well are to be destroyed. One has to transcend the activities of the mind and rest in a peaceful state, and take up 'dhyana' and meditation.

We may pray and practice 'japam' leading to meditation. There must be constant awareness of the meaning of the holy words filling the mind. Prayer and japa, when methodically practiced, create a new harmony that purifies our thinking, feeling and willing, a great step towards meditation. When the mind is fed with spiritual food it yields greater tranquility. Spiritual food consists of prayer, contemplation, japam and meditation. One must be aware of the Supreme Lord who guides our lives and get rid of ego. Free from fear, attachment or anger, heart remains filled with love and compassions for all beings. Long-lasting peace is thus built on a strong foundation of love and compassion and this helps in attaining divine Consciousness.

Basic Yoga scriptures insist that the strict adherence to'Ashtanga Yoga Sutras' will easily enable the aspirant to control his Mind.

Thought Control Technique

A very simple technique of thought control is briefly given here. This can be followed without much difficulty. First, select a secluded place with a calm and serene atmosphere. Sit in a slightl elevated place in a comfortable position with back, neck and head straight allowing circulation of blood without any hindrance. Curved back and bent head may cause discomfort in the long run and even cause pain. Use a mattress or deer skin, if available, or some dry grass and pout a cloth on it and sit comfortably in 'Padmasana'. Once you are settled in a comfortable sitting pcsture, observe your thoughts, simultaneously having a rhythmic breathing. *Rhythmic breathing will calm the mind.*

Watch your thoughts pass by. Do not obstruct them. By watching the thoughts come and go you can kill them one by one. The thoughts, when they come under the watchfulness of the 'Saakshi'or witnessing self, will disappear one by one; finally you will reach a state of thoughtlessness. When you are fully aware of this state, you will get into a state of 'choiceless awareness'. This technique is known as '*mano-nigraha*' or '*manonasha*'.

Once you attain this state, contemplate on a mahat tatva or maha vaakya like "*So'ham*", or "*Aham Brahmaasmi*", or "*Thou Art That*". Even a rational continuous thought like the 'existence of a vast space, stars and planets, and myriads of life and the divine force behind these' may be entertained. This will lead to a state of divine bliss and supreme happiness. If one contemplates on his Ishta Devatha in this state, he can even visualize Him! Such is the strength of thought control through contemplation, dhyan, and meditation.

Manoniyantrana Tantra (Yoga for Mind Control)

In the Vedic times, Yoga was adopted along with Ayurveda and Jyotishya as a way of life. Thus, Yoga is the age-old secret technique, 'tantra' of Mind control. It is in vogue since time immemorial. The Paatanajali Yoga Sutra is a codified Yoga Text and a very useful guide to Yoga. Bhagavad Gita gives a detailed account of Karma Yoga, Bhakti Yoga, and the Jnyaana Yoga. Sri Krishna says, "I am the Yogacharya and Yoga is the easiest way to emancipation". Yoga brings about harmony in the function of Body, Mind and Spirit (Soul), and, hence, an integrated personality.

What is Yoga?

'Yoga' means 'yuj' the union of the object with the subject through concentration; it is 'Meditation'. Concentration on anything is in fact '*yoga*'. If one concentrates on a flower it is 'pushpa yoga'; and, if one concentrates on the fragrance of the flower, it is 'Pushpa sugandha yoga'. If one concentrates on dhyan, it is called 'Dhyana Yoga'. Whatever that brings about good of the union is 'Suyoga' and the opportunity that brings about the 'Yuj,' union is '*Samyoga*'. In fact everybody should practise some or the other type of Yoga in order to obtain concentration and success in work. It is difficult to achieve success without concentration. '*Sankalpa Yoga*' is thus very useful for it helps to concentrate on the task decided to pursue. Hence, one need not be frightened with the use of the word 'Yoga' in the context of our day- to- day life. Further, there are different types of Hatha Yoga that are practiced by Sadhus in the Himalayas.The '*Surya Yoga*' is a very simple but very useful Yoga. It is all about concentrating or gazing on the Sun for a few seconds daily at the time of sunrise and sunset. Walking barefoot on warm ground and gazing at the rising sun or sunset for just five seconds everyday is enough. The period of gazing may be gradually increased but not more than a few minutes. Enormous power is stored in brain cells by Surya Yoga technique and one can reduce dependence on food for physical upkeep of the body.

Similarly, there are many types of '*Hatha Yoga*' by which certain mystical powers are obtained. Clairvoyance, Omniscience, and Omnipresence, Levitation, Thought Reading, Floating in air, and walking on water, etc. are possible by very severe practise of these Yogic exercises. There are atleast a dozen Yoga Upanishads that explain the techniques of these different types of yogic practices. But, it is also warned here, that these occult practices should not be practiced for selfish ends. The mystic powers are the by-products of spiritual attainments and should be disregarded for, the ultimate goal is to seek, attain, and merge in the Brahman. One should not desert the supreme goal for immediate temporary siddhis and mystic powers; miracles happen and they are not important!

Again, by Yogic practices, Mind can be used as a tool to control the mind just as the diamond is used to cut the diamond. One can attain the state in which the Mind succeeds in stilling the clamour of the sense organs and, in turn, the mind itself becomes pure, steady, and still. This is the inner condition that all the spiritual aspirants seek; and, some are even successful to the extent of perceiving God as affirmed by Shri Krishna in Bhagavad Gita, "Freed from attachment, fear and anger, absorbed in Me –the One Self in all, and taking refuge in me, very many people, purified by the tapas of jnyana, or discipline of spiritual knowledge, have attained to oneness with Me". [Bhagavad Gita, IV.10]

The Upanishads have declared the great truth ***'Tat tvam asi', (Thou art that')*** i.e., 'Man is divine', or divinity is inherent in Man. If divinity is the innermost core of man, the path to it lies through the withdrawal of the senses and the mind from the world of sensate experience and diverting their energies inward in a supreme effort of concentration. By such inward penetration, man achieves realization of his true nature, the non-dual, immortal, changeless and pure 'Atman' behind his apparent self of changeful individuality. This is the well known *Adhyatma Yoga.*

In Mandukya Upanishad Karika, Shri Goudapada, Guruji of Shri Shankara has affirmed this truth. "The transcendental non-dual state, in which relative existence is overcome has been attained by sages who were free from attachment, fear and anger, and who had gone beyond the Veda".

Hinduism has four well-defined 'Purusharthas' viz, Dharma, Artha, Kama, and Moksha to be realized during one's lifetime. Of these, the last one, i.e., 'Moksha' is very important and it comes at the later stage of life, i.e., in 'Vaanaprasthashram' and it aims at spiritual perfection that brings peace and immortality. But, a beginning has to be made very early in life in order to achieve this higher state of spiritual exercise. There are different pathways to spiritual attainments. These paths lead direct to higher intuitive experience. These are called Yoga. Adhyatma Yoga helps to unite the microcosmic Consciousness with the macrocosmic or Universal Consciousness. By practicing the principles of Yoga as per Sage Paatanjali's 'Yoga Sutra', one can attain the state of Supreme-Consciousness and Supreme Bliss. *Kurma Purana* gives details of yoga. It is said that Yogi Paatanjali Rishi learnt Yoga at the feet of Lord Brahma and handed over these Yoga Sutras to future generations with his lucid commenataries. Paatanjali's Yoga Sutra is an important source on methods of practising Yoga for spiritual attainment.

Types of Yoga

There are many and different types of Yoga like the Karma Yoga, Bhakti Yoga, Jnyaana Yoga, Dhyaana Yoga, Mantra Yoga, Raaja Yoga, Hatha Yoga, Kundalini Yoga, Laya Yoga, Sankalpa Yoga, Surya Yoga, Adhyatma Yoga, etc. But, the most popular ones are: Karma Yoga, Kriya Yoga, Bhakti Yoga, Dhyaana Yoga, Jnyana Yoga and, Raja Yoga. The preliminary preparation for advanced spiritual development or Samadhi is 'Kriya Yoga'. It involves three exercises viz, Austerity (Samyama); Scriptural studies (Vedaadhyayana); and, Devotion to God (Bhakti).

Controlling the mind and the senses, and directing their energies to higher purpose comes under austerity or tapas. There should be no place for argument in any of these practices. In Yoga, the efforts are directed to rise above the sensuate level and intellect level and to reach intuition level. Repetition or chanting of the name of Ishtadevatha and absolute submission to the Lord are important. Kriya Yoga is necessary for an aspirant of spiritual attainment. MahavataraBabaji and his disciples

Swami Lahiri, Swami Yuktananda and Paramahansa Yogananda are some of the Yogins who got divine inspiration to take to spread of Kriya Yoga in India and abroad (Los Angeles, USA). Paramahansa Yogananda has established YOGADA SATSANG ASHRAMS where Kriya Yoga is taught. Atmasakshatkar is attained through Pranayama and meditation on 'Om'. Kriya Yoga is taught in these Satsang Ashrams as enunciated in Bhagavad Gita.

There are thousands of Yoga Ashrams all over India having Branches abroad, where Yoga is taught by specially trained Yoga teachers, called Yogacharyas. *The techniques vary from Ahram to Ashram and teacher to teacher. However, care must be taken while choosing the type of Yoga. Not all Yoga lessons are taught exhaustively to everybody who seeks Yoga. Preliminary lessons are for the beginners; depending on the aptitude and success, the aspirants are given higher training. Only limited number of spiritual aspirants are admitted to higher courses that lead to monkhood and seats of spiritual, religious duties, and Yoga ιeading to Atmasakshaatkar. Hence, taking to Yoga is highly discriminative and left to the Yogins who impart the Vedic doctrines leading to emancipation. It is interesting here to note that a good number of devoted Yogins living in the Himalayan States of Himachal Pradesh, Jammu and Kashmir, Leh and Tibet, Sikkim impart Yoga. Hrishikesh, Badrinath, Kedarnath, and places around Kailas are important centers for training in this spiritual discipline.*

Karma Yoga

Karma Yoga seems to be very simple in that one has to do his duty with total humility and offer it at the feet of the Lord. Karma Yoga does not lay down numerous 'do's' and don'ts. It seeks total involvement in one's duty. In the long-run, karma is binding and salvation becomes difficult. Bhakti Yoga, on the other hand, has total devotion to the Lord and there are numerous instances of Bhaktas totally merging in Him. This is, indeed, the most simple but the most difficult method, for it involves total submission to Him. It is total merger like Radha in Krishna. Love and sacrifice are the keynotes of Bhakti Yoga.

Jnyana Yoga is different from the two others- Karma yoga and Bhakti Yoga, in that it requires intellect and self-realisation. In a sense, bhakti with jnyana is the surest path to Self-Realisation. This is a difficult path. It requires lot of discipline in daily life, study of scriptures, study of one's own self, one's own mind, and keep good company (Satsang) and always think of Him. One has to realise one's own Self and the goal in life. This is a very difficult path for most of the seekers who do not have the facilities to study and get proper guidance from spiritual teachers. Jnyana Yoga along with Bhakti yoga is the best way to realise the Self.

Of all the Yoga types, i.e., the Kriya Yoga, the Karma Yoga, the Bhakti Yoga, the Jnyana Yoga and the Raja Yoga (Dhyana Yoga), the last one, the Raja Yoga is the king of Yogas. The practice of Hatha Yoga is suggested to those who opt for Raja Yoga. [Patanjali: Yoga Sutra]. It helps to control the mind since the mind is stubborn and adamant and will not take to RajaYoga so easily.

Bhakti Yoga

Bhakti means spontaneous and continuous attraction of the mind to God under all circumstances. No motivation is involved here and a sense of total surrender to Him with Love is observed here. Supreme devotion to Lord, Para-Bhakti is the basis of Bhakti Yoga. This surrender to Lord with Love comes comes from the purification of soul through renunciation and knowledge. Those who think man is just a body and has got a soul think that the sole purpose of creation is to enjoy the worldy things; even their approach to God is to obtain the worldly happiness and a heavenly life after death. They live a life of sensuousness, slaves of the senses, animal life indeed! But there are those who think that 'man is a soul and has a body'; they think otherwise. They think of obtaining the supreme bliss by renunciation. They realize that 'there is an infinite, omniscient spirit behind, that can do everything, break every bond- and, that spirit we are, and we get that power through love'. *Narada Bhakti Sutra* is a source of the 'secrets of devotion'.

Bhakti proceeds out of a real want. Ordinarily man wants only food, clothing, wealth, sex satisfaction, acquisition of power, fulfilment of ambition, etc. When all these lower desires fall off little by little, man will begin to want God in a real sense. Materialistic demands cloud the need for God. Renunciation is involved in all types of Yoga. Giving up the desires of fruits of action is the gist of Karma Yoga. In Raja Yoga, it is the eternal separation of soul from nature and in Jnyana Yoga, it is the concept of 'Maya'or illusion, that is the sum and substance.

Universal love is evident in the perspective developed by the Yogi practicing Bhakti Yoga as also in Raja Yoga. A sense of fearlessness dawns on him; he perceives all others as creation of the Lord and sees Lord in them. He experiences no pleasure or pain and feels everything including his body belongs to Him, the Lord. "Knowing that Shree Hari, the Lord is in every being, the wise have thus to manifest unswerving love towards all beings". He develops a sense of total surrender, perfect surrender, and the conviction that nothing that happens is against him. Let things come as they may. "Thy will be done". He realizes that fighting, struggling, thinking always has no meaning and the awakening of attachment of love of God effectively breaks all other bondages and he is free. The best treatise on Bhakti is *'Narada Bhakti Sutra'*.

Narada Bhakti Sutra is an exhaustive treatise on Bhakti. Sutra 25 states:

"Sa tu karma-jnyana-yogebhyopyadhikataraa".

Meaning, that, 'devotion is superior to the paths of action (karma), Knowledge (Jnyana), and Yoga (mental exercises)'. Bhakti is not merely a path to salvation but it is also the goal (of Realisation). It is not something that is produced but something which is the very essence of our being. It is the goal itself; hence it is not something to be achieved. It is the love of God; it is already there.

It should be noted that, *Narada Bhakti Sutra* 28 says, that, 'devotion can be generated through knowledge only'. Sutra 29 says that, 'knowledge and devotion depend upon one another'. This seems to be a balanced view. Mainly, however, through the grace of the great souls or through a little grace of God, can one obtain Bhakti or devotion [*Sutra* 38].

Narada Bhakti Sutra gives the methods of achieving pure Bhakti. Renunciation of the objects of desire and one's attachment to objects of desire is the first pre-requisite to obtaining Bhakti or devotion. The second requirement is undivided devotion to the Lord; and the third requirement is the continuous remembrance of God. Even when one is pre-occupied with various activities one should remain engaged in chanting, hearing and singing the glory of the Lord. This will keep the mind engaged in the thought of God; but, mainly one attains devotion through a little Grace of The Lord Himself, or the Saints and Seers. Bhagavad Gita proclaims that the Lord takes full care of those who completely surrender and erase their ego in the sharanagati (surrender) of pure bhakti.

"Ananyaschintayanto maam, ye janah paryupasate;
Tesam nityabhiyuktanam yogakshemam vahamyaham"

Meaning, "*Persons who meditate on me in a state of oneness with me, who worship me, who are constantly in a state of yoga, I carry what they lack and preserve what they already have, and thus fulfil all their desire" [Gita 9.22].*

Practice of Bhakti Yoga is as difficult as Jnyana Yoga, or for that matter, even the Karma Yoga or the Kriya yoga are not very easy. Of course, nothing is easy in the process of Self-realisation. Purity of thought, purity of mind, and total surrender to Lord are difficult to come to mortals who are after sensuous life and who are always body-conscious. It is very interesting to quote Sri Ramakrishna here: 'the whole world is a lunatic asylum. Some are mad after worldly love, some after name, some after fame, some after money, some after salvation and going to heaven. In this big lunatic asylum, I am also mad- I am mad after God; my madness is after all the best" said Sri Ramakrishna.

"We all begin as dualists in the religion of love. God is to us a separate Being. Love comes between, in the middle, and man begins to approach God and God also comes nearer and nearer to man in the form of mother, father, son, friend, master, and lover……… and the last point of progress is reached when the devotee feels that he has become absolutely merged in the object of his worship". In the discipline of Bhakti, the practice of renunciation consists not in destroying any of man's affections, but in giving them a godward turn.

So, the teachers of Bhakti have taught how to channelise human affections into forms of God-love known as 'Bhavas" These Bhavas are: 1.Santa Bhava (placid or philosophical without any human element in it), 2. Dasya Bahava (attitude of a servant), 3.Apatya (attitude of a son to a father), 4. Sakhya (friendly or mitra bhava), 5.Vatsalya (parently affection towards children), 6.Madhura Bhava or sweetness that can take the form of conjugal love, or a lover's affection to his/ her sweet-heart. In the highest state of Para-Bhakti the lover loses himself in the Beloved and attains to the state of non-duality. And, thus the highest form of knowledge and the highest from of Bhakti are one and the same in the end, though they may appear to be different at the initial disciplinary stage. Love and knowledge are thus the obverse and the reverse of the same coin even as are the personal God, Ishtadevatha and the Para Brahman.

Body consciousness is too strong in ordinary men and this constitutes a hurdle in the path of knowledge. For those who pursue the path of worship of personal God, it is easy to offer all their actions and surrender to Him and live in entire reliance on Him. Unlike in Jnyana Yoga where there is the danger of self-deception, Bhakti Yoga is natural, sweet and gentle.

Shuddha (Reverence), preeti and longing of the soul, surrender to Lord and feeling the meaningless-ness of life without Him, and a sense of belonging to Him are the essentials of Bhakti Yoga. Universal love characterizes the Bhakti Yoga.The true Bhakta does not care for the philosophical details. He goes beyond these turbulent and hazy regions of reason to the calmness and clarity of realisation. He no more reasons and believes, he almost perceives. Bhaktas even maintain that serving God in truth and in spirit is higher than even moksha. This kind of whole-hearted devotion to God is also of the highest utility.

However, there are a large number of people who do not care for Bhakti, or concede that it is of the highest value. Such people have to go through many more births and re-incarnation to learn to feel even the faintest necessity for anything higher than just eating, drinking and engaging in sexual pursuits.

Jnyana Yoga

Jnyana Yoga is for the discriminative mind. It is impossible for an ordinary person with little learning to dwell at length the Vedanta philosophy. It is through intellectual discerning that one can realize the ultimate reality and any one who wants to understand this mysterious world shall have to understand the basics of 'Maya'. In *Svetasvatara Upanishad*, the word 'Maya' appears with Nature. It says, "Know Nature to be Maya and the Ruler of Maya to be the Lord Himself". 'Maya' is not illusoriness of the world as commonly believed.

In the '*Rk Veda*', it is said that, "Indra, through his Maya, assumed various forms". Here, it is the 'magical' spell that is 'Maya'. This is the earliest one can find about Maya. In a sense, it is the 'make-believe' world that is 'Maya' and it is not 'illusory world'. The word 'illusion' came with the Buddhist interpretation; a section of the Buddhist Vijnyana-vadins maintained that 'ideas alone are there, not the external objects corresponding to them'. They considered the experience of the world outside as Maya, illusory perception, the ideas alone being real. However, for the sake of convenience, the word illusion is used in the text.

As Swami Vivekananda puts it, 'Vedanta in ts fully developed form is neither idealism nor realism, nor is it a theory. It is simply a statement of fact; it is a statement of what we are and what we see around us'. External Nature that we perceive is very real to us and we try to explain it in very rational, very scientific way, as the ultimate truth. Unfortunately, it is not so. First, the Veadanta points out that, 'our investigation of Nature is limited by our mind and its associated faculties, the senses'. Second, mind is limited by space, time, and causation. Third, the world that we actually experience exists only in relation to the minds that experience as such. In a way, there are as many worlds as there are minds; and each Purusha has a mind. Another important thing is that our experience is also limited due to the limited capacity of the faculties endowed to us. If we had more sense organs, or tools as such, to perceive or experience this world, we would see the world in a different way. Thus, the world experienced externally has therefore no unchangeable and ultimate existence. But,. it cannot be called non-existent, because it is experienced.

This world is full of contradictions. We feel 'it is' there and at the same time 'it is not' there. We do not know anything about this universe. Also, we cannot say we do not know. We stand between knowledge and ignorance, light and darkness (twilight), this mingling of truth and falsehood. It is as if we are walking in dream, half asleep and half awake. We do not know what is the reality. We try to explain it all in a very rational and scientific way; we are going in circle coming back to the same starting point. What we call matter, spirit, space, time, or mind, or anything for that matter, the fact remains the same that, 'they are', and 'they are not'. This external play of light and darkness, indiscriminate, indistinguishable, inseparable is always there. This is a statement of fact. This is what is called Maya. We are born in Maya, we live in Maya and we think and dream in it. This is the work of name and form, i.e., nama (name) and roopa (form). Everything that is bound by laws of space and time and causation is within Maya. The whole of human knowledge is generalization of Maya, even if you call it infinite knowledge, for it comes within Maya. It is a contradictory, incomprehensible nature of the world refered to as "Maya'.

If one realizes this simple truth, that this world is all 'Maya', a make-believe' world and nothing is permanent in it, the whole attitude of man, his way of life, his way of thinking, his acquisitive nature, his selfish motive, his mindless actions, stress and tension, his miseries, ailments - physical and mental, all disappear in a matter of moment. Here is a warning! This does not mean that we can be indolent and need not work; this does not mean that we need not strive for the upliftment of the other less fortunate brethren. On the contrary, we have to work harder and strive much better for the welfare of others.

But, there are people who do not believe in all these; they are the agnostics. They say that, we are living in incomprehensible, irremediable world, let us take for what it is worth and enjoy it without any thought of the ultimate nature of things. This is the 'Theory of Nature' and accepting it we become slaves of Nature. Our intellect does not permit it; our ego prevents it. Man can rise above Nature and get out of its irremediable contradictions. He can be free.

The Absolute and the Relative

It is very important to have a clear understanding of the concept of the 'Absolute' and the Relative in Jnyana Yoga. Absolute is 'Brahman' and it is the 'Absolute that is the goal, the goal of 'Jnyana Yoga'. The 'Absolute' is the 'One' and the 'Only' and it is beyond all reasoning for,

the Mind and the senses cannot reach there. All else is 'Relative'. The entire Universe, rather the multiverse is 'Relative' and 'dualistic'; it is dynamic metamorphism. The Absolute, or the 'Brahman', can be understood only in a state of transcendental meditation or super-Conscious state by Jnyana Yoga.

'Jnyana Yoga' is for intellectual contemplation. It presupposes certain basic knowledge of evolutionary processes. Persons pursuing Jnyaana Yoga should have a preliminary idea about the origin of this universe, the process of evolutfion, and the position of man in this world. However, rudimentary it might be, such knowledge would greatly help in understanding the nature of man. Unlike Bhakti Yoga, Jnyana yoga insists on 'svadhyaya', vedadhyayana. Jnyana Yoga is not for the ordinary people who cannot dwell into the ancient spiritual writings and the Veda. A number of questions remain to be answered despite the Vedic pronouncements and a Jnyani is always conscious of this. For instance, there is a controversy regarding the whole idea of the evolution of the universe. Origin of the universe is explained away by a 'Big Bang' and the consequent processes that produced space, time, etc. This leads to the idea that something (consciousness) existed even before the evolution of space and time and that must be the energy and its consequential Matter. Here, 'Absolute' is 'the Absolute' and cannot exist or manifest through time, space, and causality. 'Absolute' stands on one side and the manifesting medium on the other. There cannot be two independednt existences, without each limiting the other, according to Advaitins. This destroys the very concept of Dvaita. It can be only 'One' without a second i.e., '***Ekameva-adviteeyam***'!

So, time, space, and causation cannot have an independent status even when these three are taken together as a unified category. In their very nature also these three are found to have no existence in themselves, but in a relative sense only. Time is dependent on our state of mind. In sleep it vanishes; in dream its standard varies. Besides time cannot be thought of in abstraction. It can be experienced only in relation to two events. So also space can be thought of only as within limits, or coloured, or occupied by something. As for causation, it is felt only in relation to two events in succession and it is therefore dependent on space and time. So, extraneously, these can be conceived only as a kind of existence dependent on 'the Absolute', and intrinsically, as mutually interdependent in existence. They are shadows around everything without substantiality. They have no real existence, but yet are non-existent, seeing that, through them all, things are manifesting as the universe.

Now, the scientists have understood how the sub-microscopic particles move in a state of inter-action creating and destroying particles. Thus, energy becomes matter and vice versa. One is driven to understand that space existed for the particles to evolve and move somewhere. All these lead to confusion. The idea put forth by the Advaitins try to solve this riddle by assuming that the Absolute is without the second (Ekameva adviteeyam); and all the duality, relative existence, interdependence, could be explained as the 'Lord's Will'. That is how the Biblical statement that the Lord said,'Let there be Light, and there was Light', assumed importance. Here, the 'Lord's Will' is also to be taken as a product of meditation, or Tapas, 'tapa' meaning heat generated by concentration.

Here again, there is some objection to the use of the concept of 'Will'. The idea of equating the 'Will' with 'the Absolute' (Schopenhauer) and speaking of the 'Will' as the cause of the universe causes confusion. 'Will' is something changeable. It is also the fact that, 'Will' manifests in consciousness and is thus a secondary product; it cannot come before time, space and causation. It cannot be equated with the Absolute. Hence, the question of 'how' and 'why' the Absolute has become the finite world of plurality has never been explained satisfactorily.

The ancient Seers have maintained that the Absolute is unknown and is unknowable. This is explained in the Vedantic way as –"the 'Absolute' or 'God' is more intimate than objects and it is only through Him we perceive this world. He is the witness, the witness of all knowledge. Whatever we know, we have to know in and through Him". He is the essence of our own Self, of our ego, this 'I', and we cannot know anything except in and through that 'I'. He is nearer to us than our own limbs; He is infinitely nearer to us, yet He is infinitely higher. He is neither known nor unknown, but infinitely higher than either. In and through Him we breathe, in and through Him we exist. He is the essence of all this, the soul of my soul.

"He that is the Essence of your soul, He is the self. He is the truth. And, 'Thou art that'!" *O Svetaketu, implores the Sage, try to attain that Knowledge of the Self.*

He is the eternal subject and it is this we often refere to as 'I', ignorantly attributing the "I" to the physical, degenerating, decaying, body, everchanging mind, and the ever moving prana. He is our real Self. Nothing exists, moves, inter-acts, without 'His Grace'. This is the sum and substance of Jnyana Yoga. This has to be contemplated upon. A number of mantra, statements, mahat tattvas, are given at the end of the book to think over, contemplate, and chant; these will help to realize the Self. This is for Dhyan, Contemplation, and Meditation.

Pathanjali's *Yoga Sutra* is a treatise on 'Yoga' and his '*Eight Steps to Supreme Bliss*' is very popular. Patanjali has laid down certain ethical rules to be followed in the pursuit of spiritual life. Each system is suited to different types of persons and one can select any of these paths to attain Super-Consciousness. There is nothing to prove that one system is superior to the other since all these help us to reach the same goal. Since Jnyan and Bhakti are indispensable, Raja Yoga is described in detail here.

Raja Yoga (Dhyana Yoga)

Raja Yoga starts with the Mind. The central theme of Raja Yoga is *Mind control* through dhyaan, japa, and meditation. Raja Yoga is called the 'Dhyana Yoga' since it involves Mind and it is the Yoga of Meditation. It involves awakened intelligence, or developing Buddhi. '*Dhi*' stands for Buddhi in Veda, and its power of truth perception. It gives us enormous power to understand the universe and the human being as integral unfoldments of cosmic intelligence. This higher intelligence arises through the energisation of speech and Prana and brings an extraordinary transformative power into the deepest level of the Mind. In Dhyana Yoga the light of truth floods the Mind and we come to know the unitary nature of all reality.

Dhyana Yoga as depicted in the Vedic Yoga is slightly different from Patanjali's Ashtanga Yoga Sutra. Dhyana Yoga of Vedic Yoga does include the preliminary requirements like yama, niyama, prathyahara, but not as separate limbs of Yoga. Even Asana and Pranayama constitute an integral part of Dhyana Yoga, but not as separate limbs as in Ashtanga Yoga. Vedic Dhyana Yoga includes Dharana, Dhyana, and Samadhi, (concentration, meditation and realisation) of Raja Yoga that are the three aspects of merging the Mind into the Divine Self.

For Dhyana Yoga, the expanse of the Sun, or 'truth- consciousness' must be created. One must contact the Divine Self or 'Paramatman' within the heart. We should meditate on the Prana- energized Mantras and use them to move deeper into higher states of consciousness. The space of light or light of space must be opened for the realisation process to continue. Meditate on Indra, Agni, Soma and surya; Gayathri mantra is highly suited for this purpose. It will make our inner light glow and make us literally shine for shining is one of the attriburtes of the Brahman. The spark is already there within us. It has to be kindled by Tapas, concentration, meditation, dhyan with pure heart and mind.

Paatanjali's Raja Yoga has eight steps to attain Supreme-Consciousness. Hence, it is called the *Ashtanga Yoga*. The eight steps are:

1.Yama 2.Niyama 3. Asana 4. Pranayama 5. Prathyahara 6. Dharana 7. Dhyana (Meditation), and 8. Samaadhi, or Superconsciousness.

There are many books on Yoga and the best are the original Yoga Upanishads that are almost a dozen and each of them describes the different types of Yoga in minute detail. A good book on Yoga is by Shri S.Chaturvedi- "Yoga Pradeepa". Shri Sudhakara Chaturvedi, now 111 (in 2003), a bachelor, an expert on Yoga, a Vedic scholar and a close associate of Gandhiji, is a living legend. He has edited a number of Volmes of Rk Veda Samhita and the Sama Veda. His book 'Yoga Pradeepa' (in Kannada) is an excellent Treatise on Yoga. It is authoritative, written in a very lucid, simple style and easy to understand.

According to Yoga Sutra, there are eight steps to Samaadhi. The first two steps, i.e., Yama and Niyama are the ethical rules. Yama consists of five disciplines that are to be strictly practiced by all people at all times. Yama consists of: i. Ahimsa, ii. Continence (Brahmacharya), iii. Satya (truth), iv. Asteya (non-stealing), and, v. Aparigraha. In aparigraha, one should not even accept gifts; if it is inevitable, some thing in return should be given, may be it is some sort of service, if not in kind.

The terms, 'ahimsa' covers all aspects of piety, compassion and fellow-feeling for all the creatures of the world; one should not injure, or even think of hurting the feelings of the fellow beings kaaya, vaacha, manasa and indriyas- i.e., in body, mind, words, thoughts, and deeds. Similarly, continence is such a difficult exercise. At the outset, it seems impossible for ordinary mortals to practice it. One should abstain from sex even with one's own wife after begetting one child or two children; the couple should live like brother and sister for, the purpose of sex is only for procreation and not for sport and self- indulgence. Since sexual activity is dwelling at lower plane involving not much of energy, one is easily aroused in sexual thoughts and activity at the least instigation of the mind or fantasies of the mind.

Yoga demands diversion of sexual energies towards higher planes for, spiritual practices and demand higher energy. Energy should not be dissipated in illusory fascinations and tantalizing dreams initiated by hidden desires. Concentration is affected by attractions of forms and figures, fascinations and wishful dreams. It is the confirmed fact according to the realized souls that continence gives enormous strength to practice japa, tapa, dharana or dhyana, and meditation. Since abstinence of sex gives a superior happiness, all spiritual seekers should abstain from sexual thoughts, avoid company of opposite sex, and lead a very pure life. Total purity of inner body, senses, mind and heart is the basic foundation of spiritual life.

The two other ethical rules viz, *Satya* and *Asteya* are also very difficult to practice in ordinary day-to-day life. Not only one should not indulge in untruth, one should not even abate or support others to think of, or speak 'asat' or lies. *Asteya* means not only coveting what rightly belongs to others, but also gaining anything by unfair means. So also, Aparigraha; here it is very difficult to practice self-less life. One should give away every thing that one does not need in spiritual way of life. ***Attachment is the greatest stumbling block in spiritual exercises.***

The second ethical principle is Niyama and it consists of:

i. Shoucha, purity of both body and mind: Discipline in life is the first requisite for a happy and successful life. Many people do not consider the importance of physical and mental purity and, thus indulge in sensuous life without care. The spread of Aids and such other dreadful diseases is alarming. If laziness is the cause of neglect of physical cleanliness, it is also true that a sense of happiness is derived from abandoning all routine duties like taking bath, prayer and meditation; this is the result of the prepondering tamasic guna of the person. But, the end result is diseases, illness of both body and mind. Hence, the first priority goes to purity of body.

ii. Santhosha or contentment: Some people are in the habit of complaining about everything. Since there is no harmony within, there is discontent everywhere for such people. They complain about their environment, about their surroundings, about their social circle. They also make it an excuse to abandon the spiritual exercises. Contentment with oneself, with what one has got, and santhosha (happiness) in daily life is very important. It is the frame of the mind, the attitude and mental disposition that decides about the ultimate happiness; all mental energies should be directed towards dhyana, meditation and tapas in order to get the full result.

iii. Tapas: 'Tapa' is heat. When the physical and mental energies are directed towards understanding the Self, the body gets heated. This heat is the 'unifying' factor. It brings harmony. It removes all dirt; virtually it burns away all mental rubbish. When the body and mind is thus cleaned, it is ready for receiving the Divine Light. It is an essential part of the yoga. It facilitates easy flow, an unobstructed flow of energies. Nerves are cleansed by tapas. All the nadis and the nerves should be cleansed by strict yogic practices. Shuddha Ahara or proper sattvic diet, and shudhdha vichara or good thoughts are important in tapas. Food here stands for food not only for the body but also for the senses. All the senses should be brought under control and should be fed only by pure thoughts, divine thoughts.

iv. *Svaadhyaya*: The Upanishads says '*Shrotvyaha manthravyaaha*', meaning, 'you hear or read and then reflect on what you have heard or read'. Making our own what we have heard or read is 'Svaadhyaaya'. Study of Veda and Upanishads, as well as sacred works like Bhagavad Gita, Bible, Khoran, Bhagavata, Puranas, Preachings of Great Teachers like Budhdha, Mahavira, Confucious, Lao Tse or Tao, are all very important. Study of one's own mind is much more Important than all these scriptures; it helps to dwell deep within oneself. Study of scriptures, sacred books, and one's own mind is stressed in Svaadhyaya.

' *Isvara Pranidhaana*' is Self-surrender to God'. Individual will should be subordinate to Divine will in order to get the best out of our work. Our individual will is like a small ray of the universal will power and we must always remember that the Infinite will is working in the universe. We should learn to move with this divine force. We can achieve better results with the surrender of our ego and moving with the divine will ('daivecche'). In other words, faith and trust in God is very important.

Asanas:

There are a dozen postures that are described in Yoga shastra. Of these, Padmasana and Vajrasana are the most popular ones for meditation. Different postures or asanas prescribed for different types of Yoga. These are found in the Yoga Upanishads that are twelve or more in number. Practice of Asanas is elaborately dealt in 'Hata Yoga'. Hata Yoga is mainly concerned with the maintenance of health and attainment of longevity of the body. But it is cautioned here that too much of attention to the body might nullify the efforts towards the ultimate goal. One may end up in perfecting 'yogasanas' for body fitness neglecting the spiritual exercises. Any comfortable sitting posture will do for meditation; but, it should enable us to sit for long hours without causing discomfort and pain.

Pranayama

Prajapati created the Jeeva and found that it was not functioning. This did not bring any joy and He decided to enter into the body as vayu. Even then it did not work. So He divided Himself into five vital breaths and the body startèd function and this brought Him joy. These five vital breaths are the Prana, Apana, Samana, Vgyana and Udana. Controlling the Prana by regulated breathing is Praanaayaama. One who controls Praana becomes immortal and achieves all the powers.

Pranayama, as the name suggests, is controlling 'Prana', vital breaths-Prana. Apana, Vyana, Udana and Samana. Prana is vital breath that sustains the body by supplying oxygen. The in-breath called *Pranavayu* takes oxygen to the lungs, which in turn supplies it to the blood in order to get rid of its impurities like carbon dioxide. The impurities of blood are removed by the supply of oxygen through deep in-breathing, called 'Pooraka', of fresh air and impurities are removed by out-breath called 'Rechaka'. The circulation of the five vital breaths helps the body to perform different functions. The air that mixes with food in the stomach helps in metabolism and assists assimilation of food and nutrients and then, the impure air goes out as *apanavayu* downword and goes out of anus. The subtlest part of the vital breath is conducted through all parts of the limbs is the 'Samana'. The 'Vyana' holds the 'Prana' that goes upward and the Apana that goes downward Controlling the movement of these vital breaths in the body will give enormous strength and power. Prana is the life-sustaining force. Pranayama helps in purifying the nerves, the carriers of energy in the body. Although 'Prana' exists everywhere, it cannot be perceived. It exists in the akasha. Akasha is the ultimate basic stuff out of which all the gross forms, from atoms to galaxies, from microscopic cells to the perfected human and divine bodies, take shape and in to which they resolve when they are dissolved or disintegrated to the pristine condition. Prana and Akasha are the two ultimate entities of the manifested universe. What works upon thę Akasha and shapes it into all forms or manifestations is called '*Prana*'.

Prana is the all-inclusive basic energy into which all forms of energy known to us as manifesting in matter and mind are reduced at the end of the cycle. It is Prana vibrating at the beginning of the cycle that shapes Akasha, the basic condition of matter, into a new universe of diverse forms of and states of subtlety. Out of 'Prana' is evolved all forms of energy, physical or mental. Thus, all physical forces like motion, electricity, magnetism, etc. are the expressions of 'Prana'. Thus, the sum total of all forces in the universe, physical or mental, when resolved back to their original state, is 'Prana' and the knowledge and control of this 'Prana' is Pranayama.

Thus, it is also clear that the quantum of Prana working our mind and body is the nearest to us of all the waves of the infinite ocean of Prana. Any person is capable of establishing control over the quantum of Prana constituting his being, will be able to establish a kind of mastery over 'Prana'. Such a Yogi will be in touch of the Whole, as the whole universe is one mass of 'Prana' and 'Akasha'.

Pranayama is the control of universal energy, the prana. Breath control is a method of achieving the optimum flow of this energy in the body. It helps in cleansing the nerves that carry energy to different parts of the body.

Pranayama is the means for establishing control over the nerves and muscles involved in breathing, and through that control, over all the finer movements of the Prana in the body. The ultimate purpose of 'Pranayama' is to arouse Kundalini, the one and the only way to attain Divine wisdom, superconscious perception- realisation of the spirit. This may come through the love of God, through the mercy of a spiritual leader or saint, or merely through analytical will of the thinker. When by the power of long meditation the vast mass of energy stored up travels along the Sushumna, - and strikes the centres, the reaction is tremendous, immensely superior to the reaction of dream or imagination, or even more intense than the reaction of even sense perception. It is supersensuous perception. When this energy reaches the head, the 'Sahasrara Chakra', a thousand-petalled Lotus, the whole brain reacts, and the result is full blaze of *illumination*, the perception of the Self. This is the result of rousing the Kundalini by Pranayama.

The purpose of selecting a suitable sitting posture or 'asana' is to perform dhyana (meditation) comfortably. In the course of meditation, the body, the neck and the head should be in a straight line so as to allow an easy and free flow of blood. It will be dangerous to sit in a curved position. 'Pranayama' is performed for purification of nerves.

Pranayama should be learnt under an expert teacher. Although it seems very simple at the outset it should be started under guidance only. The lining stomach and the diaphram should be strong enough to hold the air that is powerfully driven in and out while inhaling and breathing out, respectively.

'Yogasanas and Pranayama Techniques' in 'Yoga Pradeepa'. [Vaidika Prakashana Samithi, Kunji bettu Udupi]

There are several exercises in Pranayama, at least eight are important and three are commonly practiced. These should be practiced under expert advice only.

The first method is very simple and can be performed by any person without much difficulty and any danger. Sit straight in a comfortable position in a secluded place and breath in and breath out in a measured way uttering 'OM' in the process. Deep Breathing should be done with awareness, unlike it is normally done, and the breath is not held in. By doing this several times, four or five or seven times, the mind and body becomes calm, restful and rhythmic.

The second exercise may be started after one has practiced the first exercise regularly for some days.

First, hold your palm close to the nose and press the right nostril with the thumb and breath in by the left nostril for 4 seconds retain it in lungs for sixteen seconds, and breath out through the right nostril for eight seconds. Imagine that you are drawing in energy through the Ida and sending the nerve current down the spinal column and striking forcibly on the 'Muladhara', the seat of Kundalini. Holding the current there for a while, then breath out slowly through the right nostril, the Pingala. Next, do it in the reverse manner. Again, close the left nostril (Ida) byt the ring finger and small finger together and breath in for 4 seconds retain breath for 16 seconds and breath out for 8 seconds. Repeat this procedure four times or for five times twice a day. This is called 'Sukha Pranayama'. Physical and moral fitness must be ensured before embarking on Pranayama for rousing the Kundalini. It is risky for people who are not fit for it. It may cause insanity.

There is another very simple method. It is breathing in from one nostril and breathing out by the other nostril alternately. Thumb is used to press the right nostril at a time while breathing in and little finger and ring finger together are used in breathing out leaving no gap in time. These exercises should be performed early in the morning and late in the evening in a cool secluded open place. It can be performed at mid-day and mid-night also for better results. 'Pranayama' helps to purify nerves in about two weeks. It is suggested that Japa, or 'Shree Hari Nama-smarane' (chanting the Lord's name) also should be simultaneously performed with pranayama for better results. But it must always be remembered here that mere Pranayama and Yogasanas are mere physical exercises; these will nothelp to make any spiritual progress unless meditation too, goes hand in hand.

Benefits of Pranayama are many and varied. By the control of Prana one can achieve such power that can cure dreadful diseases; faith cure or Reki is one such. Prana has the power of bringing it into a certain state of vibration that can be conveyed to others, arousing in them a similar vibration. It is also the secret of power of great men over others.

If a country is great and can sway its power over others, it is because of the immense will- power of its leaders. The leaders of great countries have such will -power, that they can bring their Prana into a high state of vibration, and it is so great and powerful that it catches others in a moment, and thousands are drawn towards them, and half the world thinks as they do. It is also true of the Great Saints and Prophets whose teachings catch the world over; they had brought their Prana to the highest state of motion, and this is what gave them power to sway the world. All manifestations of power arise from this control.

Manipulation of the power of 'Prana' is very much evident in spirituality. The universe perceived by our senses is the manifestation of Akasha by the vibration of Prana at a certain intensity, wavelength. We are all in a state of vibration at certain wave- lengths. There are innumerable other universes like ours operating at different vibrations of Prana in Akasha; only the degree of intensity of vibration they represent is different. If a Yogi can change the vibration of his mind and attune himself to any of these vibrations representing any of the spheres, he can become aware of those spheres while simultaneously becoming shut off from his earthly contacts. All these kinds of supra-conscious experiences come under Samadhi. The highest grade of Samadhi is when we realise that substance out of which all these vibrations and beings representing them have come. The method adopted for controlling the manifestation of 'Prana' as vital and mental force, through psychical means, is the Raja Yoga.

One of the most important prerequisites of Pranayama is contenance, celebacy or strict avoidence of sex, i.e., Brahmacharya. This is advocated for householders as well, since it is the basis of Pranayama. The semen ejected in sexual intercourse is a loss of energy, which would otherwise become 'Ojas' more useful for rousing Kundalini. It is the semen or 'veerya' (Dhatu) that is converted into 'ojas' (psychic energy) that brings in turn 'tejas' (Chaitanya). By channelising the creative force, the psychic energy or vital energy, through Sushumna to Sahasraara that one gains access to the hidden powers of the brain. If semen (dhatu) is wasted in masturbation by youth, they will lose concentration and physical and mental strength; their yogic exercises will be futile. So also, indulgence in sex, either in thought or action, by householder is detrimental to spiritual practices.

Vatsayana's Kama Sutra clearly lays down the principles of sexual practices as far as it helps Self Realisation. It is approved for procreation up to two children and none thereafter. First is the dharma putra/putri and the rest are all results of Kama, or lust. It is advocated that sexual indulgence is avoided at all cost and this can be achieved by raising oneself to higher planes of spiritual life. Reaching Kundalini (hidden energy of the plexus or level of consciousness) to heart level and staying there will help in controlling sexual thoughts and action. The extreme step of abstaining from sex in youthful stage is neither possible nor advised. The very purpose of birth on this earth is fulfilment of desires (Kama- one of the Purusharthas) and 'desire of the flesh' is one of them. According to Buddha, it is the desire of the flesh that is at the root of repeated births and death. Sexual energy can at best be channelised otherwise it will be wasted in different ways. Sex is one of the most powerful basic needs like thirst and hunger. After one has fully experienced this basic urge, he should develop detachment. That is real 'Prathyaahaara'.

Some uphold the view that there is a fourth aspect in the study of life of Man. Body, mind, and soul are the three aspects with which we are familiar. The fourth is the '*energy-flow*' aspect. This is also the 'life-force'. This flow is in the form of sex-energy. There is a very interesting account of the Brahman appearing in the form of Yaksha to teach a lesson to the proud Devas, particularly Agni and Vayu, for the elated behaviour. The Devas were proud and boasted of their powers and took all the credit of retrieving Amrit from the churning of the ocean. When Brahman appeared as Yaksha, Indra and others could not recognize him. Indra sent Agni to find out who it was. When Agni appeared before Yaksha (Brahman) and proudly identified himself as Jataveda, Brahman placed a piece straw and asked Agni to burn it. Agni used all his powers to burn it and failed; he returned humiliated to Indra and said he could not know that adorable Spirit. Then, Indra sent Vayu. Vayu approached Brahman and faced the same problem; The Indomitable Brahman placed a piece of grass and asked Vayu to move it. Vayu used all his force but could not move the straw a bit and returned humiliated. Indra personally came to test the Yaksha and found instead a beautiful lady, Uma, the daughter of the snow-clad Himavat.

Both Agni and Vayu are the deities of the Indriyas, eyes and ears, respectively; and Indra is the Lord, Mind under whose control the indriyas function. Indra, the mind (ignorance), cannot function in the face of Buddhi or intellect or the Light of the Self. Mind is only matter and gets burnt under the fire of the Supreme-Consciousness. But, who is this beautiful Uma, daughter of Himavat? In Himavat, Hima stands for cold. Woman stands for prakriti. Beauty stands for the captivating force of the Prakriti. Woman stands for Sex. Thus, 'Indra seeing beautiful Uma' stands for 'the Mind coming under the grip of the captivating sex'. Sex is the over-powering and dominating force captivating the senses.

Sex is a powerful instinct. It exercises a captivating force and governs the life of humans throughout life. The sexual energy is the mainstay of life. If the sexual energy ceases, the life of the person ceases. A person will become aware of his/her sex very early in life, say by about a year or so after birth, and continues to be aware of it till ripe old age. This sexual energy has been the central idea of the works of Sigmund Freud. He went to the extreme of identifying sex as the center of study of man. But, one cannot deny the fact that for most part of life, sex energy controls the life and activity of man. Much remains to be done in the field of sexual energy, although the ancient Seers have realised it and laid much stress on strict adherence to contenance, Brahmacharya.

Prana and Mind

Prana is one of the ingredients of the living beings. It is accompanied by Consciousness, Intelligence, Mind and Awareness (Sakshi). Thought is the highest expression of Prana. Its expression is three-fold. First, there is instinct, which may be called conscious thought. At a higher level is reason in which thought is a conscious and well- regulated effort. But the circle within which it runs is very limited.'That', '*that is beyond*', can be grasped by super-conscious, or Samadhi. All manifestations of the subtle forces of the body, which are different manifestations of Prana, give a push to the mind to assume vibrations that reveal facts at subtle level of existence. The whole universe is one unbroken mass of matter in flux beaten into different states of vibrations by the Prana. The Sun, the Moon, the Man, the plant, the animal, the mineral, the atom are all mere points of this one huge mass, *the Mahat*. When the action of Prana on Akasha is most subtle, it is called *Mind*. Mind is also one unbroken continuum. If one gets into the subtle vibration through the regulation of Prana within oneself, then that whole universe is seen as composed of subtle vibrations of thought. Samadhi brings the individual's mind to those vibrations that enable it to apprehend the facts of these subtle levels of existence.

Prana is generally, but often loosely, translated as 'vital-breath', the life-force or the vital force. The term is applied to both transcendental principle, the subtle cause, as well as to its effects, the forces moving to activity the organs- physical and mental. *[Brahmopansihad 2].According to Brahma Sutra, both Prana and Mind are Brahman.*

In *Prashnopanishad*, Pippalaada unfolds the whole philosophy of this Prana. Prana is espressly identified with the Atman; it is not just the manifested aspect of the Atman. The manifested aspect, Prana, is in reality is the same as the Atman; for purposes of intellectual comprehension, it is distinguished as a process of manifestation or creation. In the Upanishads, Prana is used as synonymous with the Atman or Brahman [*Brahma Sutras* I. 23 and I .28-31]. Prana is identified as the life of the Devas (Indriyas), because the latter embody only its manifested functions that go to make up the macrocosm and the microcosm, the external and the internal world. It is also their death, because their dissolution means nothing but resolution into it.

'Prana' is the Devatha (Deity) of the Nadis, because they represent its functions. Prana cvolvcs thc complex of man's psychophysical activity. The Nadis form the media for evolution as well as involution. Thus, we have the conception that Prana becomes many and then functions through determinate channels built up with matter- Brahman in its self-manifesting process becoming determined as action and reaction, as Prana and Akasha, force and matter.

Pranayama and Kundalini

Human body is a web of nerves, the 'nara-mandala'. Prana or vital energy working in the nervous system is called 'Psychic Prana'. There is the latent or coiled up energy at the base of the spinal column (Mulaadhaara) technically called 'Kundalini'. Pranayama initiates the flow of this coiled up energy up-wards from the base to the brain, utilizing the power generated by the control established over the breath. The control of the breathing process works similarly on all the functioning of the Prana in the body. By rhythmic breathing all the molecules of the body gradually begin to move in the same direction and this makes a man a tremendous battery of will power. When all the electrons in a body flow in the same direction, electric power is generated. Similarly, by Pranayama, the energies of the body and mind are controlled and directed towards the base of the spinal column, called 'Mulaadhaara', and thereby Kundalini, the coiled up power, is activated. Once Kundalini is activated, its energy begins to flow upwards from *moolaadhaara* (at the base of the spinal cord) and passes through plexus or chakras of *svaadhishtaana* (behind the genitals) *manipuraka* (in the navel region) *anahata* (heart), *vishudhdha* (throat), *ajnya* (between eye-brows), and finally, *sahasraara* (top of the head).

The vertebral column has the spinal cord running through it and it starts from moolaadhaara and ends up in the brain in the lumbar vertebrae as fine nerve fibres. Two nerve currents flow on two sides of the spinal cord, called '*Ida*' (*the afferent nerve*) and '*Pingala*' (*the efferent nerve*) carrying sensations to the brain and in turn convey the reactions of the brain to the body. Between these two nerve currents is '*Sushumna*' (*canal centralis*). This canal is closed at the bottom and ordinarily does not perform any function unless it is aroused to do. Yogis who practice Kundalini open this canal and let the nerve current pass through this hollow canal without the help of nerves. This is the medium that established contact with Super-Consciousness with the environment during evolution but finally got entrapped. The release of the bondage of the body and to establish the contact with the 'Universal Consciousness' is the purpose of practice of Kundalini Yoga. When the Sushumna canal is opened up and mental currents are passed through its empty space, the bondage of the body is released and the yogi establishes the contact with the Super-Consciousness. This brings the knowledge of the Brahman, a clear understanding of the Reality or "Truth", an extraordinary sense of happiness, the 'Supreme Bliss' that cannot be expressed by words!

The Mulaadhaara (the sacral plexus) is the root receptacle, the seat of Kundalini. Enormous power of evolutionary impulses is coiled up here. It is this energy that enables the evolutionary process to continue devising the new forms and functions like the one that ended in devising man from the monkey. This is also the key that holds the future of mankind. This is attained by tremendous concentrated will power generated by Praanaayaama. The manifestation of a little of this is seen in the creative instincts and the sense of reality one gets in the experience of dreams and vivid imagination.

From Muladhara at the bottom, to the Sahasrara in the brain there are in all seven chakras, centres of consciousness. The body, mind, and the spirit meet at these junctions and influence each other. These centres of consciousness are: *the Muladhara, Swadhishthana, Manipuraka, Anahata, Visudhdha and Ajna, and the last one is the Brain, called Sahasrara*, where the thousand- petalled lotus blooms on 'enlightenment'. These Yogic centers are located in the regions of anus, root of genital, navel, heart, throat, in between the two eye- brows, and crown of head, respectively. The seven plexus called chakras are the centers of Consciousness that create different vibrations associated with different Gunas. Some knowledgeable persons associate these chakras with different Puraana Purushas and the cities or centers of their activity like Shree Rama and Ayodhya, Shree Krishna and Dwarka. Haridwar is the place associated with Muladhara, the base of the spine. Tamas is associated with this plexus and when inertia (jadata) is overcome some sort of spirit or enthusiasm starts energizing the person to action, Kanchi is associated with Svaadhishtaana located behind the genitals and Kaamaakshi, Goddess of desire is the presiding deity. Desire or Kaama originates from this plexus. Ayodhya city is associated with Manipuraka plexus and Sri Rama, son of Dasharatha. Shree Rama and Kaikeyi stand out prominently in the story of Ramayan. The gunas of generosity and joy (Shree Rama), greed, and jealousy (Kaikeyi) meet in the region of navel (nabhi) where the manipuraka plexus is located. Peace is associated with this plexus. Mathura is associated with the heart plexus 'anahata'. Love, fear and hatred are the Gunas of this region. Mathura symbolizes the love and devotion of Gopikas for Krishna as well as the hatred and fear of Kansa. Ujjain (Avantika) is the seat of 'vishuddha' plexus or chakra around throat region. It is the seat of grief, glory and gratitude and one gets choked and words do not come out when one is filled with grief or gratitude. Kaashi also known as Varanaasi is associated with the ajnya chakra where the third eye or Jnyaan Chakshu is located. It is the seat of knowledge. The city of Dwarka is the Sahasraara where the thousand petalled Lotus blooms when the Kundalini energy culminates at this center. Thus, the Kundalini power (serpent or the coiled up energy) is released when the Yogi successfully completes the spiritual exercise of Kundalini Yoga. Enormous energy is released from the muladhara (Haridwar) and passes through the chakras and finally enters sahasraar (Dwarka) at the top of the head. In this process of Kundalini Yoga, the vital breath, Prana moves through different centers of Consciousness or the chakras and the negative feelings cease to exist, thus leading to liberation or freedom from bondage. Ultimately, it is vibrations! Vibrations generated by spiritual exercises are the cause of joy, peace and happiness.

In ordinary people the first three chakras, the centers of consciousness from the bottom upwards are active and the higher ones are dormant. The first three are connected with the animal life of man like eating, drinking, sense enjoyment or sexual pleasures. Selfish animal thoughts and emotions influence the lower centres. Tamas and Rajas gunas are dominant at lower chakras and, satva guna gains ascendency at higher centres of consciousness. Sushumna becomes active only when we become satvic. When the conscious level rises to the centre in the heart, the spirituality is awakened in man.

Kundalini Yoga is also known as *Laya Yoga*. Laya is dissolution, dissolution of vrittis, thought-waves. Raja Yoga is restraint of Vrittis. *Hatha Yoga* helps to control Vrittis by rigorous spiritual, ethical and moral practices. The words 'Ha' and 'Tha' mean union of the Sun and moon, the Prana Vayu and the Apana Vayu (vital airs). It is also known as '*Kriya Yoga*'. One should not be carried away by the names of Yoga. It is the effect of the spiritual exercise that is very important. All that is required is steadfastness, and sincere concerted effort.

Rising Kundalini is not easy in the beginning and it requires enormous will- power and discipline. It is difficult to force the psychic energy along the Sushumna canal by will power alone. It is very important to note that these centres of consciousness at higher levels are extremely subtle centres which vitalize and control the gross bodily tracts indicated by the various regions of the vertebral column and the ganglia, plexus, nerves, arteries, and the organs situated in those respective regions. In a way, these are not to be disturbed unless one is physically and mentally fit to handle the enormous energy released by the control of Prana that enters this canal of Sushumna and reach the higher charkas or centers of consciousness. One must live a pure life of truth, love, sacrifice, and regulate the habits in order to operate the Kundalini, 'the Serpent Power'.

Kundalini or the latent energy hidden in the plexus or chakras can be activated by control of breathing i.e., 'Praanayaama' by Hatha Yoga, or by Mind control by Raja Yoga, i.e. dhyaan, meditation. Both the techniques are ideally suited to energise the naadis and plexus. But, care must be taken to see that the physical body, the nervous system, the muscles, the will power are a capable of sustaining the surge or sudden flooding of energy.

The adverse effects of Kundalini are such that they may cause nervous break down in introverts, or lead to uncontrolled misadventures in extroverts. It may lead to insanity in weak persons. It may cause boosted egotism in physically strong but morally weak persons with the consequence that they become a threat to society. Some persons may gain cheap psychic powers like mind reading and gain control over other weak persons. They may, with practice of japa, meditation with namasmaranam, and a disciplined life will enjoy peace and happiness.

Surya Yoga is the technique of absorbing the solar energy and energizing the brain cells. This is a very simple technique. One has to spend about 45 minutes walking barefoot on the warm ground absorbing the earth energy; at the same time, one should gaze at the Sun for a few seconds only. The time suitable for gazing at the Sun is at the time of sunrise or sunset. The period of gazing at the Sun should be five seconds at a time, and may be gradually increased over a period of 45 days; and, it should not exceed 45 seconds. Constant gazing at the Sun, at a stretch, is not advisable for it will affect the eyes damaging the retina . By this method, solar energy is stored up in brain cells and it will help reduce dependence on solid food for the phyical sustaenance of the body. Such persons who have mastered this technique live for thousands of years and attain superb control over their self. They also obtain certain spiritual occult power like clairvoyance, levitation and 'parakaya pravesh' (entering other's body). Pranayama, Gayatri and Kundalini are also associated with Surya Yoga and this is a very powerful technique of Yogic exercise.

Prathyahara and Dharana

'*Prathyahara*' means '*gathering towards*'. 'When the senses giving up their own objects take the form of the mind, as it were, it is 'Prathyahara', according to Patanjali [*Yoga Sutra* II. 54].

It is detachment from all sensuous objects, thoughts, fantasies, indulgences in things that bind the mind and concentration on the Almighty. With-holding the mind from its going along the channels of perception and in gathering, it is called '*Prathyahara*'.

Moral instruction consisting in forbidding the doing of certain things is ineffective, because the power to detach the mind from the object of the senses is not present in the person. Establishing control over the mind is not easy. Mind is active like a monkey drunk and bitten by a scorpion. So it is suggested here that one should allow the mind to wander and simply watch it. After a strenuous senseless pursuit it will come to rest on its own. Thus, one can get control over the mind gradually by constant observation. This is Prathyahara in practice. This can also be done by creating an aversion to the sense objects just like one is fed up when constantly fed by same food, may be one's most favourite dish. For a spiritual aspirant, too much indulgence in sex should bring about aversion to sex. Similarly, too much of loose talks, drinks, entertainment, television viewing, and other habits should be nauseating. By autosuggestion, one can develop aversion to all these and turn the mind to God.

By '*Dharana*', we mean concentration on a particular object, i.e., holding the mind on a single point. May be it is one's own heart, or a picture of Ishtadevatha, or a flower. Even a lit-candle will serve the purpose. Long and arduous practice is required for success in Dharana. Spiritual aspirants practising dharana should be strict in their food habits, talk less, and live alone, if possible. The results of dharana can be seen very early. They become calm, develop clear voice and good temperament. With increase in practice, they can hear anahata dhwani, sounds from distance. One can hear mantras in the right ear. The senses become very sharp and pointed and even a pin drop will be a thunderbolt! Some aspirants select one idea and concentrate wholly on it and achieve extraordinary success. The results of Dharana are unbelievable!

It is difficult to say when concentration ends and meditation begins. Meditation follows concentration. Ethical practices like Yama and Niyama are important before Dharana is practised. Concentration without purity of mind is of no use. Taking to Dharana without preliminary ethical training is like taking to long jump without practice that will end in disasters.

Concentration is steadfastness of mind. Continence, Brahmacharya (preserving virya), is necessary for Dharana (concentration) for it will give strength of mind. Those who practise Dharana, i.e., concentration evolve quickly and can do any work efficiently, with scientific accuracy and much quicker than others. They will gain clarity and extra in-depth perception of jobs on hand. Concentration helps in attaining material prosperity. Nothing is impossible to a person who practises Dharana regularly. But setting a goal is very important in Dharana and the process of concentration should be continuous and without break like the flow of oil.

Dharana, Japa, and Dhyaan (Meditation)

Dharana is concentration. 'Dharana is holding the mind on to some particular object' [Patanjali Yoga Sutra III.1]. Discarding the names and forms that have been superimposed on objects by ignorance, and realizing the Brahman behind every object that the mind the and senses come into contact, is the culmination of Dharana. Concentration is very important. Without concentration, it is impossible to achieve anything. Since the mind is always searching for more and more exciting things, it shifts from thought to thought and object to object. Unless a person learns to concentrate on one object or one thought at a time, it is very difficult to achieve success in anything. Regular practice is necessary to concentrate the mind on any task or thought or object. One may concentrate on any external object, or internal Chakras or Plexus. Concentrate on Trikuti, or the Ajnya chakra at varanasi- the junction of the two eyebrows. The space between the two eyebrows is normally the one used in Dharana. The picture of 'Om' is another good icon. Picture of Guruji is also good for those who have great faith in their master.

To start with, one should hold a flower and gaze at it, or gaze at the idol, or photo of one's Ishtadevatha, Krishna, Rama, Ganesha, Radha Krishna, Vishnu, or Ishvara, Jesus, Mary or the picture of Buddha; or simply gaze at a candle-lit light for five minutes and learn to hold the mind under control. One can concentrate on the sound of a wall-clock, or any spot on the wall in front, or the tip of a pencil. All these are concrete concentration. Normally, there can be no concentration without something upon which the mind may rest. The mind can rest only on a pleasing object. It is difficult to fix the mind in the beginning and dharana should be practiced till the mind is well established on the object of concentration. Watch the thoughts pass by. Rhythmic breathing will also help in this process. Once concentration becomes easy, japa and meditation can be started.

The mind of worldly persons is gross. It is unfit for concentration and introspection. Sattvic mind is calm, sharp and subtle. Rajasic mind is passionate, restless and turbulent. It agitates the body and the senses and makes them subject to foreign influences. The mind of a subtle seer is like a lamp that does not flicker. So one has to sharpen the mind by practice of daily meditation. There are different methods to discipline the wayward mind and try them. One should not give up even if he fails to control the mind in the initial stages. Gradually one will succeed. Control of one vasana (the subtle desire) or one vritti (thought) will give strength to control another vasana or another vritti. Patience and perseverance is all that is needed.

Remember, it is important to purify the mind by Yama and Niyama before Dharana is attempted. Concentration of mind without purity is of no use. Some persons attempt dharana without purification of mind and get into trouble. Concentration without a goal is dangerous. Proper method is to take up ethical practices before concentration is practiced.

Dharana, concentration is steadfastness of mind. Those who practice Dharana (concentration) evolve quickly and can do any work with scientific accuracy and great efficiency. Power of concentration will greatly increase when all causes of distractions are removed. Contenence, or Brahmacharya is another pre-requisite of Dharana. A true Brahmachari will have wonderful power of concentration. Attention is another important element of Dharana. One should develop the knack of visualizing things even if they are absent; one must be able to retrieve the mental picture at any moment. Only good practice of concentration will enable one to have sharp memory. Prathyahara will be of great help in sharpening Dharana. Thus, Yama, Niyama, Asana, Pranayama and Prathyahara are to be practiced before coming to Dharana, Meditation and Samadhi. Dhyana and Samadhi become easy and successful only when one is properly equipped with all these ethical and spiritual practices.

The benefits of Dharana are many. One who can concentrate for half-an hour or one hour will have tremendous psychic powers; Will power will be very strong. Work efficiency will be several times better and quality will be superb. What was cloudy and hazy before becomes very clear and definite. What was difficult before becomes very easy now; what was complex, bewildering and confusing before comes easily within the mental grasp. The outcome of the effort can be easily estimated with a little concentration on the pros and cons. Nothing is impossible to a man who regularly practices Dharana (concentration). Besides, the persons who practise Dharana will have good health and very good mental vision.

Dhyana, Japa, and Samadhi

Dhyana is the continuous flow of divine thought in an unbroken chain [*Paatanajli Yoga Sutra* **III**.2]. This is achieved by concentration on a particular location, may be the tip of the nose, or preferably between the eyebrows. It leads to Samadhi. Patanjali, the yoga teacher, says '*By 'Ishvarapranidhana', sacrificing all to Ishvara, comes samadhi*'. Learn to surrender all of your labour of your spiritual practice to the Supreme Being. *Surrender yourself completely; offer all fruits of your action, connect your little will to the divine will, and then a miracle takes place.* That Truth, that Reality which shines within, which also shines outside in all beings, reveals itself in all its glory, and then comes communion between the soul and the Oversoul.

Dharana, Dhyana and Samadhi, the three together is called '*Samyama*'. Meditation should begin with gross objects and slowly rise to finer and finer ones until it becomes objectless. It should lead to a state of 'choiceless awareness'. The meditative state is the highest state of existence. It brings total happiness and real enjoyment incomparable to any the senses could bring.

Regularity in meditation is a *sine qua non*. One should select a suitable place and time, take the appropriate asana, like the Padmasana, and practice dhyana with utter sincere devotion. Concentration on a physical law like the law of gravitation, flow of light, expanse of space, or a spiritual idea like the mahat tattva with clarity and bhavartha will yield immense joy and happiness. Through concentration, one can gain penetrative insight; subtle esoteric meanings will flash out in the field of mental consciousness. Inner depths of meaning and philosophical significance become very clear. One has to train the mind in concentration on various subjects, gross and subtle, big and small and in the end a strong mind and will power will emerge.

Meditation will become habitual and brings supreme joy after some time. Discussions and arguments result in hostility and mental disturbance. Much energy is wasted. Nothing is gained of endless talks. Everybody wants to show his scholarly learning and intelligence. In the end both the parties fight. A wise man will never enter into arguments and discussion. He will take every opportunity to dwell in meditation and will not entertain any thought of participating in debates and discussions and will avoid them. It is very important to note that much study of Veda and the shastras is also not necessary and much intelligence and retentive memory is also not needed for self -realisation. Only meditation is enough. One should have a calm and tranquil mind. No meditation is possible without serenity of mind. Serenity is a rare virtue. It is acquired by eradication of vasanas. With serenity, one can enjoy unruffled abiding peace of mind. When all vasanas are eradicated, mind becomes calm and serene, just as the lake becomes calm and serene as the waves subside. Hence, the Mind Management Rule here is: "*Meditate as much as possible and wherever it is possible*".

One should meditate on the Universe bearing in mind the interior relations of the earth, the air and the atmosphere. The air is the means of joining the posterior form the earth with the atmosphere, the junction. By meditating on this Infinite Universe, the mind goes beyond the trifling preoccupations and attunes itself to the Infinite,

One should meditate upon the Light. Fire is the prior form, the Sun is the posterior form, water is the junction, and lightning is the means of joining.

One should meditate upon Learning. The Teacher is the prior form, the pupil (student) is the posterior form and the Learning is the junction. Imparting of instruction is the means of joining.

One should meditate upon the Progeny. Mother is the prior form, father is the posterior form, progeny is the junction and procreation is the means of joining.

One should meditate upon the Self. The lower Jaw is the prior form, the upper jaw is the posterior, Speech, or the vocal organ is the junction. Tongue is the means of the union.

These are called the 'Great Combinations'. He who meditates upon these conjunctions, as expounded above, will attain progeny, wealth, and the abode of heaven. There is no hard and fast rule regarding the time, place and postures, but based on the facility available and agreeableness one can meditate. All meditations except that on Paramatman are symbolic.

"Om", the symbol and designation of Brahman- the Object of profound meditation and the highest spiritual efficiency attributed to it is the quintessence of Veda. Veda is derived from 'Vid' meaning Knowledge [*Chhandogya Upanishad II 23*].

"Oh! The Supreme Lord, cheer me with the intellectual vigour. Oh! Lord, may I be the possessor of the immortal Revelation. May I be able and active in my body; may my speech be sweet and agreeable to the highest degree; and, may I, with my ears, listen abundantly clear (so that I may learn). Thou art the sheath of the Supreme Being, the "Om", I pray to thee, to preserve my learning".

This is a prayer addressed to the Supreme Being, the Grantor of all wishes, asking for mental power and physical fitness without which Knowledge of Brahman is not possible. [*Kathopanishad I 15-17; Prashnopanishad V 2-7; Brihadaranyaka Upanishad V 1.1; Mundakopanishad II 2.6; Mandukyopanishad V. 11; Bhagavad Gita Ch. IX. 17; and Manu Smriti XI*].

Meditation and Self-culture are ancient practices, as old as the Veda. The preliminary process of attaining purity of mind by a life of self-control (Righteousness) is given in the following:

"Yunjjana prathamam Manasthatvaya savithadhiya;
Agnerjyotirnichayya Prithvya Adhyabhavat."

First, harnessing the Mind and the senses with a view to realize the Truth, and then having found out the Light, of the fire, the evolving soul brought itself out of the earth. The Sun is used as a synonym for 'Antaryamin' (the Ultimate Principle) as the source of all creation, working constantly and eternally in the hearts of all beings to raise them to higher and higher levels of life (thus evolution is caused behind the scene). All evolution is to be traced ultimately to the working of divinity 'within'. Only those rare few who know the glory of the Immanent Soul (All-pervading, all-knowing, Infinite and the Self- Luminous) undergo the necessary discipline and spiritual practices. The wise do, indeed, control the activities of the intellect, and practise meditation and Dharana, Concentration.

Sit down for a few minutes and pray:

"Tejosi tejo mayi dehi, veeryamasi veerya mayi dehi;
Balamasi balam mayi dehi, ojosi ojo mayi dehi!"

This is a very simple prayer mantra to ask for purity, energy, strength and peace of mind. This is a very effective mantra from *Shukla Yajur Veda Samhita* 19.9.

It gives enormous strength of mind and self-confidence. Meditation gives good relaxation to tired mind and body. Close your eyes and take the name of the Lord and chant. If you get sleep, it is good. Continue meditation when you get up. But this going to sleep in meditation should not be developed into a habit. It will not, help spiritual attainments. Meditation should be done with total awareness, not in sleep. A man getting up from sleep may be fresh and look refreshed; but a man coming out of mediation looks bright, radiant, and more energetic. Meditation helps to calm nerves and reduce tension. Very nervous people cannot meditate. So, first the tense nerves should be calmed down. We should control all our sentiments and feelings, good or bad. And make the mind passive. We should concentrate on the Infinite and tune our mind towards the Supreme Lord. Fill the mind with the holy image and the harmonizing vibrations of the holy sound, 'Om'.

Before we go to bed, concentrate on some holy idea or think of some divine form; this will help to get a sound sleep. Keep the mind engaged in the Divine, by chanting Lord's name or 'Om'. It is not good to combine Japa with sleep. Japa before and after sleep is good. Normally, japa of the required number of chantings should be completed for good results. Find the center of consciousness at the heart level, 'Ajnya' level, and concentrate on this at the time of japam and meditation for excellent results.

Sattvic food, rhythmic breathing, constant awareness of mind, or alertness and feeling one with the environment are the important requirements for success of meditation. Patience, good disposition, kind and benevolent attitude towards others are virtues. Establishing in oneself is important for a harmonious and peaceful life. Impatience, anger, dissatisfaction and digruntled behaviour will spoil the mood and bring unhappiness to self as well as others. Pleasant mood should be practiced despite any odds and, it is very difficult. But, it comes easy with meditation. Our own mental impurities, desires and passions, tendencies and impressions, attachments are major obstacles to meditation. Meditation requires a pure mind and meditation creates a pure mind!

Japa

'Japa' means chanting of a mantra. The word comprises of 'Ja' meaning, 'destroys birth and death cycle' and the syllable 'Pa' meaning, 'destroys all the sins' [Agni Purana]. Thus, Japa has the potential to unite the soul with the Supreme Being. It has miraculous powers that infuse us with courage and confidence. Vedic mantra are very sacred. Hymns of the Veda are known as mantra. Some of the mantras are the prayer mantra. One such hymn in the Yajur Veda is the Gayatri mantra. It is a beeja mantra or seed syllable, derived from ancient primeval sounds. Lord Shree Krishna says in the Bhagavad Gita, amongst the mantras I am Gayatri. Gayatri mantra has the latent spiritual power by which regular japa and meditation can transform the mind into prajnya or wisdom. Chanting of this mantra, the 'Gayatri', with concentration and understanding, brings inexplicable peace, calm and solace to the disturbed mind.

Japam or chanting Mantra is the most smple form of Meditation. Maa Sharada Devi used to get excited and emotionally disturbed when somebody said that he cannot meditate, she advised him to chant Twenty-thousand times daily the name of any Shiva, Rama, or Krishna, or any God he likes and feel the Bliss, experience the effect of Meditation.

Samadhi* - *'Sushupti'

As already stated, there are different layers of consciousness. Normally, we work within a circle of what appears to be rational and this comes within the conscious sphere. Here, self-consciousness accompanied by an individualized will is functioning. There are the sub-conscious and super-conscious levels besides the unconscious and, we are rarely aware of these in our normal work. Yogis claim that even the internal organs of our body that are normally independent of our control like breathing, pumping blood, pulses can be brought under conscious control of man. This is the ego-prompted rational level and self-conscious. This is in contrast to the ego-less and uncontrolled instinctive level commonly found in animals.

"The Yogis hold that the mind can go beyond the self-conscious level of the mind". Just as unconscious work is beneath consciousness, so there is another kind of work which is above consciousness and which also is not accompanied with the feeling of egoism. The feeling of egoism is only in the middle plane. When the mind is above or below this line, there is no feeling of ego and yet the mind works. When the mind goes beyond this line of self-consciousness it is called 'Samadhi' or Super-consciousness. When a fool goes into Samadhi he wakes up an enlightened person. This will be the effect of Samadhi on persons who practises all the eight steps of yoga to the point of culmination in Samadhi.

'Samadhi' is the culmination of the steps to 'Self Realisation', the last stage. It leads to Paramananda or supreme Bliss, Brahmananda; but it is very difficult to reach this stage in the ordinary way of life. It is said, that the culmination of spiritual exercises in 'samadhi' will bring immense happiness and bliss that is un-surpassed by any other effort. This bliss is not comparable to any other joy. Those few who have experienced this bliss will be ever ready to share their happiness and bliss with their devotees. They see divinity in all souls and make no distinction of caste, creed, birth, or worldly accomplishments in their devotees. In the Hindu way of life, this is the ultimate one can achieve and it is the aspiration of all spiritual seekers to reach this stage, called 'turiya', and experience

the Bliss of 'Sat-Chit-Ananda', i.e., Brahmananda.Although this is what Buddha calls 'Nirvana', it is not the 'void' that' nirvana',(the negative aspect) indicates. It is positive happening, energizing, refreshing, enlightening and fulfilling experience. It is "SILENCE" not the one experienced by Buddha, but the one experienced by a fulfilled soul, emancipated, or liberated soul. It is attainment of 'the Brahm'. This supreme position can be attained either by RajaYoga through Meditation, or Hatha Yoga by Praanaayaama (Breath-control) or by any other Yogic exercise as directed in the Yoga Upanishads. .

The meditative state is the highest state of existence. It is only the contemplative 'witness-like' study of objects (Saakshi-bhava) that bring us real enjoyment and happiness. 'Samadhi' is also known as enlightenment or attainment of 'Divya Jnyana' ('Supreme Knowledge') or 'Realisation', or Knowledge of the Self (Aparokshaanubhuti). It is not a state of unconsciousness; it is a transcendental state attaining super Consciousness. Samadhi is the complete forgetfulness of all thoughts by first making it changeless and then identifying it with Brahman [Patanjali Yoga Sutra]. It is 'Pure Consciousness'.

The state of Samadhi is the final stage of spiritual attainment. But, it is very difficult to reach this stage without much effort. Many obstacles such as idleness, desire for sensual pleasure, sleep, dullness, distraction, lack of inquiry, sudden disinterestedness or loss of enthusiasm to pursue it further and eagerness to taste joy and a sense of blank-mindedness appear while practicing Samadhi. So, one has to guard against all these obstacles and get rid of them; one has to pursue the effort to reach the state of Samadhi with steadfastness and with firm determination.

The next highest state after '*Turiya*' (Samadhi) is '*Sushupti*'. One attains the Brahman in this state. There will be no body-consciousness or mind-consciousness in this state. It is Absolute Brahman! It is not possible to stay in this state for long. One has to come back to 'Turiya' and constantly strive for the 'Eternal Bliss"

It is not the intention here to go into the details of 'Samadhi', or 'Turiya' state, and its benefits since the main objective of this book is to live and work in this sensate world happily, peacefully, and successfully. It is with this intention that the householders' approach to 'Self Realisation' is stressed. Without taking recourse to going to forest ('*vanaprasthashrama*'), staying in the family and achieving the fulfilment is the goal of this book, 'Manoniyantran or 'Mind Management Techniques'. The 'sat' (True) 'nyasa' (maarg) i.e.,' sanyas' through mind control or mind management is the real pathway to Self Realisation. It is not Sanyas with ochre robe and total abandonment of family responsibilities that is advocated or sought for here. Life is to enjoy and everyone should enjoy it fully; the Veda and Upanishads fully support and encourage fulfillment of this purushartha and offer a number of mantras or techniques for this purpose. A few such mantra are given in the opening pages of this book. For more mantra, one can always refer to Mahnarayana Upanishad.

9
The Mind Console Techniques
Mantra, Yantra, and Tantra

When it comes to a distressed Mind and the problem of consoling it, we find many interesting things that cannot be explained by the scientists with all the so called advancements made in modern physical and mental sciences. A bruised mind or a wounded mind can be easily cured left to itself. But the modern psychiatrists and medical practitioners, administer sedatives, try to drive it to rest that will not help the problem. Modern science cannot penetrate deep into the subconscious mind or explore the superconscious states. It is the simple technique of Meditation that helps in consoling the disturbed mind. Modern science is objective in that it can explain what is generally visible and, in special cases, certain things that come within the purview of the senses, that too with the help of specially designed equipments such as the microscope, the endoscope, spectroscope, and such sorts of aids. We have to remember that science can deal with matter only since matter is finite and limted and comes within the grasp of the mind and the senses that are also finite and limited. But, man is partly matter and partly spirit; and, that part of the man that is matter can be explained scientifically, whereas, that part of the spirit, the soul, can be explained only spiritually. But, science does not consider things that do not come within its grasp, i.e., spirit. Hence, the difficulty arises when we want to explain the 'real nature of Mind' that falls outside the purview of material science. The problem becomes more complicated when it comes to the sub-conscious Mind. Mind is not only matter but it is also energy, vibrating fiercefully when excited and heated up.

Mind is Chitta Vritti, thought waves, and the vibration of these waves creates different minds and moods. Another important thing that complicates the matter is that the behaviour of Mind of a person is closely connected with the rhythm of his breathing. Raja Yoga explains that by controlling breathing the Mind can be controlled. Mind cleansed of all impurities such as thoughts, desires, imagination and fantasies becomes pure Mind. Impure Mind can be cleansed by Japa, tapa, vrata, nema (discipline), niyama (order), and dhyaana meditation. It should always be remembered that pure Mind is Prajnya, Consciousness; and, pure Consciousness is the 'Self', or the 'Atma'. And, the Atma 'knows all', and the Atma is Veda; and, 'Atma' knows all - 'KNOWLEDGE' personified as the '*Spirit*', *par excellence*. Purity is the decisive factor here. A blemished Soul is one full of karmic particles knit close by the silken thread of desires. Mind that is full of desire is thus impure and does not get the light of

Buddhi and Prajnya (Intellect and Consciousness) and the sense of discrimination. It is the pure 'Atma' that sheds powerful lght, the light of knowledge, and the 'Prajnya'. Consciousness, acts as a mirror that reflects this light to Buddhi that guides the Mind. In the absence of this light, Mind is in dark as to know what to do under circumstances of dire strait and distress. Mind becomes overstretched and distressed, and hence, sick. The Doctors who treat a sick person disturbed by Mind with sedatives, that only drives the Mind to rest, but will not help in curing the cause of the distressed mind. The ancient Sages were conscious of this problem and have evolved beautiful techniques of consoling the Mind. They use very simple Mantra, Yantra, or Tantra to stabilize the distressed Mind. Meditation is one simple and sure method of Mind control and Mind console.

Vedanta is the panacea for all human problems and ailments. Vedanta holds the key for happiness and success in life. ***'Vedanta' - 'the Knowledge Supreme'***, holds a different view, than the one held by Science, of this material world. The Veda go deep into the structure of the Multiverse, hither to considered as the Universe, and identify the physical, metaphysical, the spiritual, and the invisible, too! The spiritual and the invisible may be experienced in a super-conscious state of samadhi and is 'experienced' rather than explained. There are secrets of nature that cannot be explained since they do not come within the grasp of words and sounds. Further, the experience of the Yogins who visualize these spiritual and invisible subtle matter that lie on the border of energy can neither be communicated to others nor can the experience be transferred to others. At best, it is one's own experience and rests with the Yogin who visualized it. Further, this exclusive knowledge gained by very strenuous Yogic exercises cannot be questioned by one who is not well versed in the science of spirit, also known as 'mysticism' or occult sciences. The Mantra, Yantra, and Tantra come under this branch of science. Atharvaveda deals with all these aspects in great detail.

The 'Mantra' is Richa, the structure of Veda, the 'Akshara', as in th first mantra "Agnimeelay purohitam..." where, the Richa 'A' and 'k' go to make it 'Agnim'- self evolved, full of knowledge and consciousness. The first single-lettered Richa (word) 'Om' is a very powerful mantra and it has emanated from deep silence, '*Abhaava*' is bhaava-less; bhaava is *expression of will, desire*, intention of Mind; 'manobhaava' is also the trend or attitude of Mind. It is the source of all intentions, desires, thoughts, images, and words and sounds. The whole of Rk Veda consisting of 10,552 Mantra spread in Ten Mandalas (evolving and revolving) emerge and again merge only to re-emerge afresh with new impulses, desires, thoughts, images, words, sounds and objects, thereby creating the whole of this material objective world from the simple mantra "*Richo Ak*'-kshare". [See Mahrishi's 'Apaurusheya Bhashya', 'Wholeness on the Move', and 'Heaven on Earth'.]

"Richo Ak-kshare parame vyoman yasmin Deva adhi vishve nishedhuh;

Yastanna veda kim Ruchaa karishyati ya it tad vidus ta ime samaasate."[Rk Veda 1.164.39]

Meaning, The verses of Veda exist in the collapse of fullness (the 'kshara' of 'A') in the transcendent field in which reside all the Devas, the impulses of Creative Intelligence, the Laws of Nature responsible for the whole of manifest universe. He whose awareness is not open to this field, what can the verses accomplish for him? Those who know this level of reality are established in evenness, wholeness of life."

The first mantra of 'Rk Veda' is so powerful that it contains all the mystery of this universe in it. The entire universe has emanated from it, contained in it, sustained in it and, may be discarded by it one day! The first 'Akshara' of the Rk Veda is 'Ak' as in *"Agnimeelay purohitam ...." wherein the letter 'A' is the Universe, the macrocosm, and the letter 'k' is the 'kana' or microcosm and the entire Brahmanda is held in this word 'Ak'. All the multifarious diverse objects have emanated from the word 'Ak'. The GAP between the letter 'A' and the letter 'k' is the source of all the 33 million objects of the objective world. The GAP is Silence between the sounds of two letters and it has all the KNOWLEDGE and has immense possibilities and power of creation or CREATIVE INTELLIGENCE. It is called 'Purusha'. It is the meeting place of Purusha and Prakriti, the dynamic force that generates universe. One who understands this becomes the generating force himself capable of creating the objective world. This is the secret of the Yogins who create objects in mystic ways and the power of the mantra is evident in this creative process. The GAP or SILENCE between the sounds is the seat of Supreme-Consciousness, the seat of the ' Self-Referral', ' all-knowing' Consciousness –a simple word 'GOD' is used here for want of any other suitable one.*

The Mantra is associated with Brahmana. Both Mantra and Brahmana constitutes the Veda. The mechanics of transformation, the organising power of the Mantra is the Brahmana. Swara, the Mantra is also inherent in the Brahmana, from where it emerges. The definition of Veda is:

"Mantrabraahmanayorvedanaamadheyam", meaning, Mantra and Brahmana together constitute the Veda.[Apastamaba Shrauta Sutram 24.1.31].

To quote Maharishi, 'The Mantra' are the structure of Veda, and in the GAPS between the Mantra are the structuring dynamics, the Brahmana. GAPS or Silence between Mantra is the mechanics of transformation of the unmanifest non-specific field of intelligence and this will emerge as 'Swara' (Sound), the specific Mantra; and, this is the Brahmana aspect of the Veda.

This Brahmana aspect of Veda is the Technology of Consciousness according to Maharishi Mahesh Yogi. [Apaurusheya Bhaashya, pp. 150-151] "The structuring dynamics of the Mantra is the basis of Vedic Technology, which uses the Mantra to create anything from Veda, or to create anything from consciousness. As Mantra is the expression of consciousness, and consciousness is the most basic element of life-everything is the expression of mantra, expression of the Vedam expression of the consciousness. Therefore, one's consciousness when fully awake *within himself has the natural ability to create anything within his own consciousness" (Ibid) Yo jaagaar tam richah kaamayante" [Rk Veda, 5.44.14] meaning, "He who is awake,the Richah zoom forth in his awareness and uphold his thoughts, speech, and action. [Richah is Mantra, ('Rk') expressions of Veda, consciousness].**

Mental Aberrations - Play of Mind

The Samkhya Philosophy holds that, 'this heterogenous Multiverse is the development, or 'Srushti' borne out of homogenous Prakriti and, ultimately it returns to Prakriti only. Thus, it is clear that there has been no creation nor there will be any destruction of this objective world. It has always been in existence and will continue in one form or the other. There has been a continuous process of evolution and involution; everything emanating out of the black hole and merging into it at interval of what may be called 'kaala' (Time). Actually, there is neither Kaala (Time) nor Desha (Space) since Kaala or time is the interval between two events and, Desha, or Space is 'that' which is created by objects (that occupy it)! These are again illusion created by relativity, play of the Mind. Remember, it is just the play of Mind! Here, an illustration will help to understand these aspects of space and time, clearly. Supposing you are caught in a traffic jam in a crowded city, you will say, 'just cannot move' because there is no space. How come there is no space in a big city? Second, we say, 'there is lack of communication' in a traffic jam. How come 'lack of communication' when you are actually in communication virtually touching each other? Now, about time, there is all the time in the world when you are alone and you have no time when you are in a crowded city! What makes you feel these things? Similarly, there is vast, unlimited space when you are alone in a village and the space is squeezed when you are with others in a city that is quite large! Yet another simple illustration is that of a train that appears moving although it stands still. When you are in a stationary train and the other train on the neighbouring track starts moving slowly, you feel that your train is moving. These are all illusions created by relativity, the play of the mind that normally we all experience. Remember that these are just play of the Mind!

Pure Mind is the Atman that is blemishless, desireless, gets entangled with the desires and fears and feels bonded due to ignorance and, hence suffers. When knowledge of 'Reality' dawns the disturbed mind is freed from illusions, confusion, bondage, and all its ailments disappear. A healthy mind is one that sees 'things as they are'. In other words, when the Purusha recognizes his svaroopa, innate quality of omniscience, permanence, freedom, and immortality, he is released from the clutches of the non-intelligent Prakruti, the attractions of this material world.

There is a supreme Coordinator who sits and coordinates all experiences and thus enables us to experience the objective world. When the Reality is experienced, the screen disappears and the Coordinator stands 'revealed'. Prakriti is mainly responsible for our bondage as well as freedom. When one identifies himself with Prakriti, he is in bondage;

and, when one recognizes the Purusha in himself, he becomes free. One is born to experience the Prakriti (the objective sensate world) and he has got all the freedom to get released from bondage of Prakruti. That way, each one of us is here at our own sweet will and pleasure and remain here as long as we desire. To enjoy or suffer is according to our good deeds or bad deeds at present or in the past! Mantra, yantra, tantra, dhyaan, and Meditation, japa and tapas will go a long way in recognizing the Purusha, the Self within, and thereby redeeming oneself from the clutches of Prakrti. All these are tricky questions and one needs to contemplate on them.

It is the play of Mind since it believes in 'things' that do not exist in 'reality' whatsoever! The things that did not exist earlier, and that will not exist in future, also do not exist in the present in 'Reality'. "*Reality*" is 'That' which exists always beyond the constraints of time, space and causality. In the absence of this reality, it is all mental aberrations that cause sickness of mind.

There are two aspects of what is called '*Existence*'- one is the physical and the other psychic. The physical deals with matter such as the atom or the sub-atomic particles, and the psychic deals with the Mind. Mind is the thing! Mind is matter and Mind is energy. Matter such as photons or electrons (sub-atomic particle) are produced from radiation (light). The ultimate constituent of the universe of the physicist is energy of radiation, i.e., light. The Vedantin or a Jnyaani (Yogin) goes a little beyond this material science. He visualizes in his meditative super-conscious state, the energy that emanates from the Brahman, the supreme Consciousness, or the supreme source of energy, 'Narayana'. This energy radiated as light, illumination, enlightenment, or 'jnyaan' is the ' Reality' of existence, and it is the Only "Truth". All else is illusion. Mind is the screen on which the objects of the world are projected. It is the objective world, the illusory world that projects matter (objects) on the Mind and, it is a sensate world since the senses can grasp it. The Mind is Akasha or Maha Sagara, or vast endless apace called 'mahadaakasha'. It is the 'chittaakasha', or the ocean of 'thought waves'.

To repeat, Mind is also energy in its pure state, and is called 'Consciousness'. Energy radiates as heat, light, consciousness (prajnya), and Prana. Mind, that is energy, becomes matter as electrons of thought waves. Thus, the entire mechanism is one of interplay of Mind as matter and energy. Energy radiates and creates matter. Waves and vibrations of radiation cause different gunas that produce forms and functions of matter. Matter acquires quality (gunas) as 'Gunas' accumulate in matter according to the velocity and intensity of waves and vibrations of energy. It is gunas that constantly evolve and not the soul. It is said that, matter behaves according to its quality. *"Gunaanu gunavartante"*, meaning, the objects possess qualities according to the vibrations and behave accordingly. A cat cannot behave like a Lion. Gunas are infinite in number and quality. However, three major groups of Gunas have been identified- the Sattva, the Rajas, and the Tamas. These gunas combine and recombine in different degrees by permutation and combination to form the objects of different qualities. Hence, it is all the *play of the mind* that project different forms and functions. It is here that, the Mantra, Tantra and Yantra play their role in erasing the illusion and establishing "Reality". Once the mind-screen vanishes, the pictures (objective world) on the mind screen also vanish. With 'manonasha', or cessation of the vibration of 'chitta vritti' the sensate world of make-believe objects disappear. In Bhagavad Gita, Shree Krishna makes it very clear that He is the Purusha behind all this magic, wielding the magic wand. Don"t be carried away by this make-believe world, says Krishna to Arjuna. It is 'avidya' or ignorance that makes you believe that as real. In reality, nothing exists and all that exists is only 'Him' in different forms, name, and function. It is the 'One' and the only 'Truth'.

'Enlightenment' comes with the cessation of the vibration. The Mind is chitta Vrittis, or the thought waves with vibrations. The Mantra are also vibrations of sound and the vibrations match in intensity and wavelength of Gunas causing reactions. Annihilation or cancelling the effect of projection of objects on the mental screen is possible by matching vibrations of Mantra and this is called 'manonasha'. Thus, the projection of thoughts and images cease with the cessation of the vibration with the help of mantra, tantra and yantra.

Thus, the most interesting aspect of the Mantra is that they can control the Mind. The mechanism is very simple. The Mind is 'antahkarana' that has its source in the heart. Mind and the heart are the source of vibration of thoughts, emotions, sentiments, ego, etc. Certain mantra originate sounds from navel, heart, and throat each with different effects. So also, the Yantras that have magical numbers and colours that vibrate with the blood flow from the heart and affect the thought waves. Rajo guna has red colour, Sattva guna has white colour, and the tamo guna has yellow colour and these define the emotions of anger, pity, or indolence, respectively, to name a few. Predominant gunas give the respective quality to the objects. This explains why a tiger and a sheep differ in their form and function. Mantra can be used in dhyan and meditation to transcend these gunas and attain the guna-less state of Super-Consciousness.

Now, the Mind, the heart, the blood flow, breath control (Pranayama), the mantra, the yantra and the tantra all work in a beautiful, harmonious way to reduce the vibrations to almost a state of stillness. With the stillness of the vibration, the mind ceases to vibrate and the thought waves stop removing the screen of neiscience or 'avidya'. The result is the removal of ignorance or avidya and dawn of enlightenment. "Enlightenment", Illumination, or " dawn of "Knowledge" comes with this "manonasha" caused by the Mantra, Yantra, and/or Tantra.

How about attaining emancipation or liberation from the cycle of rebirth from mantra, yantra, and tantra? It is very simple. It is certain that 'desire' is the cause of birth and rebirths. Desire is matter like the sub-atomic particles, like the electrons. These are the blemishes of the soul. The embedded soul is polluted by the flux of minute particles of 'desire' that cling to it (just like dust on glass) as memory, sanskaar, or the impressions of the past, or simply "Karma". Unless prompted by desire, the embedded soul does not take a body to fulfill its desire. The Upanishads declare that, *'Desire is Brahman'* and desire is embedded in the soul and assumes the form and function it desires most. Desire selects a body and enters it as prana, vital breath and remains there till that body is useful to fulfill its objecticve. Thus, it is 'Karma' and 'Desire' that dictate the form and function of the next birth. Whatever is uppermost in the mind at the time of death of the jeeva becomes a possibility in the next brith. Now, this 'seed', or the 'germ cell', the 'desire' that is the cause of rebirth can be burnt by pratyahara, 'japa', dhyana, and 'tapas' (heat), of chanting of Mantra. The vibration caused by the mantra, tantra, and yantra can destroy the 'germ cell' and thereby 'immortality' is attained. All sorts of chitta vrittis, desires, karma- prarabhda or samchita, can be reduced to ash by the tapas. The mantra, tantra, and yantra help in this process. These techniques are beyond the comprehension of scientists who depend on their mind and senses for these tools are finite and limited. Only the yogins who withdraw their mind and the senses from their outward projections, and transcend time, space, and causality by transcending gunas, will attain the Absolute. Cessation of vibration, or 'manonasha' is essential for emancipation. This is removal, or the 'root out' of the causes like desire, karma, and sanskaar that cause rebirth. Scientists do not believe in this aspect of tantric exercise. They reject it as rubbish! It is sheer ignorance at that!

Another important thing is 'Yogic Perception'. Yogins, or Siddhi Purushas can perceive the past and future by their intuition, a power derived from rigorous practice of dharana and meditation. This yogic perception is attained without the aid of mind and the senses since the Purusha or the witnessing Self ('Sakshin') perceives it. Remember what Sri Krishna tells Arjuna in the Kurukshetra battlefield.

"Kaunteya, they are 'asat', i.e., the embodied souls- bound by time, space and causality, not real; they are already dead and do not be under the impression that they are going to die at your hands". The Lord as 'Antaryamin', or the witnessing 'Self' knows everything- past and future, because He witnesses all changes or modifications of the chitta vrittis (mind stuff). Trust me and do your duty.

Scientists dealing with 'physical' objects, or 'matter', do not comprehend the 'metaphysical' aspects since they keep 'Spirit' outside the purview of Physics. They search and re-search into 'matter' and get deeper and deeper into the tiniest of the sub-atomic particles. They fail to notice the 'nothingness' (involution in latent form) that emanates as energy, as the by-product of supreme-consciousness, latent or hidden in the microns just as 'oil is latent in the sesame seeds', or 'the banyan tree hidden in the seeds of the tiny banyan seeds'. This simple 'truth' is hidden from the normal sense organs and the Mind that always look outward towards the 'objects' for the answers. The Veda and the Upanishads make these points amply clear and one should be sensible enough to know the difference between the 'spiritual' and the 'materialistic'. Any effort to discard 'spiritual' from the existential reality is foolish. Mind, Consciousness, Prana, Breathing, the 'anthahkarana', the subtle body, and the subtler aspects of the Heart, etc. are beyond the purview of physical or biological science, since the science looks only at the 'objects' that are physical and biological and that are subject to investigation by the senses and the mind. But, spiritual implorations are a science of a different kind that can be personally experienced which needs no proof, confirmation, and no experimentation. The truth holds good for eternity!

All the Sciences, Arts, and Commerce on the one hand, and all the sciences of Physics, Chemistry, Human Physiology and Mathematics on the other, come within the ambit of human understanding and can be traced to one single source. This source of all Knowledge is the 'Veda'- that is holistic and Samhita (Totality). In Samhita the Knower, the Knowledge, and the means of Knowing (the illumining Principle)- become one. It is three-in –one. It is the Samhita of the Rishi (the Seer or Knower), the Devata (the Illumining Principle-Light), and the Chhandas- the Knowledge. Thus, Totality is established in this Yoga. The four Veda and the thirty-six Vedic literature constitute the total Knowledge and all these exist in the intelligence of Man. Man is Rk Veda, the embodiment of all Knowledge. The Mantra emanate from different parts of the body as 'sounds or vibrations of sounds' or neurons carrying messages of Vedic literature i.e. quality of intelligence having its source in Atma. Thus, it is this 'totality of Knowledge' that is Veda Samhita – 'Rk Veda Samhita'.

Thus, the Veda and Upanishads give the most authentic and the most beautiful account of the mysteries of the universe as also explains the techniques to unravel them. Through the Mantra.

There are the 'Yantra', the 'Mantra', and the 'Tantra' for interpreting this Universe. The 'Mantra' generate vibrations that create mystic experiences in the Yogins and the powerful thought-force could be employed to many desired ends. The chanting of '*Mantra*' cures diseases. There are powerful Mantra that ward off death or prevent untimely death of children while the parents are alive. Poison in the body, particularly by snakebite, is extricated by chanting of particular 'Mantra'. Extra-sensorial Perceptions, telepathy, faith- healing, or touch therapy and other techniques are very popular even today. The yogins employed these methods for alleviating the sufferings of mankind. Magical numbers and colours that created or absorbed the universal vibrations could be deciphered by contemplation or Meditation and /or the formulae of the powerful 'Mantra' of Atharva Veda. Thus, the entire field of Vedic learning constituted the "Vedic way of life" of the ancient Indians. In a way, it was a life of prayers, prayer for the welfare of the humanity, prayer for the wellbeing of the person, and prayer for a life of fulfillment. This holistic approach to learning as well as living is absent in modern times anywhere in the world.

Mantra, Its Significance

Mantra is any word or words that emanated intuitionally from the bottom of the heart. It may be simple ordinary words but they beocome powerful when charged with the power of spiritual attainment, by the fire of the persons purity of thought; it may be invoking the Lord's blessings. Mantra literally means that which frees the soul through reflection, '*Mananat thraayate iti mantra*'. Utterance of a mantra, a divine name, is the simple and easiest way of self- realisation. Maharshi Paatanjali, speaking about the effect of repeating 'Om' and other holy names says that, *"It removes the various obstacles (like doubt, illness, mental disturbances) on the path and leads to the awareness of the individual Spirit" [Yoga Sutra*, 1.29]. Repetition of the Mantra calms the nerves and unifies the powers of the mind and finally awakens the Spirit within. Each mantra contains a special syllable called the bija (seed). The bija is believed to arouse special power of our deity in us. Every individual has a *bija mantra* or a personal divine name which is very potent and effective; but this has to be revealed by an accomplished Guru or, should be initiated to by a person of spiritual attainment. Even parents can initiate as is usually done during the upanayanam. Sometimes, mantra is heard as 'anahata dhvani' in the right ear, or in a dream, and it tallies with the one given by the Guru. In tantric tradition the mantra is a secret and never to be revealed to others for it loses its power and sanctity. It becomes a common- place utterance when revealed to everyone.

The efficacy of the chanting of Mantra cannot be under-estimated. There is enormous strength in the Mantra and it helps us to see through our inner eye. It enables one to make the ordinary extraordinary, profane profound, and the sensuous sacred. The vibrations generated from japam or chanting of mantra help cure the sickness of body and mind andestablish harmony in the function of the body, mind and soul. It helps unlock the hidden centers of energy (plexus) and helps us to develop our personality, develop our potentialities. It helps us to see *things as they are* and see the world free from illusion. Chanting of Mantra with devotion and understanding, as in Japam, makes possible transformation. It removes the 'ego'. Thus, it is a source of great transformation from 'I-ness' to 'Thyness'.

'Shanti Mantra' is the invocation to peace. Peace is where there is harmony, when there is acceptance, when there is Truth. The body is made up of five elements viz the air, water, fire, earth and prana (the vital force). There is harmony among these five great elements. A slight impairment in any one of these five great elements will cause sickness and death. The Supreme Being, the Self unites and joins and keeps them in harmony in the body and the person is healthy and happy. These elements that are inside the body are also outside the body. There is harmony and balance between the outside and the inside. This Shanti Mantra is for the continuance of that balance and harmony.

The Mantra states:

"May Mitra, Varuna, Aryaman, Indra, Brihaspati, All-pervading Vishnu be propitious to us and grant us welfare and Bliss. I bow down to Brahman in reverence; Oh, Vayu, I bow down to thee in adoration. Thou art verily perceptible Brahman. I shall declare thou art Right. Thou art the True and the Good. May that Supreme Being, adored as Vayu preserve me. May He preserve the Teacher. May He protect 'Om'. May He protect both of us. May He nourish us both together. May we work conjointly with great Energy. May our study be vigorous and be effective. May we not mutually dispute or we not hate any. Om! Let there be Peace and

peace and Peace in me, in my environment, and the forces that act on me." Some of the most potent Mantra are:

The first Mantra is SILENCE"................." i.e, Silence, "Absolute Silence". Silence is the most effective of all the mantra. The entire universe, or the Brahmanda has emanated from silence. The Prashaant Prajnaya Saagara, Abstract Silence is the source of all KNOWLEDGE. The first manifest form of this Shaanti, Absolute Silence is Svaar (Sound, the 'Om'. The sacred Mantra 'Om' emanates from Atma. The sounds that emanate from pure heart is very effective. The vibration of sound emanating from Atma is capable of creating anythong from nothing! In fact, the objective material world has emanated from 'Rk' 'Mantra', the sound emanating from pure Consciousness, One must practise this mantra perodically, if not regularly in order to utilize the potential inherent in it. Atharva Veda is full of Mantra that is capable of transforming anything! It wards off dangers and protects; it removes poison and prevent harm done by enemies. It cures diseases and regulates flow in the body keeping it healthy. There are Mantra of different metere or Chhandas that reveal the hidden power and strength.

"Om" (one-and-a-half letter word); or the "AUM" (3- letter word); or the "AUMm" (Three-and-a-half letter word); and these sounds produce different results. Metre or Chhandas of the Mantra has its own effect. This aspect has already been discussed elaborately. However, it is repeated here for reference. The efficacy of the Mantra, it should always be remembered, depends on the purity of the heart and purity of mind and the degree of austerity of the person. Spiritual exercises are greatly facilitated by this mantra.

"Om is the Pranava mantra and it is connected with Prana; it flows through the vital breath and is very effective in meditation.

"Sri Harih! (2 words) Om!"Om is the prefix and the mantra always ends with a Shanti mantra and Om.

"Om namah Shivaaya"(3 words); "Om namo Naaraayanaaya"(3 words of 8 letters);

"Om namo Bhagavate Vaasudevaaya" (4 words of 12 letters)

"Om Bhur bhuvah svah, Tatsaviturvareneeyam,
Bhargo devasya dheemahi, dheeyo yo nah prachodayat!"

"Om, Ghruneeh, Suryah, Adityaaya namah, Om"

"Om, Vishveshvaraaya Namah, Om"

"Om, Gam Ganeshaya namah, Om"

"Shree Ram Jaya Ram, Jaya Jaya Ram",

"Hare Rama, Hare Rama, Rama Rama, Hare Hare,
Hare Krishna, Hare Krishna, Krishna Krishna Hare Hare"

"Ramaaya Ramabhadraaya Ramachandraaya vedhase
Raghunaathaaya Naathaaya Seetaayapataye namah, Om"

"Kalyanaadbhutagaatraaya kaamitaartha pradhaayine
Sreemad Venkatanaathaaya Sreenivaaasaaya te namah. Om"

"Poojyaaya Raghavendraaya Satya Dharma Ritaaya cha
Bhajataam kalpavrukshaaya namataam Kaamadhenave"

In the above Mantra, there are: one letter word, two letter words, three letter words, four letter words, eight letter words, and twelve, twenty-four and thirty-two or thirty-six letter words. Each mantra is suited to certain persons whose date of birth or janma nakshatra matches numerologically. Normally, a spiritually attained person, or the persons's father can initiate a person with a mantra and such mantra are fruitful. All mantra are not useful to all persons always. There are Mantra for different occasions and Maha Narayana Upanishad has mantra for different purposes. These mantra are in different Chhandas (metres) and they are effective only when they are pronounced phoenetically correctly creating the appropriate vibrations.

Well, if the mantra are to give the desired results, it is very essential that the person should be pure kaaya, vaacha, manasa i.e., pure in heart and mind and deeds; he should observe certain rituals like cleaning the surroundings, particularly temples. He should take bath very early in the morning and sit in Padmasana (cross- legged) in a serene atmosphere, prefereably in front of a deity of his choice. He should always live an austere life, if any mantra is to be effective. Indisciplined persons cannot get any benefit out of these Mantra. Only a religious person of trained mind, controlled manas can help us in this matter and, as such, one needs a 'guru' in the initial stages.

Sometimes, even a word uttered by a Saint or Saadhu, or spiritually attained person, or even the elders becomes a very effective 'Mantra'. Hence, one must be very respectful and careful while talking to these persons. Humility is very essential for spiritual success. These Mantra help to ward off dangers from natural elements (like floods, strong winds lightning), wild beasts, poisonous creatures, and enemies who are bent on harming us. Persons of weak mind should always chant these Mantra to strengthen their mind. These Mantra also bring material wealth, better health, and spiritual progress. As prayers, the mantra are very useful and mitigate the hardships, sufferings, and pain of others.

The mantra formed the foundation of life during the Vedic Period. The religious persons started their day with mantra and ended it with mantra. There are mantra for almost every activity like plucking flowers for pooja, taking bath, siting for dhyan, eating food, and bless the youngsters ('asheervad'). Asheervada-mantra are very effective and bring great luck and success and ward of dangers.

Since these mantra are counted by their syllables (Bija mantra) that have numerological significance one should know which mantra is very effective and must use regularly in dhyan, japa and meditation to gain full benefit from it. The mantra arouse the latent spiritual tendencies in every man. Thus, one can contemplate, or meditate on the 'Bija mantra'that is suitable and appropriate and this will give very good results. Continuous repetition of mantra with concentration produces what may be called 'molecular vibration', that which will persist even when there is no external repetition with effort. Repetition of the mantra and contemplation of the meaning of the mantra should go on simultaneously. Vishnu Purana says, 'after the repetition of 'Om', one should have recourse to meditation, and after meditation, one should again take to chanting of Om! Through perfection of repetition and meditation, the Supreme Spirit becomes manifest'. This sort of using 'bija mantra', or 'Ishta devatha namasmarane', reciting the name of God in japa, dhyaana, or meditation is not restricted to Hindusim. In Islam, the Sufi mystics have for centuries employed the repetition of 'Allah' meaning God, or 'Ali' as a means of getting spiritual illumination. In Buddhist sect Shin, the spiritual aspirants recite the mantra, Namo Amitabha Buddhaya (Namu-amida-butsu). One can repeat the name of Amida in any posture. The Catholics use the rosary in repeating ' Ave Maria, Hail Mary'. The Greek Saints perfected the system of prayer. Jesus Prayer [The Way of a Piligrim] is similar to the Hindu japa. The name of the Lord should be repeated constantly without break, with full heart, and contemplation. Meditation with bhavartha, imploring the Lord's Grace keeping His picture in mind is very effective. The Holy Mother used to practice japa, over a lakh a day, during the sadhana period and had demonstrated the power of the divine name (naamasmarane). Through japa and dhyana one can rise from body consciousness to super-consciousness.

The technique of meditation should be perfected in order to realize its full powers. That is, 'if the mind can first concentrate on an object, and then is able to continue in that concentration for some length of time, and then, by continued concentration, is able to dwell only on the internal part of the perception of which the object was the effect, everything comes under the control of such a mind'. 'At first, meditation must begin with some gross objects and slowly rise to finer or subtler ones until finally it becomes 'object-less'. The mind must be employed to perceive the external causes of sensations, and then move on to internal motions and then to its own reactions. When it has succeeded in perceiving the motions inside by themselves, it will gain the control of all the mental waves in itself or others, even before they have translated themselves into physical energy; and, when he will be able to perceive the mental reactions by itself, the Yogi will acquire the knowledge of everything, as every sensible object and even though it is the result of this reaction. Then he will have seen the very foundation of his mind and it will be under his control. This is the perfect method of mind control.

As regards, Meditation techniques, no single method is perfect and final. All the methods explained here are for the beginners. For those accomplished, there is no meditation. Meditation is their way of life. Any spiritual seeker can follow any method suited to his temperament, after all it is to destroy the 'ego' and still the mind that these exercises are practiced. The highest state of meditation is one where a single vichara dominates and all thoughts are destroyed by that single 'vichara'. So, Contemplate on any single concept or 'mahat tattva' and dwell in it. You will reach the basis of the Truth. Mantra are very helpful in this regard.

Mahanarayana Upanishad contains a number of Mantra to propitiate the various Deities. The most significant of them are the Mantra in Gayatri, Trishthub chhandas. Persons desirous of materialistic or paaramaarthic benefits are advised to keep a Text of this Upanishad and use it for japam and meditation, tapas.

So, meditate; practise dharana, japam and tapas, dhyana and

meditation. The golden rule is Japam-japam-japam; practice japam all the time and experience the result! This will give immense peace and happiness.

The Mantra "Om", Its Special Significance

The sound that emanated from the Prashanta Prajnya Saagara abstract silence 'Brhm' at the time of the 'Sphota' is "OM". This "Om" is considered to be the most potential 'mantra'. *"Om" is affixed and prefixed to all other Mantra by Brahmanas. By the way, one should clearly know what are these 'Mantra' and 'Beahmana'. Maharishi Mahesh Yogi has defined 'Mantra' as:*

"Mantra Brahmanayor- Veda naamadheyam",

Mantra and Brahmana together constitute Veda- Mantra, the structure of Veda, and Brahmana, the structuring dynamics of Mantra.The structuring dynamics of the Mantra is the basis of Vedic Technology, which uses the Mantra to create anything from Veda, or to create anything from consciousness. That is why Vedic Technology is Technology of Consciousness. Mantra (Svara) and everything is the expression of Veda; everything is expression of consciousness. Consciousness is the most basic thing in life. Everyone is bestowed with this wonderful gift of creative ability and anyone can tap this eternal source in the state of pure wakefulness, full awareness, pure Consciousness.

"Ýo jaagaar tam richah kaamyante". [Rk Veda 5.44.14]

He who is awake, the Richa zoom forth in his awareness and uphold his thought, speech, and action. The mechanics of transformation is the Brahmana aspect of the Vedic structure. ***Brahmana is the organizing power of the Mantra.*** *In fact, the persons who exhibited this quality of structural dynamics came to be known as Brahmins or 'Iyyas' (knowledgeable persons).*

Mahanarayana Upanishad has clearly mentioned the source of "Om". Accordingly, "the name designating the self-luminous Reality and consisting of the syllable 'Om' is hidden in the Veda. By contemplating on the Supreme alongwith the slow repetition of "Om", one attains to immortality. "Om" is the central support of the undying spirit and supreme Bliss. This is evident from 'Rk Veda' [IV.58.1-2] that states: "Om" is the means of attaining release from the cycle of birth and death and the Pranava, the "Om", is the nama (name) expressing the Self-luminous Reality, Adtya, or Ghruta". Taittiriya Upanishad says, "the four-horned bull is the AUMm ("Om"), the four horns of the bull represent the sound elements in the "AUMm". The syllable "Om" is conceived in the form of Bull of four horns, three feet and two heads; it has seven hands and has entered the mortals everywhere. [Rk Veda IV.58.3; Mahanarayana Upanishad XII.10]. Here, the four horns are the four Vedas; three feet are the states of waking, dream, and sleep of the individual soul, as also, three vyahritis- the earth, the sky, and the heaven (Bhur, bhuvar, and svar); the two heads are higher and the lower aspects of Prakriti, as also, the unevolved cause and the soul embodied in the universe. The seven hands are the seven worlds- bhur, bhuvar, svar, mahat, janah, tapah and satya. The loud bellowing of the Bull is "Om" that declares Paramatman is present in all creatures protecting and sustaining them. The Lord Himself has entered the human beings through the sacrifices in which He is worshipped. "Om" is also used as the mantra in sacrificial sense in priase of water (ghruta' that which has trickled)– rather, in praise of the Lord, glorification of Paramatman who created water. Water has a special significance since it supports life.

'Om' is Brahman. 'Om' is a primeaval sound. 'Om' is the imperishable Brahman, and it constitutes the universe. All Vedic prayers emerged from Om! Om is used as prefix to all mantra as it is synonymous with Brahman. Whatsoever existed, whatsoever that exists now, and whatsoever shall exist hereafter is 'Om'. [Mandukya Upanishad, 1]. 'Om' represents all the physical and astral bodies, both manifested and unmanifested, from the external-most physical to the internal-most spiritual on four cosmic planes. 'He who knows it attains the highest fulfilment of life' [Katha Upanishad, 1. 2. 15-16]. 'Om' is the symbol of Ishwara or God according to the Yoga Sutra of Patanjali. Paatanjali says that constant repetition of this mantra leads to awakening of the soul removing all obstacles. "Om" is called the Pranava Mantra" since it is Prana flowing through the body. Praana is the vital breath and its flow is pravahana. Pranava is the life-sustaining force and as such, the most important.

As of repeated, *Om* is the most sacred mantra ever known and the origin of the word is closely linked to the origin of the universe. It is the first word that came out of Brahman. It came out with the explosion of primordial matter 'the Big Bang', or 'the Sphota'. 'Om' is the symbol of this sphota and the 'Om' and the sphota cannot be separated. It is the mother of all names and forms and the whole universe may be supposed to have been created out of this holiest of the holy word 'Om'. The divine spirit expresses itself through the divine Idea, and the Divine Idea through divine sound or word 'Om'. During his meditation, Sri Ramakrishna got the revelation of the Nada Brahman or the manifestation of Brahman as sound.

The Katha Upanishad[1.2.15-16] says 'Om is the supreme, immutable Brahman Itself'. He who knows it attains the highest fulfilment in life. The *Mundaka Upanishad* [2. 2. 4] compares 'Om' to a bow, and the purified and concentrated mind to an arrow, and exhorts us to shoot the arrow with intense alertness so that it may hit the target which is Brahman and become one with it. 'Om' here stands for the entire meaning of the Upanishads. The *Mandukya Upanishad* declares that, "the syllable 'Om' is the Universe. Whatsoever that existed, whatsoever now exists, whatsoever shall exist hereafter is 'Om'. The syllables A, U, and M that constitutes 'Om' stands for the vast physical universe, the vast mental universe and the causal substratum of both these universes, respectively. The soundless or the unmanifested 'Om', the amatra, however, transcends them".

'Om', represents the whole phenomenon of sound production and no other word can do this. This is the fittest symbol of the sphota. *Sphota* and 'Om' are the same according to Swami Vivekananda. 'Om' is truly symbolic of God. Therefore one should contemplate and meditate on *Om*!

'Om' is the only word that reached where nothing else could reach, and it is the word that originated where everything else is consequential. The mantra shastra or the science of mantra, which is a division of the Tantra, is based on the theory that the whole universe is created out of vibrations. What we call sound is only physical vibrations. Subtler than audible sound are the electromagnetic waves like the instruments within the radio-receiving sets. Subtler still are the thought waves. Thought itself is a manifestation of the eternal supersensuous cosmic pulsations of the Nada Brahman or Shabda Brahman, or the cosmic mind. Nada Brahman can be heard through the subtle mind. It only needs a highly purified mind.

Some times these mantra are counted by their syllables (Bija mantra) that have numerological significance. The mantra arouse the latent spiritual tendencies in every man. Thus, one can contemplate or meditate on his 'Bija mantra' and this will give very good results. Continuous repetition of mantra with concentration produces what may be called 'molecular vibration', that which will persist even when there is no external repetition with effort. Repetition and contemplation of the meaning can go on simultaneously. *Vishnu Purana* says, 'after the repetition of Om, one should have recourse to meditation, and after meditation, one should again take to chanting of Om! Through perfection of repetition and meditation, the Supreme Spirit becomes manifest'.

This sort of using 'Bija mantra', 'Ishta devatha namasmarane', and reciting the name of God in japa or meditation are not restricted to Hindusim. The Sufi mystics and the followers of Islam have for centuries employed the repetition of 'Allah' meaning God, or 'Ali' as a means of getting spiritual illumination. In Buddhist sect Shin, the spiritual aspirants recite the mantra, *Namo Amitabha Buddhaya (Namu-amida-butsu)*. One can repeat the name of *Amida* in any posture. The Catholics use the rosary in repeating '*Ave Maria, Hail Mary*'. The Greek saints of the Middle Ages perfected the system of prayer, *Jesus Prayer [The Way of a Piligrim] is similar to the Hindu japa*. The name of the Lord should be repeated constantly without break, with full heart, and contemplation. Meditation with bhavartha, imploring the Lord's Grace keeping His picture in mind is very effective. The Holy Mother used to practice japa, over a lakh a day, during the sadhana period and had demonstrated the power of the divine Name. Through japa and dhyana one can rise from body consciousness to super-consciousness.

The Gayatri Mantra

Manu Smriti has elaborately dealt with the Gayatri mantra. It is culled out of the three Vedas- the Rig Veda, Yajur Veda, and Sama Veda, by none else than Brahman, Himself. It starts with the 'OM' that emanated with the sphota or Big Bang at the time of the origin of the Universe and the sound still persists in the cosmic space. The Gayatri mantra has been constructed by letters "A', 'U', and 'M' extracted out of the three Vedas and by their coalition with the three mysterious words- 'Bhur', Bhuvah, and Svah, meaning earth, sky and heaven, respectively. Thus the text of the Gayatri mantra was composed as:

"Om! Bhur bhuva svah, tatsaviturvareneeyam, Bhargodevasya dheemahi, dheeyo yonah prachodayat".

This mantra is conceived as the worship of Shree Hari, of Aditya (the Sun), and also as pure Nirguna worship of Brahman. Bhisma Pitamaha advises Yudhistir to recite this spiritually powerful Mantra in the battle-field of Kurukshetra. The Goddess Gayatri Devi is the incarnation and manifestation of Brahman who resides as intelligence in all human beings, rather in all living beings. *Gayatri mantra* is also known as Savitri mantra or Surya mantra and is addressed to the divine power of the Star of our Solar System, the Sun.

The *Shvetasvatara Upanishad* proclaims that, "the one affluent divinity is hidden in all beings. He is All-pervading and is the inner-self of all creatures. He presides over all actions and all beings reside in Him. He is the inner-witness. He endows all with the consciousness and is Nirguna, or free from all three gunas- the tamas, Rajas and the Sattvic". *Isavasya Upanishad* also gives a similar exposition of the Gayatri mantra. However, the *Rig Veda* has defined this Gayatri mantra differently. Accordingly, " the illumined sages like Surayah constantly see that infinite all-pervading supreme reality Vishnu without any obstruction as though their vast intuitive eye or vision was spread over the spiritual sky". Before Gayatri japa is chanted, it is beneficial to practice Pranayama. This helps in concentration. Of the three methods of chanting the mantra, the Vachik (chanting loudly), Upansu (in low voice) and Mansic (mental chanting), the last one is more effective. Gayatri is a spiritual weapon that protects one who chants it, and blesses him with brilliant light of the highest spiritual illumination. It should forma nitya karma for one and all, a means of realisation of the self; it leads to realisation of the divinity of the self and it is salvation.

The effect of Japa and meditation are direct. Japa and meditation keep the mind engaged. The mind dwells, at least for a little while, on the supreme spirit, dwells on divine blissful form, on the noble attributes. Then comes the time, when one feels the divine Presence. Many blessed souls get the spiritual vision of the divine Form. Such persons then become the Guru. *Spiritual life is like mountain climbing. One has to go slowly higher and higher, carefully.* No one can become a realized soul overnight. One has to begin with a simple thing like repetition of the name of the *Ishtadevatha.* This is called *Japa*. Repetition of the name should not be mechanical. It should be done with total devotion and bhaavartha. The significance of the name uttered should be contemplated upon. Think of the Lord as pure, blissful, luminous, all-pervading spirit. Gradually the inner meaning will unfold by itself. It will be a very enlightening experience. It brings with it cheerfulness and peace.

Meditation is contemplation on the Divine. It is a continuous flow of thoughts towards a higher spiritual ideal in a higher spiritual 'centre of Consciousness'. One must be absorbed in the thought of the divine, but it does not come easily in the beginning. Japa is the first step in this direction. Repetition of the name of Ishtadevatha, thinking of Him, deeply absorbed in Him, will gradually lead to supreme Spirit 'Sat- Chit- Ananda'. God will appear to his devotee in the form of his Ishtadevatha.

Yama, Niyama, and Prathyahara should be practiced before attempting serious meditation. If one attempts meditation without having attained purity of mind, it is likely that he will concentrate more on impurities of the mind than God. The higher centers of consciousness must open in order to enable one to dwell on higher thoughts for long. Prayer and doing good work helps here.

Meditation is a fully conscious process, an exercise of the will. Meditation means concentration on a spiritual idea that presupposes that the aspirant is capable of rising above worldly ideas. Meditation is done usually at a particular center of consciousness, preferably the heart. It is a long drawn process and the results come automatically in due course and one should not be too eager to experience the results. Real dhyan or meditation is possible only when the outgoing tendencies are controlled and the mind flows continuously as a current in the contemplation of God.

In the beginning, we may need some support like the picture of our Ishtadevatha. We have to remember in our mind this picture as we repeat the name and gradually install this picture in our heart. Then, it becomes easy to look inward and pray; we can take His form, then His attributes, and then His infinite Svaroopa or nature. Thus, progress in meditation will be made step by step. The inner shrine will be gradually revealed to us as we make progress in meditation. The seat of consciousness is the space, contentless. It is called 'Chidakasha' in the heart as compared to the 'mahakasha', external space (Mahat or vast outer space).

So long as one is notable to control his thoughts, one should not take to meditation. In early stages forbidden impure thoughts rise in the mind and overpower the aspirant leading to confusion. One should go very slowly about meditation and gain control over wandering mind. The concentrated mind, if it is not pointed, becomes a veritable demon and creates lot of trouble. Once again, it is reiterated here, that 'purity of mind and purity of heart with a disciplined austere sattvic life', are essential for a purposeful and fruitful meditation.

We have to meditate within the shrine of our heart, the 'chidakasha', or heart, or the seat of pure consciousness. If we perform Japa and dhyana, obstacles will be removed and a new spiritual consciousness awaken'. Our tendency to worry will disappear. The evil thoughts and anxiety that sicken our mind and body will be removed and holy thoughts take their place. Harmony is established. With the improvement in mental health, physical health will also improve. With the awakening of the spiritual consciousness we will discover that we are not mere physical body but the spirit, a part of the universal spirit, and the 'Ishtadevatha' is no other than the 'Paramatman', the source of supreme bliss, supreme peace, and supreme love.

Often we hear the complaint that, 'in spite of all my sincere efforts, there is no progress; nothing happens, and the like'. It should be made very clear that nothing happens in the beginning. But one should not feel disappointed. The path to spiritual progress is very slow and difficult.

There shall be the effect of meditation if one does his meditation or japa with devotion, sincerely. First the physical health will improve and the mental peace prevails. In the early stages of meditation it is like waging a war with the mind. The restless mind has to be brought under control. Any attempt to resist thoughts is of no use. Thoughts should be allowed to come and go on their own; simply watch the thoughts. That will do.

Unless we meditate, we cannot control the mind and unless we control mind, it is difficult to meditate. So, we must start meditation with firm determination and should not leave it even for a day. It is enough if we meditate for 15 minutes every day in the beginning. At best, one should meditate for 2 hours in the morning and 2 hours in the evening, in a selected secluded place without any disturbance. But, it must be remembered that we should not grumble about the environment and complain about it. We should accept whatever comes our way. That is the 'law of least effort'. One should not exert too much and strain the brain in early stages. One has to go slowly and then gradually intensify the effort. Once it becomes a regular habit, it becomes easy to sit for long hours in meditation. Happiness and a feeling of freshness are the results of deep meditation.

Meditation is not easy to those who indulge in worldly affairs too much. Too much of anything is bad- whether eating, sleeping, talking, indulgence in sex, or pursuit of sensual happiness. In *Bhagavad Gita*, Sri Krishna says, *"Yoga destroys sorrow for a man who is regulated in his food, recreation, work, sleep and wakefulness"*. [*Bhagavad Gita* VI, 17]. There should be a golden mean; '*this far and no further*'. One should create hunger for God; meditate on Him, Ishtadevatha'. One can visualize his God with perseverance and patience. There is nothing superior to the happiness one derives from 'God-visualisation' through meditation with a pure heart, pure mind, and pure body. Purity is the mainstay of spirituality. ***One should always be pure in thoughts (mind), words (vaacha) and deeds (Kaya) and perform his action in total submission to the Lord. Then only, the effect of mantra, japa and meditation will yield good results.***

Slightest ego will spoil the whole effort. Vedas and Upanishads make it clear that one should build-up his 'ego' only to be offered at the Lotus Feet of the Lord. One must work hard to earn material wealth, earn name and fame. With all humility, he should spend his wealth to the welfare of the other less fortunate. Otherwise, what can you offer Him? Love and sacrifice are the hallmarks of a spiritual aspirant. This will bring enormous peace and happiness.

The Tantra

Srimad Bhagavata states that the 'Tantra' are scriptures by means of which knowledge is spread in order to save humanity from ignorance. [Bhagavatam XI. xix. 32-45]. These are better known as Agamas, or revelations in conformity with the revelations of the Vedas.

The origin of the Tantra is traced to Maheswara as revealed to his consort Parvati, or Shakti. It has come to be known as the 'Shakti' cult since the Tantra came to us through the Divine Mother, 'Shakti Maa'. There are, however, Vishnu Tantra where the chosen deity is Vishnu and Shiva Tantra called Shaiva Agamas where the deity chosen is Shiva, in addition to the Shakti Tantra or Shakta Agamas. The Vaishnava Agamas are also known as '*Pancharatras*'. But, the Shakta group is very powerful and popular and the Shakta Agama has attained the status of a 'cult' in many parts of Eastern India and extreme southern parts of India.

The *'Tantra'* are practices, or Sadhana, the philosophy of which is derived from the Upanishads. Here, the individual soul is identified with *Shiva –Shakti*, the Universal self. This is the creative power, also called 'Maya' derived from Shakti, the Goddess 'Maa', or 'Maata' or 'Durga' or 'Kaali Maata'. It is her divine play when she herself assumes the role of Mind and matter and it is all an illusion possessing in itself no absolute reality. Indeed, it is Shree Ramanuja who identified this illusory power with the transformation of Brahman. It is in effect, rather, the body of God. Any discerning person or jnyaani will not make any distinction between this 'Shakti', or Goddess Maa, and the Brahman, the Absolute. The power of the Absolute is the Shakti and the Purusha behind it is Shiva. Or Brahman. Shiva is the static or the potential, transcendental plane; it is the Absolute Existence-Knowledge-Bliss, (Sachit anand). In the immanent or the active plane, the play of the Shakti is evident in the objective dualistic world. 'One is the Fire and the other is its burning power', as Shree Ramakrishna would put it: “Brahman is the Absolute state without the activities of creation, protection and dissolution and a person meditating on Brahman will attain that Absolute state.” On the other hand, a person meditating on the creative power of Shakti Maa will attain all the powers of creation. The difference lies in the Absolute and the Creative, the essence both are one and the same- i.e., the Shiva-Shakti Brahman. The Goddess Maa is both the container and the contained and holds the seed of creation as desire.

There are the Saadhus called 'Aghoris' who are totally devoted to this Shakti cult and they practise very difficult spiritual exercises. These powerful exercises give them enormous power and strength. Interestingly, very few of the Aghoris have learnt the techniques or tantra of converting energy into matter and matter in to energy; they also transform matter like sand and pebbles into sugar, almond (badam) and the like. They can easily convert inorganic matter into organic matter and vice versa. These Aghoris live in West Bengal. Some others using the Tantra or Shakti tantra live in Malabar coast of Kerala. However powerful, effective, or useful, these tantra are always dangerous and, invariably do much harm to both the tantrics and their followers. The Tantra are derived from Atharva Veda and there are hardly a few real Tantrics in the world.

Goddess Uma is the source of all Knowledge and offers 'jnyaan' and liberation to whomsoever she is pleased with. The *Kenaupanishad* has the story where, "Hyamavati Uma brought the proud and arrogant gods to their senses and offered them supreme Knowledge." Rk Veda praises the Divine Mother. *"I remain always the all-intelligent primal energy, as well as the one intelligent being, perfect and untouched by my magic creation". [Rk Veda* X.125.3-7]

According to Tantra philosophy, the Infinite knowledge, power, and bliss are latent in every person. Only by sadhana, attainment of this supreme knowledge is possible. The ' Truth' is vsible in one's own soul. There are four types of sadhana according to Tantra philosophy. The first one is 'Brahma-sadbhaava. It is meditating on the inner self of one's self, feeling the Brahman as the resident of the heart-space 'Goodhaakesha'. The second is constant chanting of the name of a chosen deity within one's own heart. The third is japa. It is repetition of the 'mantra' and prayer. The last one is the worship of a symbol or image of God. It is only in an advanced stage of Consciousness or spiritual awareness that it is possible to take to meditation on the inner self, the Atman or the Brahman. In the initial stages, it is necessary to hold on to some image or a picture, or a design and graph called the "Yantra". The Yantras are specially prepared using the bijamantra, the colour and magic number suitable for the person as per his zodiacal positions of stars at the time of birth. There are the "Shree Chakra", the "Sudarshan Chakra" etc.

The Shakta Tantra has the Kaali Maa, or the Divine Mother as the Deity. It is the supreme power of creation as well as destruction and absorbs everything, or dissolves the universe into her self. It is often experienced as terror, death, and destruction, the obverse of bliss, life and creation. All spiritual aspirants look to Divine Mother as the source of liberation. These spiritual aspirants take to Kundalini Yoga to achieve their goal and finally experience the supreme Bliss. Mystic powers are gained in the course of these spiritual sadhana and these are not to be used for personal gains if one wants to advance in the main spiritual goal of attaining "Self Realisation". Mystic powers gained in Shakta Tantra may be more harmful than blissful, if used for personal gains.

However, there is a great danger in misinterpreting these Vedic formulae and already some unscrupulous persons have misused it. The perverted use of these techniques has come to be known as 'vamamaachaara' and is despised by the spiritual leaders. They take to women and wine, and worship Kaali at the dead of night on New Moon nights and indulge in orgies as tantric sex. These are occult practices that have no sanction in the Upanishads and the Upanishadic doctrines forbid indulegence in sex for they uphold continence. It is only with absolute shoucha and purity of mind and body that one can attain spiritual goal. However, it is important to note here that, the power gained in this sort of occult practices are very powerful, but harmful in the long-run. One should avoid it at any cost. It is very effective when one thiks ill of others. This will only boomerang and bring immense misery to those who take to occult practices in the hope of harming others. Atharvaveda has wide ranging formulae of mantra and tantra to get whatever one wishes in the materialistic or spiritual world.

As already stated, the *Atharva Veda* is believed to be the Veda dictated by Brahma to his eldest son and pupil, Atharvan. Thus, Veda is 'One' only and it is '*Atharvaveda*'; the other three, i.e., Rk, Saman and the Yajus are its divisions based on mantra yantra and Tantra. *Atharvaveda* is said to be the essence of the other three Vedas and the Atharva mantra are called 'Sidhdha Mantra'. *One who performs Japa with Atharva mantra with shrudhdha and bhakti gets all desires fulfilled. [Kamalaalaya Khanda, Skanda Puarana].*

"Yasthathraatharvanaan japedchadhadhasamanvitaa; Tejaam arthodhbhavam kruthsnamphalam praapnothi sadhruvam."

The Mantra of'Atharva Veda' are very potent and mystic; and, sparingly used by yogins for the welfare of society. There are many result-oriented mantra like Shanti and Mahashanti mantra with details of methods of performance (vidhi-vidhana) of Shanti extolling the respective deities, like the Raja Karma, etc. from which abundant riches are obtained. Only those well- versed in Atharva Veda are permitted to perform Homa, Havana, etc in Kings' Court. Pourohitya in Rajabhisheka is described in Atharva Veda [*Vishnu Purana*].

The *Atharva Veda* has several mantra for specific purposes such as ward of death, jala gandaantha, ward of burglary and theft, to find the lost things, prevent diseases and cure diseases, cure body pains and ailments, remove toxic materials and extract poison from infected parts, getting relief from 'black magic', for achieving desired ambitions, getting married, getting children (Shruti of Prajapathi Mantra), money, education, jobs or position, power, fame and other earthly possessions and 'purushaarthas'. There are Shanti such as 'Mahendri', 'Kubera', 'Achintya' Vyashnavi, Roudri with Vaasthu (for wealth), Varuna (those facing jalagandanth), Yamya (for those fearing loss of life), Varuni, Aparajitha (to obtain success), Gandharva, Kumari Maha Shanti (to overcome diseases of children), Abhaya, Vaasthu samskara Mahashanti (to obtain wealth), and many other Shanti and Maha Shanti Mantra in Atharva Veda. It is specifically mentionfed that 'pumasarana and other Karmas are to be performed in homes only on the Full Moon Day (Pournima), and / or New Moon Days (Amavasya) and other auspices days. Performing 'Black Magic' is also given prominence in Kaushika Sutra.

Normally, diseases are caused due to two reasons. One reason is due to food that is contaminated and poisonous. The second reason is traced to past karma or sins. The latter can be cured by means of Atharva Veda through Homa. *Kaushiki Sutra* 4.8 has a mantra:

"Oushadhi vanaspathinaam anukthaanyaprathii. Bheshajyaanam O holidaghbhih I Thathaa sano muchchthvaram haraa."

This is a Papanivaraka mantra (Formula for eradicating sin) that is used as medicine through the Homa Karma. This mantra is also useful in begetting children and saving children that have little or short span of life. There are certain instructions regarding the methods of performing the Homa Karma and the food to be taken after the Homa Karma.

In *Nakshatra Kalpa Sutra*, the poojas and Homas starting from Kriththika (Star) is advocated and the Mahasmruti is performed. Vyashradeva Shanti is performed for the departed souls. Mahashanti is performed for purposes of getting over fear of agni and getting all the desires fulfilled. By performing *Bhargavi Mahashanti* all the fear and diseases caused by stars, planets and satellites or upagrahas are warded off. *Kubera Mahashanti* is performed to obtain wealth and prevent loss of money. *Achintya Mahashanti* is performed to get education, wealth and good health. *Vyashnavi shanti* is performed to get food.

In *Angirasa Kalpa*, the method of performing Homa for prevention of 'Black Magic", is explained with all the details of types of firewood, ghee, etc. that are to be used.

In Shanti Kalpa, *Vinayaka Homa* is explained. The Atharvan Mantra are Sarva siddha mantra and can be used for various purposes. The very first mantra of the Atharva Veda, Shomakeeya Shakha, "*Ye thrishaptham*.......", is the first Anuvaka that finds place in all the actions relating to acquisition of intelligence or production or increase of budhdhi shakti. According to Kaushik this can be done in Hastha Homa. There are three types of Hastha Homa viz Darvi Homa, Hastha Homa and Purna Homa [*Kaushika Sutra* 14-3; 7-8]. These manthras should be recited with great care.

Some of the present-day mystics have abused these powers for self-aggrandizement despite severe warnings not to use these for personal gains. The ultimate goal of all these Vedas is to reveal the 'Grandiose Plan' of the Lord in creating this universe and Man. In a way, it speaks volumes and volumes of the evolutionary history of the universe.

The 'Mantra' that sums up these basic concepts is:

" Om, Mahat Pradhaana Purusha Kaalaroopine
Sat chit ananda svaroopaaya namo Naaraayane namah, Om."

Mauna (Silence), Its Significance

"Mauna (Silence) is the Brahman, the source of all that we see, hear and know. It is the cause of all causes and everything is borne out of Silence. In Silence one can see the 'Sat' (Truth), experince the 'Chit' (Knowledge), and enjoy 'Anand' (the supreme Bliss). Silence is 'Satchidaanand', the Brahman.

Sound is heard only in silence and sound is a disturbance. The Buddha would not answer any questions and would simply ask the questioner to sit near him for two or three years in silence till it was total. And then ask any question. Those who dared to do so found that when total silence engulfed them, all the questions they had vanished too. Verily, ultimate reality is beyond words. Silence is Bliss. Silence is Existence. **"Silence is Brhm". The Yogins who have attained to 'Brhm' become totally silent! They are called the 'Muni'.**

The significance of 'mauna' is that words have their origin in the mind and the mind has no relationship with the unknown. Hence what all mind thinks is only repetition of the memory. It cannot think of the unknown. It stands-still in the wake of anything that is wonderful, magnificent, magnanimous, huge, astounding, and 'Mahat'. Only Silence is aware of all great things. *Kathoupanishad* puts it thus: *'The Ultimate Reality cannot be known through speech or through eyes. Who but the one who says 'It Is', can know it? And that 'It Is', cannot be known by logic or words; it can only be known through silence. The silence does not reside in the mind, that is ever shifting process, but it resides in the heart. Discussion involves using words and these words collide with the mind or head and rebound to the seeker or the questioner".*

Words can perform only one function; they can make the seeker

aware of the need to be silent or wordless. After the dawn of this awareness, the words are useless as far as the seeker is concerned. As silence lies beyond the parameters in which words and sound operate, the latter cannot express that which is known in silence. For words and sound can only describe the known. The ultimate reality is unknowable to words and sounds. One should practice vow of silence ('mouna vrat') atleast one day in a month, and, gradually make it once in a week. This will keep the mind cool and steady. This is the method of cleansing the mind. Chanting the Lord's name within the heart is very effecticve in cleanisng the mind and heart. Purity of mind and heart is very important.

Buddha never wrote anything and his preachings are also few and of limited use of words. He always advocated silence. His sessions always started with silence and ended in silence. Silence with him conveyed more than what the words would. In fact, later Buddhist monks also practiced the same technique. Buddha's silence speaks volumes and volumes of 'nirvana'. There is enormous strength in silence.

Transcendental Meditation (TM)

This is a very simple but very effective method of controlling the mind. Maha Rishi Mahesh Yogi developed this technique based on the Vedic Science of Consciousness during the later part of the last Century and, this technique caught the whole world like wild fire. In Maha Rishi's own words, "Transcendental Meditation [TM] is a simple, natural programme for the mind; a spontaneous, effortless march of the mind unfolds its potential for unlimited awareness, transcendental awareness, Unity Consciousness- a lively field of all potential, where every possibility is naturally available to the conscious mind. The conscious mind becomes aware of its own un-bounded dignity, its unbounded essence, and its infinite potential. Transcendental Meditation provides a way for the conscious mind to fathom the whole range of its existence- active and silent, point and infinity. It is not a philosophy or a religion; it is an experience, a mental technique one practices everyday for fifteen or twenty minutes".

In Maha Rishis's own words, ***"the technique of Transcendental Meditation, when practiced regularly, tends to produce normalization in all areas of life. It reduces stress, improves health, enriches mental functioning, enhances personal relationships, and increases job productivity and gives job satisfaction; besides, it is extremely simple for everyone to practice. It is well known that creative intelligence is the cause of this universe and the manifestation of this intelligence is the physical and psychological features of everyday world. Transcendental Meditation approaches directly this creative intelligence aspect of creation rather than the creatures, the manifestation of intelligence. It induces the much-needed harmony and well being at the very basic level of existence. Hence, it deals with the humans rather than their problems; hence, it is very wholesome, covering all the three aspects- psychological, intellectual, and the spiritual. Thus, it is very effective in harnessing the full potential of the divine gift of human life.***

Transcendental Meditation [TM] directly deals with the mind only. It does not involve any additional aspects with which the mind is associated, such as breathing, yoga or physical exercises. Transcendental Meditation helps to fathom the whole range of its existence unhindered by any extraneous factors. There is no interference of any sort in this process of TM. The technique of TM ranges from active mind or the performing mind to- quiet mind or resting mind. In resting mind, there is purity and simplicity, and no other involvement. All expressions of intelligence are nourished since only the mind is involved. The mind meditates, gains Transcendental-Consciousness and brings about transformation in different fields of manifestation. All fields of life, which are the expression of intelligence, are nourished or transformed and made better through experiencing Transcendental Meditation [TM].

In Maha Rishi's own words, ***"the nature of transcendental consciousness is unity of consciousness, an encounter with the field of unified consciousness. In transcendental consciousness, the mind experiences itself; intelligence experiences itself. The mind is the observer of its own reality. In that state, the mind is transcendental consciousness. Transcendental consciousness is the self-fulfilled state of mind; it is the source of all activity, just as the surface of the quiet ocean is the source from which all waves rise. It is called the unified field of natural law, from which all the different laws of nature emerge and conduct their specific activities in the relative world".***

Through regular practice of Transcendental Meditation [TM], ***'that unbounded awareness, that pure consciousness, the field of all the laws of nature, becomes ingrained in all activities of the mind'. 'Then the mind begins to live in Unity Consciousness; it becomes a living reality'. [Maha Rishi Mahesh Yogi]***

The best thing is to take a course in Transcendental Meditation in any of the TM Schools run by the Maha Rishi Mahesh Yogi. This will help the aspirant to experience himself whatever happens; what happens is that the mind, in its active state, learns to experience its own less active states, experience its progressively minimized active states, until eventually it cognizes the transcendental state of consciousness. In order to realize what is the natural state, the aspirant has to be first liberated from unnatural programs, performances, and experiences. Most people have no experience with Transcendental Consciousness, pure consciousness, which is the nature of pure mind. They are aware of active mind, which is the waking state of consciousness. They are also aware of forgetful state of mind, the sleep state of mind. They are aware of the dream state of mind. But they are not aware of pure state or Transcendental Consciousness. This is taught in Transcendental Meditation courses; it is a course in natural state of mind, rather, a nature of mind.

Transcendental Meditation [TM] does not involve intellect. It is an experience of the mind from the active levels to the unified level. It is just an innocent experience of active mind and an innocent experience of settled mind, silent mind. Try it under some trained persons and experience it. There is nothing superior to Transcendental Meditation.

Neuro-Linguistic Programming (NLP)

Neuro-Linguistic Programming (NLP) is a technique of 'Mind Management'. It is an age-old practice among the Hindus to gather in small groups on auspicious days like Saturday and Thursday at regular intervals and sing and clap (bhajan) for an hour with total devotion. The modern terms 'Neuro' stands for nerves (that represents behaviour), 'linguistic' is for language that means structure; and, 'Programming', used in computer science language stands for creating 'change'. Thus, NLP creates 'structural behavioural changes' in our attitudes using techniques like Meditation, creative Visualisation, and 'auto-suggestion' depending on the person's mental map. Here, the five senses can be controlled by the technique of Neuro-Linguistic Programming (NLP) according to Dr. Bandier and Dr. Grinder. All the successful persons use certain common traits with the help of the five senses. These traits can be studied, decoded and programmed to produce success.

According to Neuro-Linguistic Programming (NLP), if you have a negative memory you have to programme it out of your system. This can be done by sitting in a comfortable position, closing the eyes and listening to special mind power music and visualizing the event that the person wants to forget, like watching a movie. This helps one to forget all unwanted memories or sad events. Like re-winding a film, by this revisualization process, the negative energy associated with a particular memory goes into trash. This technique is very helpful in eliminating fear, emerging out of trauma, sad events, or tragic events like accidents and death.

The visual, the auditory, and the kinesthetic are involved in the Neuro-linguistic Programming (NLP). A simple bhajan or a 'sastang namaskar' (prostrating, all parts of the body touching the ground) is the simplest method of NLP. If the whole family does this regularly it would give wonderful results. Meditation for a few minutes chanting "Om" and singing together clapping hands for a few minutes everyday is fine. It brings cohesion, understanding, mutual respect and affection, and will greatly promote peace and happiness in the family. Spirituality rules and spirituality binds the family.

Neuro-linguistic Programming (NLP) helps to keep the mind cool and fresh. It helps concentration and increases efficiency in all daily activities. In fact, this is a regular practice in any Hindu family.

The origin of the Neuro-linguistic Programming is found in Rik Veda. Meditation and exercise, that is regularly practiced, enables one to vibrate with the energy of the universe. Diet is a very important factor in NLP. It has been observed that a certain kind of food interferes with the brain's function and hence avoided. Extreme Rajasic and Tamasic foods, i.e., too hot or too cold a food are avoided; Sattvic food creates ideal conditions for noble thoughts and noble deeds.

Need For Spiritual Life

Where is the need for spiritual life if one is happy and contented? Yes, this is the most perplexing question. Most of the mortals are happy and contented; even if they are not happy, they are resigned to fate and live as their fate decides. Even in day-to-day struggle, it never occurs to them that there is a simple and beautiful way to get out of all this rut. It is sheer ignorance that they enjoy, for '*ignorance is bliss*' to these persons. Some spiritual leaders like Sri Madhwacharya and Sri Shankara are of the opinion that, 'Divine Grace' is required to turn to Him. Without His grace, nothing can move. May be it is true that is the way many people think!

In *Vivekachudamani*, Shri Shankara says, "*a human birth, desire for emancipation, and contact with holy men- these three are very rare and are attained only through the Grace of the Lord*".

'Divine Grace' is something very powerful that steers your life out of all pitfalls and gives you 'awareness'. Hence, it is not something that comes from outside but that is already within you. It is the light that shines when your spark kindles it. It is the result of a pure mind and a pure heart (anthahkarana) that comes with love and sacrifice. It is self-luminous; it is always present behind Self-reliance and Self-surrender; it comes in the form of divine pulsations from within and only a strong mind can receive it. It can be felt only in the absence of ego. This requires total surrender to Him.

Sri Krishna says in *Bhagavad Gita*, "abandoning all dharma, take refuge in 'Me' alone; I will liberate you from all sins; grieve not". 'Not even a blade of grass waves without my will' ['*Trinamapi na chalati* ....']. Lord's Grace is also not that easy to get. It is like the saying, 'only the crying child gets the milk'. Only those who cry for Him will get His grace. Sant Tukaram did it; Gouranga or Chaitanya Maha Prabhu did it. Tears should flow down in utter submission and total desperation; only then will He turn towards you. Where is the need for all these? One may ask. Those who do not believe in God and those who think they are already happy and successful by their poorva punya and the Lord's Grace think there is no need for crying. But Narada Bhakti Sutra clearly states that, 'happiness and peace of mind are not sufficient; one should constantly think of the Lord both in happiness and distress. It is the ultimate goal of every human being. It is easy to live happily like any other animal; but if one has to cross the ocean of sansar one has to look to Him. Gita Govinda says:

"Punarapi jananam, punarapi maranam
Punrapi janani jatare shayanam...
....
Iha Samsaare bahu dustaare,
Kripaya saare, Pahi Muraare,
Bhaja Govindam, Bhaja Govindam,
Govindam Bhaja, Mudha mate ".

There are situations when your ego stands in your way to see the Lord. You desperately need Him; but your ego will not allow you to think of Him. It is here we all come to what is called 'living on the periphery'. There is no sense of purpose of life. There is no set goal. There is absolute complacency and a false sense of satisfaction. There is no internal urge to develop spiritual life since the mundane world has a firm grip and moha does not allow to get rid of it. That is the beauty of the 'Mother Earth'!

Mother earth is the Goddess Shri Lakshmi, the bestower of everything in this sensate world. She is beautiful and bountiful. She is the supporter, the inspiration to Shriman Narayana. She is the eternal source of wealth; and, any one who prays her, praises her, will get whatever one wants. The hold of the mother over the child is astounding! Once born on this earth, even to think of the other world is very difficult. The earth is gross and finite. It is this finite world that dictates all life and activities. But no one will believe that this world is unreal!

This world is bound by space and time. Anything bound by space and time is finite and limited, a 'make-believe' world. Even the solid surface features of the earth that appear firm are not stable and give way with the earthquakes. Lofty features such as the mountains, plateaus and plains have changed over the geological time of thousands and thousands of Millenia.The Rivers have changed their course and many a lakes have dried up. There have been major convulsions and revolutions in the earth's cycle and the finest example is that of the Himalaya Mountains. These lofty mountains stand where once the Sea of Tethys stood. May be, one day our Great Ganga Plains will be raised up to lofty mountains and the Himalayas are eroded and denuded and reduced to an erosional plateau. When the lofty mountains are reduced by denudation what about the fragile life of the humans on this earth?

The tragedy of human life is that man believes that everything is eternal and permanent. For even a second, man cannot believe that he is mortal and would die anytime, any day. This idea of permanency of status is derived from the same divine source, the eternal 'Atman' who dwells in him. This taste of 'Infinite' nature is the taste that lingers in man and, it is for this infinite status his subconscious lingers on. But to fathom it out is very difficult under the earthly conditions. Swamy Vivekananda used to repeat, *'each soul is potentially divine, and the goal is to manifest the divinity within'*.

Both the body and mind are subject to constant change and cannot reach a state beyond change. But beyond the momentary sheath of gross matter, beyond the finer covering of the mind-lies the 'Atman', the true Self of man, permanent and ever free. It is His freedom that is percolating through layers of thought and Matter; and in spite of this, the colourings of name and form is ever asserting its unshackled existence. This Atman is to be realised through faith, devotion and meditation. There is no doubt, it is the same 'Atman' that shines in our souls and also shines in all souls. We all reflect the same Light. It is the one 'Infinite' spirit that manifests itself through all individual souls. Self-knowledge is the realisation that the individual self is part of the all- pervading spirit Sri Hari Narayana. Attaining it, all desires, even in the subtlest form, disappear. Once successful in this attempt, having attained this with the help of the enlightened ones, it is the duty to return to world to spread this divine knowledge, realization of God in man. It is this realization of the divinity that manifests in man is what is called true 'Religion'.

Ashtavakra Samhita is a very beautiful treatise on philosophy of life. Having born one has to simply live; Living is an ordained duty or obligation to God, the Creator. There is nothing that one can do on the face of 'prarabhdha karma' and forces of 'samskara'. But this does not mean total abandonment of one's duty. One should live a contented life (nirlipta jeevana) of minimum needs. Remember, all knowledge leads to this!

This is the '*Keep Quiet Rule*' of Mind Management Technique (MMT). Keep quiet, or talk less if there is need to talk. Silence speaks much better than sound. There is a very interesting account of a rich and powerful person. He was going in the vicinity of an ashram and felt like meeting the saint. He went to him and asked him to tell him some secret mantra. The saint looked at him and smiled. Again this gentleman asked him to tell him quickly for he had no time to spare. Again, he smiled at him. When he persisted further, the saint said only one word 'Om' ("meditate"). The saint said, even uttering one word is half-truth and you have made me utter it. The more words you use, the more untruth will fall out. A meaningful glance or an all-knowing smile is enough. Never enter into discussion or argument. Take to meditation at the earliest opportunity and contemplate on Him. A wise man will never indulge in worldy affairs for he knows the futility of it all.

We all know that Man is a human being; but, in reality, as men, neither we are 'Human' nor we know how to be a 'Being'. Too much of ego, too much of senseless talks, arguments, take away our energy. These have no place in this philosophy of Self Realisation. We are always restless. We keep on dabbling in things consciously or without it. Keeping a calm and cool disposition with total awareness is the Mind Management Technique. Here, it is reiterated that 'happiness is not rejoicing and unhappiness is being dull and morose. It is a state unperturbed by happenings- success or failure.

Equanimity is equipoise as it is said in Gita- *'Sukha dukhe samekrutva, laabhaalaabhau jayaajayau'* [*Bhagavad-Gita* II.38]. It is maintaining equanimity under all circumstances. It is treating happiness and sorrow, gain and loss, and conquest and defeat with equanimity; One has to engage in battle (of life), thus he will not incur sin (sorrow). This is the way to be happy and successful. Happiness is normally believed to be a state of joyfulness with elated ego; extroverts expressing it in jumping, singing and dancing and introverts enjoying it within unmindful of the goings on in the outside world. Both the expressions are not happiness. *Happiness is a cool and contemplated, meditative mind, an undisturbed state of mind, a state of equilibrium. Neither jumping with joy, nor being morose and dull with sadness are stated to be real 'happiness'. It may be called a 'nirliptata', happy and contented state of mind.*

There are two types of '*nirliptata*' or '*simply being*'; one, just like a fool who keeps quite for he knows not what to do, and the other, a Jnyani who knows the reality as also, that he is at the mercy of the Lord. A jnyani will neither brood about the past nor get anxious about the future. He just lives–now and here, at the present. Past is dead and future is unborn to a jnyaani. Arjuna was advised even to forget the episode of 'Visvaroopa Darshan' and get down to the practical duty. To dwell on the memory of the vision of God is to prevent the experience of the present. Even the 'vision' of the God will not bring one's duty to an end, and one has to constantly remember Him and do his duty. Here, there is no choice; there is no role to the play of the quixotic and fickle mind. There is absolute resolute mind, concentrating on the ordained duty. This is the sure way of achieving success and happiness in life. 'Duty first' is the Rule of Mind Management Technique (MMT). One cannot abandon one's duty under any circumstance.

Peace and Happiness

Peace is the state of a tranquil mind. A person's Mind is at rest while he is enjoying peace. Peace is an undisturbed state of mind. Ordinarily, the mind is always agitated and there will be no peace. Peace or 'Shanti' comes with enlightenment. Peace is a calm state of Mind that comes with Jnyan, Knowledge. It can be achieved by ethical principles, Sama and Dama. It is an experience that comes with Self-Realisation. Such a' peace' of mind cannot be disturbed by any worldly disturbances caused by desire, or the enemies within, the'Ari-shadvargas'.

Ashtavakra Samhita [XI. 2] says,

"He who has known for certain that 'Ishvara is the Creator of all and that there is none else' becomes peaceful with all his inner desires set at rest, and is not attached to anything whatsoever".

Desires arise from thinking that there are desirable things and attractive existences outside of one self. Mind rests on them (objects) and feels restless untill it covets them and enjoys them. But, when one knows that the universe is pervaded by the Self- that there is only 'the Self' and nothing else- the feeling of 'otherness' goes and there is no desire, and hence there is peace. A person who is perfectly happy with him self contented, and calm and peaceful even under dire provocations, is not at all perturbed even when ridiculed and despised by his servants, sons, wife, daughters and their children and other relations. He is a Yogi, a man of knowledge.

Although outwardly appearing to feel pleasure and pain, a yogi is not at all affected by anything. It is only a person of dull intellect, even without doing anything, is ever agitated by distraction; but, the knowledgeable one, even doing his duties, is verily unperturbed, peaceful. His Mind is always calm and peaceful. The pure one knows for cetain that this universe is the product of illusion and that nothing exists. Self is revealed to him, and he naturally enjoys peace. Bliss and peace are the very essence of the Self, the 'Atman'. Hence, one has to realize that peace is already there within oneself. Self-knowledge is not a thing to be obtained by practice of control. The wise one neither longs for gain nor grieves at non-attainment. His cool mind is verily filled with nectar. [*Ashtavakra Samhita* XVIII 75, 82].

One has to realize the totality of existence. The unity of existence is the key to a happy and successful life on this planet. Those who do not realize this will have repeated births and deaths; no doubt they will have some glimpse of happiness and success here and there; but the higher they go deeper they fall. Every feeling of happiness is followed by misery, unhappiness. The Buddha is an example; he says that he has taken atleast a- 500 rebirths as narrated in the jataka stories. Gautama was distressed at the sight of human sufferings, old age and death and wanted to get himself redeemed from it and help others to get what he called 'nirvana' (liberation). He did not aspire for wealth, power or fame for he was a prince by birth. He was not aspiring for any worldly happiness for he had everything! Although this world offers everything to everybody, the unhappiness and misery is sure to haunt some time or the other and we have to find a permanent solution to the problems of life. One must realize the Reality of life and find fullness in oneself.

Contemplate on this mantra from Ishavaasya Upanishad:

"Om! Poornamadah Poornamidham Poornaath
Poornamudhachyate
Poornasya Poornamadhaaya Poornamevaavashishyate".
Om! Shantih, Shantih, Shantih!

"Om! That is the complete; this too is complete. From the complete has come out the complete. The complete remains complete even though the complete has come out of the complete. It may be surprising that, some times, what we think as the part of the complete is more than the complete. This is the greatest mystery of this Universe! Everything we perceive is the complete in it self, may it be a unicellular amoeba or the Man". We have to realize this completeness, of this great opportunity of being born in human life form, and should strive for attainment of Supreme Bliss.

"Engrossment with the many without knowing the One behind it is the bane of ignorant life. The secret of the many (avidya) is that the One (vidya) can appear to be many without losing its unity" [*Isavasya Upanisad* 10]. One who understands this attains the spiritual felicity of transcendence by absorption in the One (avidya), having overcome the weakness and delusions of mortal life by knowing how 'the many are the becomings of the One'. [*Isavasya Upanisad* 11]. This sense of oneness, unity, homogeneity, all-comprehensiveness, totality, fullness, completeness, should be realized.

Select a serene, secluded place and contemplate on this idea with bhaavartha in order to get an inner vision of the Self. Meditation should be practiced regularly in a selected serene place and at regular times. One should meditate four times a day- in the early morning around 5 a.m., around 12 in the noon, around 6 in the evening, and 10 p.m. or before going to bed. Each meditation should last for about 45 minutes at a stretch. There should be complete concentration on the Lord and nothing should disturb the mind. No effort shall be made to ward off the unwanted thoughts that occur in the mind spontaneously; just watching them is sufficient to drive them off. Mind shall be calm and serene in a few days after regular practice. It will give supreme strength and self-confidence in all other activities. It will increase efficiency and creative intelligence will take over inertia and indolence. It will give a new turn to life. It gives new energy and makes life more enjoyable.

10
Goal of Life

"Know *thy*self"
"The *Self indeed serves as his Light"*
[*Brihadaranyaka Upanishad*, 4.3. 2-6]

Whether it is Science, or Religion and Philosophy, the goal is the same. It is the search for "Truth". It is the main objective of every sensible inquisitive mind to know the "Truth", the truth or reality of our existence. It is common experience that we repeatedly touch and try to feel the existence of things for we are not sure of its existence in our deeper consciousness. Whenever we see a table or a chair, we first feel its existence and then try to know its quality. This is a deep-seated inner urge 'to know'. Are we sure of our existence? Definitely not; otherwise, there would have been no effort 'to know', 'to undertsand', or to realize the "Reality". Man is the only thinking animal gifted with the rare ability to think, contemplate, and visualize the divinity within.

"All this world, deluded as it is by things made of the 'gunas' (qualities), does not know 'Me' (the Lord) who is transcendental to these and undecaying." [*Bhagavad Gita*]

The Veda declare that, '*whatever that is transcient, not permanent, not 'Sat' is not the 'Truth'. "Truth only exists*" and nothing else really exist. This is the reason why we try to confirm the existence of an object by repeartedly touching it, feeling it and confirming its existence. Despite our repeated exercise we fail to perceive the real objects! We do not see the objects if something intervenes between our sight and the object; so also, we do not see the objects if we close our eyes. In fact, we do not know whether the objects really exist and do not see them due to many reasons. The objects cease to exist even when we are seeing them and many times we see objects of our own imagination! There is 'virtual reality', hallucination, and 'day dreams' and ' make-believe' things that we believe as real. This makes the whole universe complex and complicated and we are perplexed. This is called, '*Maaya*' in Bhagavad Gita, or 'illusion ' in Budhdhism. The letter '*Maa*' means 'not' and '*ya*' means 'that'; it (the world) is 'not that' what we see. For instance, the 'one' single unicellular amoeba has multiplied itself to form the 'many'; and, it is also true that the 'first ever-formed amoeba' still exists in different forms and continues to proliferate! Another important thing is that the Universal Soul is one and it takes numerous forms and names and do different functions giving us the illusion of the multifarious objective world. This is the 'Truth", the Veda proclaim. That which is unmanifest ('avyakta') is the 'Sat'. In the light of this Vedic dictum, it is made clear that "Nothing that is 'sat' is ever born, die, or decay". Similarly, nothing that is 'sat' can be ever created or invented; it can only be discovered since everything exists in the universe as an illusion or Maya; and, it is all a 'myth' not the 'Truth'! 'Know' this truth, the Sages implore! What is the philosophical import of these implorations? Human sanity, avoiding rash and negligent actions, sensitivity to preserve and protect lives of fellow living beings, banishing thoughts of violence, strife and war, rather, knowing our limitations, and a sensible living at that!

According to Vedanta, the goal of human life is "Self Realisation". It is called Moksha, one of the four purusharthas; it is also known as 'mukti' or release from bondage, or simply, 'liberation'. It is very difficult to understand why we should seek liberation unless we feel the 'bondage' of our existence. There are a number of theories such as the 'social contract theory' put forth by Hobbes, Locke, and Roussou. Of these, the most famous one is by Hobbes, who says, "man is born free, but everywhere he is in chains". Unless one feels the bondage, the slavery, the helplessness, there is no question of 'liberation'. The famous Raikva, the cartman, also holds the same view. There is no question of 'liberation', or release from 'bondage' for one who is already free. It is only a play of our mind! If the mind feels that there is bondage, there is bondage and the struggle starts for release from this imaginary bondage! The Upanishads also stress this aspect of 'play of mind' and implores us to realize our Self or the 'Atman'. Ultimately, it is the realisation of the "Truth" that releases from bondage, if at all we feel we are in bondage.

There is another interesting side of the same story. It is the desire that prompts us to get into this bondage. A person devoid of desire is 'free'. *Desire is the cause, the source of all our bondage*. To get rid of this bondage is to get rid of the desires that cause the bondage. The attachment (Raga, Lobha, Moha) to the mundane, the worldly objects that offer no permanent happiness is the key to bondage. One has to get released from the bonds of '*anthahkarana*', the strings of heart that bind us to this objective sensuous world in order to be completely free, to become a 'jeevan mukta'. Only one Shuka, or a Narada, or a Raikva and a Vemana are free in that sense of the term; no one else!

Freedom, or 'liberation' is the product of realisation of the Self. It is the dawn of knowledge, the 'Reality' of this objective world that brings liberation. Once this 'reality' that this is a 'make-believe' world and it is not 'Real' is realised, the 'desire' for existence itself ceases to exist! Of course, who wants a 'make-believe' world when the 'Real' world is in sight! There is the memory of the "Supreme Bliss" of a "Real' world somewhere in our subconscious mind since we have enjoyed this happiness sometime in our past life and we hanker after that! That is the fact! That happiness is estimated to be of the value of 1 to the power of 20, 1 followed by twenty zeros, and cannot be compared to anything on this earth!

The goal of life is the 'Realisation of the Atman', or the Brahman, the supreme-Consciousness. It is the ***"Supreme Bliss". or, the "Sat-chit-anand".*** This is achieved by '*jnyaan*' (Knowledge) and, Raja Yoga helps us to achieve this supreme happiness only in a state of 'nirvikalpa samadhi'. Only when one transcends all the three gunas in the state of samadhi, one can realize this real 'liberation' or release from bondage. This requires a thorough training in the art of '*manonasha*' (stilling the mind) or 'manoniyantran' (Mind Control) and many Yogis have achieved this by practice of 'Hatha Yoga'.

Remember ***"Manonasha"*** is not the destruction of the Mind. Neither it is possible, nor is it desirable to 'kill' the Mind, for Mind itself is 'existence'. The term 'nasha' is used here to denote the state of Mind that is devoid of any vibration or chitta vrittis. It is a silent Mind or a Mind that is 'stand still'. Rather, to be precise, it is raisng the Mind to the state of super-consciousness where it ceases to be matter and becomes energy. Pure Mind is pure Consciousness. Consciousness polluted with kaamana, vaasana, or desire is matter and Mind devoid of sanskaar is pure Consciousness, i.e., the Atman, or the Self.

Thus, "*Realisation of the Atman*" is the goal of life. This Atman is so subtle and as consciousness, it is identified with the Brahman, the Supreme-Consciousness. The Atman is experienced in deep contemplation only. Meditation on the Atman will help us to realise this Atman in deep samadhi. It is the energy, the "***Light within us***".

Enlightenment, the 'Light Within Us'

Enlightenment is the realisation of the Self. The Self is a very subtle force that serves as the source of light to Buddhi, the Intellect. It is this Intellect that gives the discriminatory power to man and enables him to seek the 'Truth", the Eternal Brahman. Avidya or ignorance governs the life of man till the realisation of the Self within. "The Self indeed serves as his Light" [Brihadaranyaka Upanishad, 4.3. 2-6]

All the external lights can help man only in his waking state. But, during the dream state and deep sleep, it is the Self by which man knows and enjoys himself.

There is a very interesting account in *Brihadaranyaka Upanishad* regarding the 'light within us'. Janaka, the emperor of Videha asked Yajnavalkya, the great Upanishadic Sage about the '*Light that serves man in darkness*'. Janaka, a great Jnyani, wanted this answer to enlighten the common man, the man who identifies himself with his body and mind. Yajnavalkya answered this question in a very simple way. 'It is the Sun who gives light to the world and when the Sun has set, it is the moon who reflects the sunshine and sheds the moonlight that gives light in the dark. When the moonlight is not there, it is the fire that gives the light and the heat. When the Sun, the moon and the fire are not there to give light, man uses his speech and finds his way in darkness. One can shout and make his presence known when there is no light. Likewise, man can use his ears, nose and touch to make his way in darkness. The fragrance of a flower or the smell of a plant, the touch on a wall, or the sound coming from some direction will serve as light in the absence of the sun, the moon and the fire.

The most significant answer came when the Sage said that the inner light shines spreading light on our thoughts, intuition, dreams and bright ideas. Srinivasa Ramanujam, the great mathematician found answer to most of his problems in his dreams! No external light helps a man in sleep; but it is his inner light, the Consciousness, the Self, the Atman that guides him, that enlightens him.

So far, no one has gone to the depth of the mysterious mind to unearth the precious store of wealth hidden in the layers and layers of the subconscious. Super-Consciousness will shed light on all the mysteries of man and his universe. This can be achieved by constant meditation. It is the '*choiceless awareness*', the supreme-consciousness 'an atom of which is in our Self' that shines on its own and sheds light on everything within us. It is this that keeps us alive and kicking! "***The Self indeed is the light of man***", says Yajnvalkya.

The source of all light is Brahman, the Supreme Spirit, i.e., the Pure Consciousness. Atman, the knowing self of the human being is identical with the Brahman, Pure Consciousness. It is the radiance of the Pure Consciousness which manifests all things at all times. Pure mind is anthahkarana, the inner instrument of this knowing self. It is not the source of light. There is no consciousness inherent in the mind. The mind only receives the radiance of consciousness from the knowing self whose inner instrument it is, and illuminate all things including physical light. 'Though having no light of its own the mind appears to be luminous. Though it seems to cognise, the mind is not the cognizer, but only an instrument of cognition. Shining as it does with the borrowed light of consciousness, the mind is an effective instrument of knowledge'. The Self is not illumined by anything but it illumines everything else. This light shines in the state of spiritual attainment, all by itself. It is for this illumination that the spiritual aspirants crave and adopt all sorts of spiritual exercises like dhyana, japa, tapa, vrata, meditation, and goes into the state of Samadhi. No one can stay in that state for long, and no one can leave that effort either. Hence, it is the desire of every aspirant to gain that state of supreme bliss and remain there forever.

The Cosmic Energy

'Cosmic energy' is flowing through us all. We are all instruments, more or less. But, when we consciously stop the expression of this energy through the lower centers (of consciousness) and let it find expression through the higher ones, we always feel fresh, then there is no old age for us so far as thought life is concerned. Sometimes we are not able to maintain the activity at higher centers (of Consciousness) because of our old impressions (samskaras or memories) and tendencies, and then there is a strong downward pull, a real tug-of-war that cannot be avoided if we are to grow at all. We can never stop the energy, but we can give it a higher direction, consciously, intelligently, with an effort of the will.

Conscious intelligent thinking is necessary. Conscious intelligent thinking removes the barrier, and when the obstruction is removed, more psychic energy flows in us.

The Importance of 'Being'

The '*Supreme Being*' is the Lord Himself. He is the '*Purushottama*', the *Mahapurusha.*It is also true that the species *Homosapiens* sapiens are human beings. 'Being' means '*Purusha*', a divine personality, a spiritual personality. But, it is very clear from this study that we are neither 'human' nor 'beings; we have to evolve from the animal to man, and man to human first. And, then we have to learn how to 'Be' (svastha- establish in one's Self), because we are always struggling without 'be'-ing (calm and peaceful). We are a confused lot and we do not know what we are doing and what we want. We madly run after things and get disillusioned when we do not get what we want. Unfortunately, it is also the experience of most of us that we are not happy even when we get what we want! It is all a mad mad world! We have not understood the meaning of this 'Being".

'Being' is to dwell in the present. If we look at the old people, they are always talking of their past; and, if we look at the youngsters, they are always talking of their future. Nobody is conscious of the present. It is the conscious living, being aware of oneself in the present that is very important. This *conscious awareness* is the meaning of the 'being'. Such persons are the real 'Beings'.

Unity of Being or "Samata"

'I"-ness merged in the Self is Unity ('yuj'). Sages Vashishta and Patanjali have beautifully explained the 'Unity of Being, also known as the Principle of "Samata", the Samata spirit of the Upanishads. "Kartapan" should be eradicated in order to attain the Self; kartapan is the sense of 'I am the doer'. As long as the sense of 'I am the doer' exists, there is duality- 'I' and the 'other'. As long as the other exists, there is strife, misery, and unhappiness. As soon as the other merges in the Self, the duality ceases to exist. Here the Principle is "na karta, Hari karta"- I am not the doer, Sri Hari is the doer. As long as the 'I'-ness exist, or ego exists, the 'other' exists; it is this 'I'-ness that gives rise to dualistic forms of thinking; the other is treated as an object that has to be possessed and so has to be looked upon as something inferior. So the sense of doership should go. As soon as this 'ego' (sense of 'I am the doer') is erased, the cosmic vision is opened up revealing the 'Unity of Being'. In this state of revelation, the 'other' ceases to exist and becomes a part of the Self. Such yogins who get this revelation see all others as their own self and do not see duality. This is the principle of 'Samata' or 'equanimity', unity of Being, coincidentia oppositarum.

"Om", Brahman alone is 'Being', 'niraakara', without shape and form, the One without a second, all- pervasive, blessing incarnate. To Him, the Supreme Lord, we offer our Salutations".

'Self Realisation' can be attained by smaran, dhyan and samadhi. One of the interesting results of this Meditation is the revelation, the descent of the revelation of the word. The flow of revelation would continue like the flow of water in a stream. "*When divine rapture pours out, the intellect becomes inoperative- it does not think in terms of dualities. In that state of wakefulness, no wrong word can possibly be uttered. Only he who has realized the blissful state within can know what the freedom from thinking is. When the intellect is merged into the word, right thoughts rise up spontaneously and without thought-activity, the revelatory words rush out on their own. Nothing remains concealed in that state- neither the world nor its Creator. Hidden secrets reveal themselves with absolute clarity*".

The Path of Self Realisation is very smooth to those who have realized the 'Truth'. Five cardinal principles can help in this spiritual attainment. These are: ***Sat*** (truthfulness), ***Sadgi*** (simplicity or austerity), ***seva*** (selfless service), ***Satsang*** (right association), and ***Satsmaran*** (right remembrance of God. In conclusion, with all the volumes of literature laid before us, the questions still remain: What is Self Realisation? How to attain to it? Is it ever possible for we the mortals to attain the Supreme Self? The answers are very simple and direct: May or may not!

First of all, the concept of *Self Realization* has to be clearly understood. This is a spiritual aspect that each one has to understand only by personal effort. In fact, it is a personal experience only. No amount of reading of the scriptures, guidance from the revered Guru or teachers will help in this matter. One has to develop an interest, an attitude, a feverish desire to attain it and move steadfast in that direction. It all starts with a few simple exercises: Number One: "*Keep Quiet*".

Practise to sit in a comfortable posture, in a calm and serene atmosphere, close your eyes and keep the mind calm and undisturbed or still atleast for a few minutes in the beginning. This seems to be very difficult in the beginning; gradually, with practise, it becomes easy. One has to sit atleast 45 minutes- three to four times a day. The ideal timings are: 4 a.m. to 6 a.m.; around mid-day; in the evening; and before mid-night. Gradually the duration should be increased. Sitting posture in Padmasana, preferably in front of a candlelight or Ishta Devatha is advantageous. No effort should be made to stop the thoughts passing in the mind; only, these thoughts should be observed as a 'witness'. Rest will automatically follow.

Number two: Raise the level of Consciousness. We all live and work at very low level of consciousness and this has to be raised from the navel level to heart level, then on to throat, ajnya and sirsa levels. We must try to live at a higher level of Consciousness as much as possible; remember, it is difficult unless concerted effort is made in this direction.

Number Three: One has to cultivate the moral and ethical values of life. Keep the body and mind by clean food and clean thoughts. There should be a 'choiceless awareness' of all our thoughts and actions. Mind should give place to intellect and intellect should take the guidance of the inner Spirit, Atman.

Number Four: Desire is the cause of misery. The destruction of desires is liberation, and this is considered to be the first priority in attaining liberation. Keep away from sense objects and keep your sense organs rivetted to divine and divine activity only. Be selfless in all your thoughts and actions. Entertain no desire for self-enjoyment or self-aggrandisement. "Owing to the desire to run after society, the passion for too much study of scriptures, and the desire to keep the body trim, people cannot attain to proper realisation. Until the identification with the body is completely rooted out, do away with thy superimposition with watchfulness and concentrated mind". [Viveka Chudamani].

Number Five: Always think that- " I am not the body"; "I am not the Mind"; "I am not the Prana"; "I am not the individual soul, but the Supreme Brahman";" I am the Eternal Spirit". Meditate on the Mahat Tattvas. Always chant the name of your Ishta Devatha, day-in and day-out, 24 hours of the day and 365 days of the year and see the results!

Number Six: Meditate on any of the divine thoughts. See 'Think it over' given in this book' Meditate on the pranas the self, the Atman. As the mind becomes gradually established in the Inner Self, it proportionately gives up the desires for external objects. And when all such desires have been eliminated there takes place the unobstructed realisation of the Atman. 'Merging the finite soul in the Supreme Self by means of meditation on their identity, always keep quiet'.

Do not care for the universe, which is' other' than the Self, before whose majesty it pales into insignificance."The three bodies- the gross, the subtle and the causal, are also false. This objective universe is absolutely unreal; neither is egoism a reality, for it is observed to be momentary. Therefore give up the identification with this physical body that is a lump of flesh, as well as with the ego, or the subtle body, which are both imagined by buddhi. Realising thy own self, which is Knowledge Absolute and not to be denied in the past, present or future, attain to peace". [Viveka Chudamani].

Tamas is destroyed by sattva and rajas, the rajas is destroyed by sattva, and the Sattva is destroyed by Pure Consciousness, Brahman. 'Nistraiguna bhava'. Try to transcend all the three Gunas that are the cause of desire that causes repeated births and deaths in this world. Knowing for certain that the Prarabhda karma (work) will maintain the body, remain quiet and do away with thy superimposition carefully and with patience.

Shri Shankara says, "Even after the Truth has been realized, there remains that strong, beginningless, obstinate impression that one is the agent and experiencer, which is the cause of one's transmigration. It has to be carefully removed by living in a state of constant identification with the Supreme Self. Sages call that 'Liberation' which is attenuation of sanskaras here and now." This will burn all 'Prarabhda Karmas' and kill desires that cause repeated births and deaths. A man who has no selfish desires will easily attain mukti.

There are as many ways of attaining mukti or moksha, liberation or release from bondage as many jeevas are there. So do not be perturbed. Follow any means of Self Realisation! All paths lead to salvation and much depends on the sincereity and devotion of the aspirant.

The 3 'V's of Success

There are thre 'K's that keep us in eternal darkmess. Kaama. Karma, and Krodha and there are three 'V's to overcome them. These are very important requirements for achieving success in life as also attaining spiritual knowledge are: (1) Vicharra, (2) Viveka, and (3) Vairagya, and to these may be added Sama and Dama, and Uparati. Whether one is a

Grihasta, or a sanyasi, whatever be the station of his life, Jnyana, Bhakti, and Vairagya are essential besides moral and ethical requirements such as purity of body, mind, heart and soul. Remember, it is the blemishes of the soul, due to attachment (moha), due to desires (kama) that one gets into this world of birth and death, the 'Mrutyuloka'.

Vairagya is dispassion, a sense of indifference to all objects of enjoyment. Abandonment of all desires at all times is called 'Sama'; and, restraint of the external functions sense organs is called 'Dama'. Turning away completely from all sense objects is the height of 'uparati'. As compared to Sama and Dama where effort is needed to control the mind, '*Uparati*' brings a calm and peaceful state, a state of equipoise of the mind spontaneously, effortlessly.

The choice before the householder is to live and work for materialistic prosperity as also gain spirituality, or to decide about spiritual path, 'sanyas', liberation from 'sansara', or the worldly bondage. The householders' path has been clearly laid and there is no doubt about the duties and obligations of a householder. Veda and Upanishads never teach one to abandon his duties in the pursuit of spiritual goal. But it is certainly true that it is extremely difficult, if not impossible, to pursue the spiritual goal living in the '*Grihasthashrama*' with the full responsibilities of running a family. It is also true that old age will be too late for starting a spiritual life. This is the paradox. We want spiritual progress in family life. How to attain it?

There is an eight-fold path to spiritual goal of 'liberation'. Even a householder can regularly practice these in a limited way and attain spiritual progress enjoying the family life. Sri Ramakrishna says, "Do all your duties, but keep your mind on God. Live with all- with wife and children, parents, brothers and sisters. Treat them with love and affection, but know in your heart of hearts that they do not belong to you". Love of God should be upper-most on the mind and a sense of detachment (remember, not neglect) should rule the life.

Only at later stages in life, as and when the inner urge becomes too strong, one must take to ascetic life, that too, with the permission from the family members, and, then spiritual practice can be made rigorous. But, nothing is possible without a concerted effort, disciplined rigid yogic exercises. Patanjali's eight-fold path to liberation is the path to be followed. Thus, there shall be no conflict of interest; the balancing act requires, of course, strong determination, steadfastness, purity of mind, and love of God; Divine Will and His Grace will take care of the rest. Purity of mind and heart is the basic necessity.

It is indeed very difficult to understand what exactly is this Mind and how it functions. The Mind is a biological computer and, all the inputs to mind come through the five senses. Desire and prana are inter-related. Prana depends on the desire. If there is no desire, there is no purpose or need for prana to exist. The moment all desires are fulfilled, prana ceases to function. Breathing is controlled by desire and prana is breathing fuelled by desire. And, '***Desire is Brahman***'

Desire leads to action. Repeated action becomes a habit; habit defines character and ones character decides the destiny. So, in a way, one's desire leads to his destiny. The biologically- evolved super computer called the human mind is an extraordinary storage reservoir,'*the Manas Sarovar*' of memories, experiences and crave for fulfilment of its desires through the senses; and, as such, the human mind is always in search of fulfilment of unfulfilled desires of the past births. But unfortunately, these are mere impressions and far from reality separated by time and space. Even when the desires are fulfilled the person is sure to be disappointed due to the gap in time his achievements do not match his desires.

Making a distinction between mind and the physical basis of mind, Sir Charles Sherrington says:

"Knowledge of the physical basis of mind is making great strides in these days. Knowledge of the brain is growing, and our theme is almost equivalent to the physiology of the brain. Mind, meaning by that thoughts, feelings, memories, reasoning, and so on, is difficult to bring into the class of physical things. Physiology, a natural science, tends to be silent about all outside the physical. And, so the study of the physical basis of mind suffers from falling between two stools."

Nuclear physicist Erwin Schrodinger in his book 'What is Life?' has explained that, "Consciousness is never experienced in the plural, only in the singular... Consciousness is a singular of which the plural is unknown; that there is only one thing, what seems to be a plurality is merely a series of different aspects of this one thing, produced by a deception, *the Indian Maya*".

The quantum energy field or the four-dimensional space-time, which twentieth century physics presents as beyond sensory verification, finds its counterpart in Vedanta in its 'chittaakaasha', the 'akaasha' - the 'space-time continuum'. This is what mind reveals in dreams. This is the knowledge-field, or 'consciousness field', of which all seer (drik) or subject and all objects, or the seen (drishyam) are but two poles as the observer and the observed. The subject of modern sub-atomic physics is now the position of the ancient *Samkhya Philosophy of India in its reduction of the observed into the unity of the quantum energy field, while retaining the multiplicity in the dimension of the observer.* The Samkhyas achieved the unification of all the 'not-self' in its Pradhana or Prakriti, or Nature, while retaining, however, multiplicity in the realm of the *Purusha*, the observer, the self Atman-Brahman unity or the subject.

Atman-Brahman unity is 'Sat'. This can be put as A = B. This is the unity of existence. Veda proclaim that what all that exists on this earth is Brahman. This 'unity of existence' can be experienced in transcendental meditation or 'Samadhi'. Remember what Shree Krishna says, "I am the kshetra and I am the kshetrajnya', meaning I (Brahman) am the 'field' and I am the 'knower of the field'. Modern physics has come out with a *'unified field theory' in the sagrangian superstring theory.* In physical nature, comprehending electromagnetic, nuclear, and gravitational, and other phenomena, completely and successfully is very difficult; it is difficult to solve the problem of unifying, man and nature, '*Prakriti*' and '*Purusha*', the observed and the observer. Einstein spent his last years searching for such a unified field theory. '*Chittaakaasha*', referred to as the space-time continuum, still involves duality of the subject and the object. But, the Vedantic view of Consciousness, the Infinite, Non-dual, the 'Aakaasha', or void of 'chit', or Pure Consciousness which is the same as 'Chittaakaasha' viewed non-causally overcomes the limitations of physics. By presenting this way, neither the Universe nor its matter, and separate intelligent beings, is destroyed, but is only illumined of its true nature.

Non-duality is the answer to all our problems. Non-duality is better explained in *Mandukyakarika* of Gaudapada as:

"Beyond all conceptual thinking, and beyond all causal relations, is' jnyanam', Prajnya, Pure Consciousness, which is ever non-different from the object of knowledge. Brahman, the sole object of knowledge, is unborn (beyond causality) and eternal; the non-causal (knowledge) realizes the non-causal (Brahman). All higher spiritual truth are obtained only through inner penetration and the raising of consciousness to higher and higher levels."

"All those that have been expounded earlier (about the realisation, of the Atman, of the nature of the Non-dual Pure Consciousness), or the products of dhyana, meditation, none bereft of the knowledge of the Atman, can verily enjoy the fruits of one's labour in peace and joy."

One can see this truth in the present day world where the high material prosperity through an efficient technology, alienated from higher spiritual values, has led to increasing psychic and social distortions and the people's inability to enjoy life in peace and joy, however rich and prosperous they may be.

Romain Roland says, 'the true vedantic spirit does not start out with a system of preconceived ideas. It possesses absolute liberty and unrivaled courage, among religions with regard to the facts to be observed and the diverse hypotheses it has laid down, for their coordination. Never having been hampered by a priestly class order, each man has been entirely free to search wherever he pleased for the spiritual explanation of the spectacle of the Universe'.

Lincoln Barnett has observed in his lecture on 'The Universe and Dr.Einstein' that, "in the evolution of scientific thought, one fact has become impressively clear: there is no mystery of the physical world which does not point to a mystery beyond itself. All highroads of intellect, all by ways of theory and conjecture, lead ultimately to an abyss that human ingenuity can never span". We are both spectators and actors in the great drama of existence". Man is thus 'his own greatest mystery'. He does not understand the vast veiled universe into which he has been cast, for the reason he does not understand himself. He comprehends but little of his organic process and even less of his unique capacity to perceive the world around him, to reason and to dream; the ability to transcend himself and perceive himself in the act of perception.

Katha Upanishad IV.1 clearly states that, "the self-existent One created the sense organs, including the mind, with the defect of an out-going disposition. Therefore, beings perceive perishable things outside, but not the immortal Atman (the Self) within. A certain wise and heroic seeker, desiring to achieve immortal self, realized the inner self by turning his senses (including mind) inward". One should look to Sri Krishna in Gita Ch.XII.2 where it is clearly explained that 'the knowledge of the kshetra, the object (the known or 'without' of things) and of kshetrajnya, the subject (the knower, or, the 'within' of things) is jnyana, wisdom or philosophy. In a sense, it is '*Brahm vidya*'; *it is sarva vidya, or 'samvat'*.

Here, the concept of 'Triputi' is important. *Triputi* is the triple group consisting of Jnyana, Jneya and the jnyata, i.e., the knowledge, the object of knowledge, and the knower. Anubhava is experience. Vedanta discovered anubhava or jnyana as the conscious field and all objects or jnyeya and all subjects or jnyatas as its passing configurations and which resolved the triputi distinctions. And, it termed the Ultimate Reality, or Atman or Brahman, as Anubhava -Swaroopa, or Jnyana -Swaroopa, or Chit-Swaroopa – of the very nature of knowledge', of the very nature of Consciousness. This is conveyed in Upanishads as:

" Satyasya Satyam", in Brihadaranyaka Upanishad 2.1.20;
"Prajnyaanam Brahmaa" *–Brahma is Pure Consciousness.*
Aitareya Upanishad 5.3.

"Satyam Jnyanam Anantam Brahmaa"
"Brahman is Truth, Consciousness and Infinity"
Taittiriya Upanishad 2.1

"Ayamaatma Brahmaa so yam atma chatushpat"
All this manifestations is Brahman Himself is Brahman.
This self manifests itself through the four states viz,
Waking, dream, deep sleep, and the turiya or the transcendental.
Manduka Upanishad 2.

The human body is made of gross matter. It is this gross body that undergoes births and deaths. There is a subtle body and a causal body. When the gross body falls, the remaining two bodies still form a combination. The physical sense organs like the eyes, ears, etc. belong to the gross body; but, if by the senses we mean the subtle power of which the eye and the outer organs are but instruments, then they belong to the subtle body. The causal body forms the support of even the subtle body (sookshma sharira).

Sri Krishna says that '***the true Self of man is unborn, immortal and eternal, (Bhagavad Gita: Ch.II verse 16). He asks Arjuna to "transcend the dualities of experience like the heat and cold, pain and pleasure, and identify himself with the permanent and unchanging Being, the 'Sakshi'. The Sakshi being the Ultimate Subject, there is considerable difficulty in comprehending truly".*** [*Bhagavad Gita*, Ch.II Verse 29].

Brahma Rahasya of Happiness

The secrets of knowing the Self, the '*Brahman*' are beautifully explained in the '*Brahma Rahasya Upanishad*'. This Upanishad contains mantras that help in understanding the attributes or the swabhava of the jeevas, and the methods of overcoming the obstacles that prevent realization of the Brahman. This whole world is a make-believe theatre of action. All are actors who come and go and the stage remains. This make-believe world, rather this unreal world or '*maya prapancha*' is the product of the mind. If the mind vanishes, the world vanishes. There is a beautiful mantra in *Brahma Rahasya Upanishad* where in '*Manonasha*' is described. [Mantra 12]

"Jeevanmuktesu manasah saroopanashah videhamukteshu svaroopanashah".

This means, "*There is a Saroopanasha of mind in jeevanmuktas. In Videhamuktas, i.e., who have attained disembodied liberation, there is' aroopanasha' of mind*". Janaka, the King of Videaha was a 'Jeevanmukta'.

Thus, there are two kinds of 'manonasha', or destruction of mind: (1)Saroopanasha (Mind with form) and (2) Aroopanasha, (Mind without form).

If one is free from desires, from sensual objects, raga (attachment), dvesha (hatred), ahamkara (egotism), anger, lust, 'mama'-ta (mine-ness), pride, jealousy, greed and attachment, such a person has achieved '*manonasha*' (mumukshutva) or liberation. It is the Vasanas that cause bondage and attachment to sensual objects. Vasana-kshaya is extinction of Vasanas. *Manonasha* is destruction of mind. Tatva-Jnyana is knowledge of truth. As long as these are not equally practiced regularly and continuously, the knowledge of the Self cannot be achieved. Extinction of Vasanas that causes annihilation of mind cannot be achieved easily. It requires discrimination (Viveka), meditation on the Self (Atma-Chintana), Vichara (enquiry of Atman), Sama (control of mind), control of senses (dama), Vairagya (dispassion), Tyaga (renunciation) – all these, to destroy Vasanas.

Attainment of Brahman, i.e., Self- realisation can be achieved through the mind alone after abandoning its Sankalpas (Resolutions), or Vrittis (thoughts) and Vikalpas (Imaginations). When the five organs of knowledge are subdued, when the mind is controlled, and when incessant meditation is practiced, Brahman is revealed. Then alone one becomes immortal. *Brahma Jnyana* is the release from the trammels of one's own mind. Such a release alone leads to the attainment of *Moksha (emancipation)*.

The purpose of Brahman-realisation is self-perfection and the attainment is illumination and liberation from the meshes of ignorance, desire and rebirth. "***He who realizes Brahman becomes Brahman***" [*Mundaka Upanishad* III-2-9]. He realizes the final goal of evolution. This realisation of Brahman is not limited to mere intellectual apprehension. It is really a profound working experience in which ordinary Consciousness working in the realm of time and space through subject-object relation is transcended, indeed, deepened into its essence, i.e., Brahman. Such a state is realized in the highest mode of in-drawn concentration known as '*Nirvikalpa Samadhi*' or '*Asamprajnyata*'.

One who has attained this realisation has a true and immediate vision of the divine unity, and is the possessor of supreme felicity, free as he becomes, from all cravings and evanescent interests. ***Only when the Mind ceases from its preoccupations with the sense objects and turns to Brahman, it can enjoy the Bliss; for, Brahman is the source of the reflected happiness that the mind experiences even in the sense contact***. One has to realize the Mahat tattvas: ***'So 'ham', "Aham Brahmasmi", and 'Tat tvam asi'***'(Brahman' as one's own very Self). Then and then alone one can attain perfect independence. Real swarajya, or independence of the soul, can be achieved by manonasha (destruction of the mind), and burning of the Vasanas. Meditation alone can help in the control of the mind. This gives eternal happiness. This is the Brahmarahasya of supreme bliss.

Mukti! What is it?

"Bondage and Liberation, which are conjured up by Maya, do not really exist in the Atman, one's Reality. Bondage and Liberation are attributes of the buddhi that ignorant people falsely superimpose on the Reality. For this Immutable Brahman is Knowledge Absolute, the One without a second, and unattached" [Viveka Chudamani 569- 71].

Liberation is possible only with the identification of oneself with Brahman and by no other means. No amount of yoga or study of scriptures mechanically will help here. *Svetasvatara Upanishad* ***says, "Seeing Him alone one transcends death, there is no other way".*** [*Svetasvatara Upanishad III*.8].

Mahanarayana Upanishad gives some of the means of salvation, rather, the well laid paths to liberation. These are: Truthfulness, austerity (Tapas), dama, shama, daana, dharma (religious rites), procreation, protection and offerings to Vedic Fires, Agnihotra, Yajnya (Sacrifice), Maanasa Pooja (Mental worship), nyaasa (sarva karma phalatyaaga), Sanyasa.

'Satya', or Truth is the supreme means of liberation, Prajapati told his sons, Aruni and Suparna. By truth the wind blows and the sun shines in the sky. Truth is the foundation of speech. Everything in practical life depends on truth. Truth is the supreme means of liberation [Mahanarayana Upanishad Anuvaka 79.2]

'Mukti' is liberation. Liberation from what? It is quite obvious that everybody wants some freedom. Freedom from bondage is what everybody aspires for, for it is the real quality, the swaroopa of Brahman. You are liberated the moment you realize the Truth, the Reality; you feel you are happy and contented; the moment you decide you do not want any more rebirth you will be released. But, this comes with a rider. First, you have to prepare yourself for this. You have to burn all your desires, sanskaras; you have to burn all your vasanas, be aware of the pull of the sense objects and control the drive of the sense organs. This can be done by purification of the mind only by constant dhyan, dharana and meditation. The arishadvargas that include raga, dvesha, moha, lobha, mada, matsarya, should be annihilated by prathyahara and constant dhyan, japa, tapa and vrata. All the prarabhda karma and sanchita karma should be burnt by constant chanting of the name of Ishtadevatha.

Ashtavakra says, "it is bondage when the mind desires or grieves at anything, rejects or accepts anything, feels happy or angry at anything. Liberation is attained when the mind does not desire or grieve or reject or accept or feel happy or angry. It is bondage when the mind is attached to any sense experience. It is liberation, mukti, when the mind is detached from all sense experiences". These desires, rejoicing, grieving are the modifications, thoughts, or function of the chitta, the mindstuff; they are like the waves or ripples on the water of the lakes. The depth of water in the lake is our own true Self. We can catch a glimpse of the bottom of the lake, i.e., our own true Self, when the water is calm and clear without any ripples or waves. If the water is agitated and muddy, we cannot see the depth. Likewise, as long as our mind is under delusion, agitated under the sensual attractions, desires, due to our attachment with our body, mind and senses, we cannot see the nature of our true Self. This is ignorance and bondage. But when the mind is calm and free from all such agitations and modifications, we realize our true nature and attain mukti or liberation. Here the Rule of Mind Management is: "*Always keep a cool and collected Mind; never get perturbed. Believe it or not, the waves will subside soon and all anxiety and tension would disappear. There is nothing that can be achieved by an agitated Mind*".

Identifying the Self with the non-self this is the bondage of man, which is due to ignorance and this brings all the miseries; it is also the cause of the cycle of rebirth. It is the mistaking of transitory things as real that causes bondage. It is our own willing submission to desires that cause our bondage. It is within our power to get rid of this bondage and attain mukti. Thus, bondage and freedom are just identification and dissociation from the internal, mental modifications, respectively. Further, Ashtavakra says, "*When there is no 'I', there is liberation; when there is 'I', there is bondage". Egoism is bondage and egolessness is liberation.* When there is no ego, there is no identification of the Self with body and mind, and the Self is realized as 'One without a second', pervading the whole universe. Having this knowledge, one becomes perfectly tranquil in mind and free from desires or aversions.

The liberation process begins with the process of Self-realisation and 'mukti' is attained with the spiritual attainment in 'Samadhi'. If you are prepared for this in thoughts, words and action, i.e., kaya, vacha and manasa, you will get it. No doubt about this! Always remember that,'this world is not yours'. It is not for you in the sense, you are for the world and the world does not exist for you. You may live today and die tomorrow; the world exists forever. When the world is not yours, why do you cry for it? Why do you think this is mine and that is mine when nothing is yours! You have to realize that you are a guest for a limted period of stay, may be a hundred years, and you have to live with in limits ('maryada') as a guest and get out as early as possible, the earliest the better! That is the way to live happily and successfully. Here, the Rule of MMT is: '*Live with Love and make sacrifice your goal. Thus, you will enjoy supreme happiness*'.

Further, 'Atma Jnyana' alone can give Mukti or salvation. Jnyana, the knowledge of the Self, is the only direct means to freedom. Shrutis, Upanishads emphatically declare:

"*Rite Jnyananna muktih", meaning, 'there is no liberation without wisdom'*.

Nishkama karma can at best help Chitta Shuddhi very much required for mukti; it canot give Mukti. Karma or action cannot remove

ignorance. Only knowledge of the Brahman, 'Brahma Jnyan', can totally remove ignorance. Rigid discipline, right conduct, austerity and meditation, or a drastic sadhana like 'hatha yoga' with pure mind, is needed for eradication of ignorance, fear, and desire of the flesh; the belief of 'Deha-adhyasa', meaning 'I am the body' is the product of ignorance. This one idea 'I am the body' has created so much havoc that we go on taking birth after birth. It is a mysterious Avidya, ignorance.

Moksha! What is it?

Sarvopanishad, the quintessence of the Upanishads, gives answer to some of the most important questions like: What is Moksha? What is bondage of the Soul? What is Vidya? What is Sakshi? What is Kutastha? What is Paramatman or Supreme Self? What is Atman? What is Maya?

Shri Shankaracharya's 'Viveka Chudamani' gives a beautiful description of this 'make-believe' world and shows the way out of the 'Samsara tapatrayas'. "***All this universe which through ignorance appears as of diverse forms, is nothing but Brahman that is free from all limitations of human thought***". [*Atharva Veda*]. If this universe be true, let it then be perceived in the state of deep sleep also. As it is not at all perceived, it must be unreal and false, like dreams. Therefore, the universe does not exist apart from the Supreme Self; and the perception of its separateness is false like the blue colour of the sky. Hence, whatever is manifested, viz. this universe, is the Supreme Brahman Itself, the Real, the One without a second, pure, taintless, calm, serene, adimadhyantarahita, the Essence of Knowledge, 'Sat-Chit-Ananda'. '*Sages realize the Supreme Truth, Brahman, in which there is no differentiation of knower, knowledge, and known, which is Infinite, transcendent, and the Essence of Knowledge Absolute". [Viveka Chudamani]. When the Jnyaata, Jnyeya, and Jnyaana become one, unite in transcendental meditation, the supreme Brahman is realized; and, there is nothing else to realize!*

"That which is beyond caste and creed, family and lineage; devoid of name and form, merit and demerit; transcending space, time, and sense objects- that Brahman, art thou, meditate on this in thy mind. That Supreme Brahman which is beyond the range of all speech, but accessible to the eye of pure illumination; which is pure, the embodiment of knowledge, the beginningless entity- that Brahman art thou, meditate on this in thy mind. That which is untouched by decay, death, hunger, thirst, grief, and delusion; meditated upon by the Yogi's heart, but not grasped by the sense-organs; which the buddhi cannot know; and which is unimpeachable- that Brahman art thou, meditate on this in thy mind. That which, though One only, is the cause of the many; which refutes all other causes, but is itself without cause; distinct from Maya and its effect, the universe; and, independent – that 'Brahman art thou', meditate on this in thy mind. That which is free from duality; which is Infinite and indestructible; distinct from the universe and Maya, supreme, eternal; which is undying Bliss; taintless- that 'Brahman art thou', meditate on this in thy mind. On the Truth inculcated above, one must oneself meditate in one's mind, through the intellect, by means of the recognised argument as provided in the Vedas. By this method, one can realize the Truth". One must live in constant identification with the Supreme Self. Sages call that Liberation here and now. Thus, the techniques as envisaged by Shri Shankara are very clear. "***The master of Self, the Paramatman dwelling in the body, looks upon the body and such like things other than the Self as Itself; this egoism is the bondage of the soul. The cessation of that egoism is 'Moksha', liberation***".

Inspite of the above, we, the mortals, feel it is wellneigh impossible to attain the state of 'Supreme Self'; here again, our ego forms an adamantine wall in perceiving the Truth. There is a very interesting story that helps to understand the predicament of a common man. There was a King who had only one son. That son took to bad habits and the King was so angry that he finally banished him from his Kingdom. After several years, when the King was on his deathbed, he felt it appropriate to crown the prince. But, alas! The King had banished the prince. So he asked his men to search for the prince and bring him back to the Kingdom. The boy who was banished at a young age had forgotten that he was a Prince and, was wandering like a beggar. When the King's men were searching for the Prince, they saw the shabby looking young man and wondering whether this was the Prince! They were talking about the 'Prince' so loud that the young man could hear it. The moment he heard that the King's men were searching for him and he heard the words 'Prince', the young Prince asked them to take him to the King. This is how one can realize one's position and status: "***I am That***". *This is how a person realizes his Self in a moment!*

Moksha is not what is available some where and that can be easily achieved by some technique. Moksha is a dynamic process. It is an attitude like happiness; it is a way of looking at things. Once you attain this stage or gain this attitude in life, you will enjoy every minute of life, only if you are alive to it and are aware of what is happening.

Normally, one gets bored sooner or later in this mundane worldy life. You do not know what to do. Nothing is interesting. Nothing is thrilling. Time moves very slowly and you are aware of that every minute; it seems endless and it is killing. You are asking when this boring state is going to end. You want to know when there is liberation or mukti from this life. But, if you are enjoying life, you will not ask when it is going to end. You do not want that blissful state to end. You are enjoying every minute and you do not ask when it is going end. You are already free. In the very enjoyment of life has come your freedom. You feel it is good when it ends. It is also fine if it does not end. You are enjoying it; you are living it. You accept it totally. This is moksha, the state.

Here, the Mind Management technique is:

"One has to develop this attitude of happiness from 'living' in the present every moment of life. Do not dwell on the past memories, fantasies and sanskaras; so also, do not live on hopes, dreams and aspirations. Live now and here and enjoy every moment of this life without attaching your mind and senses to life. Attachment brings misery. Live every moment of your life; observe it as a witness or 'Sakshi'. Watch it like a drama unfolding in front of you. Do not add colour to it, do not attach meaning to it. Observe it in a trance as a mesmerizing act of the Lord! It is the

cosmic drama of life on earth. You will enjoy the Sat, Chit and Ananda. This is supreme bliss that never ends. But you have to live it. Past second is dead the next second has not arrived as yet. That very second of time you are watching has all the essence of life; it is Hiranyagarbha! Try to enter into it and experience yourself". And, this is the secret. This is Moksha here and now! What more do you want?

Ashtavakra Samhita is a very beautiful treatise on philosophy of practical life. It is the equivalent of Bhagavad Gita, but very little of this is known due to inaccessibility of the original scripture. It first came in an Indian Vernacular, Kannada and later in English versions, and till today, no satisfactory true version has come out! It is a very very practical way of living peacefully, happily, and successfully in the modern day huzzle buzzle of life. In a nutshell, *Ashtavakra says*:

"Be calm and serene; don't be agitated. Do not go after anything. If anything comes your way accept it gracefully, happily, and be contented. Be humble and hear your inner voice. Problems crop up when you run after things and get them; of course, disappointment and unhappiness are there if you do not get them". This holds good even to the aspects of liberation and salvation. You will be soon disillusioned for leberation and salvation are not easy to get! As long as that desire to achieve some thing is there, that desire itself acts as the stumbling block. If you just 'keep quiet' you will get everything, including mukti (liberation), moksha or salvation. If you run after it, even if you take to Yoga and Meditation, you will not get it! Because you are always aware that you are doing yoga and meditation to achieve salvation and that 'desire' acts as a deterrent to concentration of mind and fulfilment. As soon as the desire is erased completely from the subconscious fulfilment is experienced.

The essence of this philosophy is very simple but very difficult to understand. It is so simple that '*anything you strive for eludes you due to the fact that your 'desire', the conscious mental effort, itself becomes a hurdle; if you approach the same without the involvement of the Mind and the senses, the Self (the Pure Conscious) takes over and achieves it very easily*'. There is nothing that is impossible for the Self (Pure Conscious) to achieve, for the simple reason that 'the Self is Brahman'! But, it is also made clear here, that '*there is nothing to go after, there is nothing to achieve, and, there is nothing to strive for in terms of material progress and achievement in this 'make-believe', illusory world (Maya Prapancha)', as also, material prosperity, worldy fame, and power and position are not the goal of life.*

What even if a Nobel Prize is awarded and National Honours are showered on you when you feel hollow internally and do not enjoy the internal peace and happiness? These honours may bring a few US $ and scrolls of paper inscribing your name boosting your ego. Unless you surrender all this ego to Him it is a waste. All external aggrandizement will only enhance the ego and create more problems. It is very essential to realize this 'Sat', the Truth! Ultimately, you may die as a person widely known all over the world but not knowing your own Self! That will be a great tragedy.

The Reality is this. It is so very simple. Once you realize that '*Thou art That*' *there is nothing more to achieve! You are already That, "Tat Tvam Asi*". Just realize the Self in you. It is your total awareness that "the Lord dwells in you; He is the guiding force. He is the Effulgent Self that sheds light and erases your ignorance. He is Omniscient".

It is sheer ignorance that prevents you from realizing Him in your self, rather visualizing Him! Look inward. Watch your Self; watch your mind; observe closely the behaviour of your mind. Watch your thoughts. Be a witness or 'Sakshi' to all your thoughts and actions. You will realize Him, the Lord within you. It is your inferiority complex; it is your lack of 'self-confidence', it is lack of trust in the Lord that hinders your vision of Him. Be courageous; be a 'dhira' and live your life, every moment of it, neither thinking of the past nor looking anxiously at the future. It is He who has created this illusory world and it is He who will take care of it. Remember He has got a Department of Protection and a Hod! have faith in Him. He is omniscient, omnipresent and sees everything and will protect you always and under all circumstances. Thus, the Mind Management Rule is: *Trust Him. Surrender totally to Him and Him alone.*

You can invent the whole set of gadgets to investigate this outer world, this physical universe; but you cannot invent yourself! Invent your Self! Discover your Self! It is now more important than ever to discover your Self and invent your Self because you do not know yourself; you are lost in delusion, in the floods of ignorance and every scientific advancement and technological progress is posing new cxhallenges and a threat to your own existence, survival.

Some body has well said, "***How wretched is the man, with honours crowned, who having not the one thing needful found, dies known to all but himself unknown***".

Total annihilation glares at the face of our modern scientific civilization. We have no other alternative but to look to salvation in spiritual attainments!

Noble Laureate Alexis Carrel, the author of "Man, the Unknown", states, "*The aim of civilization is the progress not of science and machinery, but of mankind*". He further said, "if men like Galileo, Newton, Lavosier had devoted their intellect to the study of human body, mind and consciousness the world would have been entirely different". He emphasized the need for the study of man in depth. Even Einstein is of the same opinion. He says "Objective knowledge provides us with powerful instruments for the achievements of certain ends in life. But the ultimate goal of life and longing to reach it, must come from another source".

Ultimately, the aim of life, according to the Veda and Upanishads, is to "Know thyself". Reknown Poet D.R.Bendre has explained what is meant by 'Get into thyself'; it is 'Be thyself' or 'know thyself'. He says, "*When we try to understand our true nature by means of proper thought, technique, inquiry, and experience we get immersed in the depths of our beings. Then we have a glimpse of the profound light latent within ourselves. We realize that this light is not a figment of our imagination but a matter of profound truth*".

The modern day life has become simply unbearable. Increasing madness, ego, fear frustration, challenges and competition, standing on nerves, jealousy, cut-thorat competition, greed, avarice and what not!

About the increasing mental ailments and the present day modern man's predicaments, C.G.Jung has warned Thus:

"Psychoneurosis must be understood as the suffering of a human being who has not discovered what life means to him" In the same context, T.M.Thomas, in his 'Images of Man', has opined thus:

"The twentieth century neurosis is the neurosis of purposelessness, meaninglessness, valuelessness, hollowness and emptiness".

What a great fall from 'Grace of the Lord"! Thus, it is high time we take note of the trend of the present-day developments and take all precautions to avoid the unavoidable, self-annihilation.

"Utthishtato (Arise) Jagrata (Awake)! 'A clarion call of the Veda.'

The basic message of the Vedas is "Be Open". Do not cling to the past. Do not close the door. Keep it open and wait for the unknown to happen. And, whenever it happens do not try to make it known. Whatsoever happens throw it away and be ready again. Something new will happen again. The Brahman remains unknown eternally. "*Indeed, he attains immortality who realizes it in and through pulsation of knowledge and awareness. No Knowledge is ultimate. It is just a vibration, a pulsation*".

Do not make any vibration the ultimate. In deep meditation you will come to feel a great silence. This is just a pulsation. Whatever happens, Brahman is always more. Do not identify any happening with Brahman; otherwise you will stop. Let every wave be wave; wait for the ocean.

Many people have reached deep ecstasy and they stop because then they say, "This is the Brahman. The ultimate has been reached". Remember, Brahman is never achieved! It is simply achievable; never, never achieved; approachable but never, never approached by mortals. The beautiful journey remains; it goes on and on. It is Narayana!

Do not be under false impressions. Be Aware! Be aware of Truth and strive to achieve it, realize it. Do not be carried away by delusion. 'Choiceless Awareness' is very imporant. ***"Utthishtato Jagrata!"*** *This is the clarion call of the Veda and the Upanishads. It is now more relevant than ever before.*

11
Conclusion

"If we take care of Nature, Nature takes care of us"

Our Mind is the most powerful instrument "anthahkarana' that makes or mars our lives unless we know how to harness its powers. So far, there is no easy and simple method of understanding this Mind. 'Manoniyantran', i.e., Mind Control is, indeed, the central theme, the sum and substance of Upanishadic doctrines that repeatedly implore us to live an austere way of life, know the Self, i.e., the 'Atman' and, thereby enjoy the supreme Bliss. Bhagavad Gita elaborately deals with it; it gives us the techniques of controlling the wayward, ficklish Mind, or holding the reins of the horses- the 'chitta vrittis' that disturb or spoil the peace and happiness. Our Mind is compared to a drunken monkey bitten by a scorpion and, as such, it is extremely difficult to control it.

In this psychophysical world Mind cannot be studied in isolation of either the 'world we live in' or the 'life' we live on. It is very difficult to understand the Mind since it is too vast and ever shifting, evading us. It is difficult to get the Mind in our grip unless we adopt certain techniques. Mind is one thing that travels faster than light and needs no vehicle to carry it. It has got the capacity to transform things and visulaise the virtuality. This creative ability is inherited by the Mind from the Consciousness, that is the storehouse of immense possibilities. In fact, we must use the mind as a tool to control the Mind just as the diamond cuts a diamond; we have to cajole the mind and tutor it to get into our control. These techniques are beautifully explained in this work.

All aspects of life have been covered here in order to get a complete picture of the world we live in and the way we live. It is now evident that we have changed our life style, attitudes and mores; and, our mode of thinking has changed over the centuries and very significant changes have come about in the recent past. All these changes are not for our good! Some of these changes have affected the very basis of life and come as a threat to our existence. Man is the only animal who rejoices in the sufferings of others and does not hesitate to maim or kill others for personal joy. No animal kills another unless it is extremely difficult for it to survive. But, man wages war for no reason; at times, war is said to be in the interest of peace! Even one person in position and power can bring about total annihilation of mankind just by one wrong move! These are the days of guided missiles and un-manned nuclear arms and ammunitions that are capable of destroying larger number of people over much wider areas than in the past. Now, there are new diseases and pestilences that cause immediate viral infection. The Kyasanoor Forest Disease (kfd fever) caused by the monkeys displaced from their habitat in Shimoga District of Karnataka is an ecological problem; KFD causes brain fever and has already killed many children. And there is the SARS, the Severe Acute Respiratory Syndrome, that started somewhere in China and took a heavy toll of life in Canada across the Pacific. Further, the widely prevailing HIV/AIDS, the DENGUE FEVER, etc. that spread fast and are of global dimension affecting larger numbers very quickly. The SARS, a disease causing sudden breathlessness and death, started somewhere in China and large number of people who contacted this and traveled to Canada have already died in Canada.

An austere way of life and striving for the establishment of peace and universal brotherhood through the practice of Upanishadic doctrines and techniques of Manoniyantran is the only answer to all these problems. Our behaviour and action, unmindful of consequences, is mainly responsible for this sort of new problems. Most of our problems are due to our Mind, i.e., our attitudes, moods, way of thinking- mostly negative thinking, and selfishness in every thought and action. All these are performed under the influence of Mind than Buddhi or Intellect. Our Ignorance (Avidya) is at the root of the problem. Unless someone Knowledgeable and Selfless, say a Guru, takes a lead and educates us as to all these intricacies of Mind, Intellect, Consciousness, it is very difficult for us to live an intelligent, sane and sensible way.

As already said, our life is of our own making. To live a happy or a miserable life is in our hands. As far as others are concerned, it is immaterial whether they like it or not, take it or leave it; one has to live his life to the best of his potentialities. This requires enormous will power, strength of Mind and determination and devotion to God. Spirituality is the most important factor that brings immense happiness and peace in life. Materialistic progress is important insofar as it provides wherewithal to serve the society. But it is not very important for the evolutionary progress of Man. Spiritual progress is vertical growth that leads us to the 'Brahman' (Kaivalya) while materialistic progress is horizontal growth that takes us nowhere. Always, one should aspire for the spiritual growth and development and strive for that supreme Bliss. Ultimately it is liberation, or Mukti, and Moksha, i.e., Immortality, getting rid of the shackles of repeated births, that is important. One should enjoy the beauty and the bounties of the earth as an honoured guest and quit at the earliest opportunity to enjoy the higher divine 'Bliss'. This is the purpose of '*Manoniyantran*', a technique of spiritual attainment. "Harih, Om. Tat Sat!"

Think It Over

Contemplate on the following

Meditate on any one of thesewhichever you like most

Space manifests first, then comes time.

When there is time, events come in succession.

Our mind thinks in terms of space, time, and events. Prana acts upon the ether.

Then the five elements come into being.

The elements combine and various objects are formed.

Even if you imagine that nothing exists, there will be space.

You will have to transcend space to realize the 'Self'.

Transcending time and space is Realising the Self.

Try to experience this!

GOD IS EVERYWHERE!

Time and space are eternal.

The Supreme spirit covering all time and space is Shree Hari Narayana.

All matter- fire, water, air, earth and mind
and their respective Qualities emanate from
the Supreme Spirit. Soul, the Jeeva
is the infinitesmal part and parcel of Shree Hari,
The Supreme Spirit pervading the Universe.
Realisation of the fact that the whole world including the Creator
Is a play of matter and spirit,
and is a cosmic joke is the key to Freedom and
escape from Sansara or cycle of life and death.

Any devotee who wants to see God in the name and Form he wants to See, can see and experience Him in that name and form. In reality, the devotee and his mind itself is also a part and parcel of The Supreme Spirit encompassing the whole Universe. Realisation of this Truth is "Aham Brahmasmi". Or "Tat Tvam Asi". God has no particular name or form and is not attached to any Since He pervades everything. "Choiceless Total Awareness is True Living". Observe this phenomenon within yourself and practise it "The Atman is hidden in the hearts of all. It is seen only by the Seers through their pure subtle intuition"

[Katha Upanishad 1.3.12]

Each one of us is a part of the infinite Spirit. As our mind and heart becomes pure, we come to get hold of Our individual inner- self. As we move further and further, We find that we are all really parts of a greater Whole And this is the greatest truth we need. We, as souls, are inseparable parts of the Oversoul, The Supreme Spirit. Let us try to awaken in us the consciousness that we are the Spirit. Let us try to find that we are all parts of the one Oversoul.

GOD KNOWS EVERYTHING!

"A playwright knows the plot and the sequences well before drafting his play. It is only the spectator who has to wait for sequences to be unraveled on the stage. So also, a Yogi can perceive by his contemplation, meditation, And, yogic powers foresee the things to come. The Lord knows the past, prese nt and the future. He has simultaneous knowledge of all events at all times at all places.

Self- realisation means the union of the individual spirit with The supreme Spirit. Spiritual initiation brings the individual Self into harmony with the supreme Self. Mind purified of thought is 'Self'. 'Self' filled with thoughts and desires, is the mind. [Gita VI-35] Mind is the enemy of one who cannot control the mind. Mind is the friend who has won the mind.

Brihadaaranyaka Upa.[1-5-9]

Mind is made up of food. [Chaandogya Upanishad]

Pure food helps to keep purity of mind.

Pure mind is energy. Pure mind shines as consciousness.

Indians beware, stale and contaminated non-vegetarian food Lead to impure mind leading to impure thoughts and inhuman actions.

All dead animals are contaminated with germs and microbes.

And, human digestive system is not meant for hard food from non-vegetarian sources. One should avoid non-vegetarian food.

He who covets the desirable things, while brooding on their virtues, is born amidst these very surroundings along with the desires.

But for one who has got his wishes fulfilled and is self-poised, all Longings vanish even here. [Mundaka Upanishad III- ii- 2]

Mind is the world and world is our Mind.

If we want to win the world, we have to win our Mind.

For a person who has overcome the mind, he rests peacefully within Himself; he has no preference for time and place.

He has no choice since the time and space have become one.

He is one with Pure Consciousness.

When Mind is merged with consciousness, there is no 'becoming' or 'attaining'. There is nothing to be achieved. All this is in the Mind and that Mind is no more. This consciousness is the background and support of mind and all thoughts that exist.

Mind is to be treated very kindly, tenderly and should be tutored.

It is the knowledge that frees the mind and dissolves the Mind.

"The 'fear' is the resistance to movement.

Fear is the feeling, for loss of attachment, for loss of what we have, and loss of whom we have.

We are afraid to lose something and someone since we ourselves do not matter.

Since we ourselves do not have self-esteem, we do not value Our selves and want someone whom we value higher and by whom our value increases.

We by ourselves are worthless.

We have to be identified with wealth, power, position, or by recognition of some higher achievement for us to have value and faith in ourselves or by others.

This self-abnegation, this ignorance that something, or somebody is higher, and something makes us higher, and the fear of losing that, that makes us feel higher and better, is the achievement, an illusion of our Mind.

Otherwise, we have no where to go, and there is nothing to attain, to attain and to become.Then there is no fear, since there is no 'becoming' and 'attaining'.

Conquer fear by knowing fear There is only one being which is fearless.

This fearless and deathless entity is our 'Self', whose nature is consciousness and bliss. Its nature is also intelligence".

"*Antar Pragnyam Bahor Pragnyam, Pragnyam pragnyam eva cha*"

"The inner consciousness and the outer consciousness is one and the same consciousness".

If the individual consciousness is different from outerconscious ness , then each individual would have seen different sizes of objects, depending upon the size of the image etched in their memory".

"Since all persons and beings see the same objects, hear the same sound, taste the same taste, and experience the same touch of an object, the seer, the hearer, the taster and smeller,and experiencer is one and the same in all the bodies. But, the interpretation of the quality of objects being different from person to persondepending upon one's likes and dislikes, the play of the mind".

"It is the Universal Consciousness that is reflected in the

Creative intelligence or consciousness of innumerable beings".

Just as the reflection changes according to the quality of the Reflecting surface, even though the object is the same, each

Individual soul seated in all the different beings being one and the same, sees the same life-size objects".

"Going beyond Mind is going beyond space and time;

Going beyond space and timeis going beyond Light".

"*Brahmam Satyam, Jagat Mithyam*". Shri Shankara.

"Brahma is Real and the world is unreal".

"Everything exists within Him; we are in this world and the entire world is within us, in the microcosm".

"Mind is made up of time and space, the environment in which

The person lives. Mind is a product of his past experiences, living conditions, desires and urges and future ambitions.

A Hindu has a Hindu mind steeped in rituals, beliefs and superstition.

A Muslim has a Muslim mind indoctrinated, fanatic, and blindly following system irrespective of time and place.

A Christian Mind has Christian Mind trying to measure the immeasurable and judge the infinite with the finite.

Mind does not change the path and goes on in a trodden path by its past memories and experiences".

" Mind is the servant of the ego. The ego is the feeling of supremacy identified with the limited adjuncts of the body.

'Ego' is truly the master of the Mind. The Mind has found its true master in the ego and serves the ego day in day out.

Ego is based on ignorance and exists only in isolation.

This ego is not accepted by any one, since it promotes only isolation and exclusiveness".

"Sangaat samjaayate kaamah, kaamaat khrodhobhijaayate,
Khrodaatbhavati sammoha, sammohat smrityvibhramah;
Smritibhramshat buddhinaasha, buddhinaashat pranashyati!

[Bhagavad Gita, Ch.II –62-63]

"By dwelling in objects therewith, man develops attachment, From attachment is born desire, from thwarted desires comes Anger; from anger ariseth delusion, there from confusion of memory, loss of reason; when reason is gone, the man is lost"

"Veeta raagabhayakrodha sthithahdhir muniruchyate"-

"That sage who is free from attachment, fear and anger,
Is a 'Muni', of stable mind, or poised understanding"

Man of self-control and real peace is described as

"One whose thoughts shine like the cool moon-beams, whose mind remains unruffled when confronted with fighting in death, even as at the prospect of festivity- he indeed is called a self-controlled man of peace".

[Yoga Vasishta Mumukshu Khanda 14. 75]

"Blessed are the pure in heart, for they shall see God".

[Bible, St,Mathews 5:8]

Acknowledgements

My salutations to Sri Ramakrishna Paramahansa and Swami Vivekananda, Shri Swami Shivananda, Swami Ranganathananda, and Swami Yatishwarananda and the great monks of the Ramakrishna Mission who have been the guiding spirit and light showing us the path of sensible life. Day in day out, we have to remember them and pray. Their contributions to mankind are of immense value and cannot be assessed by any means. I have quoted exhaustively from their looks and by debt of gratitude to all the monks and swamijis of the Ramakrishna Mission.

Bhagavad Gita is the eternal source of knowledge. Many great thinkers and spiritual leaders have interpreted the Gita in different ways. It is an important source of inspiration to all who seek solace in times of distress. It lightens the path when left in darkness, and gives enormous moral and spiritual strength. This source is quoted at length in my Text.

Rig Veda and the Sama Veda, the Upanishads, the Brahma Sutra, the Vishnu Purana, the Bhagavad Gita, are all parts of the cultural and spiritual heritage of India. They are the rich source of knowledge. Sudhakara Chaturvedi has given a beautiful translation and commentary on the Sanskrit verses to *Rig Veda Samhita* and *Sama Veda*, published by Veda prakashan samiti, Bangalore. I am indebted to Sri Sudhakar Chaturvedi. Raghavendra, T.N. has given a more modern and scientific commentary to Rig Veda and Sama Veda, and the Upanishads, the Bhagavad Gita, Vishnu Sahasra Nama, I am indebted to him. His book (un- published) "The Creative Power Within Us" is the most comprehensive book on Mind and his 'Vidyas in Bhagavad-Gita' is quite refreshing. The most significant contribution to our knowledge of veda and vedic literature has come from Bhagwan Maharishi Mahesh Yogi. His 'Apaurusheya Bhashya', 'whdeners on the move' and 'Heaven on Earth' are very important. I have quoted some passages from his 'vision of total knowledge' for which I owe my debt and gratitude. By respectful pranams to Bhagawan.

Besides, a number of authors like Swami Vivekananda, Swami Shivananda, Swami Rama, Swami Abhedananda, Swami Ranganathananda, Swami Yogananda, Swami Yatiswarananda, Narayanasvami Iyar, Padmanabha, C.S, Fritjof Capra, Aldous Huxley, Thomas Huxley, Julius Huxley, Sigmund Freud, Schroedinger, Carl Jung Stephen Hawkins and a host of others have been quoted at length in the text in order to bring out the diverse opinions and commentaries as also guide the interested readers to their original works. I owe my debt of gratitude to these authors and their publishers. My thankfulness to Shreyas Kulkarni for his help in correction and my gratitude to all those who have made this work possible and see in print.

Selected References

Achyuta Rao, T.N. : VEDANTA - The knowledge Supreme, Gyan Book New Delhi - 2004

References

Arthur J. Thomson : Introduction to Science
Bertrand Russel : The Impact of Science on Society
: The Scientific utlook
Capra, Fritjof, : Uncommon Wisdom,
: The Turning Point
: The Tao of Physics
Charles Darwin : Origin of the Species
Chardin, Teilhard de : The Phenomenon of Man
Chaturvedi, Sudhakar : Yoga Pradeepa, Udupi.
Rig veda Samhita, Sama Veda, Arya Samaja, Bangalore, 2001
Daniel Goleman & R.J. Davidson : Consciousness: The Brain. States of Awareness, and Alternate Realities
Fritjof Capra : The Turning Point
Tao of Physics
Uncommon Wisdom, Bantam Age Publications.
Gaudapada : Mandukya-karika,
John Welwood : Meeting of the Ways: Explorations in East/ West Psychology
Jennings, J.G., : The Vedantic Buddhism of the Buddha, Oxford University Press
Julian Huxley : The Uniqueness of Man,
Evolution after Darwin, (Vols. I -III)
Maha Rishi Mahesh Yogi : The Science of Being and Art of Living.
Settled Mind and Silent Mind,
[An interview with Maha Rishi Mahesh Yogi, by Kathy Juline in Science of Mind, Nov. 1993, pp. 1-7]
Max Muller : Three Lectures on Vedanta Philosophy,
Narayanaswami Iyar, K : Thirty Upanishads, Parimal Publications, Delhi
Padmanabhachar, C.M. : Life and Teachings of Shri Madhvacharya, Bombay, 1909.
Paul Deussen : Sixty Upanishads, Germany
Penfield, Wilder. : The Cerebral Cortex and the Mind of Man,
Peter Laslet (Ed.) : The Physical Basis of Mind
Raghavendra, T.N. : The Power of Creation Within Us.*(Unpublished)
Rig Veda Samhita* (Un-Published)
Gods of Veda*
Ishavaasya Upanishad, Gayatri Publication, Bangalore
Atmavan, Gayatri Publication, Bangalore, 2001
Chandogya Upanishad*
Mandukya Upanishad*

		Vidyas in Bhagavad Gita *
		Vishnu Sahasranama *
		Lalita Sahasranama*
		Brihadaranyaka Upanishad *
		Vishnua Purana *
		Mahanarayana Upanishad *
		Ashtavakra Samhita*
		Krishna* [*Un-published]
Radhakrishnan, S.	:	The Bhagavad Gita, Bharatiya Vidya Bhavan, Bombay
Richard Devenport	:	An Outline of Animal Development,
Schrodinger, Erwin.	:	What is Life? Mind and Matter
Siu, R.G.H.	:	Tao of Science, M.I.T., Mass., U.S.A.,
Swami Abhedananda	:	Yoga Psychology
Swami Gambhirananda	:	Prasna Upanishad, Pub.: Advaita Ashrama, 1995 Bhgavad Gita (Commen taries of Shri Shankaracharya), Tr., Advaita Ashrama, Calcutta, 1991.
Swami Madhavananda	:	Minor Upanishads, Advaita Ashrama,
Swami Nityaswaroopananda	:	Ashtavakra Samhita, Advaita Ashrama, Calcutta 1998.
Swami Ranganathananda	:	Message of the Upanishads,
Swami Shivananda	:	Ten Upanishads, The Divine Life Society Shivanandnagar, U.P. 1973.
Swami Sarvananda	:	Isavasya Upanishad, Shri Ramakrishna Math, (Tr.) Mylapore, Chennai- 4 Taittirypanishad, Madras
Swami Vimuktananda	:	Aparokshanubhuti, Adavaita Ashrama, Calcutta 1996
Swami Vivekananda	:	The Complete Works of Swami Vivekananda, Advaita Ashrama, Calcutta 1973.
Upanishads cited	:	Advaitamruta Upanishad Aithareya Upanishad. [1.1.4] 24; [2] 80; [IV-1] 82. Amrutabindu Upanishad. [2] 80. Ananadabindu Upanishad Aparokashanubhuti Aruneyi Upanishad Ashtavakra Samhita [1.2] 88, 157-8, 193. Atmopanishad Badarayana Brahmasutra [4-1-7] 133. Bhagavad Gita [II-29] [II 7-8] [III-17] [IV 18],[XII-13,4,18-19] [XVII-40] 26, 31. Brahmanubhava Upanishad Brahma Sutra [4-1-7] 133. Brahmopanishad [III-13] 77. Brahmendra Upanishad

Glossory of Samskrut Words

A: Akhand (Rk Veda)
Ak: The Macrocosm (Mahat) and the microcosm (subatomic particles) or 'anu' (RkVeda)
Anu: Subatomic particles, photon,
Agnim; Fire
Ahara: Food
Aakasha: Sky, space.
Abhinivesha: Clinging to life
Abhokta: Non-enjoyer
Achyuta: ' That' which does not wear out,. That which has no 'Chyuti' or end; The Omniscient and Omnipotent.
Adhyatma: The reality underlying the innermost individual self.
Advaita: Monism
Ahara: Food, Food for body, Food for thought.
Aithareya Upanishad: deals with the spiritual character of the Absolute
Aja: Unborn
Akarta; Non-doer
Akshara: Imperishable
Alambana: Support for the mind to lean upon
Ananth: Endless; refers to time and space and the power behind the unifying force. Actually time and space are borne put of the same Eternal called Ananth
Antaryami: Yama inside the body
Anusandhana: Enquiry
Anthahkarana: Internal organ that includes mind and intellect, i.e., manas and buddhi
Aptakama: One in whom all desires are gratified
Asambhuti : Maya, Prakruti
Asamsakthi: Non-attachment for objects
Asmita: Egoism, with sense of Responsibility
Ashtanga Yoga: Yoga with eight limbs
Asura: Demon
Atman: Soul, the divine energy with Creative intelligence and bliss that pervades through nature having different qualities, create bodies having qualities of nature through which it (creative energy) pervades. Atman: the Soul, the Self; the Supreme Spirit.
Avidya: Nescience, Ignorance.
Bhaya: Fear
Bhakta: Devotee
Brahma: the Creator, the first manifestation of Brahman.
Brahaman: The Supreme Self, Supreme Being; the cosmic

Intelligence; Supreme-Consciousness; Supreme Knowledge; the Self-luminous power,Cosmic flow, i.e., Sri Hari Narayana

Brahmacharya: Continence, Abstinence from sex

Brahma Srotri: Person having Knowledge of Brahman by studying books.

Brahma Nishta: One who has direct Perception of Brahman through Self-Realisation

Brahmanda: Hiranyagarbha, Cosmic Space; The first manifestation of Brahman, Sambhuti.

Bruhadaranyaka Upanishad:
deals with the Unity of Being; inherent purity and diversity of soul; Absolute is fearless.

Chhandogya Upanishad:
deals with True Nature of Self; It is in the form of a dialogue between
Satyakama and Svetaketu;
'The knower of the Self crosses all sorrow' [VII 1.8].

Chitta: Thought, Mind-set; manas.

Chitta Vritti: Thought Waves

Dama: Self Restraint; Self- control; control of senses. Turning Jnanendriyas and Karmendriyas away from sense objects and placing them in their respective centers is called Dama or self-control.

Ego: Ahamkara in ordinary sense; but, means more than that. It is the ignorance that makes one identify himself with Body and mind, and not the spirit or self within.

Egotism: Prepondering 'I'-ness. All defects arising from Ahamkara.

Ekadandi: One who always carries one staff, Sage or Saint, Danda is staff of authority God; That Supreme Power behind the Universe; The all-pervading Vishnu the cosmic flow; the energy that sustains this universe.

Guna: Attributes such as: Saguna and Nirguna- with or without attributes.

Hatha Yoga: Yoga of physical- vital culture.

Heredity: The theory of heredity is that the impression registered in the 'Germ cell' are transferred from generation to generation, as there is continuity in the germ cell. In the bioplasmic cell, the limitless impressions of all time are compressed and transmitted to the offspring.

Hiranyagarbha: The Cosmic Sace; the Supreme Lord of the Universe Hatha; in popular parlance, firm minded, determination; 'Ha' means Sun, and 'Tha' means moon, energu and food, respectively. Union of Prana Vayu and Apana vayu.

Ishavasya Upanishad:
The First Upanishad of great spiritual significance; deals

with the Divinity of man, nature, and the inherent spiritual nature of life. Also known as Samhitopanishad, or Manthropanishad par *excellence*.

Ishwara: Tat Pada, literally meaning Brahman (indicative)

Jada: Inert; inertia; laziness.

Japa: Higher form of worship

Jeevatma: Individual soul

Jnyana: Knowledge, Wisdom, Knowledge of the Self

Jnyani: the Knower of the Self, the wise man

Kama: Desire, lust. Kaamana.

Karma: Impressions of actions.

Karma Kanda: Karma Kanda of the Vedas comprise of Samhitas and Brahmanas; Forms the source of inspiration for one sect. As compared to Jnyana Kanda of the Vedas comprising of Aranyakas and Upanishads.

Karma Yoni: Birth for action.

Karta: Doer (Akarta- Non-doer).

Katha Upanishad: Deals with Fear, Death and After in the form of a dialogue between Yama and Nachikethas.

Kenopanishad: deals with Ultimate Reality- the Inner Self.

Knowledge: The union of subject and object; Supreme Knowledge is the Unity of subject and object in the Absolute; here neither the Subject nor the object exist. It is Realisation of the Pure Consciousness or the Supreme self.

Kshama: Forgiveness, ethical conduct

Laya Yoga: Yoga of absorption of mind.

Mahavakyas: Great sayings of Shritis.

Mandukya Upanishad: Deals with Divinity of Man ; self same reality.

Manonasha: Destruction of Mind; Stilling of Mind

Manolaya: Temporary absorption of mind in the object of meditation, Vasanas are still present; only in manonasha, vasanas are destroyed.

Mantra Yoga: Yoga of recitation of sacred syllable OM.

Mauna: Silence; method of cleansing impure mind.

Moksha: Deliverance from cycle of birth and death.

Mundaka Upanishad: deals with Para and Apara Vidya; Sage Angiras teaches Saunaka (Atharva Veda) Freedom and Delight; Summons to battle of life equipped properly with Upanishadic thoughts, and Meditation.

Nada Anusandhana: Concentration of Anahata or mystic sounds of heart and channelising energy.

Nature: Unmanifested Ether; Prakruti, Maya. Shakti, Ajnyana.

Nidra : Ignorance, Sleep.

Nishkama Karma: Yoga of selfless service

Om: The sound that emanated with the Sphota at the time of Origin of the Universe, the Brahman the Nada Brahman

Paramatman: The Supreme Soul, the Lord, The Supreme-Consciousness Pure Consciousness.

Paramahansa: Yogi who neither carries Danda (the Staff) nor the hair stuff, Nor the holy thread,who has attained nirliptata.

Patanjali : Maharishi who compiled Yogic Principles and tenets Taught by Hiranyagarbha according to Yagnyavalkya Smriti. Patanjali Yoga Sutra is the treatise on Yoga.

Prakuti: Nature, the universe, a manifest form of the Lord.

Prana: First Principle of life, then as Principle of Consciousness, then equated with Ultimate Reality, namely Atman.

Prashnopanishad: deals with Philosophical problems in diaogue form.

Prathyahara: Yogic practice of drawing mind to self; drawing in of sense organs into the Chitta or mind stuff, by detaching from their objects

Purusha: Dweller in the body (referred to as Brahmapura), refers to the Supreme Being, Purushottama

Purushottama : The Lord, Supreme Being

Raja yoga: Dhyana Yoga, Yoga of meditation and Samadhi.

Rebirth: There is heredity transmission so far as furnishing the materials to the soul for embodiment is concerned. But, the soul migrates and manufactures body after body, and each thought we think and each deed of ours, is stored as moral efficiency in the soul. Ready to spring again and take shape at proper time. The sum total of these impressions give the soul the direction for the next birth. If these impressions are such that they have to manufacture a new body for further experience, the soul will go to those parenets who are ready to supply it with material for that body. Thus, from body to body it will go, sometimes to heaven and back again to earth; this way it will go on till it has finished its experience and completed the circle.

Revelation: It is a divine afflatus springing from within, the result of inspira tion through God-intoxication.It is not a message received from outside. [Ranade]. Only he whose heart is purified and made ready can receive the revelation. [Katha Upanishad, II. 5. 23].

Rishi: Wise Seer.

Salvation: The search for a new body and fulfilment of desires come to an end when the Soul comes to know of its true nature, its Ignorance vanishes, its power becomes manifest; it becomes perfect and there is no need to work through physical bodies or through finer mental bodies. It shines in its own light, and is free, no more to be born or to die. It is the desire, the ignorance that causes rebirth. Salvation lies in cleansing the soul of its blemishes of desires and samskaras (impressions).

Sama: The resting of the mind steadfastly on its goal, viz. Brahman after it has detached itself from manifold sense-objects by continuously observing the defects, is called Sama or calmness.

Samadhi: Highest State of Consciousness; Height of spiritual attainment; Yogic achievement. Nirvikalapa Samadhi-without triputi and alambana Thought-less Super Conscious (Choiceless Awareness) state. Samprajnayata Samadhi

Sabija or savikalpa S: Samadhi with triputi and alambana.

Samhita: Collection.

Sama: Tranquility of Mind.

Samadhana: One pointed Mind.

Samadhi: Super-conscious State wherein super sensual experiences occur Ultimate in Yoga.

Samsara: Realm of births and deaths.

Samskaras: Latent Impressions, experiences, memories stored in sub- conscious.

Sanyasins: Spiritually consecrated seekers.

Sat: Truth, Real, the real foundation of the universe.

Satsang: Company of spiritual thinkers, seers, sages, sants, spiritual aspirants

Shikha: Tuft of hair on the crown of head (Govinda?)

Shriddha: Faith.

Siddhi: Perfection in Raja Yoga entering Asamprajnya Samadhi

Soul: The self-luminous entity that forms the core of man's personality. It can reveal itself and reveal others simultaneously and give the awareness that 'one is experiencing'. This is the spiritual Essence, the Atman in man. It is beyond causation; it is not the product of anything (not a compound of anything) and it is indestructible.

Suras: Gods; stands for noble, divine and other higher qualities.

Svastha: One who is established in oneself, Sthithaprajnya.

Taittiriya Upanishad: deals with Nature of man the Five Koshas.

Tanmatras: Subtle elements.

Time: Time has been calculated in terms of the rotation of the earth around the Sun in our Solar System. Once we get out of this earth and enter space, the basis of our calculation is lost. In Vedanta, time is calculated according to the wheel of time wielded by Sriman Narayana. It consists of Brahma's 100 years of life; each year consists of 360 days and each day consists of Krita, Treta, Dvapara and Kali ages; added together and multiplied 994 times. In terms of human years it works out to: Krita Yuga 1.728 million years; Treta Yuga 1.080; Dvapara Yuga 0.72 million years and Kali Yuga 0.36 million years. Together it works out to 3 million 888 thousand years a single age of the Gods (Divine Age). 71 Divine ages make-up one Manvantara-, i.e., one day of Brahma, the four-faced creator, the manifestation of the Brahman, the Supreme Spirit. 100 years of Brahma (36000 Kalpas) end up in a Mahapralaya (deluge) lasting equal duration. Indras, Manus, and Rishis change at the end of every Manvantara. It seems that 21 Krita, Treta and Dvapara Yugas have already passed in revolution since the origin of this Universe. That is why Shri Krishna refers to the cycle and says that He will take birth at every dawn of a Dvapara Yuga to restore Dharma (Dharma Samsthapanar-thaya Sambhavami Yuge Yuge). The great wheel of Mahapralaya and Maha kalpa has millions of smaller ones, wheel within wheel, rotating at the propulsion of the Supreme Spirit in the center of all, the processes of nature taking place right through in rotations. This is the Celestial Time as distinct from the time calculated in our solar and lunar calendars, based on rotation and revolution of earth and its satellite, the Moon, respectively.

Titiksha : Endurance.

Trataka: Steady Gazing, Dharana, Concentration Chitta ekagrata, steadiness of mind..

Trikuti: Concentrating between eye brows

Triputi; Triad, The knower, the knowledge and the knowable. (in Savikalpa Samadhi); Tome.Space and Causation are the Triputi of Vedanta.

Turiya: Super –conscious State.

Upanishads: Constitute the end and aim of Vedas (Vedanta); the sum and substance of all true wisdom; 1180 in number one for each Shakha of the Vedas, but only 200 brought to light. Upanishads in Mantras are called Manthropanishad.See list at end

Uparati: Renunciation.

Upasana: Bhakti, Devotion.

Vairagya: Renunciation, Dispassion, Non attachment as opposed to Raga (Attachment). It is the desire to give up all transitory enjoyments. It includes the desire to attain Brahmanhod.

Veda: "Ved" means Knowledge, Divine knowledge.

Veda: Literature that sheds light on the transcendental means of Achieving what is wished for and avoiding what is disliked According to Sayanacharya, Vedas are transmitted by word of mouth since time immemorial, beginningless antiquity, believed to be the first received

	from Brahma, the creator.
Vedas:	Rig Veda, Saama Veda, Yajur Veda and Atharva Veda.
Vichara Shakti:	Power of enquiry
Vikshepa Shakti:	Projecting capacity of Mind.
Vikruti:	Indriyas; Pancha bhutas.
Vimochana:	Release from Bondage, Mukti.
Viveka:	Discrimination
Vrittis:	Thought waves; mental modifications.
Wisdom:	The discriminatory power. According to Vedas, Brahma, the Creator, is the first manifestation, born of fire of Wisdom; wisdom, thus, existed before the other five elements were formed.
Yoga:	Restraint of thought waves, union with God, Union of (Jeeva) atma and Paramatma, Union of he individual soul and the Supreme-Consciousness.
Yoga Nadis:	Astral nerves
Yogi:	One who practices yoga; a wise man.
Yuj:	to join, Knowledge. Unity.

Index